équipe nouvelle 2

Livre du professeur

Danièle Bourdais
Sue Finnie
Anna Lise Gordon
with Pat Dunn

OXFORD
UNIVERSITY PRESS

OXFORD
UNIVERSITY PRESS

Great Clarendon Street, Oxford OX2 6DP

Oxford University Press is a department of the University of Oxford.
It furthers the University's objective of excellence in research,
scholarship, and education by publishing worldwide in

Oxford New York

Auckland Bangkok Buenos Aires Cape Town Chennai
Dar es Salaam Delhi Hong Kong Istanbul Karachi Kolkata
Kuala Lumpur Madrid Melbourne Mexico City Mumbai
Nairobi São Paulo Shanghai Taipei Tokyo Toronto

Oxford is a registered trade mark of Oxford University Press
in the UK and in certain other countries

© Danièle Bourdais, Pat Dunn, Sue Finnie, Anna Lise Gordon 2005
The moral rights of the authors have been asserted

Database right Oxford University Press (maker)

First published 2005

All rights reserved. No part of this publication may be reproduced,
stored in a retrieval system, or transmitted, in any form or by any means,
without the prior permission in writing of Oxford University Press, or as
expressly permitted by law, or under terms agreed with the appropriate
reprographics rights organization. Enquiries concerning reproduction
outside the scope of the above should be sent to the Rights Department,
Oxford University Press, at the address above

You must not circulate this book in any other binding or cover
and you must impose this same condition on any acquirer

British Library Cataloguing in Publication Data

Data available

ISBN-13: 978-0-19-912460-2
ISBN-10: 0-19-912460-4

10 9 8 7 6 5 4 3 2

Page make-up by Kamae Design, Oxford

Printed in Great Britain by Ashford Colour Press Ltd, Gosport

Acknowledgements

Front cover photograph by Martin Sookins.
The authors would like to thank the following people for their help and advice:
Rachel Sauvain (project manager), David Buckland (course consultant),
Marie-Thérèse Bougard (language consultant).
Songs: Laurent Magloire, Eric Moulineuf, Dorothée Rascle, Vanessa Seydoux.
Speech: Jérôme Ambroggi, Laetitia Ambroggi, Yves Aubert, Jean-Pierre Blanchard,
Marie-Thérèse Bougard, Henry de Boysson, Clémence Brunet, Eléonore Buffet,
Adrien Carré, Aurélia Carré, Raphaël Carré, Jean-Sébastien Conil-Lacoste, Olivia
Conil-Lacoste, Louis Daillencourt, Juliet Dante, Barbara Dewast, Caroline Dewast,
Louise Dewast, Marvin Dez, Laurent Dury, Samuel Freeman, Victoria Girardot,
Alexandra Goddard, Pierre-Matthieu Gompertz, Rob Gould, Catherine Graham,
Thierry Harcourt, Guillaume Jouinot, Antoine Lecocq, Laura Lecocq, Phil McComish,
Nicholas Mead, Daniel Pageon, Sophie Pageon, Christine Potts, Julien Rose, Carolle
Rousseau, Mathieu Sagnier, Jessica Schinazi, Mikaël Schinazi, Jean-Baptiste Thubert,
Thibault Thubert.
Music: Laurent Dury.
Studios: Post Sound, London W3; Air-Edel, London W1.
Production: Marie-Thérèse Bougard, Simon Humphries and Charlie Waygood.

Contents

Summary of unit contents	4
Introduction	**5**
The course	5
The components of **Équipe nouvelle**	5
Course progression	8
Équipe nouvelle and the Modern Languages Framework	8
Teaching with **Équipe nouvelle**	16
Summary of main characters	16
Features of an **Équipe nouvelle** unit	16
Presentation and practice of new language	17
Using the soap story: *La belle équipe*	19
Target language	20
Differentiation	21
Independent learning	21
Thinking skills	22
Assessment	22
Équipe nouvelle and the National Curriculum	23
Équipe nouvelle and the QCA Scheme of Work	23
Teaching in Scotland	23
Teaching in Wales	23
Équipe nouvelle and ICT	23

Teaching notes for Équipe nouvelle 2	
Unité 1 Mode ado	24
Unité 2 En forme!	54
Révisions Unités 1–2	84
Contrôle Unités 1–2	86
Unité 3 On se relaxe!	90
Unité 4 Tous les jours	120
Révisions Unités 3–4	153
Contrôle Unités 3–4	155
Unité 5 Voyages et vacances	159
Unité 6 Une visite en France	189
Révisions Unités 5–6	218
Contrôle Unités 5–6	220

Symbols used in this Teacher's Book:

- 🎧 listening materials
- **C1** copymaster materials available
- **W1** consolidation and extension activities available in Workbooks
- **AT 1.1** reference to National Curriculum attainment level

ÉQUIPE NOUVELLE 2 — SUMMARY OF UNIT CONTENTS

	Contexts	Grammar	Skills	Pronunciation	Culture	PoS coverage	Framework
Unit 1	• Revision of self • Clothes and colours • Types and styles of clothes • What you wear for different occasions/in different weather	• Revision of present tense of *être* and *avoir* • Colour adjectives • Present tense of *-er* verbs • Possessive adjectives • Present tense of *mettre* • *Super-challenge!* comparative adjectives	• Revision of how to ask questions • Using *parce que* • Using *quand*	• Revision of sound–spelling links • Pronunciation of *un* and *une*	• History of fashion	1a, 1b, 1c, 2a, 2b, 2c, 2d, 2f, 2g, 2h, 2i, 3a, 3b, 3c, 3d, 3e, 4a, 4c, 4d, 5a, 5c, 5d, 5e, 5f, 5g, 5i	8W2, 8W4, 8W5, 8S1, 8S2, 8S4, 8S7, 8T2, 8L2, 8L4, 8C1, 8C4 – **L**
Unit 2	• Parts of the body • How you feel and what is wrong with you • Healthy living • What you did to be healthy	• Revision of masculine, feminine and plural forms • *à + la/le/l'/les* • Imperatives • The perfect tense 1	• Using a dictionary 1 • Translating idioms • Understanding and adapting texts	• Sounding French 1 • Accents	• *Tour de France*	1a, 1b, 1c, 2a, 2b, 2c, 2d, 2e, 2f, 2g, 2h, 2i, 3a, 3b, 3c, 3d, 4a, 4c, 4d, 5a, 5c, 5d, 5e, 5f, 5g, 5i	8W7, 8W8, 8S8, 8T4, 8T6, 8L1, 8L6, 8C2, 8C5 – **L** 8W5, 8S7, 8T2, 8L2, 8C4 – **R**
Unit 3	• TV programmes, likes/dislikes • Types of film, 24-hour clock • Arranging to go out • Making a telephone call • Giving excuses not to go out	• *aller + infinitive* • *vouloir* • *pouvoir, vouloir, devoir 1* • *Super-challenge! pouvoir, vouloir, devoir 2*	• Using connectives • Listening for gist and detail	• Sound-spelling exceptions	• The 24-hour clock • French TV channels	1a, 1b, 1c, 2a, 2b, 2c, 2d, 2e, 2f, 2g, 2h, 2i, 3a, 3b, 3c, 3d, 3e, 4a, 4c, 4d, 5a, 5b, 5c, 5d, 5e, 5f, 5g, 5i	8W1, 8W3, 8W6, 8S3, 8L3, 8L5, 8C3 – **L** 8W2, 8W5, 8S7, 8C2 – **R**
Unit 4	• Revision of sports • Musical instruments • Daily routine • Household chores • What you have/haven't done to help at home	• *jouer à/de* • Reflexive verbs 1 • The perfect tense in negative statements • *Super-challenge!* reflexive verbs 2	• Expressions of time • Writing a longer description • Using verb tables • Adapting a text	• Sounding French 2 • *-ent* verb endings	• Football	1a, 1b, 1c, 2a, 2b, 2c, 2d, 2f, 2g, 2h, 2i, 2j, 3a, 3b, 3c, 3d, 3e, 4a, 4c, 4d, 5a, 5c, 5d, 5e, 5f, 5g, 5i	8S5, 8S6, 8T1, 8T3, 8T5, 8T7 – **L** 8W1, 8W2, 8W4, 8W5, 8W6, 8W8, 8S1, 8S2, 8S3, 8S7, 8L1, 8L5, 8C3 – **R**
Unit 5	• Countries and capital cities • Means of transport • Basic details of a holiday • Describing a holiday in more detail	• *aller à + ville* • *aller en/au/aux + pays* • *à/en + transport* • The perfect tense 2 • *Super-challenge!* plural forms of the perfect tense	• Writing a detailed description	• *Point lecture* *-ille, -eil, -agne* sounds	• *La Francophonie*	1a, 1b, 1c, 2a, 2b, 2c, 2d, 2f, 2g, 2h, 2i, 2j, 3a, 3b, 3c, 3e, 4a, 4c, 4d, 5a, 5c, 5d, 5e, 5f, 5g, 5i	8W3, 8W4, 8W5, 8S1, 8S2, 8S4, 8S5, 8S6, 8S7, 8T5, 8L4, 8L6, 8C5 – **R**
Unit 6	• What's available in town • Directions • Paris monuments • Describing a visit to France	• Revision of imperatives • *c'est/c'était + adjective*	• Using a dictionary 2 • Improving written work	• The French *r* sound	• Facts about Paris	1a, 1b, 1c, 2a, 2b, 2c, 2d, 2e, 2f, 2g, 2h, 2i, 2j, 3a, 3b, 3c, 3d, 3e, 4a, 4c, 4d, 5a, 5c, 5d, 5e, 5f, 5g, 5i	8W5, 8W7, 8W8, 8S7, 8S8, 8T1, 8T3, 8T4, 8T5, 8T6, 8T7, 8L3, 8C1 – **R**

Introduction

The course

Welcome to **Équipe nouvelle 2**!

Équipe nouvelle is a broad-ability course for 11–14 year olds with a single volume Students' Book in Parts 1–3 that provides differentiation in particular via the *Challenge!* and *Super-challenge!* sections, the *Encore/En plus* pages at the end of the Students' Book, and the parallel Workbooks. The course:
- has been revised to meet the requirements of the MFL Framework
- is now even easier to use
- is fully differentiated to teach the whole ability range.

Équipe nouvelle 2 retains many of the popular features of **Équipe**:
- a familiar structure and content coverage
- the focus on a group of four friends via *La belle équipe* – the regular soap story
- the most popular songs from the original **Équipe** have been reused
- the *Zoom grammaire*, *Guide pratique*, *Expressions-clés*, *Mots-clés* and *Ça se dit comme ça!* sections still play a central role in the course
- there are extended *Encore* (reinforcement) as well as *En plus* (extension) pages at the back of the Students' Book.

Rationale

The aims of **Équipe nouvelle** are to provide:

- **a clear structure**
    - There are six units per Part, which makes it easy to teach one unit per half-term.
    - There are four core spreads in each unit, which makes it easy to teach one core spread per week.
    - Regular assessment is provided via the end-of-unit checklists, and termly revision sections and differentiated formal assessment.

- **clear progression**
    - Clear teaching and learning objectives are provided to show students exactly what they will learn.
    - There is careful and systematic presentation and practice of key grammar, skills and pronunciation points.
    - The *La belle équipe* soap story recycles key language of the unit and provides more reading and listening practice.

- **clear differentiation**
    - The core material that all students must cover is clearly identified.
    - There are *Challenge!* plenary activities at three levels of difficulty on each spread.
    - There is a *Super-challenge!* page of extension material that extends the language of each unit.
    - There are *Encore* and *En plus* differentiated activities at the end of each unit that students can work through on their own.
    - There is a 12-page extended *Point lecture* reading section at the back of the Students' Book.
    - Parallel Workbooks at *Encore* and *En plus* levels accompany each part of the course.
    - There are termly assessment copymasters at different levels of difficulty.

- **clear presentation**
    - The bright and attractive location photos provide a vivid cultural backdrop that will motivate students.
    - The Students' Book activities are colour-coded by skill so that students can find their way easily around a spread.
    - All the language that students will need to use is highlighted in the *Expressions-clés* and *Mots-clés*.

- **clear and comprehensive support**
    - For students, there is an end-of-unit vocabulary page and checklist together with a clear grammar section and French–English, English–French glossary.
    - For teachers, full support is provided with Scheme of Work and lesson planning via the Teacher's Book and **Coursemaster** CD-ROM.

The components of Équipe nouvelle

Students' Book

The Students' Book is 160 pages long and consists of six units: one unit per half-term's work. Each unit is divided into four core spreads: one spread per week. This then allows time to cover the additional practice material provided in the course, including revision and assessment. Part 2 ensures that students have appropriate activities for their second year of learning French, providing the necessary programme of teaching, practice, revision and reference materials.

Full attention has been given throughout the course to the Modern Languages Framework (see page 8) and to the National Curriculum, the QCA Scheme of Work, and Scottish and Welsh curricula (see page 23).

The Students' Book contains the following sections:

Bienvenue à Équipe nouvelle 2!
This page provides a guide to the symbols, headings and typical rubrics that feature in the Students' Book to support learning.

Unités 1–6
There are six 14-page units set in different contexts. Each unit has been planned to be interesting and motivating, as well as providing a coherent and systematic approach to language development, e.g. grammar, pronunciation and study skills. An outline of the content of each unit is given on page 4 of the Teacher's Book. For a detailed description of the features of an **Équipe nouvelle 2** unit, please refer to pages 16–17 of this book.

Introduction

Révisions
At the end of every second unit, there is a revision section containing activities across the four skills, aimed at providing consolidation and further practice of the language of the preceding units. Students can work on these activities independently, with a partner or as a whole class with you. Some of the activities (reading, writing, grammar) can also be done as homework activities.

The revision pages cannot cover all the language of the preceding units, but together with the assessment copymasters (*Contrôle*), they provide the opportunity for students to demonstrate most of what they have learned.

Encore and En plus
Each unit has two pages of reinforcement activities (*Encore*) and two pages of extension activities (*En plus*) at the back of the Students' Book. The *Encore* pages are intended for learners who require more support and further consolidation of core language from the unit. The *En plus* pages are intended for motivated and more able learners who are confident with the core language of the unit. For further notes on differentiation, see page 21 of this book.

Point lecture
Équipe nouvelle has a substantial 12-page reading section at the end of the Students' Book. There are two pages of reading per unit at graded levels of difficulty. These pages are intended to encourage independent reading. Students should attempt them once they are confident with the core language of the unit. The activities can be used by students who finish other activities quickly or as alternative class and homework activities.

Grammaire
This detailed grammar reference section is located at the back of the Students' Book and complements the explanations given within the main teaching units. The grammar points are presented simply, but in a way that will help students using reference materials later on. The grammar reference section is in English to ensure that all students can use it independently. An important feature of the **Équipe nouvelle** grammar section is the additional grammar practice activities, which are integrated in the appropriate grammatical explanation for students wishing to consolidate or revise further their grammatical knowledge. The answers for these activities are at the end of the grammar section in the Students' Book for self-checking.

Expressions utiles
Following the grammar reference section, there is a small section containing useful general vocabulary for easy reference, including greetings, numbers, times, days, months, quantities, connectives and countries.

Glossaire
A French–English and English–French glossary contains the words in the Students' Book for students' reference.

Teacher's Book
Each unit contains the following detailed teaching notes:
- a unit overview grid
- a Medium Term Plan showing coverage of Framework objectives
- notes to accompany the unit opening page including unit objectives and assessment opportunities
- a Planning Page for each core teaching spread for ease of lesson planning
- ideas for presenting and practising new language
- detailed suggestions for using the material in the Students' Book
- ideas for additional differentiated activities
- some background information on the topics covered in the Students' Book
- answers to all the Students' Book activities
- suggestions for further activities to reinforce and extend the content of the Students' Book
- information about the copymasters, including answers
- information about the Workbooks, including answers
- transcripts for all recorded material.

The notes for the *Révisions* and *Contrôle* sections occur at the end of every second unit to reflect the position of the *Révisions* sections in the Students' Book. They include answers and a mark scheme with assessment criteria for the assessment activities.

Cassettes and CDs
The cassettes and CDs provide the listening material to accompany the Students' Book, copymasters and assessment material. The listening material was recorded by native French speakers. The material is scripted and contains a range of types, including monologues, short dialogues, longer conversations, and songs. All recorded material may be copied within the purchasing institution for use by teachers and students.

Cassette contents:
Cassette 1 side 1: Unit 1
Cassette 1 side 2: Unit 2, revision and assessment Units 1–2
Cassette 2 side 1: Unit 3
Cassette 2 side 2: Unit 4, revision and assessment Units 3–4
Cassette 3 side 1: Unit 5
Cassette 3 side 2: Unit 6, revision and assessment Units 5–6
Cassette 4 side 1: copymasters Units 1–3
Cassette 4 side 2: copymasters Units 4–6

CD contents:
CD 1: Units 1–3, revision Units 1–2
CD 2: Units 4–6, revision Units 3–4 and 5–6
CD 3: Copymasters, including assessment Units 1–2, 3–4, 5–6

Coursemaster
This CD-ROM is available to accompany all Parts of **Équipe nouvelle**. It provides teachers with an instant library of ready-made files accessible on both PC and Apple Macintosh platforms to produce Schemes of Work, Students' Records of Progress, and Class Records of Progress for **Équipe nouvelle** Parts 1–4. The aim is to provide maximum support for the course, and to minimize the need to rewrite departmental documentation. Special Welsh and Scottish versions of the **Coursemaster** are also available.

Introduction

Copymasters

The copymasters are an integral part of **Équipe nouvelle** and there are cross-references to them throughout the Teacher's Book. Notes and transcripts for each unit's copymasters are provided together at the end of each unit's notes in the Teacher's Book. The copymasters provide opportunities for further practice and extension of the language of the unit.
Each unit has the following copymasters:

Vocabulaire – this copymaster summarizes the core language of the unit and provides a record of vocabulary learned. Students can customize the list, for instance colour-coding the words and phrases according to the level of difficulty they have at remembering them, e.g. green for words they always remember, blue for those they sometimes forget and red for words they regularly get wrong or forget. Encourage students to note any other useful language of their own, either in a vocabulary book or on the back of this copymaster.

Podium checklist – use this checklist of the core language of the unit in class and/or at home for self- and peer-assessment. Students read each point and do the checking activity on the right-hand side. It is important to allow enough time for this activity, as students will need to go back over their previous work to check what they have forgotten. Students should identify any areas of weakness and revise these at home before having another go at the checking activity on the checklist.

À vos marques – starter activities.
Challenge! – plenary activities.
Écoute Encore, Écoute En plus – two sheets of listening activities for lower and higher attainers.
Parle Encore, Parle En plus – two sheets of speaking activities for lower and higher attainers.
Lis et écris Encore 1, Lis et écris Encore 2 – two sheets of reading and writing activities for lower attainers.
Lis et écris En plus 1, Lis et écris En plus 2 – two sheets of reading and writing activities for higher attainers.
Grammaire 1, Grammaire 2 – differentiated consolidation and practice of grammatical points. Each sheet covers a different grammar point from the unit.
Guide pratique 1, Guide pratique 2 – graded skills activities. Each sheet covers a different skills point from the unit.
Ça se dit comme ça! – a sheet to focus on the pronunciation points of the unit.

Contrôles – At the end of the copymasters there are 24 assessment *Contrôles* copymasters for use after every second unit. Each test has eight sheets – two sheets per skill at differentiated levels (*Encore* and *En plus*) for lower and higher attainers respectively. The *Encore* sheets cover levels 1–4 and the *En plus* sheets cover levels 3–5. Students complete a test at either *Encore* or *En plus* level for each skill.

Workbooks

Reinforcement and extension activities are provided in the two Workbooks that accompany **Équipe nouvelle 2**: *Cahier d'activités Encore* (reinforcement) and *Cahier d'activités En plus* (extension). These Workbooks are designed for students to write in, so are ideal for setting homework.

There is one page in each of the Workbooks for each main spread in the Students' Book. This is followed by: *Grammaire*, a page which focuses on a particular grammar point of the unit; *Méli-mélo*, a page combining various grammar points from the unit; *Challenge!* (*Encore* Workbook) and *Super-challenge!* (*En plus* Workbook), a page to provide reading material that recycles the language of the unit in the *Encore* Workbook and extends the language of the unit in the *En plus* Workbook; *Vocabulaire*, key vocabulary from the unit; *Podium*, a checklist of the language, skills and grammar learned in the unit. At the end of each unit there is *Pour écrire*, a blank page to use for writing activities.

The Workbooks contain many reading and writing activities which can be completed without a lot of teacher input and there are also a few speaking activities. Bilingual rubrics are provided for all activities, with clear examples as support for students.

Flashcards

A complete list of flashcards accompanying the course is provided on an index card included in the **Équipe nouvelle 1 and 2 Flashcards** pack.

OHTs

OHT number and title	Context/Image
1A, 1B *L'équipe, c'est qui?*	Introduction to the four characters
2 *Je me présente*	Enlarged letter from Students' Book, page 7
3A, 3B, 3C *Ma tenue préférée*	Clothes and colours
4 *J'adore le look sport*	Favourite outfits
5 *Point lecture Unité 1*	Lyrics to song on Students' Book, page 120
6A, 6B, 6C *Ça va?*	Parts of the body, where something hurts
7A, 7B *Qu'est-ce qui ne va pas?*	Symptoms and ailments
8A, 8B *Bon ou mauvais pour la santé*	Healthy living advice
9 *Le journal de Natacha*	Enlarged diary extract from Students' Book, page 26
10A, 10B *Le passé composé*	Comparing the present and perfect tenses
11 *Sélection télé*	TV programmes
12A, 12B *Guide pratique*	Using connectives in longer descriptions
13A, 13B *On va au cinéma?*	Types of film and showing times
14A, 14B *On organise un rendez-vous*	Arranging to go out
15 *Que d'excuses*	Reasons for not going out
16A, 16B, 16C *Elle joue au foot*	Sports you play and how often
17A, 17B *Ma journée*	Daily routine
18A, 18B *À la maison*	Household chores
19A, 19B, 19C *J'ai donné un coup de main*	Enlarged text from Students' Book, page 56
20A, 20B, 20C *Les pays*	Countries and capital cities
21 *À l'étranger*	Enlarged conversation from Students' Book, page 66
22 *À pied ou en voiture*	Transport and opinions

Introduction

23A, 23B, 23C *Le passé composé avec être*	The perfect tense with *être*
24 *C'était vraiment sympa!*	Enlarged texts from Students' Book, page 72
25 *Les vacances*	Holidays
26 *Qu'est-ce qu'il y a ici?*	Places in town
27A, 27B, 27C *Les directions*	Directions using *tu* and *vous* imperative forms
28 *C'est où, la plage?*	Directions around Dieppe
29 *Visite à Paris*	Paris monuments
30 *Le journal de Mélanie*	Enlarged diary extract from Students' Book, page 86
31 *Les souvenirs*	Souvenirs

Équipe nouvelle en clair

Équipe nouvelle en clair complements **Équipe nouvelle** and provides a wealth of motivating materials to support slower and low-attaining students. It is a resource file that contains copymasters, teacher's notes and a CD of recorded material at a deliberately slow pace. A resource file accompanies each Part of **Équipe nouvelle 1–3**.

Interactive CD-ROM with integrated video

The **Équipe nouvelle 2 Interactive CD-ROM** provides a series of short authentic video clips of interviews with French teenagers. There are quick, easy-to-complete activities to assess understanding of grammar, vocabulary, pronunciation and listening. The results are saved to provide a full assessment profile for each of your students.

There is a Students' Interactive CD-ROM for independent study in class or at home and a Teacher's Interactive CD-ROM for network use, which includes an end-of-year assessment package.

Course progression

Completing Équipe nouvelle 2 in a year

Équipe nouvelle has been designed so that it is possible to complete each Part in a single year. There are six units and each unit is divided into four core spreads. It is estimated that each spread will take a week to complete and each unit will cover approximately half a term's work. The **Équipe nouvelle Coursemaster** CD-ROM provides detailed guidance on how to plan and write your Scheme of Work to suit your timetable needs. If you have limited contact time with your students, the flexible structure of **Équipe nouvelle** will allow you to cover the essential language points within a single year: concentrate on teaching the four core spreads in class and use the material from the end sections selectively for students to work on independently. The *Encore*, *En plus*, *Point lecture* and activities in the Grammar reference section are ideal for cover or homework as are the activities in the copymasters and Workbooks, which all contain further practice.

Équipe nouvelle and the Modern Languages Framework

Background to the Framework

The Framework for teaching Modern Foreign Languages in Key Stage 3 lies at the heart of MFL as a strand in Foundation Subjects. It is part of the Government's overall strategy to improve standards of teaching and learning in schools. The aim of **Équipe nouvelle** is to provide a practical and motivating way to teach the Framework objectives within familiar contexts. The Framework for MFL aims to build directly on the greater knowledge of the way language works that students are bringing with them from primary school through the Literacy Strategy. As the term "Framework" suggests, the focus is not on a prescribed body of language items, but on a structure for learning.

The Framework objectives are those considered to be most useful to the more general skills of language acquisition. They are not specific to any one language, but to all languages. Students may progress through objectives in different sequences and at different speeds, but the emphasis is on making the process of language learning *transparent* and *accessible to all*. The long-term aim is to encourage mastery, and to make students independent language learners.

The objectives cover three years, which can be viewed broadly as:
- Year 7 – Foundation
- Year 8 – Acceleration
- Year 9 – Independence.

This pattern will vary from school to school and from class to class, but serves to illustrate the progression through objectives.

The Framework objectives

Objectives are grouped in five strands:
- Words
- Sentences
- Texts: Reading and writing
- Listening and speaking
- Cultural knowledge and contact.

Each strand has between five and nine objectives for the year. It is not suggested that learners start with words, then go on to sentences, then texts. Rather, the five strands were chosen to illustrate the interrelated nature of the skills needed to master the basics of a foreign language. They have also been carefully matched against the objectives mapped out in other Key Stage 3 strands, especially literacy in both primary and secondary schools. So the Framework for MFL should enable closer cooperation between Modern Languages and English departments. There is a glossary in the DfES guidance file *Framework for teaching modern foreign languages* explaining the meaning of such terms as "connective", now in common use in English lessons.

Introduction

How will it benefit your students?

The MFL Framework will give teachers and departments a mental map of language learning over Key Stage 3. Many teachers will already be able to recognize and engage with many of the objectives and it will help them focus on the aspects of language learning which are really at the heart of what it means to learn a language.

It encourages a move away from learning language in a topic-based way, where the emphasis is placed on learning nouns and set phrases, towards an emphasis on understanding the underlying structures of the language: in short, the big picture. This does not mean the end of topic-based work, but what teachers and departments deliver within these contexts may be somewhat different.

The key message for teachers is that the objectives give us a clear picture of where we want to be. It will also help departments to track students' progress at Key Stage 3 when teachers are familiar with the objectives.

What are the characteristics of a typical lesson?

Much of what takes place in the classroom will be similar to what already takes place in effective MFL lessons. The emphasis is on adhering to underlying principles as outlined below to provide greater coherence. Lessons are focused and tightly structured: students are set clear objectives so they know where they are; similarly, challenging expectations are set to ensure they surpass previous levels of achievement.

The lesson is phased, beginning with a brief "starter" activity that may link with the previous lesson, or set the stage for what is to come. It is short, pacy and interactive. The main body of the lesson is devoted to ensuring that the central objective or objectives are set, introduced and then practised. This will often involve whole-class teaching, with the teacher playing a central role in setting up and modelling tasks in such a way that each stage is explicit before students are required to work in groups or independently. Talk, both in the target language and in the mother tongue*, is used extensively. Students are invited to elaborate concepts and develop understanding through problem solving, investigation and enquiry. The final phase, lasting perhaps five to ten minutes, takes the form of a plenary, where the students reflect on what they have learned, and understanding is checked.

* Where this is used, it should be for a planned purpose and the reason for its use should be evident to students.

Methods and resources

The principles for teaching and learning inherent within the Foundation Subjects strand that informs the MFL Framework are:

- **Focus the teaching**
  Put the objectives at the forefront of planning and make sure that students are aware of what they are. (See Long, Medium and Short Term Plans on the **Équipe nouvelle Coursemaster** CD-ROM and the teacher's notes for individual units, in particular the Planning Pages for each core spread.)

- **Provide challenge**
  By having an idea and higher expectations of where we want students to be, they are more likely to exceed previous levels of attainment.

- **Make concepts and conventions explicit**
  Through the process of questioning, explaining and modelling, students are made aware of the underlying skills that need to be mastered if they are to become successful language learners.

- **Structure the learning**
  Use starters and plenaries within an episodic lesson structure.

- **Make learning active**
  Use classroom activities which enable students to develop their understanding through problem solving, enquiry and investigation.

- **Make learning engaging and motivating**
  Use stimulating materials.

- **Develop well-paced lessons with high levels of interaction**
  Have plenty of opportunities for group- and pairwork and build in times for reflection on what students have learned. Develop a language for this reflection.

- **Support students' application and independent learning**
  Use modelling techniques and other forms of support, and intervene when necessary to clear up any misconceptions.

- **Build reflection**
  Encourage students to reflect on what they have learned. Involve them in assessing where they should go next.

The aim of **Équipe nouvelle** is to show how these principles can be addressed in a clear and practical way that is motivating to teachers and students alike. See **How to teach the Framework with Équipe nouvelle** on page 10 for more details.

How does Équipe nouvelle link to the DfES Optional training folder?

In addition to the guidance file *Framework for teaching modern foreign languages*, the DfES has published an *Optional training folder* for schools that have completed the core training. In many LEAs these materials will be provided by the Advisory service, but they are also available as a folder and accompanying video obtainable through the DfES Standards website (www.standards.dfes.gov.uk).

The aim of these optional training modules is to help teachers gain a deeper understanding of the Framework objectives, of how to teach them, and of how to support lesson planning and action planning.

There are 10 modules in the folder: Starters, Lesson objectives, Modelling, Questioning, Practice, Plenaries, Creativity, Target language, Planning lessons, Action planning. They do not need to be done in any particular order as they are intended to be flexible both in timing and in mode of delivery. Departments can choose the modules that meet their own training needs and priorities. In addition, the principles for teaching and learning within the Key Stage 3 Strategy, and in particular within Foundation Subjects MFL, focus on key areas of teaching and learning.

Introduction

When you read the **Équipe nouvelle** teacher's notes, including the Long, Medium, and Short Term Plans, you will see terms such as "starters", "plenaries", and "modelling" mentioned. There are suggestions in the **Équipe nouvelle** teacher's notes about possible ways of delivering these elements, but the optional training modules directly address the terms, explain what they mean, investigate ways of integrating them into your own teaching and give suggestions for further work. They also have supporting video material of teachers setting lesson objectives in a variety of ways, using different starter activities, etc., and are therefore a good starting point for further work.

How to teach the Framework with Équipe nouvelle

Équipe nouvelle has been carefully planned to ensure that all Framework objectives are covered in familiar contexts.

- **The Long Term Plans (LTPs)**
  See page 13 of this book. These provide an overview of objectives to be covered, typically, in each year of Key Stage 3. Each objective is to be specifically launched (**L**) and reinforced (**R**) at least once within that year.
  - Year 7 objectives are covered in **Équipe nouvelle 1** Units 1–6.
  - Year 8 objectives are covered in **Équipe nouvelle 2** Units 1–6.
  - Year 9 objectives are covered in **Équipe nouvelle 3** Units 1–6.

- **The Medium Term Plans (MTPs)**
  These relate to individual units within the course and aim to cover six weeks' work. The MTPs provide a clear picture of the context for learning and give an outline of how the Framework objectives, identified in the LTP, might be taught.

- **The Short Term Plans (STPs)**
  These are planning guides designed to focus on whole-class teaching strategies, specific resources and activities to meet objectives within each unit. They typically cover a week's work, and facilitate the easy generation of individual lesson plans.

To help you plan and write all your departmental documentation, the Long, Medium and Short Term Plans are all provided on the **Équipe nouvelle Coursemaster** CD-ROM in an editable format. In addition, annotated examples of lesson plans and an editable lesson plan template are also provided on CD-ROM.

This Teacher's Book includes copies of the relevant Medium Term Plans at the start of each unit, as well as Planning Pages for each core spread that mirror the Short Term Plan format.

The **Équipe nouvelle** teacher's notes reflect the focus of the MFL Framework on key areas of teaching and learning. These include:

- Starters
- Setting lesson objectives
- Modelling
- Questioning
- Practice
- Plenaries.

Each area is described in greater detail below.

Starters

Each double-page spread of the **Équipe nouvelle** Students' Book contains an on-the-page starter activity entitled *À vos marques*. In addition, suggestions for starter activities are provided in the relevant Short Term Plans and Planning Pages, and some starter activities are available on the *À vos marques* copymasters. The following is a reference list of simple starter activities:

- **Odd-one-out**: students need to learn the language for responding in the target language. As they become more sophisticated in their learning, they should be encouraged to find as many different reasons as possible for a word or phrase being the odd-one-out, e.g. *c'est masculin/féminin; il n'y a pas de -s*, etc.
- **Gap-fill**: the number of letters to fill in can be varied to suit the ability of the group.
- **Match up ...**: French/English; two halves of sentences; questions and answers.
- **Unjumble**: words/phrases.
- **Sequence**: a dialogue; numbers; words – alphabetical order.
- **Picture**: speculate; ask questions about the person/place; give nouns/adjectives, etc.
- **Categorize**: nouns; phrases.
- **Word snakes**.
- **Find the mistake**.
- **Sound patterns**: categorize words that contain the same sound–spelling patterns.
- **Punctuate the text**.
- **Team games**:
  - Noughts and Crosses.
  - Blockbusters.
  - Formulate questions to match answers.
  - With more able students: divide the class into groups. Each group chooses one word/phrase from each section on the relevant Students' Book *Vocabulaire* page. They must then invent a short exchange, attempting to incorporate their chosen word/phrase into the exchange as naturally as possible. The rest of the class listen and try to identify the chosen word/phrase.
  - Word Tennis – each team takes it in turns to ask a question, and a member of the other team must give an answer without hesitating. The activity can be further extended by telling students they must keep the "rally" going by asking another question. The aim is to be the last to speak.
  - Pairs – use the empty Pairs grid on OHTs 1A or 6A of the **Équipe nouvelle 1 OHTs** with an overlay containing pairs of words/phrases such as on OHTs 1B or 6B. Cover the grid squares with coins, sticky notes or cards. Students take it in turns to give two sets of coordinates, e.g. A2, B4; if the two words/phrases that are revealed match up they have to say them correctly in order to win a point.

Setting lesson objectives

Setting lesson objectives for students is an integral part of the effective cycle of learning. Setting objectives that are accessible for students lets them see where they are in a sequence of lessons, how their prior learning informs their current work, and what they will achieve by the end of a lesson or sequence of lessons. If possible, keep the lesson objectives displayed, or on OHT, so that they can be referred to during the lesson. It will be necessary to teach the essential vocabulary related to learning objectives, e.g. *apprendre/vous allez apprendre, lire, écrire*, etc., and aim to add to this essential vocabulary over time. This book provides initial guidance for the teaching and learning of classroom management language on page 20, as well as suggestions for teaching additional vocabulary. All the Short Term Plans and Planning Pages provide a list of learning objectives that can be easily adapted into individual lesson objectives. See the **Annotated lesson plans** on the **Équipe nouvelle 2 Coursemaster** CD-ROM.

Setting lesson objectives is an ideal time to practise the meaning and construction of "*on* + verb": *On va apprendre, écouter, parler, lire, écrire, chanter,* etc. Using the following classroom routine on a regular basis introduces students to the perfect tense in a fun, communicative way and supports speaking and listening using the language of learning:
Teacher: *Aujourd'hui, on a lu, écrit, parlé, compris, appris, chanté …*
or
Teacher: *Aujourd'hui, on a lu ou on n'a pas lu?*
Class: *On a lu.*
Teacher: *On a chanté ou on n'a pas chanté?*
Class: *On n'a pas chanté.*

Modelling

Modelling efficient ways of working can play a key role in helping the whole class to move forward together by reducing the gap between the highest and lowest achievers. It involves doing more than just providing a "good example" (e.g. a recorded dialogue or a paragraph of writing) for the student to emulate. It has to include:

- showing students precisely how this "good example" was achieved
- helping students to achieve a similar "good example" for themselves.

Good modelling techniques include:

- giving visual demonstrations
- thinking aloud whilst speaking in the first person
- slowing the process down
- deliberately using subject-specific vocabulary
- inviting questions and discussion
- helping students to practise new skills and processes with prompts and scaffolds
- withdrawing support so that students can operate independently.

Équipe nouvelle makes the process of modelling easier in the following ways:

- by providing examples, where necessary, for all activities so that students have a visual demonstration of how to complete the activity
- through specific guidance in the teacher's notes
- by providing selected written texts from the Students' Book on OHT to work on with the whole class. See **Ideas for working on longer texts** on page 19.

Questioning

Well-planned questions in the target language can do much to raise the challenge of lessons. The teacher's notes in this book provide specific guidance on how to use questioning techniques to great effect when teaching.

Practice

Équipe nouvelle provides a wealth of meaningful practice activities for students to work on as a class, in pairs or on their own in order to learn and memorize new language.

Plenary activities

Plenaries can play an important part in helping teachers and students put into practice key principles of assessment *for* learning (as distinct from assessment *of* learning). The purpose of plenary activities is to:

- confirm what has been learned (informal assessment) by referring back to learning objectives
- confirm/apply what has been learned by completing a specific task, by taking part in a game/challenge
- confirm that targets set at the start of a lesson have been achieved at the end
- reflect on how the learning has taken place
- explain a specific rule/point of language
- provide/reinforce/apply specific terminology (e.g. agreement, cognate, irregular)
- identify links with previous learning/prior knowledge
- predict the application of learning in everyday communicative contexts
- identify links with other curriculum areas
- understand what could be improved
- understand how improvement might be brought about
- set targets for future lessons
- communicate feelings/opinions about the lesson, e.g. its difficulty, how students felt at the beginning (nervous about challenge?) and at the end (satisfaction over what was achieved)
- understand the "big picture" (key concepts, general principles).

Plenary activities are often cited as being a weaker element in lessons across the curriculum. It is important to plan sufficient time for activities that really allow students to review whether objectives have been met, to focus on the success of their learning, and to look forward to future learning. Using English is not necessarily the most useful or challenging way to conduct the plenary session. Many of the activities suggested below and in the main teaching notes of this book can be conducted in the target language – careful planning is therefore the key to a successful plenary.

Introduction

Each double-page spread of the **Équipe nouvelle** Students' Book contains on-the-page plenary activities entitled *Challenge!* In addition, suggestions for plenary activities are provided in the relevant Short Term Plans and Planning Pages, and some plenary activities are available on the *Challenge!* copymasters.

The following is a reference list of simple plenary activities:

- Opportunities for students to work in pairs/small groups (and then feed back, perhaps to the whole class, perhaps by sending an envoy to another group to compare findings).
- Opportunities to make written notes/provide written responses to questions (and then feed back orally).
- Opportunities for students to question the teacher/other students.
- Opportunities for self- or peer-evaluation.
- In pairs, students draw up a list of the different strategies they have used to learn new language. Pairs exchange their ideas and draw up a list of their Top Five suggestions for effective learning.
- **Show cards**: traffic-light cards (green = completely understand; orange = understand mostly; red = having difficulty). Alternatively, students could simply use a thumbs up or down movement.
- **Odd-one-out**: with a reason from what has been learned in the lesson.
- **Spot the mistake**: with a reason from what has been learned in the lesson.
- **Team games**: see **Starter activities**.
- **Thinking skills**: students summarize what they have learned in the lesson; they suggest other contexts within which they could use this new language.
- **Pairwork**: ask a partner three questions from the lesson/tell your partner three things you have learned in the lesson. Then work with another two students. In groups of four, students feed back to the class.
- **Gap-fill activity**: graduated texts that have increasingly more letters omitted.
- **Hot Seat**: individuals or groups are put in the Hot Seat and have to: a) identify three key points from the lesson; b) answer questions posed by the rest of the class.
- **Mind maps**: often useful towards the end of a unit of work: students draw together what has been learned. They can be used in displays, and added to throughout the year.
- **Written plenary**: students complete a writing frame or questionnaire.

Launching and reinforcing Framework objectives

All Year 8 Framework objectives are launched and reinforced via the *Zoom grammaire*, *Guide pratique*, *Ça se dit comme ça!* and *Point culture* sections in the core spreads of each unit. Cross-references are provided in the Long Term Plan (see page 13), the Medium and Short Term Plans, the unit overview grids, the Planning Pages for each double-page spread and in the teacher's notes themselves.

The following sequence (on pages 13–15) shows how the Framework objective **8S2** (**connectives in extended sentences**) is taught using **Équipe nouvelle 2**. Annotated lesson plans for different ability levels are available on the **Équipe nouvelle 2 Coursemaster**.

YEAR 8 LONG TERM PLAN						
	Unit 1	Unit 2	Unit 3	Unit 4	Unit 5	Unit 6
W1: adding abstract words			L	R		
W2: connectives	L		R	R		
W3: words about progress			L		R	
W4: word endings	L			R	R	
W5: verb tenses	L	R	R	R	R	R
W6: sound–spelling exceptions			L	R		
W7: dictionary detail			L			R
W8: non-literal meanings			L	R		R
S1: word, phrase and clause sequencing	L			R	R	
S2: connectives in extended sentences	L			R	R	
S3: modal verbs			L	R		
S4: question types	L				R	
S5: negative forms and words				L	R	
S6: substituting and adding				L	R	
S7: present, past and future	L	R	R	R	R	R
S8: using high-frequency words and punctuation clues		L				R
T1: meanings in context				L		R
T2: expression in text	L	R				
T3: language and text types					L	R
T4: dictionary use			L			R
T5: writing continuous text				L	R	R
T6: text as model and source			L			R
T7: checking inflections and word order				L		R
L1: listening for subtleties			L	R		
L2: media listening skills	L	R				
L3: relaying gist and detail				L		R
L4: extending sentences	L				R	
L5: unscripted speech			L	R		
L6: expression in speech			L		R	
C1: historical facts	L					R
C2: famous people			L	R		
C3: daily life and young people			L	R		
C4: poems, jokes, songs and stories	L	R				
C5: colloquialisms		L			R	

L = where a Framework objective is **launched**

R = where a Framework objective is **reinforced**

Introduction

YEAR 8 LONG TERM PLAN

	Unit 1	Unit 2	Unit 3	Unit 4	Unit 5	Unit 6
W1: adding abstract words			L	R		
W2: connectives		R	R			
W3: words about progress			L		R	
W4: word endings	L			R	R	
W5: verb tenses	L	R	R	R	R	R
W6: sound–spelling exceptions				L	R	
W7: dictionary detail		L				R
W8: non-literal meanings		L		R		R
S1: word, phrase and clause sequencing	L			R	R	
S2: connectives in extended sentences	L			R	R	
S3: modal verbs			L	R		
S4: question types	L				R	
S5: negative forms and words				L	R	
S6: substituting and adding				L	R	
S7: present, past and future	L	R	R	R	R	R
S8: using high-frequency words and punctuation clues		L				R
T1: meanings in context				L	R	
T2: expression in text	L	R				R
T3: language and text types				L		R
T4: dictionary use		L				R
T5: writing continuous text				L	R	
T6: text as model and source			L			R
T7: checking inflections and word order				L		R
L1: listening for subtleties			L	R		
L2: media listening skills	L	R				
L3: relaying gist and detail			L			R
L4: extending sentences	L				R	
L5: unscripted speech			L	R		
L6: expression in speech			L		R	
C1: historical facts	L					R
C2: famous people		L	R			
C3: daily life and young people		L	R			
C4: poems, jokes, songs and stories	L	R				
C5: colloquialisms		L			R	

L = where a Framework objective is **launched**
R = where a Framework objective is **reinforced**

> The Long Term Plan shows how objective **8S2** will be specifically launched in Unit 1 and reinforced in Units 4 and 5.

> The Medium Term Plan for Unit 1 provides the context and teaching focus to launch objective **8S2**.

ÉQUIPE NOUVELLE 2 UNIT 1 MEDIUM TERM PLAN

About this unit: In this unit students work in the context of personal descriptions, clothes and fashion. They revise personal details and learn to describe what they wear for different occasions, name different styles and give their preferences. At the same time, they develop and consolidate their understanding of gender and adjectives, the present tense of regular and key irregular verbs (*avoir* and *être*) and how to form questions. Students also learn how to use a new irregular verb (*mettre*) and how to use connectives for building extended sentences. They consolidate their ability to pronounce and learn new vocabulary and develop their listening and reading skills, in particular in the contexts of a French song and text about French fashion through the ages. Students learn to understand and use simple comparative expressions on the extension *Super-challenge!* page.

Framework objectives (launch)	Teaching and learning	Week-by-week overview (assuming 6 weeks' work or 10–12.5 hours)
8W2: connectives	Use of *parce que* to support expression of opinions. Use of *quand*, e.g. *Quand il fait beau, je mets mon short bleu et mes sandales*.	**Week 1** Introduction to unit objectives. Revise how to introduce and describe yourself and someone else. Say your nationality. Revise the present tense of *être*. Revise how to ask questions. Revise some sound–spelling links and how to pronounce new words.
8W4: word endings	Singular and plural adjectival agreements (regular and irregular). Reflect on how the verb *mettre* is constructed.	
8W5: verb tenses	Revision of the present tense of *être*, *avoir* and regular *-er* verbs. The present tense of *mettre*.	
8S1: word, phrase and clause sequencing	Position of adjectives.	**Week 2** Name items of clothing. Say what you're wearing. Say what your favourite clothes are. Describe clothes and colours. Revise gender, adjectival agreement and position. Revise the present tense of *avoir*.
8S2: connectives in extended sentences	*Quand il fait beau, je mets …* *Quand je vais au collège, je mets …* *J'aime le look (décontracté) parce que c'est (pratique).*	
8S4: question types	Identify and analyse different question types and revise intonation.	**Week 3** Ask and say what types of clothes you like. Say what you think about clothes/fashions using *parce que*. Revise the present tense of regular *-er* verbs. Pronounce the sounds *un/une*.
8S7: present, past and future	Recognize and use the present tense of *être*, *avoir*, *mettre* and regular *-er* verbs.	
8T2: expression in text	Understand and use the comparative.	
8L2: media listening skills	*La belle équipe* episode 1: students cope with a mixture of familiar and unfamiliar language and different voices, and use visual clues to help them understand the soap episode.	**Week 4** Say what you wear for different occasions and in different weather. Revise going to places using *aller* + preposition + place. Revise the weather. Use connectives in longer sentences.
8L4: extending sentences	Give opinions and make statements about clothes and different styles.	
8C1: historical facts	*Point lecture*: students read and understand a text about French fashion through the ages.	
8C4: poems, jokes, songs and stories	*Point lecture*: students develop reading for pleasure via the song "Le blues du blue-jean".	**Week 5** Develop listening and reading skills via a soap episode.
	Teaching and learning (additional)	
	Personal identification: name, age, where live, hobbies, personality, nationality. Revision of sound–spelling links and how to pronounce new words. Clothes and colours. Weather expressions. *À* + places in town.	**Week 6** *Super-challenge!* for more able students. Recycle language of the unit via *Encore*, *En plus* and *Point lecture* pages. Students check progress via the *Podium* self-assessment checklist in the Students' Book and on Feuille 2.

Introduction

The Short Term Plan for Unit 1 Week 4 focuses on teaching strategies, resources and activities to launch and/or reinforce the Framework objectives.

A full list of possible resources is supplied for each week.

The Learning objectives outline what and how students will learn in that particular week.

Framework objectives are highlighted in bold stating whether they are to be specifically launched or reinforced. Where there is no extra wording, this indicates that there is a further opportunity to reinforce a Framework objective.

Suggestions for ICT and Creative activities (to be completed by students working either individually or in pairs/groups) are given for each week. Some of these activities could be used within lessons, e.g. if you have access to ICT facilities; others would be suitable for homework.

A summary of the key language for each week is given here.

The PoS reference section lists the National Curriculum Programme of Study statements that can be covered each week via the main Students' Book activities and additional suggestions given in the teacher's notes.

A variety of activities are suggested to reinforce the work that has taken place in the lesson.

Suggestions are included for possible starter activities. Some are given as generic ideas; others are accompanied by specific materials.

Suggestions are included for plenary activities. As with starter activities, they take the form either of generic ideas or of specific materials.

Équipe nouvelle 2   **1.4 Qu'est-ce que tu mets?**   **Week 4**

Resources

Students' Book, pages 12–13	*Encore/En plus* Workbooks, pages 7, 8 and 9
Teacher's Book, pages 00–00	Copymasters 6, 10, 12, 14 and 16
CD 1, tracks 00–00	OHT 4
Cassette 0, side 0	Flashcards 88–97

Learning objectives

Students will:
- Say what you wear for different occasions and in different weather (**8W5, 8S7**)
- Revise going to places using *aller* + preposition + place
- Revise the weather
- Use connectives in longer sentences (**8S2, 8L4 – launch**)

Key language

Qu'est-ce que tu mets quand …?
Quand je vais au collège, je mets mon/ma/mes …
Quand il/elle va en ville, il/elle met son/sa/ses …
en ville, au collège, à une boum, au centre sportif, chez mes/tes/ses grands-parents
Quand il fait beau/froid/chaud/gris, …
Quand il y a du soleil/du vent/du brouillard/de l'orage, …
Quand il pleut/neige/gèle, …

PoS reference

1a, 1b, 1c, 2a, 2b, 2c, 2d, 2f, 2g, 2i, 3a, 3c, 3d, 3e, 4a, 4d, 5a, 5d, 5e, 5f, 5i

Homework activities

- *Encore/En plus* Workbooks, pages 7, 8 and 9.
- Copymaster 10 *Lis et écris Encore 2*, activities 1 and 2a.
- Copymaster 12 *Lis et écris En plus 2*, 14 *Grammaire 2* and 16 *Guide pratique 2*.
- Students write a paragraph containing as many different parts of the verb *mettre* as possible.

Starter activities

- *À vos marques*, page 12.
- Say statements using *mettre* in the past, present and future tense. Students raise their hand when they hear a present tense statement. You could progress to asking students to identify the tense.
- Show **OHT 4** and ask students to imagine where each teenager is going and what they are saying, beginning with the word *quand* each time, e.g. *Quand je vais au collège, je mets …*
- Write some weather expressions on the board. Students design symbols to illustrate their meaning.

Plenary activities

- *Challenge!* page 13.
- Copymaster 4 *Challenge!* activity 2.
- Write a selection of sentence endings on the board or OHP, e.g. *… parce que c'est moche./ … mais j'aime bien le look sport./ … j'aime aussi le look décontracté./ … je mets un short.* In pairs, students suggest possible phrases to start each sentence. They should justify their choices.
- In pairs, students discuss strategies for learning and remembering the present tense of the verb *mettre*. Allow time for feedback so that students can share their ideas.

ICT suggestions

- Students design a poster with pictures and captions saying what they wear for different occasions and/or in different weathers. These can be displayed on the classroom wall in order to provide support for students throughout the rest of the unit.
- Students devise a PowerPoint® presentation to show that they understand possessive adjectives.

Creative activities

- See ICT suggestions above.
- Students devise a rap to help them revise the weather expressions.
- Students write poems where the initial letter of the place they are going to is the same as the item of clothing they wear, e.g. *Quand je vais en ville, je mets ma veste. Quand je vais à la plage, je mets mon pantalon. Quand je vais en Afrique, je mets mon anorak.* Encourage them to use their imagination to come up with unusual or wacky combinations.

Introduction

Teaching with Équipe nouvelle

Summary of main characters

The language of **Équipe nouvelle 2** is set in the context of the lives of four teenagers who live in a block of flats in Dieppe. The characters were introduced at the beginning of **Équipe nouvelle 1** and are reintroduced here in Unit 1 of **Équipe nouvelle 2**. As students progress through the book, they learn more about each of the characters in the context of an ongoing photo story at the end of each unit.

The four main characters are: Matthieu Brière, Arnaud Darriet, Natacha Delanoé and Juliette Frontelli.

Features of an Équipe nouvelle unit

Unit opening page

Each unit starts with an overview of the learning objectives to be covered and is accompanied by starter activities to introduce students to the contexts and language of the unit. The setting for each unit is the town of Dieppe and surrounding area, and the four main characters who live in the same block of flats.

Presentation and practice activities

New vocabulary is best introduced using the **Équipe nouvelle Flashcards** and **Équipe nouvelle OHTs**. For specific notes on these components see page 7.

New language is presented in the Students' Book in a variety of ways through photos featuring the four characters, other photos and illustrations. The conversations between the main characters are provided on cassette or CD and should be used for repetition by the students, as this will ensure the best possible pronunciation and intonation. Students will enjoy learning these short exchanges by heart and "performing" them to the rest of the class. More able students can adapt the conversations by substituting phrases with other items of key language.

Underpinning the course structure are the Modern Languages Framework objectives. Each objective is carefully launched and reinforced via the Students' Book units, specifically through the *Zoom grammaire, Guide pratique, Ça se dit comme ça!* and *Point culture* sections, and each spread has been written with the MFL Framework teaching and learning methodology in mind. For more information on **Équipe nouvelle and the Modern Languages Framework** see page 8 of this book.

Students should be encouraged to learn by heart on a regular basis, both items of vocabulary and short conversations. This will promote good language-learning habits and ensure that students are able to transfer language learned to new contexts. The key language of the unit is then developed through a wide variety of mixed-skill practice, with activities to ensure language development from supported/guided to more open-ended. **Équipe nouvelle** intends each activity to have a purpose for learners, to ensure that they find the activities interesting as well as useful in terms of their linguistic development. The copymasters and *Encore/En plus* Workbooks provide further consolidation and practice activities for each unit. Reinforcement and extension activities are provided on the *Encore/En plus* and *Point lecture* pages at the end of the Students' Book. Further grammar practice activities are also provided at the end of the Students' Book in the grammar reference section.

Core spreads

There are four core spreads per unit via which the key language and skills are presented and practised.

Each double-page spread includes:

- specific objectives given in English in student-friendly language to provide students with a clear understanding of what they are going to learn and to motivate them by the speed of their progress.
- a starter activity at the begining of the spread entitled *À vos marques*.
- activities in all four skills to practise the key language of the spread. The rubrics for these activities are bilingual where an instruction is first introduced, then in French only. There are colour-coded words for each skill *Écouter, Parler, Lire, Écrire*.
- *Expressions-* and *Mots-clés* in French. The key language of the spread is summarized in these boxes to provide support and reference for students. Students will find these sections useful for revision, and they may wish to copy this key language into their vocabulary books, although a summary of the key language for each unit is also provided on the *Vocabulaire* page of each unit, on copymaster and in the *Encore/En plus* Workbooks.
- plenary activities at three different levels of difficulty within a section entitled *Challenge!* These activities are ideal for informal class or group assessment. It will often be more appropriate for you, the teacher, to choose which activity or activities individual students should attempt, perhaps dividing them into pairs or small groups, rather than let them choose which one they want to have a go at on their own.

Zoom grammaire

Grammar is included as a central part of each unit, as students need to understand how the language works from an early stage if they are to manipulate and use it successfully in other contexts. Students are exposed to examples that occur naturally in context in the units and are then encouraged to reflect on these and work out the rules. There are practice activities on the page, in the grammar reference section at the back of the Students' Book, on the copymasters and in the *Encore/En plus* Workbooks. An overview of the introduction and recycling of the grammar points of **Équipe nouvelle 2** is given on page 4 of this book.

Guide pratique

This regular feature promotes language-learning skills in a systematic way throughout **Équipe nouvelle**. The learning skills are then developed further with additional practice activities on the Students' Book page and on two corresponding copymasters for each unit. The development of language-learning skills is considered to be an integral part of the language-learning process and should be given sufficient time during whole-class work. Students who are given opportunities to practise these skills from the start will develop into effective independent language learners. For an overview of the language-learning skills of Part 2, see page 4 of this book.

Ça se dit comme ça!
This regular feature encourages learners to focus on improving their pronunciation and intonation, enabling them to develop good habits in spoken French. As in Part 1, there is a great deal of emphasis on sound–spelling links. Sounds which are traditionally more difficult for the English speaker are featured. This section should be made as much fun as possible in class, with whole-class repetition, followed by group- and individual work. Students who find pronunciation difficult should be given opportunities to further practise these sections on a regular basis, perhaps by recording them for independent use. Further practice of the pronunciation points is given on the *Ça se dit comme ça!* copymaster in each unit. An overview of all the pronunciation points for Part 2 is provided in the Summary of unit contents grid on page 4 of this book.

Point culture
This feature points out items of cultural interest that are relevant to the unit, with a practice activity on the Students' Book page.

Songs
Songs and raps are a regular feature of **Équipe nouvelle** and are intended to provide enjoyment as well as to develop language skills. Where possible, encourage students to sing along with the recording, as this will provide additional pronunciation and intonation practice. Some students will enjoy writing additional verses, and more musical students should be encouraged to compose other songs to further practise the language of the unit. For ideas on how to use songs in your lessons see page 19 of this book.

Super-challenge!
This extension page is intended to stretch more able students who are confident with the core language of the unit. It combines language from the unit with unfamiliar language and develops grammar points introduced in the main body of the unit. It can be used flexibly either as part of a teacher-led lesson or as alternative independent class and homework material.

Vocabulaire
This is a full list of the key language for each unit. It is also provided on copymaster and in the *Encore/En plus* Workbooks.

Podium
This bilingual checklist summarizes the learning objectives covered within each unit and contains plenary activities at three different levels of difficulty – bronze, silver and gold – for students to check their progress. Use this checklist actively with students to help them review what they have learned in each unit and to reflect on areas for further revision and practice. Bilingual checklists for each unit are also available on copymaster and in the *Encore/En plus* Workbooks.

Presentation and practice of new language

Équipe nouvelle 2 provides extensive visual support for the purposes of presentation and practice. There are 155 A4 colour flashcards for use with **Équipe nouvelle 1** and **2**. A complete list of these is provided on an index card included in the **Équipe nouvelle 1 and 2 Flashcards** pack. The variety of presentation visuals is intended to be stimulating for students and provide flexibility for teachers. There are also 54 colour and black text OHTs (overhead projector transparencies) to accompany the six units. A contents list for the **Équipe nouvelle 2 OHTs** can be found on page 7 of this book. Comprehensive teacher's notes for using specific flashcards and OHTs can be found in the relevant section of the unit teacher's notes.

General strategies for presenting new language with flashcards/OHTs:

- Show or point to a new item of vocabulary and ask students to repeat, e.g. *C'est un stylo*. Organize new nouns into groups according to gender and introduce one set at a time. This helps to avoid confusion about gender. Make this repetition stage more interesting by varying your voice (e.g. loud/soft/squeaky) or by splitting the class into groups (e.g. boys only/right-hand side of room only).
- Using flashcards: invite a physical response from students to check initial comprehension by sticking flashcards around the room. As you say the word, students point to the relevant card. This is a particularly useful stage with more difficult vocabulary and with less able students.
- Using OHTs: check initial comprehension by naming an item and asking a student to come to the front and point to it. Alternatively, number the items and students give you the number of the item named.
- Check comprehension by asking alternative-type questions, e.g. point to a picture and ask *C'est un crayon ou c'est un stylo?* In the initial stages, it is a good idea to give the correct answer second, so that learners are able to copy the pronunciation more accurately.
- A final open-ended question will check whether learners have grasped the new vocabulary, e.g. *Qu'est-ce que c'est?* With OHTs, cover the item with a coin or piece of card for a memory check, asking *Qu'est-ce que c'est?*
- Point to an item and ask questions requiring a specific answer, for example *Ça coûte combien?*
- With a mixed-ability group, use a mixture of alternative-type questions and open-ended questions, according to the ability of the students.

Introduction

Games to practise language
Suggested games for practising language with flashcards/OHTs:

- **Répétez si c'est vrai**: This is an excellent game for helping students to concentrate. Hold up a flashcard or point to one of the OHTs and make a statement, e.g. *J'ai un rhume* (Flashcard 126). If the students agree with the statement, they repeat it. If not, they remain silent.
- Hold a collection of flashcards facing yourself and hidden from the class, or put a collection of OHTs onto the overhead projector (turned off) and point to one of the illustrations. If the visuals have been cut up, then a single item could be placed on the OHP. Ask *Qu'est-ce que c'est?* and students have to guess which flashcard is facing you or which OHT picture is being pointed to. Students will suggest lots of vocabulary on the topic, which is excellent revision. The element of chance also ensures that it is not always the more able students who win. The winner is the student who guesses correctly. The winner could keep the card or come to the front and hide/select the next one.
- The previous game can be adapted by placing the flashcards in a bag or OHT pictures in an envelope: slowly reveal one flashcard or OHT picture. The winner is the first student to correctly identify it.
- **Qu'est-ce qui manque?**: This suggestion works best with OHTs but could be adapted to include a set of flashcards stuck on the board. Place a selection of OHTs on the overhead projector. Give the class a limited amount of time to look at the visuals, then turn off the overhead projector and remove one item. As soon as the overhead projector is turned on again, the students try to guess which item is missing.
- **Morpion**: Flashcards stuck on the board or OHTs arranged in a grid (using the grid on OHT 10B from the **Équipe nouvelle 1 OHTs**) can be used for playing Noughts and Crosses, with the class divided into two teams. If a team gives the correct word for one of the illustrations, their symbol can be entered, either by removing the flashcard and writing the the team's symbol on the board, or by marking a small nought or cross on an overlay next to the illustration. This game can also be played in pairs or small groups.
- **Loto**: Students play a game of bingo in groups of four or five. One student is the "caller". One set of OHTs can be copied and cut up and used as the "caller's cards". The other students then draw five quick sketches of items for their own Bingo card. The caller then selects cards at random. Any student with the item on their own card crosses it out. Bingo cards for the players could be prepared in advance and students could cover up the picture with a counter when it is called out.

Activities to present, consolidate and revise the alphabet
It is important to reinforce the alphabet frequently, so try to build in the following activities on a regular basis:

- At the start of lessons, ask students to do a quick choral chant (e.g. letters a–g on one occasion, k–t on another, u–z on a third; or use the US marines chant: a, b, c, d, e, f, g – h, i, j, k, l, m, n – o, p, q, r, s, t, u – v, w, x, y, z).
- The class say the alphabet as a loop, each student saying one letter at a time, as a Mexican wave.
- Play a game where students stand up and say the letters one at a time as above, but the students saying vowels must sit down. The last student standing wins. Remind students that *y* is a vowel in French.
- Make opportunities in lessons to practise the alphabet in a communicative context, e.g. by
  - spelling words aloud and asking students to name the words
  - working with students or the whole class (chorally) to spell words aloud (e.g. words on the board or OHP)
  - spelling aloud the first part of the word only and students name the word or complete the spelling
  - naming a student by spelling rather than saying the name.
- Play Hangman or *Loto* with letters of the alphabet.

Activities to practise numbers
It is important to reinforce numbers frequently, so try to build in the following activities on a regular basis:

- Play Mini-battleships or Hand-on-the-buzzer using OHTs 6A and 6B of the **Équipe nouvelle 1 OHTs**. Divide the class into two teams, A and B. Give the coordinates of a number in figures, e.g. 3A. Students must say the number in the square (17) and find the coordinates of its written form (2F). The fastest to give the answer is the winner.
- Play Noughts and Crosses using a grid with a different number in each of the nine squares: when students say the name of the number correctly or write it in figures on the board or on their mini-whiteboards, you circle it or put a cross on it. The aim is to have three numbers in a row.
- Play Pelmanism using OHTs 1A and 1B or 6A and 6B from the **Équipe nouvelle 1 OHTs**. Cover all the squares with small sticky notes and divide the class into two teams. The teams take turns at giving the coordinates of a number. They must find the matching number, reading out the coordinates and the number to win the pair.
- Organize students into pairs and ask them to say alternate numbers up to a given number – 31, 69, 100, etc.
- Play *Loto* by asking students to make their own lottery ticket and listen as you call the winning numbers.
- Conduct a mental arithmetic contest in class.
- Ask students to make small number playing cards for use in games such as Snap (they must say the appropriate number instead of the word "snap") and Pelmanism (pairs of cards are placed face down on the desk and they take turns to try to turn over and name a matching pair in order to win the cards).
- Time students to see who can say a certain string of numbers, e.g. 40–50, in the shortest time.
- Photocopy a newspaper report of temperatures around the world and have students dictate the temperatures to their partner.

Useful language for playing games in French

It is worth spending time on a regular basis revising the language for pairwork to ensure that learners are able to play their games in the target language. Other useful expressions for playing games are listed below.

On commence?	Shall we start?
Je commence.	I'll start.
Tu commences.	You start.
Vas-y.	Go on.
Attends/Attendez.	Wait.
Où est la tableau?	Where is the board?
Je n'ai pas de jeton.	I haven't got a counter.
Donne-moi le dé.	Give me the die.
Jette le dé.	Throw the die.
Encore une fois.	Again.
C'est à qui?	Whose turn is it?
(C'est) à moi.	(It's) my turn.
(C'est) à toi.	(It's) your turn.
Avance d'une case.	Move forward one square.
Recule de deux cases.	Move back two squares.
Tu as les cartes?	Have you got the cards?
Distribue les cartes.	Deal the cards.
Prends une carte.	Take a card.
Ne regarde pas la carte.	Don't look at the card.
Cache tes cartes.	Hide your cards.
Pose une carte.	Put down a card.
Arrête.	Stop.
Continue.	Carry on.
Comme ça.	Like that.
Pas comme ça.	Not like that.
Tricheur!	Cheat! (for a boy)
Tricheuse!	Cheat! (for a girl)
En français!	In French!
J'ai gagné.	I've won.
On a fini.	We've finished.

Using songs

Using songs is a very important and motivating way to practise new language with students. The rhythm of the music and musical rhymes can help students with different learning styles to memorize the sound and pronunciation of key language. General ideas and ways of using songs:

- Start the lesson with a familiar song to get students in the mood and all using the target language.
- Allow students to hear the whole song before working on it in smaller sections, perhaps starting with the chorus where applicable.
- Don't worry if you're no good at singing – mouthing the words of the song will encourage students to join in.
- Use flashcards or visuals to provide support for a new song.
- Encourage students to make up actions for a song if appropriate.
- Split the class into two groups – who can sing the loudest/the most tunefully?
- Present the song lyrics as a gapped passage – students listen and write in the missing words.
- Perform the songs (e.g. to another class, at an assembly, at an open evening).
- If students enjoy singing, encourage them to set key language to well-known tunes, e.g. school subjects to the tune of "John Brown's body". Use the words of the song as a reading text for students to illustrate or make up questions to test a partner.
- End the lesson with a song. Students will leave the classroom humming the tune and singing the song!

Ideas for working on longer texts

Équipe nouvelle provides some of its longer texts on OHT to be used for whole-class teaching. General ideas and ways to teach texts on OHT include:

- Students look at the text and try to work out who it is aimed at by using available clues: title, layout of the text, artwork or photos used.
- Challenge students to find as many cognates as they can within a set time limit.
- Give students a list of key words to look for. They note the line where the word features or underline the word if they have their own copy of the text. They then either guess its meaning or look up the meaning in the glossary or a dictionary.
- Ask students to note down or underline in one colour any words they already know. They then identify words they could guess because they look like English words (cognates or near-cognates), and note these down or underline them in a different colour.
- If there is a recording to accompany the text, display the OHT while students listen to the recording and gradually start to blank out some key words (with small pieces of paper or putty adhesive) and ask students to listen for them. Play the recording again, this time pausing before each blanked out word, and ask students to supply the missing word.
- Present a summary in English that contains one or two discrepancies, which students identify and correct.
- Ask comprehension questions: true/false statements, questions which require specific detail in the answer.
- Make a copy of the OHT and cut it up for sequencing: students come to the OHP and reorder the elements.

Using the soap story: *La belle équipe*

At the end of the core spreads in each of the six units in **Équipe nouvelle 2** there is an episode of the soap story, *La belle équipe*, featuring four teenage friends. Language from the unit is recycled in the context of events in their lives, and the episode will motivate students by offering characters for them to identify with and a storyline to follow. There are activities on the page to help them cope with the unfamiliar and also to help develop their reading strategies.

Introduction

A summary of the storyline for each episode is included in the teacher's notes.

There are many ways to approach using the story and you will need to select those most appropriate for your students. The following suggestions may be useful:

- Ask students to work through the exploitation activities individually or in pairs. The first activity is always a gist reading activity and is then followed by more detailed comprehension activities.
- Students read the soap and, working with a partner, identify new language they have learned in the unit.
- Allow students to listen to the recording while reading. In this way they will be encouraged to read for gist and won't have time to stop and worry about individual words.
- Develop reading strategies by asking open-ended questions such as *Qui peut expliquer un peu l'histoire … en anglais, bien sûr?* Encourage students to deduce the meanings of new words that are cognates; ask students to look up a maximum of five words in the glossary and share their findings with a partner; ask students to pick out key words; ask students to make a list of any questions occurring in the soap episode, to ask a partner who can either answer from the story or give another appropriate answer.
- When students have listened to the episode and read it several times, divide the class into groups who each take one of the parts. Choral reading gives all students the opportunity to practise reading aloud, without putting any individual on the spot.
- More confident students could take a part each. Each student reads his/her part along with the recording. This will encourage fluency as students try to keep up with the speed of the recording. Turn down the volume every now and then, so that the students continue to speak unaccompanied, and then turn the volume back up again to see if they have managed to keep up with the recording.
- Students could work in groups to act out each episode or record their own version on cassette digitally using the sound recorder or on video.
- After each episode, write a brief summary of it on OHT with the help of the students. The OHT can then be shown at the start of the next episode to remind students of the storyline so far. For the first few units, you may have to prompt the summary with oral questions for the students to answer. Creating a summary in this collaborative way allows you to accept suggestions from the students, while at the same time correcting any inaccuracies and improving the quality of language as you write the suggestions onto OHT for the class to see. As they become more used to this process, some students might like to draft their own summary of the story.
- Students work in pairs to word-process a summary of the episode in exactly 40 words. The limited word count encourages them to really think about their choice of vocabulary, etc.
- Alternatively, ask students to write a "photo brief" for each scene, e.g. in Unit 3 Photo 1: *Matthieu est malade. Il est dans son lit. Il parle avec Natacha au téléphone.*

Target language in the classroom

Équipe nouvelle aims to maximize the use of French as the means of communication in the classroom by providing rubrics in French. Planned progression ensures that students have opportunities to develop their ability to use language spontaneously.

Some suggestions for revising target language phrases:

- Play *Ça se dit comment?* at the start or end of the lesson. Two students come to the front of the class and the teacher asks a question (e.g. *Ça se dit comment* "I haven't got a partner" *en français?*). The winner is the first one to answer correctly. Another student then comes to the front to challenge the winner. Who can stay out at the front the longest? As students become more confident, place greater emphasis on correct pronunciation and intonation. Some students will enjoy assuming the role of the teacher, too.
- Choose, as a class, a *phrase de la semaine* to display at the front of the class. Every time a student uses the phrase in a relevant way a point is awarded. The points are added together at the end of the week. Can the score be beaten by the phrase for the following week?
- Display key target language phrases in the classroom for students to refer to easily. To ensure that students don't rely on these phrases too much, cover up particular words (perhaps using sticky notes) on a rotational basis.
- Use brainstorming of target language phrases as a team game on a regular basis. Students work in pairs or teams to complete a phrase (e.g. *J'ai oublié …*) with as many possibilities as they can in three minutes. This could be varied to incorporate phrases for pairwork (*Note les phrases pour le travail avec un/une partenaire*) or questions (*Note des questions pour le professeur ou un/une partenaire*). Again, a time limit provides a useful element of competition.

A systematic and gradual introduction of key target language phrases will ensure that students recognize instructions quickly. Refer to your departmental policy for target language, but the following phrases might prove a useful starting point:

Assieds-toi/Asseyez-vous!
Lève-toi/Levez-vous!
Viens ici/Venez ici!
Tu comprends/Vous comprenez?
Silence, s'il te plaît/Silence, s'il vous plaît.
Écoutez la cassette/le CD/les instructions.
Regardez …
Distribue(z) les cahiers.
Ouvrez vos livres à la page x.
Faites l'activité x, page x.
Écrivez …
Remplissez la feuille de travail.
Copiez la grille dans vos cahiers.
Notez les devoirs maintenant.
Préparez …
Rangez vos affaires.
Travaillez avec un/une partenaire.
Travaillez en groupes de trois.
Changez de rôle.
Fermez/Ouvrez la porte!
Fermez/Ouvrez la fenêtre!

The following are useful phrases for students to use to communicate in the target language:

Bonjour!
Au revoir!
Merci.
S'il vous plaît.
Oui.
Non.
C'est quelle page?
J'ai oublié … (mon cahier).
Tu as/Vous avez (un stylo)?
Je n'ai pas de …
Ça se dit comment "pen" en français?
Ça se dit comment "stylo" en anglais?
Qu'est-ce que c'est?
C'est qui?
J'ai fini.
Je ne comprends pas.
Il est absent.
Elle est absente.
Le week-end dernier, (j'ai regardé la télé).
Hier soir, (je suis allé(e) au cinéma).

Differentiation

There will be a broad range of students within most classes. Ideas for consolidation and extension activities are given for each unit in the Teacher's Book.

There are particular features of **Équipe nouvelle** which will make it easier to differentiate work:

- On each double-page spread there are *Challenge!* activities at three levels of difficulty. These activities always occur at the end of the spread to consolidate and extend the key language.
- At the end of each unit there is a *Super-challenge!* page to extend the language of the unit in a new context.
- For each unit, there are *Encore* and *En plus* pages at the back of the Students' Book. The *Encore* pages are intended for students who require more support, and who may need to take some of the points of the main unit at a slower pace. The *En plus* pages are intended for more able students and could be used in several ways. More able students could do the activities on these pages when they have completed other activities quickly. Both sections could be used for homework or independent work in class including cover work. For some of the activities, students will need a copy of the cassette or CD.
- The *Podium* checklist provides activities at three levels of difficulty to test students' knowledge, so students can choose the one they feel most comfortable with. Differentiation by outcome will play a major part of the assessment of these activities.
- The *Point lecture* reading section at the back of the Students' Book provides two pages of graded reading material per unit.
- The copymasters provide differentiated activities on the *Écoute*, *Parle*, *Lis et écris* and *Contrôles* sheets.
- Within the teaching notes for individual activities, there are often suggestions for differentiation, e.g. varying the amount of support offered and adapting the tasks slightly to suit different students.

- The *Encore* and *En plus* Workbooks provide differentiated support material for each unit. The *Encore* Workbooks provide consolidation and reinforcement activities for lower attainers whilst the *En plus* Workbooks provide extension activities for more able students. Both Workbooks can be used in class or for homework.
- The **Équipe nouvelle en clair** resource file provides invaluable support material to help less able students access the core Students' Book activities.

The following additional classroom management suggestions may help teachers wishing to further differentiate activities:

- Listening activities: provide individual copies of cassettes and CDs for less able students to work at their own pace, allowing them to play the recording several times, possibly with the transcript. Encourage more able students who complete a listening task on the first hearing to note any other information they hear and check this against the transcript.
- Paired/Group listening, reading and writing: students can usefully work together on many activities. Two weaker students working together will usually tackle a task with more success than one. A more able student working with a less able student will have the dual effect of helping one student, while consolidating language for the other.
- Writing activities: encourage students to prepare a first draft of longer writing activities (e.g. the *Podium* activities). They could then improve this in consultation with you or other students. This would help less able students to avoid making basic errors and encourage more able students to use a wider variety of vocabulary and structure.
- Regular groupwork lessons: organize groupwork lessons on a regular basis to provide students with appropriate consolidation and extension work. For example, a groupwork lesson towards the end of a unit might have a group of students revising basic vocabulary playing language games (see pages 18–19 of this book for ideas), a group working on the activities on the copymasters, a group working on the soap spread, and a group of students working on the *Point lecture* pages. If a computer is available in the classroom, some students could work on drafting and redrafting written work.

Independent learning

In the early stages of learning a new language, students are reasonably dependent on their teacher for presentation of new language. However, certain features of **Équipe nouvelle** are designed to encourage learner independence:

- The *Point lecture* pages at the back of the Students' Book, with their emphasis on reading for pleasure, are an ideal opportunity for students to work independently. Bilingual rubrics are given where appropriate, for maximum clarity.
- The *Encore* and *En plus* pages at the back of the Students' Book are also ideal for students to work on independently. Again, bilingual rubrics are provided where appropriate, as support.
- The *Podium* and *Vocabulaire* pages at the end of each unit and the *Podium* copymasters could be used independently by students to review their progress and highlight any areas requiring further revision. It is worth spending time with the whole class early on to establish this practice so that students know how to review their progress.

Introduction

- The *Grammaire* section at the back of the Students' Book provides full explanations of all the grammar points in English and also provides additional practice activities. Some students will find this invaluable when revising a unit's grammar points.
- All the copymasters contain clear rubrics and the *Grammaire, Guide pratique* and *Ça se dit comme ça!* copymasters include "Flashback" explanations in English. This is to ensure that students clearly understand the concepts and can work on these copymasters independently, either on their own or with a partner.
- The **Équipe nouvelle Interactive CD-ROM** can be used in class or it can be made available for students to use independently on other occasions. Again, it encourages regular revision and recycling of previously learned language.

Thinking skills

One of the key aims of **Équipe nouvelle**, and of the MFL Framework as a whole, is that students should be able to learn in a meaningful way, to think flexibly and give reasons for their answers. Even in the early stages of language learning this can be encouraged, by allowing students time to reflect on what they have just learned and applying this knowledge to other contexts. It is important to allow students time to reflect, analyse, problem-solve and make predictions based on previous knowledge if they are to move towards becoming more independent language learners. If students take a more active role in their language learning, they make quicker progress and the thinking skills learned can be applied to other curriculum areas.

Équipe nouvelle helps students to develop their thinking skills by offering them challenging tasks on a regular basis so that they have to think through a problem which may have more than one correct answer:

- The *Zoom grammaire, Guide pratique, Ça se dit comme ça!* and *Point culture* sections all contain open-ended questions that encourage students to draw on their existing knowledge to work out a new problem. It is often best to work on these sections as a whole class with students so that you can discuss the problem or question together and listen and respond to each other's proposed solutions. By doing this, students will learn more about the thinking process involved. Suggestions are given in this book for when you could ask your students questions to challenge or confirm their thinking.
- The *Challenge!* plenary activities provide an opportunity to check learning against the spread objectives and to check students' reasoning for their answers.
- The *Podium* checklist activities on copymaster and in the Students' Book also help students to reflect on their own learning.

Assessment

Assessment of learning

Regular assessment of student progress is an integral part of the learning process. **Équipe nouvelle** offers an approach to assessment in line with the National Curriculum and the 5–14 National Guidelines.

At the start of the teacher's notes for each unit there is an **Assessment opportunities** section. This selects activities from the forthcoming unit that may be suitable to assess certain skills for formative assessment purposes. Rather than attempt to assess all four skill areas in each unit, the **Assessment opportunities** section focuses on different skill areas each time.

Équipe nouvelle also includes summative assessment material on *Contrôle* copymasters after Units 2, 4 and 6. This is designed to coincide with the *Révisions* pages in the Students' Book after every second unit. Each test has eight sheets – two sheets per skill at differentiated levels (*Encore* and *En plus*) for lower and higher attainers respectively. The *Encore* sheets cover levels 1–4 and the *En plus* sheets cover levels 3–5. Students complete a test at either *Encore* or *En plus* level for each skill. Answers, a mark scheme and assessment criteria are provided for all assessment material. Each assessment copymaster has a total of 25 marks so each test can be marked as a percentage. The assessment materials are graded, so you can easily select particular activities for some students, if appropriate.

See also **Équipe nouvelle and the National Curriculum** (page 23).

Assessment for Learning

Assessment for Learning (AFL) (which can be found in "Module 1: Training materials for the Foundation Subjects" in the MFL Framework training documentation) helps students to know and understand the standard they are aiming for, and also to understand what they need to do in order to achieve their objectives. It involves not only sharing learning goals with students, but also involving them in both peer- and self-assessment. AFL stresses the importance of ensuring that the information gained about students' progress is used, by both teachers and learners, to identify the next steps for learning. This might involve giving students opportunities to talk about what they have learned and what they have found difficult.

The *Challenge!* plenary activities, the *Podium* checklist and end-of-unit tasks at bronze, silver and gold levels provide opportunities for students to evaluate their own learning in a meaningful way.

Équipe nouvelle and the National Curriculum

National Curriculum information – Programme of Study (PoS) coverage and AT levels – is provided in the unit overview grids at the start of each unit. In addition, the Planning Pages for each double-page spread list the PoS statements covered.

AT levels are suggested for all activities where appropriate but these should be used in conjunction with the level descriptions in the National Curriculum Programme of Study. Students' achievements will vary according to the amount of support given, reference materials used and the context of the activity.

Équipe nouvelle and the QCA Scheme of Work

Équipe nouvelle has been planned and written with close reference to the QCA Scheme of Work. The **Équipe nouvelle Coursemaster** CD-ROM provides unit overviews which follow the style of the QCA Scheme of Work documentation.

Teaching in Scotland

A Scottish version of the **Équipe nouvelle Coursemaster** CD-ROM provides a Scheme of Work which has been written for the Scottish curriculum and can be adapted for the needs of your school. This includes guidance on the best way to plan for progression from primary to secondary level with Oxford University Press Modern Languages resources.

Teaching in Wales

A Welsh version of the **Équipe nouvelle Coursemaster** CD-ROM provides a Scheme of Work which has been written for the Welsh curriculum and can be adapted for the needs of your school.

Équipe nouvelle and ICT

Throughout this Teacher's Book you will find a wealth of suggestions on how to use ICT in your lessons. There are four "ICT Suggestions" sections per unit – one for each core teaching spread. They can be found on the Planning Pages for each spread. Some of the ICT ideas could be used within lessons when you have access to ICT facilities; others would be suitable for homework too.

There is also a dedicated ICT component for **Équipe nouvelle 2**, which contains a bank of video-based material featuring French teenagers in France discussing the topic areas that feature in **Équipe nouvelle**. There are student activities to accompany this material and full teacher's material to help with evaluation and assessment. See your copy of the OUP Modern Languages Catalogue or ask your local Representative for details.

Unit 1 Overview grid

National Curriculum

Pages/Contexts/Cultural focus	Objectives	Grammar	Skills and Pronunciation	Key language	Framework	PoS	AT level
6–7 **1.1 Je me présente** Personal details Describing self and others Nationality	Revise how to introduce and describe yourself and others; say your nationality; revise how to ask questions; revise the present tense of *être*; revise sound–spelling links	Present tense of *être* (revision)	Question forms Intonation in questions Pronouncing new language	*Tu es de quelle nationalité? Je suis français(e)/anglais(e)/écossais(e)/ irlandais(e)/gallois(e). Est-ce que/qu'…? Il est français. Elle est française.* Revision of personal information, e.g. name, age, birthday, where live, describing character and appearance, leisure activities	8S4 – L (7W5, 7W6, 7W7, 7S7)	1a, 1b, 1c, 2a, 2b, 2c, 2d, 2h, 3a, 3c, 3d, 3e, 4a, 4d, 5a, 5d, 5e, 5f, 5i	1.2, 2.2–4, 3.2–3, 4.2–4
8–9 **1.2 Ma tenue préférée** Clothes and colours Favourite clothes	Describe clothes and colours; say what you're wearing and what your favourite clothes are; revise gender, adjectival agreement and position; revise the present tense of *avoir*; revise how to pronounce new words	Gender, adjective agreement and position Present tense of *avoir* (revision)	Pronouncing new words	*un anorak/blouson/jean/pantalon/ pull/short/sweat/tee-shirt; une casquette/chemise/cravate/jupe/ robe/veste; des baskets/bottes/ chaussettes/chaussures/sandales C'est quoi, ta tenue préférée? Ma tenue préférée, c'est …* Colour adjectives	8W4, 8S1 – L (7W7)	1a, 1b, 1c, 2a, 2b, 2c, 2f, 3a, 3b, 3c, 3d, 3e, 4a, 4d, 5a, 5c, 5d, 5e, 5f, 5i	1.2, 2.2–3, 3.2, 4.2–3
10–11 **1.3 J'adore le look sport** Styles of clothing Opinions, likes and dislikes	Talk about the types of clothes you like; say what you think about clothes and fashions using *parce que*; revise the present tense of regular -*er* verbs; pronounce the sounds *un/une*	Present tense of regular -*er* verbs	Justifying opinions using *parce que* Pronunciation of *un* and *une*	*Qu'est-ce que tu aimes comme look? J'adore/J'aime bien/Je n'aime pas/ Je déteste le look décontracté/sport/ habillé parce que c'est pratique/ sympa/chic/moche.*	8W2, 8W5, 8S7 – L	1a, 1b, 1c, 2a, 2b, 2c, 2f, 2h, 2i, 3b, 3c, 3d, 3e, 4a, 4d, 5a, 5c, 5d, 5e, 5f, 5i	1.2–3, 2.2–3, 3.2–3, 4.2–4
12–13 **1.4 Qu'est-ce que tu mets?** Clothes for different occasions Weather	Say what you wear for different occasions and in different weather; revise going to places using *aller* + preposition + place; revise the weather; use connectives in longer sentences	Present tense of *mettre* Possessive adjectives *mon/ma/mes, ton/ta/tes, son/sa/ses*	Use of *quand* as a connective in extended sentences	*Qu'est-ce que tu mets quand …? Quand je vais au collège, je mets mon/ma/mes … Quand il/elle va en ville, il/elle met son/sa/ses … en ville, au collège, à une boum, au centre sportif, chez mes/tes/ses grands-parents Quand il fait beau/froid/chaud/ gris. … Quand il y a du soleil/du vent/du brouillard/de l'orage. … Quand il pleut/neige/gèle, …*	8S2, 8L4 – L	1a, 1b, 1c, 2a, 2b, 2c, 2d, 2f, 2g, 2i, 3a, 3c, 3d, 3e, 4a, 4d, 5a, 5d, 5e, 5f, 5i	1.2, 2.2–3, 3.1, 4.2–3
14–15 **1.5 La belle équipe, épisode 1** Soap story	Develop listening and reading skills via a soap story based on the language of the unit				8L2 – L	1a, 1c, 2a, 2b, 2c, 2g, 2h, 3b, 3c, 3e, 4a, 4d, 5a, 5d, 5e, 5g, 5i	1.2, 1.4, 2.2, 2.4, 3.2, 3.4
16 **Super-challenge!** French-speaking regions (Quebec)	Describe yourself and someone else in more detail; understand and use comparative adjectives	Comparative adjectives		*Je suis plus/moins grand(e)/ petit(e)/âgé(e)/jeune/intelligent(e) que mon frère/ma sœur/mon père*, etc.	8T2 – L	1b, 1c, 2c, 2h, 2i, 3a, 3c, 3d, 3e, 4c, 4d, 5a, 5d, 5e, 5g, 5i	2.2–3, 3.3–4, 4.4

ÉQUIPE NOUVELLE 2 UNIT 1 MEDIUM TERM PLAN

About this unit: In this unit students work in the context of personal descriptions, clothes and fashion. They revise personal details and learn to describe what they wear for different occasions, name different styles and give their preferences. At the same time, they develop and consolidate their understanding of gender and adjectives, the present tense of regular and key irregular verbs (*avoir* and *être*) and how to form questions. Students also learn how to use a new irregular verb (*mettre*) and how to use connectives for building extended sentences. They consolidate their ability to pronounce and learn new vocabulary and develop their listening and reading skills, in particular in the contexts of a French song and text about French fashion through the ages. Students learn to understand and use simple comparative expressions on the extension *Super-challenge!* page.

Framework objectives (launch)	Teaching and learning	Week-by-week overview (assuming 6 weeks' work or 10–12.5 hours)
8W2: connectives	Use of *parce que* to support expression of opinions. Use of *quand*, e.g. *Quand il fait beau, je mets mon short bleu et mes sandales*.	**Week 1** Introduction to unit objectives. Revise how to introduce and describe yourself and someone else. Say your nationality. Revise the present tense of *être*. Revise how to ask questions. Revise some sound–spelling links and how to pronounce new words.
8W4: word endings	Singular and plural adjectival agreements (regular and irregular). Reflect on how the verb *mettre* is constructed.	
8W5: verb tenses	Revision of the present tense of *être*, *avoir* and regular *-er* verbs. The present tense of *mettre*.	**Week 2** Name items of clothing. Say what you're wearing. Say what your favourite clothes are. Describe clothes and colours. Revise gender, adjectival agreement and position. Revise the present tense of *avoir*.
8S1: word, phrase and clause sequencing	Position of adjectives.	
8S2: connectives in extended sentences	*Quand il fait beau, je mets,* *Quand je vais au collège, je mets …* *J'aime le look (décontracté) parce que c'est (pratique)*.	**Week 3** Ask and say what types of clothes you like. Say what you think about clothes/fashions using *parce que*. Revise the present tense of regular *-er* verbs. Pronounce the sounds *un/une*.
8S4: question types	Identify and analyse different question types and revise intonation.	
8S7: present, past and future	Recognize and use the present tense of *être*, *avoir*, *mettre* and regular *-er* verbs.	**Week 4** Say what you wear for different occasions and in different weather. Revise going to places using *aller* + preposition + place. Revise the weather. Use connectives in longer sentences.
8T2: expression in text	Understand and use the comparative.	
8L2: media listening skills	*La belle équipe* episode 1: students cope with a mixture of familiar and unfamiliar language and different voices, and use visual clues to help them understand the soap episode.	**Week 5** Develop listening and reading skills via a soap episode.
8L4: extending sentences	Give opinions and make statements about clothes and different styles.	
8C1: historical facts	*Point lecture*: students read and understand a text about French fashion through the ages.	**Week 6** *Super-challenge!* for more able students. Recycle language of the unit via *Encore*, *En plus* and *Point lecture* pages. Students check progress via the *Podium* self-assessment checklist in the Students' Book and on Feuille 2.
8C4: poems, jokes, songs and stories	*Point lecture*: students develop reading for pleasure via the song "Le blues du blue-jean".	
Teaching and learning (additional)		
	Personal identification: name, age, where live, hobbies, personality, nationality. Revision of sound–spelling links and how to pronounce new words. Clothes and colours. Weather expressions. À + places in town.	

1 Mode ado

Unit objectives
Contexts: self, clothes
Grammar: revision of present tense of *-er* verbs, *être* and *avoir*; present tense of *mettre*; revision of adjectives (gender agreement/position); revision of *mon, ma, mes; ton, ta, tes; son, sa, ses*; comparison
Language learning: questions; giving opinions; using connectives (*parce que, quand*)
Pronunciation: *ch, s/ss*, nasal *an/on; un/une*
Cultural focus: Quebec; women's fashion in the 20th century

Assessment opportunities
Listening: Students' Book, page 97, *Encore*, activities 5a and 5b; Students' Book, page 121, *Point lecture*, activity 3
Reading: Students' Book, page 97, *Encore*, activity 6a; Students' Book, page 109, *En plus*, activities 3a and 3b

Presentation
You may like to use **OHT 1A** as a stimulus for brainstorming what students remember about the four friends and to revise some language from *Équipe nouvelle 1*. Ask students to imagine what the characters might be saying about themselves. Then put on overlay **OHT 1B** and/or move on to activity **1a** in the Students' Book.

AT 1.2
AT 3.2
1a *Écoute et lis. C'est qui?*
This opening page of the unit reminds students of the four main characters from *Équipe nouvelle 1*. Students listen to the recording while following the text in the Students' Book, then check comprehension by deciding who sentences a–e refer to. Draw attention to the use of *il* and *elle* in sentences a and d: two of the characters are aged 15, but one is male (*il*) and the other is female (*elle*). Compare this with *son anniversaire* in question e: point out that *son* can mean either "his" or "her". You could also remind students of negatives by focusing on *ne … pas* in sentence c. If appropriate, ask students further comprehension questions in either French or English.

Answers: a Natacha Delanoé; b Arnaud Darriet; c Juliette Frontelli; d Matthieu Brière; e Matthieu Brière

CD 1, track 1
Cassette 1, side 1
page 5, activité 1a

– Salut! Je m'appelle Arnaud Darriet. J'habite à Dieppe. J'ai un demi-frère et une sœur, et j'ai un chien qui s'appelle Hot-dog.
– Moi, je m'appelle Natacha Delanoé. J'ai quinze ans. Mon anniversaire, c'est le 8 mai.
– Je m'appelle Matthieu Brière. J'ai quinze ans. Mon anniversaire, c'est le 31 janvier. J'habite avec mon père.
– Bonjour. Je suis Juliette Frontelli. J'ai seize ans. J'habite à Dieppe avec ma grand-mère parce que mon père est au Canada.

AT 2.2
1b *A dit une phrase, B dit la personne.*
Students work in pairs to practise giving information about the four characters.

AT 2.2
AT 4.2
2 *Remue-méninges à deux. Vous souvenez-vous d'autre chose sur les quatre personnages?*
Students work in pairs to note down any other information they remember about the four characters from *Équipe nouvelle 1*. Ask them to feed back to the class while you record the information on the board or OHP. You could use this as an opportunity to recap on some of the language from Part 1 of the course.

Mode ado **1**

Planning Page

1.1 Je me présente — pages 6–7

Objectives
- Revise how to introduce and describe yourself and someone else
- Say your nationality
- Revise the present tense of *être* (**7W5, 7S7**)
- Revise how to ask questions (**8S4 – L**)
- Revise sound–spelling links (**7W6, 7W7**)

Resources
Students' Book, pages 6–7
CD 1, tracks 2–7; CD 3, tracks 5–6
Cassette 1, side 1; cassette 4, side 1
Encore/En plus Workbooks, page 4
OHTs 1A, 1B and 2
Copymasters 3, 11, 15 and 17

Key language
Tu es de quelle nationalité?
Je suis français(e)/anglais(e)/écossais(e)/irlandais(e)/gallois(e).
Il est français, etc. *Elle est française*, etc.
Est-ce que/qu'…?
plus revision of language for expressing personal information, e.g. name, age, birthday, where you live, describing character and appearance, leisure activities, etc.

Programme of Study reference
1a, 1b, 1c, 2a, 2b, 2c, 2d, 2h, 3a, 3c, 3d, 3e, 4a, 4d, 5a, 5d, 5e, 5f, 5i

Starters
- *À vos marques*, page 6.
- Copymaster 3 *À vos marques*, activities 1a and 1b.
- Use **OHT 1A** with **1B**. Stick blobs of putty adhesive over some of the words in the bubbles and ask students to supply the missing words. Turn this into a game of teacher versus class: a point to the class if they provide the right word first time, a point to you if they are wrong.
- Make a photocopy of **OHT 1A** for each student and ask them to write suitable sentences in the bubbles to recap on language from the previous lesson. To support less able students, you could provide some of the key words on the board or OHP.

ICT suggestions
- Students word-process the letter they write in activity **3**, using colour to highlight the cue words they have included.
- Students design a poster to show different ways of forming questions in French.

Creative activities
- In pairs or groups, students design a board or card game to practise questions and the vocabulary of the spread.
- In groups of three or four, students set the *Expressions-clés* and/or the language of describing yourself to a well-known tune, as in the *Zoom grammaire* on page 6.
- In pairs, students devise and record interviews using the questions from *À vos marques*. One plays the part of the interviewer, the other takes on the role of a famous person. They could record their interview on cassette or act it out to the class.

Plenaries
- *Challenge!* page 7.
- In pairs, students summarize in English what they have learned in the lesson and then report back to the rest of the class.
- Show the class a soft toy (a person, not an animal) or a photo of a person (not famous) cut from a magazine. Go round the class asking each student in turn to invent a piece of personal information for the character (*il s'appelle X, il a X ans, il est français, il est petit, il aime le football*, etc.). A volunteer could act as scribe and write all the statements on the board or OHP to ensure that no one repeats a detail.

Homework suggestions
- *Encore/En plus* Workbooks, page 4.
- Copymaster 15, activities 1 and 2a.
- Students write an interview with a famous person or historical character, using the questions in *À vos marques* as a stimulus. Encourage them to use a range of question types.

1 Mode ado

1.1 Je me présente
pages 6–7

À vos marques

AT 3.2 **a** *Trouve une réponse pour chaque question. Tu as 20 secondes!*
This activity revises how to ask for and express personal information. It also reminds students of question forms and serves as an introduction to the *Guide pratique*. There is one new question (*Tu es de quelle nationalité?*), which students should be able to deduce because of the cognate *nationalité*; and they should be able to work out the answer to this question (*Je suis français*) because they already know the word *français* from Part 1 of the course (see *Départ!* and Unit 3 in *Équipe nouvelle 1*). If you do this as a whole-class activity, you could add an element of suspense by counting down aloud from 20 to zero while students find the correct answers.

Answers: 1b; 2d; 3f; 4c; 5e; 6a

AT 1.2 **b** *Écoute et vérifie.*
Students listen to the recording to check their answers.

CD 1, track 2
Cassette 1, side 1
page 6, À vos marques

– Tu t'appelles comment?
– Je m'appelle Alex.
– Tu as quel âge?
– J'ai treize ans.
– Tu habites où?
– J'habite dans le sud de la France.
– Qu'est-ce que tu fais le week-end?
– J'écoute de la musique et je fais du sport.
– Tu es comment?
– Je suis grand et blond.
– Tu es de quelle nationalité?
– Je suis français.

AT 3.2 **c** *Traduis en anglais.*
Students translate the questions and answers into English.

Answers: 1 What is your name? My name is Alex. 2 How old are you? I am 13 years old. 3 Where do you live? I live in the south of France. 4 What do you do at the weekend? I listen to music and I do/play sport. 5 What are you like? I am tall and have blond hair. 6 What nationality are you? I am French.

Follow-up activity: Students could, in pairs, read aloud the question-and-answer sequence as an interview and/or write it out in full.

AT 2.2 **1** *Pose les questions d'À vos marques à un(e) partenaire. Il/Elle répond.*
Students work in pairs, asking each other the questions from *À vos marques* and answering with their own information.

Guide pratique
This section focuses on question forms and launches **8S4**.

1 Students indicate which word is the odd-one-out.

Answers: dans is the odd-one-out, because it is a preposition and all the others are question words

2 Students list as many French question words as they can. This could be done as a whole-class brainstorming session, or in pairs or small groups. If necessary, you could prompt students by referring back to topics covered in *Équipe nouvelle 1*.

Possible answers: comment, quel(s)/quelle(s), où, qui, pourquoi, quand, combien, quoi, est-ce que/qu', qu'est-ce que/qu'

3 Students listen to and repeat a series of questions, focusing on correct intonation.

CD 1, track 3
Cassette 1, side 1
page 6, Guide pratique, activité 3

a – Elle est française?
b – Ton frère est petit?
c – Est-ce qu'elle est française?
d – Est-ce que ton frère est petit?

C15 Feuille 15 *Guide pratique 1* focuses on question forms and could be used at this point.

Zoom grammaire
This grammar section focuses on the present tense of *être*. It provides an opportunity for further work on the Year 7 Framework objectives **7W5** (present tense forms of high-frequency verbs) and **7S7** (verb tense in simple sentences).

1 Students consider why it is so important to know the present tense of *être*.

Answer: It is important because it is used so frequently and is also used in the formation of other tenses, e.g. the perfect tense. As proof of this, refer students to Juliette's letter on page 7 and ask them to count the number of parts of *être* that occur.

2 Students copy out the song, filling in their own nationality and the correct present tense forms of *être*. If you have not already focused on the nationalities given in the *Expressions-clés*, this might be an appropriate point at which to do so, modelling the pronunciation if necessary (additional nationalities are given in the Unit 1 *En plus* section on pages 108–109 of the Students' Book).

Answers: see transcript

3 Students compare their version of the song with that on the recording, which is sung to the tune of "London's Burning".

Mode ado 1

CD 1, track 4
Cassette 1, side 1
page 6, Zoom grammaire, activité 3

Il est français, il est français.
Elle est française, elle est française
Française! Française!
Je suis anglaise, je suis anglaise.

Elles sont françaises, elles sont françaises
Ils sont français, ils sont français
Français! Français!
Nous sommes anglais, nous sommes anglais.

Tu es français? Tu es française?
Vous êtes français? Vous êtes françaises?
Français! Françaises!
On est anglais, on est anglais.

Refer students to the grammar section on page 139 of the Students' Book for further information on the verb *être*.

Follow-up activity: More able students could create their own song using other adjectives to replace the nationalities, e.g. to revise personality adjectives. Although the emphasis here is on *être*, you could use the song to focus on adjective agreement after completing work on pages 8–9.

AT 3.3 **2a** *Lis la lettre. C'est quel paragraphe?*
Before starting this activity, place the letter in context by drawing students' attention to the poster and photo caption at the top of the page. Students read Juliette's letter and indicate the focus of each paragraph. When checking students' answers, you could display **OHT 2**, which contains the text of Juliette's letter.

Answers: a family: paragraph 2; b leisure activities: paragraph 4; c age and nationality: paragraph 1; d appearance and personality: paragraph 3

AT 3.3 **2b** *Trouve …*
Students search the letter for the French equivalents of the English words and phrases, focusing their attention on some important high-frequency words.

Answers: a et; b mais; c parce que; d assez; e avec; f en plus

AT 1.2
AT 2.2/3
AT 4.2/3
2c *Relis la lettre et écoute. Réponds aux dix questions enregistrées.*
Before doing this activity, you could first of all use the recorded questions as a dictation exercise, in order to focus more closely on the question forms. Students could note down the different types of question: those that use question words (e.g. *quel, quand*), those that use *est-ce que* and those that rely on intonation.
Students then read the letter again to find the answers to the recorded questions. This could be done orally as a whole-class activity, with the recording being paused to allow time for volunteers to give the answers, or students could simply write their answers individually. Encourage more able students to answer in full sentences.

Answers: 1 16; 2 le 25 février; 3 elle est française; 4 son père est italien; 5 au Canada; 6 elle a une sœur et un frère; 7 oui, c'est sympa; 8 elle est mince; 9 le tennis, la natation et l'équitation; 10 regarder la télé, aller au cinéma et écouter de la musique

CD 1, track 5
Cassette 1, side 1
page 7, activité 2c

1 – Juliette a quel âge?
2 – Son anniversaire, c'est quand?
3 – Elle est de quelle nationalité?
4 – Son père est de quelle nationalité?
5 – Où est son père?
6 – Est-ce qu'elle a des frères et sœurs?
7 – Est-ce qu'elle aime Dieppe?
8 – Elle est mince ou grosse?
9 – Elle fait quels sports?
10 – Quels sont ses passe-temps préférés?

AT 4.2/3 **2d** *Écris six questions sur la lettre de Juliette. Échange avec un(e) partenaire.*
This activity enables further practice of a variety of question forms and checks comprehension of the text. Students write their own series of questions on Juliette's letter for a partner to answer. They could use the third person singular (as in the answers below), or they could write their questions in the *tu* form with responses being given in the first person, e.g. *Tu t'appelles comment? Je m'appelle Juliette.*

Some possible questions: Elle s'appelle comment? Elle habite où? Elle habite avec qui? Elle est comment? Comment est sa grand-mère? Où sont son frère et sa sœur?

AT 4.3/4 **3** *Écris une lettre pour Calum ou Shana.*
To prepare students for this activity, show them how to expand the two teenagers' details into full sentences by adapting parts of Juliette's letter. Students then choose either Calum or Shana and write a letter for them. Alternatively, they could write a third person description of Calum or Shana; or they could produce a letter for one teenager and a third person description of the other. They should include details of physical appearance, based on the photos, together with invented details of personality.

Possible answers: Je m'appelle Calum et j'ai treize ans. J'ai les cheveux courts et je suis roux. J'habite à Glasgow, je suis écossais et je suis fils unique. J'aime le football, mais mon passe-temps préféré est le patinage. En plus, j'adore le skate.

Je m'appelle Shana et j'ai quatorze ans. J'ai les cheveux longs et raides, et je suis brune. J'habite à Bradford et je suis anglaise. J'ai deux frères. J'aime aller au cinéma, mais mon passe-temps préféré est la danse. En plus, j'adore faire du vélo.

Follow-up activity: Students write a letter about themselves.

1 Mode ado

C11 Copymaster 11 *Lis et écris En plus 1* provides further practice of the language of this spread and could be used at this point.

W4 Page 4 of the *Encore* and *En plus* Workbooks could also be used here, either in class or for homework.

Ça se dit comme ça!

This section on sound–spelling links shows students that their knowledge of how to pronounce familiar French words can help them to pronounce new language. This provides an opportunity to recap on the Year 7 Framework objectives **7W6** (letters and sounds) and **7W7** (learning about words).

1 In pairs, students practise saying the words given, then listen to the recording to check their pronunciation.

CD 1, track 6 page 7, Ça se dit comme ça! activité 1
Cassette 1, side 1

a – chemise
b – pantalon
c – chaussettes

2a Working in pairs again, students practise saying the tongue-twister. Volunteers could perform a timed version to see who can say it the quickest. If appropriate, you could use this as an opportunity to revise *mon/ma/mes*.

2b Students listen to the recorded version of the tongue-twister to check their pronunciation.

CD 1, track 7 page 7, Ça se dit comme ça! activité 2b
Cassette 1, side 1

– J'ai ma chemise, mes chaussettes et mon pantalon.

C17 Feuille 17 *Ça se dit comme ça!* focuses on working out how to pronounce unknown language and could be used at this point.

Challenge!

AT 4.2/3 **A** *Écris cinq phrases pour te présenter.*
Students write five sentences to introduce themselves.

AT 4.3 **B** *Ferme le livre et écris cinq phrases sur Juliette, de mémoire.*
Students write five sentences about Juliette, from memory.

AT 2.2-4 **C** *Jeu de rôle: A est candidat(e) au Festival Jeunes Talents, B est le producteur/la productrice. Imaginez l'interview.*
In pairs, students devise and perform a role-play in which one partner plays the role of a candidate applying to take part in the talent contest (see poster at the top of page 7) and the other partner is the interviewer.

Planning Page

1.2 Ma tenue préférée — pages 8–9

Objectives
- Describe clothes and colours
- Say what you're wearing and what your favourite clothes are
- Revise gender, adjectival agreement and position (**8W4, 8S1 – L**)
- Revise the present tense of *avoir*
- Revise how to pronounce new words (**7W7**)

Resources
Students' Book, pages 8–9
CD 1, tracks 8–9; CD 3, tracks 1–2
Cassette 1, side 1; cassette 4, side 1
Encore/En plus Workbooks, page 5
OHTs 3A, 3B and 3C
Copymasters 3, 4, 5, 7, 9 and 13

Key language
un anorak, un blouson, un jean, un pantalon, un pull, un short, un sweat, un tee-shirt
une casquette, une chemise, une cravate, une jupe, une robe, une veste
des baskets, des bottes, des chaussettes, des chaussures, des sandales
blanc(s)/blanche(s), rouge(s), noir(s)/noire(s), jaune(s), gris/grise(s), rose(s), bleu(s)/bleue(s), beige(s), vert(s)/verte(s), marron, violet(s)/violette(s), orange
C'est quoi, ta tenue préférée?
Ma tenue préférée, c'est …

Programme of Study reference
1a, 1b, 1c, 2a, 2b, 2c, 2f, 3a, 3b, 3c, 3d, 3e, 4a, 4c, 4d, 5a, 5c, 5d, 5e, 5f, 5i

Starters
- *À vos marques*, page 8.
- Copymaster 3 *À vos marques*, activity 2.
- Play Hangman (*Le pendu*) using the *Mots-clés* vocabulary, either as a whole-class activity or in pairs or small groups.
- Memory game: make an outfit by placing clothes cut from **OHT 3B** onto **3A** as students watch, then switch off the OHP. Can students remember the outfits?
- Write pairs of sentences on the board or OHP, one correct, one containing an error, e.g. wrong gender for noun, wrong adjective agreement, etc. Students identify the sentence that is wrong and correct it.

ICT suggestions
- Students use colour and interesting fonts to produce a poster for display on the classroom wall to remind them of the gender of the key vocabulary.
- Students display the results of the class survey (see *Challenge!* activity **B**) using ICT to produce diagrams or bar/pie charts. Alternatively, they could make an interactive PowerPoint® presentation.

Creative activities
- Students cut pictures from fashion magazines or clothing catalogues and stick them to a frieze, writing a speech bubble for each picture similar to those in activity **1a**.
- Ask students in groups to invent a new school uniform using items from **OHT 3C** and coloured OHP pens. Each group in turn comes and places the cut-outs on **OHT 3A** with the OHP switched off. The rest of the class try to guess what the uniform is by asking yes/no questions, e.g. *Tu as un pantalon gris?* When they have guessed, switch on the OHP for the class to see.
- In pairs or small groups, students invent a rap combining a part of the verb *avoir* with clothes. You could provide some starter lines for the less able, e.g. *Je suis footballeur, j'ai un …; Il est un punk, il a …; Elle est élégante, elle a …* (NB: No determiner before a profession.)

Plenaries
- *Challenge!* page 9.
- Copymaster 4 *Challenge!* activities 1a and 1b.
- Students work in pairs. One tries to recall the *Mots-clés* without looking at the Students' Book, the other checks and awards one point for each word remembered plus a bonus point if the gender is correct. Which partner achieves the most points?
- In pairs, students discuss ways of learning and remembering new words, e.g. according to gender, in categories, as outfits, separating off words that resemble English words, etc. Allow time for feedback for students to share their ideas.

Homework suggestions
- Copymaster 9 *Lis et écris Encore 1*.
- Copymaster 13 *Grammaire 1*.
- Following discussion with a partner (see Plenary activities), students learn the *Mots-clés*. (To be checked with their partner next lesson.)
- Students write a description of their favourite outfit.
- Students write sentences describing what they are wearing and what three friends or family members are wearing.

Mode ado

1.2 Ma tenue préférée — pages 8–9

À vos marques
Trouve l'intrus et dis pourquoi.
This starter activity revises hair colour and nationality from the previous spread, together with colours from *Équipe nouvelle 1*.
Possible answers: a *mince*: it isn't a colour and/or the spelling is the same in the masculine and feminine singular; b *français*: all the other nationalities here are British; c *sandales*: it isn't a colour adjective, it is plural but all the other words here are singular

Presentation
- Look at the photos on page 8 of the Students' Book and discuss what the four young people are wearing for school. Point out that there is no school uniform in France and it is perfectly acceptable for girls to wear jeans or trousers in French schools.
- Present the clothes and colours vocabulary, perhaps using **OHTs 3A, 3B** and **3C**. For example, copy and cut up the items of clothing on **3B** and **3C**. Place **3A** on the OHP and, using the clothes from **3B**, gradually "dress" the girl and boy, presenting the new language as you do so: *J'ai une robe, j'ai des sandales*, etc. Then remove the clothes and ask students to come to the OHP and place the correct item of clothing on the transparency as you describe the outfit, e.g. *J'ai un tee-shirt et un pantalon*.
- See page 17 of the Introduction for ideas on presenting and practising new language using flashcards and OHTs.

AT 1.2 / **AT 3.2** **1a** *Lis et écoute.*
Students listen to the recorded descriptions of the young people's clothing and follow the speech bubbles in the Students' Book.

CD 1, track 8 — page 8, activité 1a
Cassette 1, side 1
– C'est quoi, ta tenue pour la rentrée, Matthieu?
– J'ai un short, un sweat et des baskets. Et toi?
– J'ai un jean, un tee-shirt et un pull.
– Salut!
– Salut, Natacha! C'est quoi, ta tenue pour la rentrée?
– J'ai une jupe, un tee-shirt et des sandales.
– Et toi, Arnaud?
– J'ai un jean, une chemise et des baskets.

AT 2.2 **1b** *Répète.*
Play the recording again. Use this repetition activity as an opportunity to focus on the pronunciation of new words, referring back if necessary to the *Ça se dit comme ça!* section on page 7. This is another opportunity to reinforce the Year 7 Framework objective **7W7** (learning about words).

Follow-up activity: Play a memory game based on the speech bubbles. Ask students to close their books, then play the recording again. Pause it at certain points and challenge students to complete the sentences.

AT 2.2 **1c** *Jeu: trouve l'erreur!*
In pairs, students make statements about what the young people are wearing and challenge their partner to spot the mistake. The example provided in the Students' Book uses the *je* and *tu* forms of the verb, but you could encourage students to use *il* and *elle*, if appropriate.

AT 4.2 **2** *Qu'est-ce que tu as dans l'armoire de tes rêves? Fais une liste!*
Students list the contents of their ideal wardrobe. See the *Encore* section on pages 96–97 of the Students' Book for further exploitation of basic clothes vocabulary.

AT 1.2 **3** *Choisis ta tenue préférée. Écoute pour voir si quelqu'un est d'accord avec toi.*
Students study the pictures and choose their favourite combination of clothes. They then listen to the recording to find out whether any of the French speakers make the same choice as themselves. They note down the speakers' choices as they listen.

Answers: Juliette: a, g, l; Matthieu: c, h, k; Arnaud: d, f, i; Natacha: b, e, j

CD 1, track 9 — page 9, activité 3
Cassette 1, side 1
– Juliette, c'est quoi, ta tenue préférée?
– Ma tenue préférée, c'est le sweat jaune, le pantalon gris et les baskets violettes.
– Matthieu, c'est quoi, ta tenue préférée?
– Ma tenue préférée, c'est le blouson rouge, le jean blanc et les bottes vertes.
– Arnaud, c'est quoi, ta tenue préférée?
– Ma tenue préférée, c'est la chemise noire, le short orange et les chaussures marron.
– Natacha, c'est quoi, ta tenue préférée?
– Ma tenue préférée, c'est le tee-shirt bleu, la jupe rose et les sandales beiges.

Follow-up activity: Students attempt to guess their partner's favourite outfit by playing a game similar to the Mastermind® peg game. Partner A tries to guess the three items that B has chosen; B says how many are correct but doesn't specify which. Partner A continues to make guesses until he/she has worked out the correct combination.

C7 / **C9** Feuille 7 *Parle Encore* and Feuille 9 *Lis et écris Encore 1* provide further basic practice of clothes vocabulary and describing what people are wearing. Both could be completed at this point.

Mode ado

Zoom grammaire

This grammar section launches **8W4** and **8S1**. Before students begin the activities, ask them what they can remember about adjectives from *Équipe nouvelle 1*.

1 Students match the sentence halves to produce four statements about adjectives.

Answers: 1b; 2c; 3d; 4a

Refer students to the grammar section on page 133 of the Students' Book for further information on this grammar point.

C13 Feuille 13 *Grammaire 1* focuses on agreement and position of adjectives and could be used after completing the *Zoom grammaire* section.

C5 Additional listening practice of clothes and colours is provided on Feuille 5 *Écoute Encore*.

W5 Page 5 of the *Encore* and *En plus* Workbooks provides further practice of the language of this spread and could also be used at this point.

Challenge!

AT 4.2 **A** *Décris ce que tu portes.*
Students write a brief description of what they are wearing. You will need to explain the verb *porter* because it has not yet been introduced.

AT 2.2/3 **B** *Fais un sondage dans la classe.*
Students conduct a survey to find out what is the most popular outfit. See ICT suggestions on the Planning Page (page 31) for ideas on how students could present the survey results.

AT 4.2/3 **C** *Invente un nouvel uniforme pour ton collège. Écris la description.*
Students describe and illustrate a new uniform for your school. Encourage them to be as outrageous as they like!

Follow-up activities:
- Following on from activity **C** above, ask a student to read out their description while others in the class draw it. Then compare the drawings: who has produced the most accurate picture? Continue this with other students reading out their descriptions.
- Alternatively, if students' drawings and descriptions have been done on separate pieces of paper, collect them all in, jumble them up and then let the class match them up again. Or you could pin the drawings around the room and give each student a description (not their own) to read and find the corresponding picture.
- Students could make up other uniforms (e.g. for a football team, for the waiters and waitresses in a fast-food place), either as homework or in pairs or groups in class.

1 Mode ado
Planning Page

1.3 J'adore le look sport — pages 10–11

Objectives
- Talk about the types of clothes you like
- Say what you think about clothes and fashions using *parce que* (**8W2 – L**)
- Revise the present tense of regular *-er* verbs (**8W5, 8S7 – L**)
- Pronounce the sounds *un/une*

Resources
Students' Book, pages 10–11
CD 1, tracks 10–12
Cassette 1, side 1
Encore/En plus Workbooks, page 6
OHT 4
Copymasters 8 and 16

Key language
Qu'est-ce que tu aimes comme look?
J'adore/J'aime bien/Je n'aime pas/Je déteste le look décontracté/sport/habillé parce que c'est pratique/sympa/chic/moche.

Programme of Study reference
1a, 1b, 1c, 2a, 2b, 2c, 2f, 2h, 2i, 3b, 3c, 3d, 3e, 4a, 4d, 5a, 5c, 5d, 5e, 5f, 5i

Starters
- *À vos marques*, page 10.
- Students answer the register by saying what their favourite style of clothing is (and why).
- Place **OHT 4** on the OHP. Students choose three of the people pictured and imagine what they would say about the type of clothes they like and why. This could be done orally in pairs or as an individual written activity.
- Write gap-fill sentences on the board/OHP for students to copy and complete.

ICT suggestions
- Students word-process a dossier of the language learned so far in this unit, using colour to highlight gender, plurals, etc. This could be kept on file on the computer and updated at the end of the unit.
- Students word-process gap-fill sentences to swap with a partner.

Creative activities
- On an A4 sheet, students draw a picture of a person wearing a defined "look" (alternatively, they could use a picture cut from a magazine). They write a caption on the back of the sheet describing the style and why the person likes it. Collect in the sheets. Show a few, one at a time, and let the class guess the caption.
- Copymaster 16 *Guide pratique 2*, activity 1.

Plenaries
- *Challenge!* page 11.
- Write up a single word from the lesson on the board or OHP. Students work in pairs to write as many questions and answers containing the word as possible in a given time.
- Students write their own opinion of the styles mentioned in the *Expressions-clés* and compare with a partner. Does any pair have all three opinions the same/different?
- Students play Word Tennis, following a model on the board or OHP, e.g.
  A: *J'adore …*
  B: *… le look décontracté …*
  A: *… parce que …*
  B: *… c'est pratique …*
  A: *… mais …*
  B: *… je déteste …*, etc.

Homework suggestions
- Copymaster 16 *Guide pratique 2*, activity 1.
- *Encore/En plus* Workbooks, page 6.
- Students write a short paragraph about the sort of clothes they like, using at least four different regular *-er* verbs.

1.3 J'adore le look sport — pages 10–11

À vos marques

Nœud de serpents. Trouve six vêtements.
Students follow the letters on each coiled snake, starting at the head, to find the six items of clothing. When checking their answers, refer to the colours of the snakes, e.g. *Le serpent vert, c'est quel vêtement?* Ask students to supply *un*, *une* or *des* with each item of clothing.

Answers: des baskets; un blouson; des bottes; une cravate; une chemise; une casquette

AT 3.2/3

1a *Trouve …*
Students search the article for the French equivalents of the English expressions.

Answers: a parce que c'est pratique; b le look décontracté; c le look habillé; d parce que c'est moche; e sa couleur préférée; f les formes simples et les matières confortables

AT 3.2/3

1b *Vrai ou faux?*
Students decide whether the statements based on the article are true or false.

Answers: a faux; b faux; c faux; d faux

AT 2.2
AT 4.2

1c *Corrige les phrases qui sont fausses.*
Referring again to the article, students now correct the false answers. They could do this orally or in writing.

Answers: a Noé <u>adore</u> le look habillé. b Clément aime son look parce que c'est <u>pratique</u>. c Emmanuelle <u>adore</u> les sweats. d Elle aime le look décontracté parce que <u>c'est sympa et c'est chic</u>.

Presentation

▶ Use **OHT 4** for further practice of the key language of the spread before students move on to activity **2**. For example, you could cover each model with a piece of paper and gradually reveal, asking students to guess what they are wearing. Once revealed, students say what "look" the person likes. Alternatively, you could name a style and students say which person you are describing.

▶ You may also like to work through the *Zoom grammaire* (see below) at this point if you feel students need help with the present tense of *-er* verbs.

AT 1.2/3
AT 4.2/3

2 *Écoute. Qui dit quoi? Fais des phrases avec les Expressions-clés.*
Students listen to the recording then write a sentence expressing each person's clothing preferences, using the *Expressions-clés* as support. If they need help, play the recording three times so that students can pick out, in order, the three parts of each sentence: on the first listening, they focus on *j'adore/j'aime bien/je n'aime pas/je déteste*; on the second listening, they focus on the style of clothing; and on the third listening, they focus on the reason given.

Answers: see transcript

CD 1, track 10 — page 11, activité 2
Cassette 1, side 1

- Juliette, qu'est-ce que tu aimes comme look?
- J'aime bien le look décontracté parce que c'est pratique.
- Matthieu, qu'est-ce que tu aimes comme look?
- Moi, j'adore le look sport parce que c'est sympa.
- Natacha, qu'est-ce que tu aimes comme look? Tu aimes le look sport?
- Ah non, je déteste le look sport parce que je ne suis pas du tout sportive … et parce que c'est moche!
- Arnaud, qu'est-ce que tu aimes comme look? Le look sport, peut-être?
- Euh non … J'aime le look habillé parce que c'est chic et c'est pratique. Je n'aime pas beaucoup le look sport. C'est moche!

AT 2.2/3

3 *Et toi, qu'est-ce que tu aimes comme look? Pourquoi?*
This activity allows students to express themselves on an issue that generally generates interest. They could prepare it at home and record themselves speaking.

Guide pratique

This section focuses on how to justify an opinion using the connective *parce que/qu'* and launches **8W2**.

1a Students use *parce que* to match up the beginnings of the sentences with their likely endings.

Answers: 1b J'aime le look sport parce que c'est pratique. 2a J'aime bien le pull vert parce que c'est ma couleur préférée. 3c Il n'a pas de pantalons parce qu'il préfère les jeans. 4d Elle habite en France parce qu'elle est française.

1b Students translate the sentences from activity **1a** into English.

Answers: 1 I like the sporty look because it's practical. 2 I love the green pullover because it's my favourite colour. 3 He doesn't have any trousers because he prefers jeans. 4 She lives in France because she's French.

C16 Activity 1 on Feuille 16 *Guide pratique 2* provides practice of *parce que* and could be used at this point.

Zoom grammaire

This grammar section focuses on the present tense of *-er* verbs and launches **8W5** and **8S7**.

1 Students write out all the present tense forms of two of the verbs given.

2 Students make up 10 sentences using different parts of the same verb. Less able students could limit themselves to one verb per sentence, whereas the more able could use two or more forms of the same verb per sentence.

Refer students to the grammar section on page 138 of the Students' Book for further information on the present tense of *-er* verbs.

1 Mode ado

C8 Feuille 8 *Parle En plus* provides additional speaking practice on the topic of clothes and expressing/justifying opinions. It could be completed towards the end of this spread, or later in the unit if preferred.

W6 Page 6 of the *Encore* and *En plus* Workbooks focuses on expressing opinions about clothes and could also be used here, either in class or for homework.

Ça se dit comme ça!

This stresses the difference in pronunciation between the nasal sound *un* and *une*. Exaggerate the position of your lips in the two words and ask students to copy. This section can be done at any appropriate stage during work on this spread.

1 Students listen and repeat the words.

> **CD 1, track 11** page 11, Ça se dit comme ça! activité 1
> **Cassette 1, side 1**
>
> – un pull … une jupe … un jean … une robe

2 Students listen to a second recording and indicate whether they hear *un* or *une*. You might like to point out that some words can have more than one gender if they have more than one meaning.

Answers: a un; b une; c une; d un; e un; f une; g un; h une

> **CD 1, track 12** page 11, Ça se dit comme ça! activité 2
> **Cassette 1, side 1**
>
> a – un livre
> b – une livre
> c – une tour
> d – un tour
> e – un poste
> f – une poste
> g – un page
> h – une page

Challenge!

AT 4.2 **A** *Décris les différents looks.*
Students prepare a brief description of each of the different styles.

AT 4.3 **B** *Qu'est-ce que tu penses des vêtements, p. 10? Donne le plus possible de détails.*
Students express their own opinion of the clothes on page 10. Encourage them to give as many details as possible and to give reasons for their opinions, using *parce que*.

AT 4.3/4 **C** *Décris l'uniforme de ton collège et donne ton opinion avec le plus possible de détails. Donne tes raisons.*
Students describe their own school uniform in as much detail as possible, expressing and justifying their opinions.

Planning Page

1.4 Qu'est-ce que tu mets? pages 12–13

Objectives

- Say what you wear for different occasions and in different weather (**8W5, 8S7**)
- Revise going to places using *aller* + preposition + place
- Revise the weather
- Use connectives in longer sentences (**8S2, 8L4 – L**)

Resources

Students' Book, pages 12–13
CD 1, tracks 13–15; CD 3, tracks 3–4
Cassette 1, side 1; cassette 4, side 1
Encore/En plus Workbooks, pages 7, 8 and 9
OHT 4
Flashcards 88–97
Copymasters 4, 6, 10, 12, 14 and 16

Key language

Qu'est-ce que tu mets quand …?
Quand je vais au collège, je mets mon/ma/mes …
Quand il/elle va en ville, il/elle met son/sa/ses …
en ville, au collège, à une boum, au centre sportif, chez mes/tes/ses grands-parents
Quand il fait beau/froid/chaud/gris, …
Quand il y a du soleil/du vent/du brouillard/de l'orage, …
Quand il pleut/neige/gèle, …

Programme of Study reference

1a, 1b, 1c, 2a, 2b, 2c, 2d, 2f, 2g, 2i, 3a, 3c, 3d, 3e, 4a, 4d, 5a, 5d, 5e, 5f, 5i

Starters

- *À vos marques*, page 12.
- Say statements using *mettre* in the past, present and future tense. Students raise their hand when they hear a present tense statement. You could progress to asking students to identify the tense.
- Show **OHT 4** and ask students to imagine where each person is going and what they are saying, beginning with the word *quand* each time, e.g. *Quand je vais au collège, je mets …*
- Write some weather expressions on the board. Students design symbols to illustrate their meaning.

ICT suggestions

- Students design a poster with pictures and captions saying what they wear for different occasions and/or in different weathers. These can be displayed on the classroom wall in order to provide support for students throughout the rest of the unit.
- Students devise a PowerPoint® presentation to show that they understand possessive adjectives.

Creative activities

- See ICT suggestions above.
- Students devise a rap to help them revise the weather expressions.
- Students write poems where the initial letter of the place they are going to is the same as the item of clothing they wear, e.g. *Quand je vais en ville, je mets ma veste. Quand je vais à la plage, je mets mon pantalon. Quand je vais en Afrique, je mets mon anorak.* Encourage them to use their imagination to come up with unusual or wacky combinations.

Plenaries

- *Challenge!* page 13.
- Copymaster 4 *Challenge!* activity 2.
- Write a selection of sentence endings on the board or OHP, e.g. *… parce que c'est moche./ … mais j'aime bien le look sport./ … j'aime aussi le look décontracté./ … je mets un short.* In pairs, students suggest possible phrases to start each sentence. They should justify their choices.
- In pairs, students discuss strategies for learning and remembering the present tense of the verb *mettre*. Allow time for feedback so that students can share their ideas.

Homework suggestions

- *Encore/En plus* Workbooks, pages 7, 8 and 9.
- Copymaster 10 *Lis et écris Encore 2*, activities 1 and 2a.
- Copymaster 12 *Lis et écris En plus 2*.
- Copymaster 14 *Grammaire 2*.
- Copymaster 16 *Guide pratique 2*, activity 2.
- Students write a paragraph containing as many different parts of the verb *mettre* as possible.

Mode ado

1.4 Qu'est-ce que tu mets? pages 12–13

À vos marques
Utilise le glossaire (page 158) ou un dictionnaire pour trouver huit nouveaux vêtements.
This quick dictionary activity gives students an element of choice and could be done in pairs. Students feed back their research to the rest of the class, perhaps spelling some of the vocabulary aloud (to practise the French alphabet) and giving the gender of each item.

AT 1.2
AT 3.1
1a *Regarde les photos et lis la liste. Ils vont où? Devine. Écoute et vérifie.*
Before beginning this activity, make sure that students understand all the places listed, including the use of *chez*. If necessary, revise how to say "to" a place: *à + le/la/les*, *en*, *chez*.
Then ask students to guess, from looking at the young people's clothes, where they might be going. (Note that there is one distractor in the list: *au centre sportif*.) They then listen to the recording to check whether their guesses were correct.
Ensure that students understand the difference between *je mets …* (I put on …) and *j'ai …* (I'm wearing … – note that *je porte* is not used here). You could perform mimes to illustrate the difference in meaning. At this point you could also elicit the meaning of *quand*, which students have already met and used as a question word but not as a connective.

Answers: Juliette: au collège; Matthieu: en ville; Natacha: à une boum; Arnaud: chez ses grands-parents

CD 1, track 13 **page 12, activité 1**
Cassette 1, side 1

- Qu'est-ce que tu mets quand tu vas au collège, Juliette?
- Alors, moi, quand je vais au collège, je mets ma jupe bleue, mon tee-shirt noir et blanc et mes baskets marron.
- Qu'est-ce que tu mets quand tu vas en ville, Matthieu?
- Quand je vais en ville, je mets mon jean, mon sweat bleu, mon blouson marron et mes baskets.
- Qu'est ce que tu mets quand tu vas à une boum, Natacha?
- Je mets ma robe bleue à fleurs, mon pull bleu et mes sandales quand je vais à une boum.
- Qu'est-ce que tu mets quand tu vas chez tes grands-parents, Arnaud?
- Quand je vais chez mes grands-parents, je mets mon jean beige, une chemise blanche et une cravate.
- Une cravate? C'est chic!

AT 1.2
AT 4.2
1b *Réécoute. Recopie et complète les bulles.*
As preparation for this activity, play the recording again and ask students to repeat only the items of clothing: *ma jupe, mon tee-shirt*, etc. Then play it through again and ask students to repeat the full sentences, while looking at the speech bubbles and pictures in the book for support.

Finally, students copy out and complete the speech bubbles.
Answers: see transcript above

AT 2.2
2 *Jeu de mémoire, livre fermé.*
Students work in pairs with the book closed, attempting to remember what the different characters wear to go to different places. This provides an opportunity to practise *son/sa/ses*, e.g. *Il/Elle met son/sa/ses …*, so you might like to look at the *Zoom grammaire* panel on possessive adjectives (see below) before students begin the activity. This memory game could also be adapted in order to practise *mon/ma/mes* and *ton/ta/tes*: Partner A: *Juliette, tu mets ton jean quand tu vas au collège?* Partner B: *Non, je mets ma jupe …*

AT 4.2/3
3 *Écris quatre bulles pour toi.*
Students write four speech bubbles for themselves, completing the bubbles from **1b** with their own details. They could extend the activity by describing what they wear on other occasions, e.g. to go to the cinema, to go on holiday, to meet a famous person/their friends, etc.

Follow-up activity: When students have written their speech bubbles for activity **3**, they could question each other in pairs to find out what their choice of clothing would be on different occasions: Partner A: *Qu'est-ce que tu mets quand tu vas en ville?* Partner B: *Je mets mon/ma/mes …*

Zoom grammaire
This section focuses on the possessive adjectives *mon/ma/mes*, *ton/ta/tes* and *son/sa/ses*.

Refer students to the grammar section on possessive adjectives on page 135 of the Students' Book.

Zoom grammaire
This section continues the launch of **8W5** and **8S7**, focusing on the conjugation and pronunciation of the present tense of the verb *mettre*. You might like to complete this section before beginning activities **4a** and **4b**.

1 Students study the present tense of *mettre* and look for any clues that might tell them it is an irregular verb.

Answers: the *je* and *tu* forms are identical; the singular forms of *mettre* have one "t" and the plural forms have two

2 Students listen to the rap. Ask them what they notice about the pronunciation of the singular and plural forms. Students then compose their own rap using the different present tense forms of *mettre* and their own choice of clothes vocabulary. Encourage more able students to include more complex sentences using the connective *quand*. Provide them with a model, if necessary.

Mode ado 1

CD 1, track 14 — page 13, Zoom grammaire, activité 2
Cassette 1, side 1

Je mets un pull
tu mets un short
il met un pantalon … un pantalon … un pantalon
elle met une robe longue … une robe longue … une robe longue.

Nous mettons des chaussures
vous mettez des baskets
ils mettent des bottes … des bottes … des bottes
elles mettent des sandales … des sandales … des sandales.

Refer students to the grammar section on page 140 of the Students' Book for further information on the verb *mettre*.

C14 Feuille 14 *Grammaire 2* could be used at this point. It focuses on verbs, pronouns and the present tense of *mettre*.

W8 Further practice of these grammar points can also be found on page 8 of the *Encore* and *En plus* Workbooks.

AT 1.2
AT 2.2 **4a** *Regarde les bulles. Quel temps il fait? Écoute et vérifie.*
As preparation for this activity, students could work in pairs to brainstorm the weather phrases taught in *Équipe nouvelle 1*. **Flashcards 88–97** could be used to remind students of the phrases they have met. Students then describe the weather depicted in each of the bubbles before listening to the recording to check their answers.

Answers: a il pleut; b il y a du soleil/il fait beau; c il y a du vent; d il neige; e il fait gris

---

CD 1, track 15 — page 13, activité 4a
Cassette 1, side 1

a – Quel temps il fait?
  – Il pleut.
  – Comment?
  – Il pleut.
  – Je n'entends rien. Je pense qu'il pleut.
b – Il fait beau?
  – Oui, il y a du soleil.
  – Il y a du soleil? Cool!
c – Quel temps il fait?
  – Il y a du vent.
d – Oh regarde … il neige.
  – Super. J'adore quand il neige.
e – Il fait beau?
  – Non, il ne fait pas beau. Il fait gris.
  – Bah!

AT 2.2/3
AT 4.2/3 **4b** *Fais une phrase pour chaque bulle.*
Students say and/or write a sentence for each of the bubbles in activity **4a**, following the example given and using the *Expressions-clés* to help them. It might be appropriate to complete the *Guide pratique* section on *quand* (see below) before students begin this activity.

Answers: a Quand il pleut, je mets mon anorak rouge et mes bottes noires. b Quand il y a du soleil, je mets mon short vert et mes sandales orange. c Quand il y a du vent, je mets mon jean gris et mon blouson bleu. d Quand il neige, je mets mes bottes/chaussures marron et mon pull violet. e Quand il fait gris, je mets mon sweat beige et mon jean bleu.

Guide pratique

This section focuses on the use of *quand* as a connective in extended sentences, launching **8S2** and **8L4**. Students use the panel of phrases to help them write as many sentences as they can using *quand*.

C16 Further practice of *quand* can be found in activity 2 on Feuille 16 *Guide pratique 2*.

C6 Feuille 6 *Écoute En plus* provides additional listening practice on the topic of clothes and could be used now.

C10 Feuille 10 *Lis et écris Encore 2* reinforces the structure *Quand je vais …, je mets …*, together with clothes vocabulary and colour adjectives. It could also be used here, either in class or for homework.

C12 Feuille 12 *Lis et écris En plus 2* could also be used at this point. It provides extension reading and writing activities based on much of the language covered so far.

W7 Further practice of weather, clothes and colours is given on page 7 of the *Encore* and *En plus* Workbooks.

W9 Page 9 of the Workbooks pulls together and mixes much of the language and grammar of Unit 1. It could be used at any point between now and the end of the unit.

Challenge!

AT 4.2 **A** *Dessine et décris une tenue pour l'été ou l'hiver.*
Students invent an outfit for summer or winter.

AT 4.2/3 **B** *Recopie et adapte les bulles de l'activité 1b pour d'autres personnes.*
Ask students to imagine what other people (e.g. their parents or grandparents, favourite celebrities, etc.) would wear on different occasions. They refer back to the speech bubbles in activity **1b** and adapt them to write their own bubbles in the third person, e.g. *Quand ma mère va au centre sportif, elle met son/sa/ses …*

C *Interviewe un(e) partenaire. Qu'est-ce qu'il/elle met quand? Pourquoi?*
Students ask and answer questions about what they wear for different occasions and in different types of weather, including reasons.

1 Mode ado

1.5 La belle équipe, épisode 1

pages 14–15

Objectives
▶ Develop listening and reading skills via a soap story based on the language of the unit (**8L2 – L**)

Resources
Students' Book, pages 14–15
CD 1, track 16
Cassette 1, side 1

Programme of Study reference
1a, 1c, 2a, 2b, 2c, 2g, 2h, 3b, 3c, 3e, 4a, 4d, 5a, 5d, 5e, 5g, 5i

For general information on introducing and exploiting the soap story, refer to page 19 of the Introduction.

This episode begins with the four friends looking at a leaflet about a talent contest. Natacha, Juliette and Matthieu are all keen to attend the auditions, but Arnaud seems very doubtful. While the others enjoy themselves trying on different clothes and deciding what to wear, Arnaud announces that he isn't going to take part. Juliette tries to persuade him, but he says he doesn't like drama and is no good at it.
The three friends (without Arnaud) later attend the auditions, where disaster almost strikes: Juliette's sandal breaks just as they are about to go on stage! Because of this, they all decide to go on stage barefoot, as if this is a planned feature of their act. The judges seem to like not only their singing but also their barefoot image … have they been chosen for the contest?!

AT 1.4   **1** *Écoute et regarde les photos. Quel est le problème?*
The soap episode launches **8L2**. It requires students to cope with a mixture of familiar and unfamiliar language, together with a range of different voices. Before listening to the recording, brainstorm with the class strategies they could use to help with understanding, e.g. using the pictures as clues, predicting language, deducing meaning from context, etc. Students could answer in French or English, depending on the ability level of the class.

Answers: The strap on Juliette's sandal breaks (*la sandale de Juliette est cassée*); so, because there is no time to repair it, the three friends all decide to take off their shoes (*ils ne mettent pas de chaussures/ils enlèvent les chaussures*) and go on stage barefoot (*ils ont les pieds nus*).

CD 1, track 16   page 14, La belle équipe, épisode 1
Cassette 1, side 1

– Concours: Festival Jeunes Talents
 1er prix: Une tournée en France et aux Antilles!
 Vous avez 15–18 ans?
 Venez auditionner (groupes de 3 ou 4)
 Samedi, 15 h – Théâtre de Dieppe
 Complétez une fiche d'inscription ou présentez-vous par lettre.

1 – Alors, on fait le concours de théâtre, c'est d'accord?
 – Oui! Les auditions sont demain, à trois heures.
 – Bien sûr, tous les quatre!
 – Ah non, pas moi.
 – Pourquoi?
2 Le lendemain, chez Matthieu …
 – Je mets mon pantalon noir et mon tee-shirt rouge. C'est joli, non?
 – Et moi, je mets ce tee-shirt rouge.
 – Ah non! Il est trop petit.
 – Et toi, Arnaud? Qu'est-ce que tu mets pour l'audition?
 – Moi, je ne viens pas.
3 – Allez, Arnaud, viens avec nous …
 – Non, je n'aime pas le théâtre!
 – S'il te plaît, Arnaud, pour moi!
 – Euh … non Juliette, je suis trop nul! Désolé. Je rentre.
4 À trois heures, au théâtre …
 – Tu t'appelles comment?
 – Je m'appelle Natacha Delanoé.
 – Et tu as quel âge, Natacha?
 – J'ai quinze ans.
 – Tu habites à Dieppe?
 – Oui, j'habite rue des Lilas.
5 – Ça commence bien … On va être des stars!
 – Ah zut! Ma sandale est cassée! Qu'est-ce qu'on va faire?
 – Ah non! Là, ça commence mal!
 – Attendez. J'ai une idée.
6 Ils enlèvent les chaussures.
7 – Ils sont drôles et j'adore le look!
 – Oui, pieds nus … c'est original!
 – Et ils chantent bien aussi.
 – Hmmm, oui, mais …
8 – Et maintenant, les résultats …
À suivre …

AT 3.4   **2** *Lis et trouve …*
Students search the text for the French equivalents of the English expressions.

Answers: a le concours; b 1er prix; c une tournée; d ça commence bien; e cassée; f ça commence mal; g j'ai une idée; h drôles; i pieds nus; j ils chantent bien

AT 3.4   **3a** *Il y a combien de questions dans le texte?*
Students search the text looking for different types of question.

Answers: There are 10 questions in the story: 1 (on the poster) Vous avez 15–18 ans? 2 Alors, on fait le concours de théâtre, c'est d'accord? 3 Pourquoi? 4 C'est joli, non? 5 Et toi, Arnaud? 6 Qu'est-ce que tu mets pour l'audition? 7 Tu t'appelles comment? 8 Et tu as quel âge, Natacha? 9 Tu habites à Dieppe? 10 Qu'est-ce qu'on va faire?

AT 1.2
AT 2.2   **3b** *Répète les questions et imite l'intonation!*
Play the recording again, pausing after the different questions so that students can repeat them, focusing on pronunciation and intonation.

Mode ado

| AT 3.2 | **4** *Relie les questions et les réponses.*
Students match the questions to the answers. This activity reinforces the use of *parce que* and its connection with *pourquoi?*-type questions.

Answers: a 2; b 4; c 5; d 3; e 1

| AT 2.4 |
| AT 3.4 | **5** *En groupes de cinq, jouez l'épisode.*
Students perform the soap episode in groups.

Super-challenge!   page 16

This extension page is intended to stretch more able students who are confident with the core language of the unit. It combines language from the unit with unfamiliar language and develops grammar points introduced in the main body of the unit. It can be used flexibly either as part of a teacher-led lesson or as alternative independent class and homework material.

Objectives
▶ Describe yourself and someone else in more detail
▶ Understand and use comparative adjectives (8T2 – L)

Resources
Students' Book, page 16
Encore/En plus Workbooks, page 10

Key language
Je suis plus grand(e)/petit(e)/âgé(e)/jeune/intelligent(e) que mon frère/ma sœur/mon père, etc.
Je suis moins grand(e)/petit(e)/âgé(e)/jeune/intelligent(e) que mon frère/ma sœur/mon père, etc.

Programme of Study reference
1b, 1c, 2c, 2h, 2i, 3a, 3c, 3d, 3e, 4c, 4d, 5a, 5d, 5e, 5g, 5i

| AT 3.3/4 | **1** *Lis la lettre de Samuel. Réponds aux questions en anglais.*
Students read Samuel's letter and answer the questions in English. The use of the comparative in Samuel's letter, together with coverage of this grammar point in the *Zoom grammaire*, launches **8T2**.

Answers: a Canadian; b French and English; c (answer will depend on student's own age; Samuel is 13); d older than him; e Martin is taller than Samuel; f Martin has blond hair, Samuel has brown hair, and Martin's hair is longer than Samuel's; g Martin is more intelligent than Samuel; h Samuel is more sporty; i yes

| AT 2.2/3 | **2** *Test de mémoire: Pose cinq questions à ton/ta partenaire sur la lettre de Samuel. Il/Elle répond, livre fermé.*
This activity reinforces the unit's focus on question forms. In pairs, students ask each other questions in French on Samuel's letter. The person answering the questions must attempt this activity from memory, with the book closed.

| AT 4.4 | **3** *Écris une lettre similaire. Réponds aux questions de la lettre. Compare-toi à un frère, une sœur ou un(e) ami(e).*
Students write a reply to Samuel's letter, answering his questions and comparing themselves with a brother, sister or friend using *plus/moins* plus adjective.

Zoom grammaire

This grammar section on comparatives develops the work done on adjectives in the main part of Unit 1. In conjunction with Samuel's letter, it launches **8T2**.

1 Students complete the chart of comparatives by selecting the appropriate words from Samuel's letter.

Answers: bigger: *plus grand*; not as hard-working: *moins travailleur*

2 Students search Samuel's letter for the French equivalents of the English comparatives.

Answers: more patient than: *plus patient que*; older than: *plus âgée que*; longer than: *plus longs que*; not as sporty as: *moins sportif que*

Refer students to the grammar section on page 134 of the Students' Book for further information on comparatives.

| W10 | Page 10 of the *Encore* and *En plus* Workbooks could be used at this point.

Vocabulaire   page 17

This page provides a summary of the key language covered in this unit. It could be used as a handy reference for students as they work through the unit. Alternatively, students could use its clear French–English format with language organized thematically when learning vocabulary.

| C1 | Feuille 1 *Vocabulaire* also contains a summary of the key language of the unit and could be given to students at this point for revision purposes. See page 7 of the Introduction for ideas on how to use this copymaster.

| W11 | Page 11 of the *Encore* and *En plus* Workbooks also provides a summary of the key language of the unit.

Podium   page 18

The *Podium* page provides students with an end-of-unit checklist of learning objectives in French and English. At the foot of the page are activities at three levels of difficulty (bronze, silver and gold) to extend the work of the unit. Encourage students to select an activity at the most appropriate level.

1 Mode ado

C2 Feuille 2 *Podium* could also be used at this point. This worksheet contains activities to help students keep track of their progress. See page 7 of the Introduction for ideas on how to use it to help self- and peer-assessment.

W12 Page 12 of the *Encore* and *En plus* Workbooks also provides an end-of-unit checklist in French and English with activities to help students keep track of their progress.

Encore Unité 1
pages 96–97

Objectives
These reinforcement pages are intended for those students requiring further practice of core language from the unit. They can be used by students who finish other activities quickly or as alternative class and homework material.

Resources
Students' Book, pages 96–97
CD 1, tracks 17–18
Cassette 1, side 1

Programme of Study reference
1a, 1b, 1c, 2a, 2b, 2h, 2i, 3e, 4a, 4d, 5a, 5c, 5d, 5e, 5i

AT 3.2 **1** *Lis les étiquettes et relie aux photos.*
Students read the labels and match them to the different outfits.

Answers: 1d; 2a; 3c; 4b

AT 1.2 **2** *Écoute. La tenue préférée de Laura, c'est quoi? Et la tenue préférée d'Aurélie?*
Referring again to the clothes pictured in activity **1**, students listen and indicate which is Laura's favourite outfit and which is Aurélie's.

Answers: Laura: 2 (la tenue "rock"); Aurélie: 1 (la tenue "charme")

🎧 **CD 1, track 17**
Cassette 1, side 1
page 96, activité 2

– C'est quoi, ta tenue préférée, Laura?
– Moi, c'est le pantalon noir, la chemise bleue, la veste noire et les sandales noires. Et toi, Aurélie, c'est quoi, ta tenue préférée?
– Moi, ma tenue préférée, c'est le pantalon noir, le pull rose, le cardigan rose et les chaussures blanches.

AT 2.2 **3** *Décris une tenue. Ton/Ta partenaire devine.*
Working in pairs, students take turns to describe one of the outfits from activity **1**; the partner listens and indicates the outfit being described.

AT 3.2
AT 4.2 **4a** *Recopie et complète la conversation avec la bonne forme du verbe "avoir".*
Students copy and complete the conversation using the correct forms of *avoir*. Refer them back, if necessary, to the *Rappel* panel on page 8 of the Students' Book.

Answers:
– Moi, j'<u>ai</u> des Adichats!
– Quoi? Tu <u>as</u> des Adichats? Eh! Il <u>a</u> des Adichats!
– Ah ah ah! On n'<u>a</u> pas d'Adichats! Nous, nous <u>avons</u> des Chatbok.
– Ah, vous <u>avez</u> des Chatbok?
– Oh là là, ils <u>ont</u> des Chatbok! Nul!

AT 2.2
AT 3.2 **4b** *À deux, lisez la conversation.*
Working in pairs, students read aloud the conversation from activity **4a**.

AT 1.2 **5a** *Écoute: à droite, c'est la tenue préférée de Julien ou de Thomas?*
Students listen to the recording to find out whether the illustration represents Julien's or Thomas's favourite outfit.

Answer: Thomas

AT 1.3
AT 4.2 **5b** *Réécoute. Recopie et complète la bulle pour Julien et pour Thomas.*
Students listen again and note down details of the two boys' favourite outfits; they complete a speech bubble for Julien and one for Thomas. Although they will be able to refer to the illustration in the Student's Book to remind them of Thomas's outfit, they will need to rely on their own notes in order to complete Julien's speech bubble.

Answers: see transcript

🎧 **CD 1, track 18**
Cassette 1, side 1
page 97, activité 5

– *[Julien:]* Quand je vais au collège, ma tenue préférée, c'est un jean, un tee-shirt blanc, un sweat vert, un blouson rouge, des chaussettes blanches et des baskets blanches. Moi, j'aime bien le look sport. C'est pratique.
– *[Thomas:]* Quand je vais au collège, ma tenue préférée, c'est un pantalon beige, un tee-shirt vert, un sweat blanc, des baskets bleues et un blouson noir. Moi, je préfère le look décontracté, c'est sympa.

AT 3.2 **6a** *Laura parle de quelle photo?*
Students read Laura's text and decide which photo she is referring to.

Answers: girl with spiky hair

AT 4.2/3 **6b** *Qu'est-ce que tu penses des tenues sur les photos?*
Students write their own opinion of the clothes in the photos.

En plus Unité 1

pages 108–109

Objectives

These extension pages are intended for more able students who are confident with the core language of the unit. They can be used by students who finish other activities quickly or as alternative class and homework material.

Resources

Students' Book, pages 108–109
CD 1, track 19
Cassette 1, side 1

Programme of Study reference

1b, 1c, 2a, 2c, 2g, 2h, 2i, 3b, 3c, 3d, 3e, 4a, 4c, 4d, 5c, 5d, 5e, 5g, 5i

AT 3.3 **AT 4.1** **1a** *Lis le test. Il y a combien de nationalités? Continue la liste.*

This activity extends the work done on nationalities on pages 6–7. Students first search the text for all the nationalities; they note them down in French together with their corresponding countries. Dictionaries should be made available for students to use if required, or they could refer to the glossary at the back of the Students' Book.

Answers: américain, les États-Unis; japonais, le Japon; suisse, la Suisse; allemand, l'Allemagne; espagnol, l'Espagne; danois, le Danemark; canadien, le Canada; français, la France; autrichien, l'Autriche; belge, la Belgique; chinois, la Chine; indien, l'Inde

AT 3.3 **1b** *Fais le test.*

Students go on to complete the quiz.

Answers: 1a; 2c; 3c; 4b; 5b; 6b; 7b; 8c

AT 1.3 **1c** *Écoute les réponses.*

The quiz answers are recorded so that students can check their answers.

CD 1, track 19 **page 108, activité 1c**
Cassette 1, side 1

1 – Les jeux vidéo sont américains, japonais, ou bien suisses?
 – Ils sont américains.
2 – Les legos sont des jouets allemands, espagnols ou bien danois?
 – Ce sont des jouets danois.
3 – Les poupées Barbie sont canadiennes, allemandes ou bien américaines?
 – Elles sont américaines.
4 – Les croissants sont français, autrichiens ou bien belges?
 – Ils sont autrichiens.
5 – Le premier ketchup est américain, chinois ou bien français?
 – Il est chinois.
6 – Les premières barres de chocolat sont françaises, suisses ou bien belges?
 – Elles sont suisses.
7 – L'Orangina est une boisson française, espagnole ou bien américaine?
 – C'est une boisson espagnole.
8 – Les premières brosses à dents sont japonaises, indiennes ou bien chinoises?
 – Elles sont chinoises.

AT 2.3 **2a** *Regarde la photo. Qu'est-ce que tu penses de la tenue de Max?*

This oral activity asks students to express their opinion of the outfit worn by Max in the photo. Encourage them to justify their opinions and to speak in as much detail as possible.

AT 3.2 **AT 4.2** **2b** *Écris l'interview avec les bonnes formes des verbes à l'infinitif.*

Students copy and complete the interview, replacing the infinitives with the correct forms of the verbs. Refer them to the grammar sections on verbs on pages 138–141 of the Students' Book.

Answers:
– Max, tu <u>as</u> 14 ans. Tu <u>es</u> mannequin depuis quand?
– Depuis trois ans, et j'<u>adore</u> ça!
– Les mannequins <u>sont</u> bien payés?
– Oui! Mais, pour moi, l'important, c'<u>est</u> la mode. Les vêtements <u>sont</u> très cools.
– Tu <u>mets</u> des vêtements à la mode?
– Oui. Mais chez moi, je <u>mets</u> des tenues décontractées. J'<u>aime</u> bien le look sport.

AT 3.3 **3a** *Lis les opinions. Qui est pour l'uniforme au collège? Qui est contre?*

Students read a selection of opinions about school uniform; they indicate who is in favour of school uniform and who is against it.

Answers: pour l'uniforme: Stephen, Charlotte; contre l'uniforme: Anne, Olivier

AT 3.3 **AT 4.2** **3b** *Recopie et complète les réponses aux questions.*

Referring back to the opinions expressed in the article, students complete the sentences about the young people's clothing preferences.

Answers: a Anne aime les jeans, les tee-shirts et les pulls. b Stephen aime l'uniforme parce que c'est simple et c'est économique. c Olivier n'aime pas les uniformes parce qu'en général ils sont moches. d L'uniforme de Charlotte est gris et bleu.

AT 4.3/4 **3c** *Donne ton opinion: pour ou contre les uniformes dans les collèges?*

Students express, in writing, their own opinions of school uniform. Encourage them to justify their opinions and to write in as much detail as possible.

1 Mode ado

Point lecture
pages 120–121

These pages are intended to encourage independent reading. Students should attempt them once they are confident with the core language of the unit. They can be used by students who finish other activities quickly or as alternative class and homework material.

Objectives
▶ Develop reading for pleasure via song lyrics (**8C4 – L**)
▶ Read and understand a text about fashion through the ages (**8C1 – L**)

Resources
Students' Book, pages 120–121
CD 1, tracks 20–21
Cassette 1, side 1
OHT 5

Programme of Study reference
1a, 1c, 2a, 2b, 2g, 2h, 2i, 3b, 3c, 3d, 3e, 4a, 4c, 4d, 5a, 5c, 5d, 5e, 5f, 5g, 5i

AT 1.4
AT 3.4
1a *Écoute et lis la chanson. Tu préfères quel titre?*
These song lyrics launch **8C4**. Students listen to the song and follow the text in the Students' Book or on **OHT 5**. From the three titles given, they select the one that best sums up the gist of the song.

Answer: b

CD 1, track 20   page 120, activité 1a
Cassette 1, side 1

Pour aller chez Noé,
Qu'est-ce que je mets?
Qu'est-ce que je mets?
Ma jolie robe rayée?
Elle est trop serrée.
Mon tee-shirt en lycra?
Ça ne me va pas.
Aïe aïe aïe, qu'est-ce que je mets?

Refrain:
Ma tenue préférée,
C'est mon jean délavé,
Mon vieux jean,
Mon blue-jean,
C'est le blues du blue-jean.

Pour aller chez Clément,
Qu'est-ce que je mets?
Qu'est-ce que je mets?
Mon beau pantalon blanc?
Il est bien trop grand.
Mon caleçon rose et gris?
Il est trop petit!
Aïe aïe aïe, qu'est-ce que je mets?
Refrain

Ça y est, j'ai une idée.
Qu'est-ce que c'est?
Qu'est-ce que c'est?
Mon vieux jean délavé!
Mon jean adoré,
Avec un nouveau sweat
Et mes vieilles baskets,
Oh là là, c'est sympa!
Refrain

AT 3.4 **1b** *Relis la chanson. Trouve …*
Students read through the song again searching for the French equivalents of the English expressions.

Answers: a elle est trop serrée; b ça ne me va pas; c ça y est

1c *Cherche les mots que tu ne connais pas dans le glossaire ou dans un dictionnaire.*
Give students the opportunity to read through the song lyrics in more detail, using dictionaries or the glossary at the back of the Students' Book to look up any unknown words.

Follow-up activity: For further comprehension practice with the song lyrics, display **OHT 5** while students listen to the song with their books closed. Start by blanking out some key words (with small pieces of paper or blobs of putty adhesive) and ask students to listen for them. Pause the recording and ask students to read a line or two, supplying the missing words.

AT 4.2/3 **1d** *Invente des bulles pour les dessins.*
Students refer back to the song lyrics to help them write a caption for each drawing.

Answers: a Mon tee-shirt en lycra? Ça ne me va pas.
b Mon beau pantalon blanc? Il est bien trop grand.
c Mon caleçon rose et gris? Il est trop petit! d Ça y est, j'ai une idée … Mon vieux jean délavé! Mon jean adoré, avec un nouveau sweat et mes vieilles baskets …

AT 3.4 **2a** *Regarde les images et lis l'article. Tu aimes quel look?*
This magazine-style article on the history of fashion launches **8C1**. Students read through the text and look at the corresponding pictures, selecting the style that they prefer.

AT 3.4 **2b** *Trouve …*
Students search the article for the French equivalents of the English words and phrases.

Answers: a les robes en nylon; b des baskets de marque; c le couturier; d longues et droites; e hauts; f les talons; g à la mode

AT 1.3/4 **3** *Écoute. Ils aiment ou pas? Écris la date et dessine* ☺ *ou* ☹ *.*
Students listen to the recording and indicate whether the speakers like or dislike the different fashions.

44

Answers: 1900: both speakers dislike the styles; 1940: the girl dislikes these styles but the boy seems to like them; 1960s: the girl loves these fashions; 1990s: this is the boy's favourite style

CD 1, track 21   page 121, activité 3
Cassette 1, side 1

- En 1900, on porte les robes longues et droites ... je n'aime pas le look. C'est trop sombre. C'est moche!
- Oui, je suis d'accord. En 1940, c'est le look très féminin ... les jupes longues, les chaussures élégantes ...
- Avec les talons hauts! Ah non, je déteste ça.
- Pourquoi?
- Parce que ce n'est pas pratique!
- Regarde ... Dans les années 60, c'est l'époque des mini-jupes. Tu aimes le look des années 60?
- Oui, j'adore ça! J'aime beaucoup les mini-jupes et les motifs géométriques. C'est super!
- Et les années 90 ...
- Jeans, tee-shirts ... c'est le look décontracté.
- C'est mon look préféré parce que c'est pratique et confortable.

AT 2.3/4   4 *Qu'est-ce que tu penses des tenues sur les photos? Ton/Ta partenaire est d'accord?*
In pairs, students express and discuss their own opinions of the different fashions.

AT 4.3/4   5 *Continue l'article. Écris un paragraphe pour décrire le look d'aujourd'hui.*
Students write an additional paragraph for the magazine article, describing the fashions of today. If appropriate, they could go on to describe the fashions 10 years into the future.

Copymasters

Feuille 3 À vos marques

There are two starter activities on this copymaster. Activities 1a and 1b could be completed while working on pages 6–7 of the Students' Book, to revise personal information. Activity 2 emphasizes the spelling of key clothing vocabulary and could be completed while working on pages 8–9.

1a *Lis la lettre. A choisit une phrase, B recopie la phrase sans fautes. Ensuite, changez de rôle. Qui n'a pas de fautes?*
Students choose a sentence from the text (the one that they think will be the most difficult!), challenge their partner to copy it out correctly, then check their partner's work against the original text. (They are allowed to copy because even this can be difficult for many to do accurately.) Apparently students are very eagle-eyed when attempting to spot flaws in each other's work!

1b *En anglais, écris dix choses que tu sais de Clément.*
Students note down 10 things that they now know about Clément. This comprehension check provides students with an element of choice. As a follow-up activity for homework, students could copy out the whole of Clément's text, aiming to do it as accurately as possible.

2 *Complète la grille.*
Students complete the crossword.

Answers: 1 chemise; 2 jupe; 3 jean; 4 pull; 5 chaussures; 6 pantalon; 7 sandales; 8 short; 9 robe; 10 baskets

Feuille 4 Challenge!

There are two plenary activities on this copymaster. Activity 1 focuses on agreement and position of colour adjectives and could be used towards the end of pages 8–9 of the Students' Book. Activity 2 could be used after working on pages 12–13. It checks comprehension of the key language of the unit and focuses on accurate copying, agreement of adjectives, etc.

1a *Complète les étiquettes avec des adjectifs de couleur.*
Students label the pictures, using their own choice of colour adjectives to describe the clothing. Stress that they can use any colours they like but they must remember to make the adjectives agree with the nouns.

1b *Colorie les vêtements.*
Students colour in the pictures so that they match the descriptions in activity **1a**.

2 *Les phrases ne sont pas logiques. Change un mot dans chaque phrase et écris des phrases logiques.*
Students alter one word in each of these illogical sentences so that they make sense. Stress that there might be a variety of possible solutions for each one and that students should use their initiative and creativity to come up with ideas. Ask them to feed back orally to the class, while you list the various options for each sentence on the board or OHP. As a follow-up activity, students could write similar illogical sentences to swap with a partner.

Some possible answers: 1 Je <u>déteste</u> le look habillé parce que c'est nul. J'aime le look habillé parce que c'est <u>chic</u>/<u>sympa</u>. 2 Elle n'a pas de <u>tee-shirts</u> parce qu'elle préfère les chemises. Elle n'a pas de sandales parce qu'elle préfère les <u>baskets</u>. 3 Je déteste les cravates parce qu'elles ne sont pas <u>confortables</u>. 4 Il met une veste quand il va <u>au collège</u>. Il met <u>un short</u> quand il va à la plage. 5 Quand il fait froid, je mets <u>un pantalon</u> et un pull. 6 Ma copine est <u>française</u> parce que ses parents sont français. Ma copine est américaine parce que ses parents sont <u>américains</u>.

1 Mode ado

Feuille 5 Écoute Encore

These activities consolidate descriptions of clothing and what people are wearing. They can be completed after working on pages 8–9 of the Students' Book.

AT 1.2/3

1a *Écoute. Note la tenue de chaque personne.*
Students listen and indicate the letters of the clothing items mentioned by each speaker.

Answers: 1 a, d, g, i; 2 b, f, h; 3 c, e, j

AT 1.2/3

1b *Réécoute. Dessine des flèches pour indiquer les couleurs.*
Students listen again and draw arrows linking the clothing items to the colours. They could later colour in the pictures to show the correct colours, perhaps for homework.

Answers: a (pantalon) bleu; b (jean) noir; c (robe) rouge; d (chemise) blanc; e (pull) bleu; f (sweat) rouge; g (veste) vert; h (baskets) blanc; i (chaussures) marron; j (bottes) gris

CD 3, track 1 — **Cassette 4, side 1** — *Feuille 5, activité 1*

1 – Ta tenue préférée, c'est quoi?
 – Ma tenue préférée, c'est un pantalon bleu … une chemise blanche … une veste verte … et des chaussures marron.
2 – Ta tenue préférée, c'est quoi?
 – Ma tenue préférée, c'est un jean noir … un sweat rouge … et des baskets blanches.
3 – Ta tenue préférée, c'est quoi?
 – Ma tenue préférée, c'est une robe rouge … un pull bleu et des bottes grises.

AT 1.2/3

2a *Lis les phrases. Écoute Salim. Entoure la lettre dans la bonne colonne après chaque phrase.*
Students read the English statements and check whether each one is true or false by listening to what Salim says on the recording. They circle the letters in the correct columns.

Answers: 1 vrai; 2 faux; 3 vrai; 4 faux; 5 vrai

CD 3, track 2 — **Cassette 4, side 1** — *Feuille 5, activité 2a*

Aujourd'hui, parce que je suis au collège, j'ai un pantalon noir … une chemise grise … un pull gris … et des chaussures noires. Par contre, ma tenue préférée, c'est un tee-shirt et un short.

2b *Arrange les lettres entourées pour trouver le vêtement préféré de Salim.*
Students unjumble the letters they circled in activity **2a** to find Salim's favourite item of clothing.

Answer: short

Feuille 6 Écoute En plus

This copymaster could be used after the main spreads have been completed, e.g. during or after pages 12–13.

AT 1.3

1 *Écoute. Relie la personne à la tenue.*
Students listen and match the speakers to the items of clothing.

Answers: Dimitri: e; 1 Marion: c; 2 Paul: d; 3 Cécile: f; 4 Nicolas: b; 5 Nathalie: a

CD 3, track 3 — **Cassette 4, side 1** — *Feuille 6, activité 1*

Exemple:
 – Bonjour, Dimitri. Qu'est-ce que tu mets quand tu pars en vacances?
 – Je mets une casquette et un sweat.
 – Tu aimes le look décontracté!
 – Oui.
1 – Bonjour, Marion. Qu'est-ce que tu mets quand tu pars en vacances?
 – Je mets une robe et des sandales.
 – Tu aimes les robes?
 – Oui.
2 – Et toi, Paul … Qu'est-ce que tu mets quand tu pars en vacances?
 – Je mets une chemise blanche …
 – Une chemise blanche … d'accord …
 – … et un pantalon noir. J'aime bien le look habillé.
3 – Cécile, qu'est-ce que tu mets quand tu pars en vacances?
 – Je mets un sweat …
 – Un sweat?
 – Oui, un sweat jaune … et une jupe bleue.
4 – Nicolas, qu'est-ce que tu mets quand tu pars en vacances?
 – Je mets un jean … et des baskets … parce que j'aime bien le look décontracté.
 – C'est confortable …
 – Oui.
5 – Nathalie, qu'est-ce que tu mets quand tu pars en vacances?
 – Moi, je préfère un short et un tee-shirt.
 – Un short et un tee-shirt.
 – Oui … quand il fait beau!

AT 1.4

2 *Écoute. Complète les bulles.*
Students listen to the speakers describing their favourite outfits and complete the speech bubbles.

Answers: see transcript

CD 3, track 4 — **Cassette 4, side 1** — *Feuille 6, activité 2*

 – Qu'est-ce que tu aimes comme look?
 – Moi, j'aime le look décontracté. C'est sympa.

Mode ado   **1**

– C'est quoi, ta tenue préférée?
– Ma tenue préférée, c'est mon jean noir, mon sweat blanc, mes baskets blanches et mon blouson noir.

– Qu'est-ce que tu mets pour aller au collège?
– Je mets un pantalon, un tee-shirt, un sweat et des chaussures.

– Tu es pour ou contre l'uniforme au collège?
– Je suis contre. C'est moche.

Feuille 7 Parle Encore

This copymaster can be used with pages 8–9 of the Students' Book. It is an information-gap activity in which students work in pairs: give the top half of the copymaster to one student and the bottom half to their partner.

AT 2.2/3

1 *Pose des questions à ton/ta partenaire et réponds à ses questions. Dessine et complète les tenues (trois choses pour chaque personne).*
Students ask each other questions to find out what the missing garments are on their section of the copymaster. As a follow-up activity, they could continue working together to describe the outfits as though in the commentary for a fashion show, either orally or in writing. The commentaries could be presented to the rest of the class. Students could add colour to the pictures on the copymaster and include these colours in their commentaries.

Feuille 8 Parle En plus

This copymaster could be completed towards the end of or after pages 10–11 of the Students' Book.

AT 2.3

1 *Quel est le look préféré de ta classe? Fais un sondage – coche la grille pour chaque personne – et présente les résultats (enregistre-toi, si possible).*
Students conduct a survey within the class to establish what the most popular style of clothing is.

AT 2.3-5

2 *Pose les questions à ton/ta partenaire et note les réponses.*
Students work in pairs, asking and answering the questions supplied. The first few questions revise the language of pages 6–7 (personal information), then the focus moves to the topic of clothes and expressing/justifying opinions of clothes. Before students begin, it might be useful to hold a brainstorming session to come up with a wider range of adjectives that students could use in their responses.
Question 10 is not modelled on pages 10–11 but is included here so as to give students scope for a more open-ended response. If appropriate, show them how to incorporate different tenses into their response, e.g. *La mode, c'est important pour moi parce que … Par exemple,* *le week-end dernier je suis allé(e) … et j'ai mis … Le week-end prochain je vais aller … et je vais mettre …* Students who are able to do this are beginning to show evidence of ability to work at level 5.

Feuille 9 Lis et écris Encore 1

This copymaster provides basic practice of clothing vocabulary and could be used with pages 8–9 of the Students' Book.

AT 3.1

1 *Range l'armoire comme dans l'exemple.*
Students allocate the scattered garments to their correct places on the shelves.

Answers: a blouson; b sweat; c chaussures; d tee-shirt; e pull; f pantalon; g chaussettes; h veste; i baskets; j chemise

AT 4.1

2 *Regarde encore les vêtements. Complète la bulle.*
Students complete the speech bubble with the names of the garments from activity **1**. They will need to supply *un, une* or *des* for each item, so encourage them to refer back to the Students' Book to check the genders.

Answers: Moi, j'ai un tee-shirt, un blouson, un sweat, des chaussures, un pull, un pantalon, des chaussettes, une veste, des baskets et une chemise.

Feuille 10 Lis et écris Encore 2

This copymaster reinforces the structure *Quand je vais …, je mets …,* together with clothes vocabulary and colour adjectives. It could be used with pages 12–13 of the Students' Book.

AT 3.2

1a *Lis la bulle. Qui parle, A ou B?*
Students read the speech bubble and decide who is speaking, person A or person B.

Answer: A

AT 3.2

1b *Colorie ses vêtements.*
Students colour in person A's clothes as described in the speech bubble.

Answers: black trousers, white shirt, black tie, yellow jacket, yellow socks, black shoes

AT 4.2

2a *Invente et écris une bulle pour l'autre personne.*
Students write a speech bubble for person B, using A's text as a model. They use their own choice of colours.

Possible answer: Quand je vais à une boum, je mets un pantalon (bleu), un tee-shirt (orange), un sweat (noir), des chaussettes (blanches), des baskets (grises).

AT 1.2
AT 3.2

2b *Lis ta bulle. Ton/Ta partenaire colorie les vêtements.*
In pairs, students take turns to read out their text from activity **2a**. Their partner colours in B's clothing accordingly.

1 Mode ado

Feuille 11 Lis et écris En plus 1

AT 3.3/4

This copymaster revises personal information and could be used towards the end of pages 6–7 of the Students' Book.

1a *Lis l'e-mail de Bruno. C'est quel paragraphe?*

Students read Bruno's letter and indicate the focus of each paragraph.

Answers: 1 son apparence/sa personnalité: paragraphe C; 2 sa famille: paragraphe D; 3 son âge/sa nationalité: paragraphe A; 4 ses passe-temps: paragraphe B

1b *Souligne toutes les parties du verbe "avoir". Il y en a combien?*

1c *Entoure toutes les parties du verbe "être". Il y en a combien?*

Students search Bruno's letter for all the different parts of the verbs *avoir* and *être*. When checking students' answers, emphasize how frequently these verbs occur and therefore how useful it is to know them.

Answers: there are 10 parts of *être* (shown in bold below) and four parts of *avoir* (underlined below):
Salut! Je m'appelle Bruno Pasquier. J'<u>ai</u> treize ans et mon anniversaire, c'**est** le trente août. Je **suis** français, mais ma mère **est** portugaise.
J'aime le vélo, la natation et le bowling. En plus, mes passe-temps préférés **sont** écouter la radio et lire des magazines sur le sport.
Je **suis** assez grand et gros. Je **suis** blond et j'<u>ai</u> les cheveux courts et raides. Je **suis** optimiste et sportif mais un peu paresseux. Et toi, tu **es** comment?
J'habite à Toulouse dans le sud de la France avec ma mère et mon beau-père. Ils **sont** sympa. J'<u>ai</u> une sœur qui s'appelle Alice. Elle <u>a</u> dix ans et elle **est** très gentille.

AT 3.3/4

1d *Réponds aux questions.*

Students answer comprehension questions on Bruno's letter.

Answers: 1 français; 2 13; 3 quatre personnes; 4 dans le sud de la France; 5 parce qu'il aime le vélo, la natation, le bowling et les magazines sur le sport; 6 il est assez grand et gros, il est blond et il a les cheveux courts et raides; 7 il est optimiste, sportif et un peu paresseux

AT 4.3/4

2 *Pour chaque mot, écris une question sur l'e-mail de Bruno sur une feuille. Échange avec un(e) partenaire.*

Students use each of the question words supplied to write a question about Bruno. They swap with a partner and write answers to their partner's questions. As a follow-up to this activity, students could adapt Bruno's letter to write a similar letter about themselves.

Possible questions: Tu habites <u>où</u>? C'est <u>quand</u>, ton anniversaire? Tu t'appelles <u>comment</u>? Tu es <u>comment</u>? Ta sœur est <u>comment</u>? Tes parents sont <u>comment</u>? <u>Est-ce que</u> tu es français/ta mere est française? <u>Est-ce que</u> tu aimes le football? <u>Quels</u> sont tes passe-temps préférés? Tu as <u>quel</u> âge? <u>Qu'est-ce que</u> tu aimes faire? Tu habites avec <u>qui</u>?

Feuille 12 Lis et écris En plus 2

This copymaster could be used with pages 12–13 of the Students' Book. It revises much of the language of the unit in the slightly different context of a magazine article on fashion, and also includes some unfamiliar language.

AT 3.4

1 *C'est qui?*

Students read the English statements and match them to the young people featured in the article.

Answers: 1 Denis; 2 Valérie; 3 Sophie; 4 Denis; 5 Pierre

AT 3.4

2 *Trouve dans le texte l'équivalent en français.*

Students search the text for the French equivalents of the English expressions.

Answers: 1 une petite jupe avec un chemisier en soie; 2 un pull à col roulé; 3 un signe de bonne qualité; 4 j'aime les couleurs vives; 5 parce que ce n'est pas si important que ça

AT 3.4

3 *Quelle opinion est la plus proche de la tienne? Traduis-la en anglais sur une feuille.*

Students are asked to choose the opinion that most closely represents their own view, and to translate it into English.

AT 4.4

4 *Écris un paragraphe pour donner ton opinion.*

Students write a paragraph in French expressing their own opinion on fashion.

Feuille 13 Grammaire 1

This copymaster focuses on agreement and position of adjectives and should be used with the *Zoom grammaire* section on page 9 of the Students' Book.

1 *Lis la bulle du chat. Barre les adjectifs qui ne vont pas.*

Students read the speech bubble and cross out the incorrect adjectives.

Answers: the correct version is: Ma tenue préférée, c'est un blouson <u>noir</u>, une chemise <u>verte</u>, une cravate <u>verte</u>, un short <u>blanc</u>, des chaussettes <u>noires</u>, des baskets <u>blanches</u> et une casquette <u>grise</u>! Hyper-cool!

2 *Complète chaque phrase avec un adjectif de la boîte.*

Students complete the sentences using the adjectives supplied.

Answers: 1 française; 2 français, algériens; 3 noirs; 4 noires, noir; 5 blanc

3 *Colorie la tenue du footballeur et décris la couleur de chaque vêtement. Attention aux accords!*

Students colour in the footballer's clothing and write a description of it, focusing on adjectival agreement.

Mode ado 1

Feuille 14 Grammaire 2

This copymaster focuses on verbs, pronouns and the present tense of *mettre*. It could be used with pages 12–13 of the Students' Book.

1a *Souligne les verbes.*
Students study the panel of jumbled words and underline all the verbs.

Answers: mettez, mettons, avez, avons, ont, as, mets, a, mettent, mets, met, ai, suis

1b *Entoure les pronoms.*
Students look again at the panel of words and circle all the pronouns. As a follow-up, more able students could link the pronouns to the corresponding parts of the verbs. Ask students if they know what type of words are left over (nouns).

Answers: je, j', tu, il, elle, on, nous, vous, ils, elles

2 *Complète la conversation avec les bons pronoms.*
Students fill in the missing pronouns in the dialogue.

Answers: je, tu, il, elle, elles, tu, je

3 *Complète les bulles avec la bonne forme du verbe "mettre".*
Students complete the speech bubbles using the correct forms of *mettre*. The paradigm is given in a box on the copymaster, but more able students could attempt this activity with the box covered, referring only to the panel of jumbled words in activity **1**.

Answers: 1 mets, mets; 2 mettons; 3 met; 4 mettent

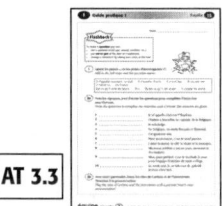

Feuille 15 Guide pratique 1

This copymaster accompanies the *Guide pratique* on question forms on page 6 of the Students' Book.

AT 3.3

1 *Ajoute les points (.) et les points d'interrogation (?).*
Students insert full stops and question marks into the appropriate places in the text.

Answers: Il s'appelle comment, ce chat? Il s'appelle Charlie. Il a quel âge? Je ne sais pas. Il habite où? En France. Est-ce qu'il aime les souris? Non. Qu'est-ce qu'il fait le soir? Il chasse les souris.

AT 4.3

2a *Voici les réponses, à toi d'écrire les questions pour compléter l'interview avec Corinne.*
Students are given a series of answers without their corresponding questions; they are asked to supply an appropriate question for each. The questions used in Charlie's text in activity **1** provide support for parts of this activity, although students will need to change the verbs from the third to the second person singular.

Answers: 1 Tu t'appelles comment? 2 Tu habites où? 3 Tu es de quelle nationalité? 4 Tu parles quelles langues? 5 Tu as quel âge? 6 C'est quand, ton anniversaire? 7 Quels sont tes passe-temps préférés? 8 C'est quoi, ta tenue préférée? 9 C'est quoi, ton sport préféré? 10 Qu'est-ce que tu fais le week-end?

AT 2.3

2b *Avec un(e) partenaire, jouez les rôles de Corinne et de l'interviewer. Attention à la prononciation!*
Students work in pairs to perform the interview, focusing on correct pronunciation and intonation.

Feuille 16 Guide pratique 2

Activity 1 can be used with the *Guide pratique* section on *parce que* on page 11 of the Students' Book. Activity 2 accompanies the focus on *quand* on pages 12–13.

AT 3.2
AT 4.3

1 *Complète les bulles avec une phrase qui commence par "parce que" (ou "parce qu'").*
Students complete each sentence using an appropriate *parce que* phrase. This open-ended task allows students to provide any reasons or opinions that make sense. Ask them to feed back their responses to the class. You could note down all the ideas on the board or OHP: which ideas are the most original and which are the most common?

Some possible answers: 1 parce que je préfère les robes noires/le look décontracté, parce qu'elle n'est pas pratique/confortable; 2 parce que je n'ai pas de chaussures, parce que je déteste le look élégant, parce que j'adore le look décontracté; 3 parce que c'est très élégant/chic; 4 parce que c'est ma couleur préférée, parce que c'est pratique/confortable

AT 3.2
AT 4.3

2 *Invente des fins de phrases.*
In this open-ended activity, students invent appropriate endings to the sentences. Remind them to pay attention to the subject pronouns and to make sure that their verbs are in the correct form. You could challenge a more able class to see who can come up with the most amusing endings. Early finishers could write additional beginnings of sentences for a partner to complete.

Some possible answers: 1 je mets un short et un tee-shirt, je vais à la plage; 2 on met un pull, on regarde la télévision; 3 je vais à une boum/au cinéma/au café, je mange du gâteau; 4 il met son uniforme scolaire; 5 nous parlons/écoutons; 6 je danse/chante

Feuille 17 Ça se dit comme ça!

This copymaster could be used with the *Ça se dit comme ça!* section on page 7 of the Students' Book. Alternatively, because the "unknown language" used here (parts of the body) will be introduced in Unit 2, you could save this copymaster until the end of Unit 1 as a reminder of the pronunciation point and as an introduction to the body vocabulary.

1 Mode ado

1a *Avec un(e) partenaire, prononcez les mots suivants.*
Students work with a partner, attempting to use their knowledge of French pronunciation to work out how to pronounce these unknown words (which will be formally introduced in Unit 2).

1b *Écoute et vérifie.*
Students listen to check their pronunciation.

CD 3, track 5 Feuille 17, activité 1b
Cassette 4, side 1

1 – ma bouche
2 – mon bras
3 – mon genou
4 – mon nez
5 – mon visage
6 – mon pouce

2a *Écoute bien la prononciation.*
Make sure that students understand the meanings of these sentences before doing this and activity **2b**.

CD 3, track 6 Feuille 17, activité 2a
Cassette 4, side 1

1 – Vous avez un nez énorme.
2 – Il met son pouce dans sa bouche.
3 – Son visage est plus sage que ton visage.

2b *Qui est le plus rapide, toi ou ton/ta partenaire? Dis vite chaque phrase trois fois.*
Students practise saying the sentences, slowly at first then faster and faster until they become a tongue-twister.

Encore Workbook

Page 4 (1.1)
Use with pages 6–7 of the Students' Book.

AT 3.2 **1** *Relie les dessins aux bulles. Écris les noms dans les bulles.*
Students match the speech bubbles to the people and give each person's name.

Answers: 1 c Blanche; 2 a Hercule; 3 d Millie; 4 b Obélix

AT 4.2 **2** *Et toi? Complète la bulle.*
Students write about themselves in the speech bubble. As a follow-up, they could write bubbles for famous people, omitting the names. They could then read out their bubbles to a partner, who attempts to guess who is being described in each one.

Page 5 (1.2)
Use with pages 8–9 of the Students' Book.

AT 3.2 **1a** *Qui parle? Relie les bulles aux personnes.*
Students match the speech bubbles to the drawings.

Answers: 1 d; 2 c; 3 a; 4 b

AT 3.2 **1b** *Colorie les vêtements. Vérifie avec ton/ta partenaire.*
Students colour in the clothes according to the descriptions, then check their work with a partner.

Answers: 1 blue trousers, yellow sweatshirt, grey jacket, yellow shoes; 2 grey skirt, pink blouse, black jacket, black boots; 3 brown shorts, red T-shirt, white trainers; 4 green dress, blue pullover, brown sandals

AT 4.2 **2** *Et toi? C'est quoi, ta tenue préférée? Dessine et écris à la page 13.*
Students draw and describe their favourite outfit on page 13 of the Workbook.

Page 6 (1.3)
Use with pages 10–11 of the Students' Book.

AT 3.2 **1** *Relie.*
Students match the expressions of likes and dislikes to the appropriate symbols.

Answers: 1 b; 2 a; 3 c; 4 d

AT 3.2 **AT 4.2** **2** *Vrai ou faux? Si c'est faux, écris la bonne phrase.*
Students read the sentences and decide whether they accurately represent the drawings and symbols. They correct the false sentences.

Answers: a vrai; b faux, je déteste le look sport; c faux, j'aime bien le look habillé

Page 7 (1.4)
Use with pages 12–13 of the Students' Book.

AT 3.2 **1a** *Lis les phrases et entoure le bon symbole.*
Students select an appropriate weather symbol for each phrase.

Answers: a fine weather; b cold weather; c rain; d windy; e sun; f hot weather

AT 4.2 **1b** *Il fait quel temps aujourd'hui?*
Students write a sentence describing today's weather.

AT 3.2 **2a** *Lis le dialogue et réponds aux questions en anglais.*
Students read the dialogue and answer comprehension questions in English.

Answers: a to a party; b white; c red boots; d a dress; e a white jacket; f a black dress, black hat and black boots

AT 2.2 **2b** *Lis le dialogue avec un(e) partenaire.*
Students read the dialogue aloud with a partner.

AT 4.2 *2c Complète la phrase pour toi.*
Students complete the sentence giving details of what they themselves would wear to a party.

Page 8 Grammaire

Use with pages 12–13 of the Students' Book.

1 Complète les phrases.
Students look at the verb endings and fill in the corresponding subject pronouns.

Answers: a je; b nous; c ils; d vous; e tu; f il

2 Écris la terminaison des verbes.
Students look at the subject pronouns and fill in the corresponding verb endings.

Answers: a aimes; b préfère; c adorons; d aime; e détestent

3 Complète avec la bonne forme d'"avoir".
Students fill in the correct forms of *avoir*.

Answers: a ai; b a; c ont; d as; e avons; f ont

Page 9 Méli-mélo

This page pulls together and mixes much of the language and grammar of the whole unit. It should therefore be used towards the end of the unit, at any point after pages 12–13.

1 Complète avec la bonne forme d'"être" ou "avoir".
Students fill in the gaps using the correct forms of *être* and *avoir*.

Answers: a suis, ai; b a, est; c sont; d sommes, avons; e êtes; f est, a; g as, es

2a Complète les phrases avec les mots de la boîte.
Students fill in the gaps using the words supplied in the box. Note that in question c, the first answer could be either *noir* or *rose*, but point out to students that pink is an unlikely colour for a pair of school uniform trousers!

Answers: a short, mon; b aimes, ma; c noir, noires; d rose; e quand, tes

2b Traduis les phrases a–e en anglais.
Students translate the sentences from activity **2a** into English.

Answers: a I love my green shorts and my yellow T-shirt. b Do you like my white skirt and my blue jacket? c When I go to school, I put on my black trousers, my black shoes and my grey socks. d Don't you like my pink and orange hat? e No, when you go into town, put on your black clothes.

Page 10 Challenge!

Use with page 16 of the Students' Book.

AT 3.3 *1 Lis l'interview. Sébastien aime la mode – oui ou non?*
Students read the interview to find out whether or not Sébastien is interested in clothes.

Answers: accept any answers that students can justify, e.g. yes, because he likes to get dressed up when he does a concert; or no, because he prefers to wear casual/comfortable clothes at home

2 Dans l'article, souligne tous les verbes au présent. Quelle phrase a le plus de verbes?
Students underline all the present tense verbs.

Answers: The sentence with the most verbs is: Je <u>suis</u> français, mais je <u>parle</u> trois langues parce que ma mère <u>est</u> italienne et mon père <u>est</u> canadien.

All present tense verbs are underlined below:
– Bonjour, Sébastien. Tu <u>as</u> quel âge?
– J'<u>ai</u> dix-sept ans.
– Et tu <u>es</u> de quelle nationalité?
– Je <u>suis</u> français, mais je <u>parle</u> trois langues parce que ma mère <u>est</u> italienne et mon père <u>est</u> canadien.
– Tu <u>aimes</u> la mode, non? Qu'<u>est</u>-ce que tu <u>mets</u> quand tu <u>as</u> un concert?
– Quand j'<u>ai</u> un concert, je <u>mets</u> un pantalon noir et une chemise blanche parce que j'<u>aime</u> beaucoup le look habillé.
– Et quand tu <u>es</u> à la maison?
– Quand je <u>suis</u> à la maison, je <u>préfère</u> le look décontracté. Je <u>mets</u> un jean et un sweat parce que c'<u>est</u> confortable. Et je <u>mets</u> un short et des sandales quand il y <u>a</u> du soleil … avec des lunettes de soleil.
– C'<u>est</u> quoi, ta tenue préférée?
– Ma tenue préférée, c'<u>est</u> probablement mon tee-shirt blanc, mon jean noir et mes baskets noires.
– Quels <u>sont</u> tes passe-temps préférés, Sébastien?
– J'<u>adore</u> écouter de la musique et j'<u>ai</u> une grande collection de CD. Le week-end, je <u>vais</u> au cinéma ou je <u>fais</u> du sport quand je n'<u>ai</u> pas de concert.

3 Dans l'article, que signifient les mots en gras?
Students give the English meanings of the bold words and phrases.
Answers: mais: but; *parce que*: because; *et*: and; *quand*: when; *ou*: or

4 À la page 13, écris en anglais 10 choses que tu sais sur Sébastien.
To show their comprehension of the text, students note down in English 10 things they know about Sébastien.

En plus Workbook

Page 4 (1.1)

Use with pages 6–7 of the Students' Book.

AT 3.2 *1 Complète les phrases avec les mots des boîtes.*
Students fill in the gaps in the descriptions using the words supplied in the boxes.

Answers: a petite et assez mince, brune, longs et frisés, gentille; b grand et mince, blond, courts et frisés, courageux; c grande et très mince, blonde, très longs et raides, sympa; d grand et gros, roux, longs et raides, marrant

1 Mode ado

AT 4.3 *2 Et toi? Écris ta description, comme ci-dessus, à la page 13.*
Students write a description of themselves. As a follow-up, they could write descriptions of famous people, omitting the names. They could then read out their texts to a partner, who attempts to guess who is being described in each one.

Page 5 (1.2)

Use with pages 8–9 of the Students' Book.

AT 3.2
AT 4.1 *1a Complète les bulles avec les bons vêtements. Plusieurs choix sont possibles, mais fais attention aux accords des adjectifs.*
Students complete the speech bubbles using the clothing vocabulary supplied. Point out that the gender of the item of clothing needs to match the adjective ending.

Answers: for most items of clothing, there are various possible positions: a un pantalon bleu, un blouson/sweat jaune, un blouson/sweat gris, des chaussures jaunes; b une jupe/chemise/veste grise, une jupe/chemise/veste rose, une jupe/chemise/veste noire et des bottes noires; c un short/tee-shirt marron, un short/tee-shirt rouge et des baskets blanches; d une robe verte, un pull bleu et des sandales marron

AT 3.2 *1b Colorie les vêtements.*
Students colour in the clothes according to the descriptions.

Answers: will depend on students' answers to activity **1a**

AT 4.3 *2a Et toi? C'est quoi, ta tenue préférée? Dessine et écris à la page 13.*
Students draw and describe their favourite outfit on page 13 of the Workbook, indicating colours.

AT 1.2
AT 2.3 *2b Lis ta description à un(e) partenaire. Il/Elle dessine. Comparez les dessins et changez de rôle.*
Students read out their description to a partner, who draws and colours in the outfit. They then compare drawings and swap roles.

Page 6 (1.3)

Use with pages 10–11 of the Students' Book.

AT 3.2
AT 4.1 *1 Écris la bonne expression de la boîte pour chaque symbole.*
Students match the symbols to the phrases expressing likes and dislikes.

Answers: a je déteste; b j'aime bien; c je n'aime pas beaucoup; d j'adore

AT 4.3 *2 Invente des phrases: opinion + look + raison.*
Students write sentences to describe the illustrations, expressing opinions and giving reasons using *parce que*.

Possible answers: a J'aime bien le look sport parce que c'est pratique. b J'adore le look décontracté parce que c'est confortable. c Je déteste le look sport parce que c'est moche. d J'aime bien le look habillé parce que c'est chic. e Je n'aime pas beaucoup le look sport parce que ce n'est pas élégant.

Page 7 (1.4)

Use with pages 12–13 of the Students' Book.

AT 3.2 *1a Lis le dialogue et barre les adjectifs qui ne vont pas.*
Students read the dialogue and cross out the adjectives that are incorrect.

Answers: the correct adjectives are: blanc, rouges, bleue, blanche, noire, noir, noires

AT 3.2
AT 4.2 *1b Réponds aux questions.*
Students answer the questions in French.

Answers: a à une boum; b un pantalon blanc; c des bottes rouges; d sa robe est bleue; e une veste blanche; f une robe noire, un chapeau noir et des bottes noires

AT 2.2 *1c Lis le dialogue avec un(e) partenaire.*
Students read the dialogue aloud with a partner.

AT 4.2 *2 Complète les phrases.*
Students complete the sentences about their own clothing preferences.

Page 8 Grammaire

Use with pages 12–13 of the Students' Book.

1 Complète les phrases. (Certaines ont plusieurs réponses possibles.)
Students complete the sentences with the correct subject pronouns. Point out that some sentences can have more than one answer, because certain pronouns are followed by the same verb ending.

Answers: a je; b nous; c ils/elles; d vous; e tu; f j'/il/elle/on

2 Écris la terminaison des verbes.
Students fill in the verb endings to match the pronouns.

Answers: a tu aimes; b je préfère; c nous adorons; d il n'aime pas; e mes parents détestent; f vous aimez

3a Complète avec la bonne forme d'"avoir".
Students complete the sentences with the correct forms of *avoir*.

Answers: a ai; b a; c avons; d ont; e as

3b Complète avec la bonne forme de "mettre".
Students complete the sentences with the correct forms of *mettre*.

Answers: a mettons; b mets; c mettent; d mettez; e met

4 Écris encore quatre phrases sur les vêtements à la page 13. Utilise les verbes "avoir" et "mettre".
Students write additional sentences about clothes on page 13 of the Workbook, using *avoir* and *mettre*.

Mode ado **1**

Page 9 Méli-mélo

This page pulls together and mixes much of the language and grammar of the whole unit. It should therefore be used towards the end of the unit, at any point after pages 12–13.

1a *Complète les phrases avec les mots de la boîte.*
Students fill in the gaps using the words supplied in the box. Note that in question c, the first answer could be either *noir* or *rose*, but point out to students that pink is an unlikely colour for a pair of school uniform trousers!

Answers: a short, mon; b aimes, ma; c noir, noires; d rose; e quand, tes

1b *Adapte les phrases b–e avec les mots en parenthèses.*
Students adapt sentences b–e from activity **1a**, substituting the words provided in brackets. Point out that they will need to alter adjectival agreement and possessive adjectives.

Answers: b Tu aimes mon jean blanc et mes bottes bleues? c Quand je vais au collège, je mets ma chemise noire, ma jupe noire et mon pull gris. d Tu n'aimes pas mes sandales roses et orange? e Non, quand tu vas en ville, mets ton chapeau noir.

2 *Entoure les erreurs, puis écris une version correcte à la page 13.*
Students circle the mistakes in the text then write out a corrected version.

Answers: the corrected text is: C'est mon anniversaire! Je mets <u>ma</u> robe noire, mon chapeau <u>blanc</u> et mes bottes <u>jaunes</u>. J'<u>aime</u> beaucoup le look habillé parce que c'est élégant. Ma sœur met <u>un</u> pantalon gris et une veste <u>verte</u>. Nous <u>sommes</u> contentes!

Page 10 Super-challenge!

Use with page 16 of the Students' Book.

AT 3.4 **1** *Lis l'article et souligne tous les verbes au présent au pluriel.*
Students underline all the plural present tense verbs. They list them on page 13 of the Workbook together with their infinitives.

Answers: plural verb forms are underlined below, with infinitives given in brackets:

Quand il fait chaud en été, <u>vous mettez</u> (mettre) un short, un tee-shirt et des sandales. <u>Vous évitez</u> (éviter) le lycra et le polyester et <u>vous préférez</u> (préférer) le coton parce que c'est plus confortable. C'est simple et logique. Mais que <u>mettez-vous</u> (mettre) cet hiver?

Émilie, 15 ans, Paris: Cet hiver, à Paris, <u>les jeunes aiment</u> (aimer) bien les gros pulls en laine quand il fait froid. <u>Nous mettons</u> (mettre) des pantalons larges ou à pattes d'éléphant. <u>Nous choisissons</u> (choisir) les bottes parce qu'<u>elles sont</u> (être) pratiques et chaudes, mais <u>les chaussures à talons reviennent</u> (revenir) à la mode pour les filles quand <u>elles sortent</u> (sortir) le soir.

<u>Les jeunes ont</u> (avoir) souvent un bonnet et des gants en laine. J'aime beaucoup ce look – c'est un peu le look skate – parce que c'est pratique et confortable.

Alex, 16 ans, Lyon: <u>Tous mes copains aiment</u> (aimer) le look gothique. <u>Ils choisissent</u> (choisir) surtout les vêtements noirs parce que c'est la couleur qu'<u>ils aiment</u> (aimer). <u>Ils mettent</u> (mettre) un tee-shirt noir à manches longues, un pantalon noir ou un jean déchiré et des baskets. <u>Nous mettons</u> (mettre) aussi des chaînes et des bijoux en argent. Quand il fait froid, je mets un blouson en cuir noir.

<u>Nous aimons</u> (aimer) ce look parce que c'est décontracté. <u>Nous détestons</u> (détester) le look habillé et le look sportif parce qu'<u>ils sont</u> (être) nuls.

2 *Trouve comment on dit en français …*
Students search the text for the French equivalents of the English phrases.

Answers: a des pantalons larges ou à pattes d'éléphant; b les chaussures à talons; c un bonnet et des gants en laine; d à manches longues; e des chaînes et des bijoux en argent

AT 3.4 **AT 4.2/3** **3** *Réponds aux questions.*
Students answer the questions in French.

Answers: a Ils mettent un short, un tee-shirt et des sandales. b Parce que c'est plus confortable. c Elles sont pratiques et chaudes. d C'est le look gothique. e Il déteste le look sportif parce que c'est nul.

4 *À la page 13, résume l'article en anglais (100 mots).*
Students summarize the article in English on page 13 of the Workbook.

Unit 2 Overview grid

National Curriculum

Pages/Contexts/ Cultural focus	Objectives	Grammar	Skills and Pronunciation	Key language	Framework	PoS	AT level
20–21 **2.1 Ça va?** Parts of the body	Name parts of the body; revise masculine, feminine and plural forms; use exclamations and sound French; use a dictionary to help with grammar and spelling	Gender and plurals	How to sound more authentic by using French exclamations Using a dictionary to find spellings, grammar and idioms	*le corps, le cou, le bras, le dos, l'œil (les yeux), le genou, le nez, le ventre, le visage, le pied, le doigt, les doigts de pied, le pouce la tête, la gorge, la main, la jambe, la bouche, la dent, l'épaule, l'oreille aïe! ouille! oh là là! mon/ma/mes*	8W7, 8T4, 8L6 – R (7W4)	1a, 1b, 1c, 2a, 2b, 2f, 2g, 3a, 3b, 3c, 3d, 3e, 4a, 5a, 5d, 5e, 5f, 5i	1.1, 2.1, 3.1–2, 4.1–2
22–23 **2.2 J'ai mal!** Illness and ailments	Ask someone what's wrong; say where it hurts; say how you feel and what is wrong with you; understand that you can't always translate literally	*au, à l', à la, aux*	Non-literal translations	*Qu'est-ce qui ne va pas? J'ai mal au/à l'/à la/aux …. J'ai chaud/froid/faim/soif, j'ai envie de vomir/dormir, j'ai de la fièvre, j'ai un rhume/le rhume des foins/la grippe, je tousse la pharmacie, l'hôpital, les urgences, le médecin*	8W8 – L	1a, 1b, 1c, 2a, 2b, 2c, 2d, 2f, 3a, 3b, 3c, 3d, 3e, 4a, 5a, 5c, 5d, 5e, 5f, 5i	1.2, 2.2–3, 3.2, 4.2–3
24–25 **2.3 C'est la forme!** Advice on a healthy lifestyle	Say what is good or bad for your health; understand and give basic advice on healthy living (using the imperative); say you agree/disagree; revise negatives	The imperative (*tu* and *vous* forms)	Agreeing and disagreeing	*C'est bon/mauvais pour la santé. manger des fruits/des bonbons, boire de l'eau, aller au collège à pied, aller au lit tard, faire du sport, fumer Je suis d'accord. Je ne suis pas d'accord.*	8L1 – L (7S5)	1b, 1c, 2a, 2c, 2d, 2e, 2f, 3b, 3c, 3e, 4a, 5a, 5c, 5d, 5e, 5f, 5i	1.2, 2.2–4, 3.1–2, 4.2–3
26–27 **2.4 Mission-santé** Health and fitness	Understand a text describing what someone did to be healthy and use it as a source for own writing; use the perfect tense; revise accents and pronunciation	The perfect tense	Using context to understand a text Using a text as a model/source Accents and pronunciation	*Qu'est-ce que tu as fait? j'ai pris, j'ai mangé, je n'ai pas mangé, j'ai bu, je n'ai pas bu, j'ai fait, je suis allé(e), je ne suis pas allé(e)*	8T6, 8S8 – L 8W5, 8S7 – R (7S5)	1a, 1b, 1c, 2a, 2b, 2c, 2d, 2f, 2g, 2h, 2i, 3a, 3b, 3c, 3e, 4a, 4c, 4d, 5a, 5c, 5d, 5e, 5f, 5i	1.4–5, 2.3–5, 3.2, 3.4–5, 4.3–5
28–29 **2.5 La belle équipe, épisode 2** Soap story	Develop listening and reading skills via a soap story based on the language of the unit; develop ability to recognize and use features that add authenticity and expression to written texts		Recognizing and using features that add authenticity and expression		8T2, 8L2 – R	1a, 1c, 2a, 2b, 2g, 2h, 2i, 3b, 3c, 3e, 4a, 4d, 5d, 5e, 5g, 5i	1.4, 3.4
30 **Super-challenge!** *Tour de France*	Develop the use of plural forms of perfect tense verbs; research and write about a famous French sports personality	Plural forms of perfect tense verbs			8C2 – L	1b, 1c, 2c, 2h, 2i, 3c, 3d, 3e, 4a, 4c, 4d, 5d, 5e, 5f, 5g, 5i	3.4–5, 4.3–5

ÉQUIPE NOUVELLE 2 UNIT 2 MEDIUM TERM PLAN

About this unit: In this unit students work in the context of body, health and fitness. They learn to understand the gist of different illnesses and describe symptoms, using set phrases and visual support. They understand and give basic advice on healthy living using the imperative, read about other people's diet, exercise regime and lifestyle, and use the perfect tense to describe what they themselves have done to stay fit. At the same time, students receive guidance on how to use a dictionary to find grammar information/plurals and idioms. They also develop their ability to read and understand a text containing previously learned language and use this as a model/source for their own writing. Progress at word level is developed by working on uses of the verb *avoir* and non-literal translations (e.g. phrases such as *j'ai mal au/à l'/à la/aux …*, idiomatic expressions); and students develop their awareness of word order in French compared with that in English. The unit also encourages students to use French exclamations and intonation to make their own speech sound more authentic.

Framework objectives (launch)	Teaching and learning	Week-by-week overview (assuming 6 weeks' work or 10–12.5 hours)
8W7: dictionary detail	Use a dictionary correctly, in particular to find plural forms and idioms.	**Week 1** Introduction to unit objectives. Name parts of the body. Revise masculine, feminine and plural forms. Use exclamations and sound French. Use a dictionary to help with grammar and spelling.
8W8: non-literal meanings	Expressions with *avoir*: *j'ai faim* = I **am** hungry, *j'ai froid* = I **am** cold, etc. *Il fait chaud, Il y a …, Ça va?*, etc.	
8S8: using high-frequency words and punctuation clues	Accents that change pronunciation, e.g. on past participles.	**Week 2** Ask someone what's wrong. Say where it hurts. Say how you feel and what is wrong with you. Understand that you can't always translate literally.
8T4: dictionary use	Use a dictionary correctly.	
8T6: text as model and source	Students develop strategies to understand and use a text to write their own.	**Week 3** Say what is good or bad for your health. Understand and give basic advice on healthy living, using the imperative. Say you agree/disagree. Negatives.
8L1: listening for subtleties	*Tu* and *vous* forms of the imperative.	
8L6: expression in speech	Use exclamations to sound French.	**Week 4** Understand a text describing what someone did to be healthy and use it as a source for own writing. Use the perfect tense. Accents and pronunciation.
8C2: famous people	The *Super-challenge!* page focuses on the fitness regime of a team of cyclists in the *Tour de France*. Students could research the fitness regime of other famous French sports personalities.	
8C5: colloquialisms	*Point lecture*: Idioms using parts of the body, e.g. *Mon œil* compared with its English equivalent "My foot!".	**Week 5** Develop listening and reading skills via a soap episode.
Framework objectives (reinforce)	**Teaching and learning**	
8W5: verb tenses	Recognize and use the perfect tense.	**Week 6** *Super-challenge!* for more able students. Recycle language of the unit via *Encore*, *En plus* and *Point lecture* pages. Students check progress via the *Podium* self-assessment checklist in the Students' Book and on Feuille 19. Use the *Révisions* and *Contrôles* sections for formal assessment of student progress.
8S7: present, past and future	Recognize and use the perfect tense.	
8T2: expression in text	Phrases that add authenticity and expression to the soap episode, e.g. *ouais, oh là là!, mais non!,* etc.	
8L2: media listening skills	In the soap episode, students imitate the expression and intonation of the four characters.	
8C4: poems, jokes, songs and stories	*Point lecture*: students develop reading for pleasure via the song "Ouille, aïe, oh là là!".	
	Teaching and learning (additional)	
	Parts of the body. Revision of masculine, feminine and plural forms of nouns. Illnesses and describing symptoms. Give advice on healthy living using the imperative. Revise negatives.	

2 En forme!

Unit objectives
Contexts: health and fitness
Grammar: revision of gender and plurals; imperative; *au, à la, à l', aux*; perfect tense
Language learning: using a dictionary; understanding a text with unfamiliar language; translating idioms
Pronunciation: sounding French; accents
Cultural focus: French idioms featuring parts of the body; *Tour de France*

Assessment opportunities
Speaking: Students' Book, page 23, activity 3d; Students' Book, page 25, *Challenge!* activity C
Writing: Students' Book, page 27, *Challenge!* activity A or B

AT 1.1 | **1a** *Écoute et lis.*
AT 3.1 | In this introduction to the themes of the unit, Matthieu appears at first to be in excruciating pain but turns out to be rehearsing for a play in which he is to act the part of Frankenstein's monster. Students listen to the recording while following the text in the Students' Book. Point out and explain the use of *si* instead of *oui* in number 7) in reply to a question containing a negation).

CD 1, track 22
Cassette 1, side 2   page 19, activité 1

- Oh! Ma tête. Aïe! Mon cou! Ouille! Mes oreilles! Oh là là! Mon ventre! Aïe aïe aïe! Ma jambe! Ouille! Mes pieds!
- Ça ne va pas, Matthieu?
- Si, ça va très bien! Je m'entraîne à faire le Monstre de Frankenstein! C'est un beau rôle pour moi!

AT 3.1 | **1b** *Trouve le nom des parties du corps. Fais trois listes.*
AT 4.1 | Students search the text for the names of parts of the body. They list them in three columns: masculine, feminine and plural.

Answers: masculine: cou, ventre; feminine: tête, jambe; plural: oreilles, pieds

AT 1.1 | **1c** *Réécoute. Joue la scène avec un(e) partenaire!*
AT 2.1 | Students listen again to the recording for activity **1a** before acting out the scene with a partner.

1d *Mime une photo. Ton/Ta partenaire devine.*
Students take turns to mime a photo for a partner to guess.

56

Planning Page

2.1 Ça va?
pages 20–21

Objectives
▶ Name parts of the body
▶ Revise masculine, feminine and plural forms (**7W4**)
▶ Use exclamations and sound French (**8L6 – L**)
▶ Use a dictionary to help with grammar and spelling (**8W7, 8T4 – L**)

Resources
Students' Book, pages 20–21
CD 1, tracks 23–24; CD 3, tracks 10–11
Cassette 1, side 2; cassette 4, side 1
Encore/En plus Workbooks, page 14
OHTs 6A and 6B
Flashcards 107–125
Copymasters 20, 26, 30, 32 and 34

Key language
le corps, le cou, le bras, le dos, l'œil (les yeux), le genou, le nez, le ventre, le visage, le pied, le doigt, les doigts de pied, le pouce
la tête, la gorge, la main, la jambe, la bouche, la dent, l'épaule, l'oreille
aïe! ouille! oh là là!
mon/ma/mes

Programme of Study reference
1a, 1b, 1c, 2a, 2b, 2f, 2g, 3a, 3b, 3c, 3d, 3e, 4a, 5a, 5d, 5e, 5f, 5i

Starters
▶ *À vos marques*, page 20.
▶ Copymaster 20 *À vos marques*, activity 1.
▶ Students adapt and sing (or invent a rap based on, if they prefer) "Head and shoulders, knees and toes", using names of parts of the body in French, e.g. *Tête, épaules, genoux, doigts de pied*, etc.
▶ Play a game with **Flashcards 107–125**: show a flashcard and name a part of the body; students repeat the name only when it matches the flashcard you show.

ICT suggestions
▶ Students could use clip art and interesting fonts to create posters for display in class to remind themselves of key target language phrases, e.g. a robot made up of body parts labelled in French.

Creative activities
▶ Working in pairs or small groups, students look at paintings by 16th century Italian painter Giuseppe Arcimboldo and do drawings in a similar style, explaining what they use for the different parts of the body (not necessarily fruit or vegetables but also objects, e.g. *les oreilles = des livres; les doigts = des crayons*).
▶ Students make a "mystery photo", cutting out pictures from magazines and making a collage to create a new person. They label this new "Frankenstein": *Il/Elle a les yeux de Brad Pitt, la bouche d'Orlando Bloom*, etc.

Plenaries
▶ *Challenge!* page 21.
▶ In pairs, students list alphabetically the parts of the body they know, from memory (with the support of flashcards if needed). Both this and the following activity require students to think in terms of spelling.
▶ Ask students to give you the names of parts of the body with three letters (e.g. *nez, dos*), four letters, five letters, etc.

Homework suggestions
▶ Students learn the names of parts of the body with correct gender (meaning, pronunciation, spelling).
▶ Students make a crossword, word square or word snake for their partner to solve in the next session.

2 En forme!

2.1 Ça va?
pages 20–21

Presentation

Prior to working on page 20 of the Students' Book, play these games using **Flashcards 107–125**:
- Divide the class into two teams. Stick two cards on the board (e.g. nose, finger) then say *le nez*. Students guess which of the two cards it is. The winning team scores a point. Continue in the same way until all the cards have been used.
- Then, draw a body and blank labels on the board. Students come out to the board and stick the flashcards on to the matching label using putty adhesive.
- Next, write the names of the body parts on the board and ask students to come out and stick the cards next to the matching names.

OHTs 6A and **6B** could also be used to present and practise the names of parts of the body:
- Photocopy the overlay **OHT 6B** onto acetate and cut it up so that students can play matching games.
- Place **OHT 6A** on the OHP, then switch off the OHP and cover one of the nine pictures with a sticky note. Switch the OHP back on and ask students to tell you which picture is missing.
- Allow students to see the pictures on **OHT 6A** for 20 seconds. Then switch off the OHP and ask students to recall the order in which the parts of the body appear on the OHT. Place **OHT 6B** on the OHP for students to check their answers, then put on both OHTs together.
- Play Noughts and Crosses using the nine pictures from **OHT 6A**.

À vos marques

AT 3.1 **a** *Devine quel Mot-clé va dans chaque bulle!*
Students select an appropriate word to fill the gap in each speech bubble.

Answers: 1 dos; 2 yeux; 3 gorge; 4 oreilles; 5 genou; 6 main

AT 1.1 **b** *Écoute et vérifie.*
Students listen to the recording to check their answers.

CD 1, track 23 — page 20, À vos marques
Cassette 1, side 2

– Ah! Salut! Ça va?
1 – Aïe, aïe, aïe, mon dos!
2 – Oh là là, mes yeux!
3 – Ouille! Ma gorge!
4 – Oh, ça ne va pas … mes oreilles!
5 – Aïe! Mon genou!
6 – Oh là là là! Ma main!
– Pffffffffff … ça ne va pas, aïe, ouille, oh là là … Eh bien moi, ça va, ça va bien, ça va très bien … merci!

AT 4.1 **1a** *Recopie et complète les bulles avec les Mots-clés.*
Students copy and complete the speech bubbles from the *À vos marques* activity, inserting the correct missing words.

Answers: see transcript above

AT 4.1 **1b** *Fais des dessins pour les autres Mots-clés! Ton/Ta partenaire devine et écrit les bulles.*
Students do drawings to represent the remaining *Mots-clés*. They exchange their drawings with a partner, who writes a speech bubble for each.

AT 2.1 **1c** *Jeu de mémoire en classe.*
This oral activity could be done as a chain game around the class or in groups of three. Student A begins by naming one body part; student B repeats A's word and adds a second; student C repeats A's and B's words, then adds a third; and so on. Make sure that students have learned the genders of parts of the body before attempting this activity.

C26 Feuille 26 *Lis et écris Encore 1* provides basic practice of the vocabulary for parts of the body and could be used during work on this spread.

W14 Additional reading and writing practice of body vocabulary is provided on page 14 of the *Encore* and *En plus* Workbooks.

Ça se dit comme ça!

This section gives students tips on how to use French exclamations (e.g. *ouille! aïe! oh là là!*) as a way of sounding more authentic when they speak French, and launches **8L6**.

1 Students provide English equivalents for the French phrases.

Answers: ouch! ow!

2 Students attempt to recall other French exclamations they have met so far. Refer them back to the soap episode on pages 14–15 of Unit 1, where several were used, e.g. *Ah non! Allez … Euh … Ah zut!*

3 Students listen to the recording and choose an appropriate symbol to match each word or phrase. Remind them that intonation can help you to understand what someone is saying.

Answers: smiley faces: 4, 6, 7, 9, 12; unhappy faces: 1, 2, 3, 5, 8, 10, 11

CD 1, track 24 — page 20, Ça se dit comme ça! activité 3
Cassette 1, side 2

1 – Ouille!
2 – Aïe!
3 – Oh là là!
4 – Oh là là!! C'est superbe!
5 – Ah non!

6 – Génial!
7 – Ouah!
8 – Zut!
9 – J'adore ça!
10 – Beurk!
11 – Je déteste ça!
12 – Bravo!

C34 Activities 1–3 of Feuille 34 *Ça se dit comme ça!* could be used at this point. They focus on the differences in intonation between exclamations, questions and statements.

Zoom grammaire

This grammar section focuses on gender and plurals. It provides an opportunity for further work on the Year 7 Framework objective **7W4** (gender and plural patterns).

1 Students identify the gender of each noun. Ask them to explain how they were able to work out the genders.

Answers: (clues to gender are given in brackets):
a masculine (*mon*); b feminine (adjective agreement); c feminine (*sa*); d masculine (*au*); e masculine (adjective agreement); f masculine (adjective agreement)

2 Students supply the plural of each noun and attempt to work out the rules. Refer them to the *Guide pratique* section for advice on using a dictionary to find plural forms.

Answers: a animaux; b gâteaux; c jeux; d cheveux; e dos; f bras; g nez; h prix; i oreilles; j cous; k genoux; l yeux

Rules: *-al* usually becomes *-aux*; *-eau* and *-eu* usually add *-x*; words ending is *-s*, *-z* and *-x* usually don't change; words ending in *-eille* add *-s*; words ending in *-ou* can add either *-s* or *-x*; *œil* is completely irregular.

Refer students to the grammar section on page 133 of the Students' Book for further information on genders and plurals.

C30 Feuille 30 *Grammaire 1* provides further practice of genders and plurals and could be used at this point.

Guide pratique

This skills section focuses on using a dictionary to find spellings, grammar information and idioms, and launches Framework objectives **8W7** and **8T4**.

1 Students follow the advice to help them find the French for the underlined words.

Answers: a chevaux; b vœux; c journaux; d bijoux

2 Students use a dictionary to find the French equivalents of some English idioms.

Answers: a pile ou face? b il est dans mes jambes; c de bouche à oreille

C32 Feuille 32 *Guide pratique 1* focuses on dictionary use and could be used at this point.

Challenge!

AT 4.1 **A** *Écris le plus possible de parties du corps de mémoire.*
Students list, from memory, as many parts of the body as they can. To encourage them to focus on accurate spelling and genders, you could award one point for each word correctly spelt and an extra point for the correct gender.

AT 4.2 **B** *Invente un monstre. Écris et lis sa description. Ton/Ta partenaire dessine ton monstre!*
Students create a monster, label it and write a simple description. They read out their description to a partner, who draws it. This provides an opportunity to recycle some of the language from Unit 1, e.g. physical appearance, colours, clothes: *Mon monstre est grand et gros. Il a deux têtes – il met deux casquettes! Il a les cheveux verts et les yeux rouges.*

AT 3.2 **C** *Lis les définitions. C'est quelle partie du corps?*
Students read the descriptions and indicate which body part each one refers to. Point out that they might need to use their knowledge of genders to work out some of the answers.

Answers: a les yeux; b la tête; c les pieds; d le nez; e les cheveux; f les dents

Follow-up activity: Students could write their own definitions, similar to those in activity **C**, for a partner to work out.

2 En forme!

Planning Page

2.2 J'ai mal!   pages 22–23

Objectives

- Ask someone what's wrong
- Say where it hurts
- Say how you feel and what is wrong with you
- Understand that you can't always translate literally (**8W8 – L**)

Resources

Students' Book, pages 22–23
CD 1, tracks 25–27; CD 3, track 7
Cassette 1, side 2; cassette 4, side 1
Encore/En plus Workbooks, pages 15 and 18
OHTs 6A and 6C, 7A and 7B
Flashcards 88, 107–135
Copymasters 21, 22, 24, 28 and 33

Key language

Qu'est-ce qui ne va pas?
J'ai mal au/à l'/à la/aux …
j'ai chaud/froid/faim/soif
j'ai envie de vomir/dormir
j'ai de la fièvre
j'ai un rhume/le rhume des foins/la grippe
je tousse
la pharmacie, l'hôpital, les urgences, le médecin

Programme of Study reference

1a, 1b, 1c, 2a, 2b, 2c, 2d, 2f, 3a, 3b, 3c, 3d, 3e, 4a, 5a, 5c, 5d, 5e, 5f, 5i

Starters

- *À vos marques*, page 22.
- Name a part of the body and ask students to mime what's wrong, e.g. by holding their head, teeth, etc. and using the exclamations they have learned: *aïe, ouille,* etc.
- Play a game using **Flashcards 107–125**. Students in pairs make three piles of cards: one with feminine words, one with masculine words and one with words usually used in the plural. Time each pair to see who is the fastest. Check each pile with the whole class.
- In pairs, students start with a noun, e.g. *le ventre*. They take turns to add another word, e.g. *au ventre, mal au ventre, j'ai mal au ventre*, etc. They check their phrases with another pair.

ICT suggestions

- Students prepare a PowerPoint® demonstration, using clip art, about sports and "aches and pains", e.g. *Quand on joue beaucoup au tennis, on a mal au coude. Quand on joue beaucoup au foot, on a mal aux genoux.*

Creative activities

- Working in groups, students create board games. Each group draws the outline of a body on a card. They number the parts of the body to be practised 1–12, and then draw those parts on to other smaller cards. They then play a dice game: they have to throw the numbers in the correct sequence, starting with number one and moving on to two, three, and so on (they will need two dice for numbers 7–12). They must say a phrase for each number, e.g. *1 = la tête: j'ai mal à la tête*. If they are able to say the phrase correctly, they "win" that body part. The winner is the first person to complete the whole body.
- Students collect phrases and idioms relating to parts of the body in either French or English, e.g. word of mouth = *le bouche à oreille*. They illustrate them for a display of Franco-English idioms.

Plenaries

- *Challenge!* page 23.
- Copymaster 21 *Challenge!* activity 1.
- Working as a whole class, play a memory game in which each student adds a new item: A: *J'ai mal à la tête.* B: *J'ai mal à la tête et au cou.* C: *J'ai mal à la tête, au cou et aux épaules*, etc.
- Give students, in pairs, two minutes to write as many statements as they can starting with *j'ai …*

Homework suggestions

- Students write verses for a song to the tune of "One finger, one thumb, keep moving", e.g. *La/Ma jambe, le/mon pied, la/ma tête, les/mes oreilles, aïe, j'ai mal …* They could perform it in class, perhaps as a rap if they prefer.
- Students write a short scene between a doctor and a teacher who doesn't want to go to school any more and is inventing all sorts of excuses, e.g. *Les élèves sont horribles, quel bruit dans la classe! J'ai mal aux oreilles, très mal! La cantine, c'est nul! J'ai envie de vomir!*

En forme! 2

2.2 J'ai mal!   pages 22–23

À vos marques

AT 2.2 **a** *Imagine la conversation entre le médecin et le Monstre.*
In pairs, students study the picture and imagine a conversation between the doctor and Frankenstein's monster. Encourage them to use language from pages 20–21 together with other known language such as greetings, e.g. *Bonjour, monsieur!*

AT 1.2 **b** *Écoute. Tu entends quoi? C'est quoi, en anglais?*
Students listen to the recording and identify what is said by the doctor and the monster. They give the English for the two expressions.

Answers: Médecin: b Qu'est-ce qui ne va pas? (What's wrong?); Monstre: c J'ai mal! (It hurts!)

CD 1, track 25   page 22, À vos marques
Cassette 1, side 2

– Bonjour, docteur!
– Bonjour, monsieur. Qu'est-ce qui ne va pas?
– Docteur, j'ai mal … j'ai très mal … Ouille! Aïe!
– Ah, vous avez mal … Vous avez mal où, monsieur?
– Oh là là, docteur! J'ai mal à la tête, j'ai mal au cou, j'ai mal aux oreilles, j'ai mal aux yeux, j'ai mal aux dents, …
– Ah, je vois …
– J'ai mal aux bras, j'ai mal aux épaules, j'ai mal au ventre …
– Euh … d'accord, euh …
– Oui, et j'ai mal aux mains, j'ai mal aux doigts …
– D'accord, d'accord!
– Et j'ai très mal à la jambe, aux genoux, aux pieds …
– AHAHAHAHAHAHAH!!!
– Docteur! Docteur! Ne partez pas! Revenez! Docteur! Docteur!!!!!

AT 3.2 **1a** *Relie les textes aux dessins.*
Students match the pictures to the texts. Draw their attention to the plural form *des antidouleur* (without an *-s* ending) in text 4, and point out that the plural *antidouleurs* (with an *-s*) is also possible.
Ask students what clues they can use to make sense of the dialogues, e.g. names of parts of the body. Ask also what they notice is happening in front of the name of the part of the body (use of the preposition *au/à l'/à la/aux*). Can students work out which form of the preposition is needed in front of masculine, feminine, plural words and words starting with a vowel? At this point, you may want to do the activities in the *Zoom grammaire* section (see below).

Answers: a 4; b 2; c 1; d 3

AT 1.2 **1b** *Écoute et vérifie. Imite l'intonation!*
AT 2.2 Students listen to the recording to check their answers. They then repeat the texts, focusing on pronunciation and intonation.

CD 1, track 26   page 22, activité 1b
Cassette 1, side 2

a À la pharmacie …
– Oh là là! J'ai vraiment mal aux dents.
– Voilà des antidouleur. Allez vite chez le dentiste!
b À l'hôpital …
– Bonjour! Ça va, ce matin? Tu n'as pas mal?
– Bof! J'ai encore un peu mal à la jambe!
c Aux urgences …
– Elle a mal?
– Oh oui, elle a très mal au cou.
d Chez le médecin …
– Qu'est-ce qui ne va pas?
– Ben … J'ai très mal à l'épaule droite.

2 *Mime un problème. Ton/Ta partenaire devine.*
Working in pairs, students take turns to mime a problem while their partner guesses what it is.

Zoom grammaire

This section focuses on *à* + *le/la/l'/les*. Look at the four dialogues in activity **1a** and ask students to spot examples of each form.

1 Students complete the two sentences using *au*, *à l'*, *à la* or *aux*.

Answers: a J'ai mal <u>à la</u> gorge et <u>au</u> ventre. b Tu as mal <u>aux</u> yeux? Oui, surtout <u>à l'</u>œil droit.

2 Students write six sentences, attempting to use *à* in a different context in each one.
Before beginning this activity, brainstorm with students the different uses of *à* from *Équipe nouvelle 1*: to say where they're going (e.g. *je vais au café*), to say where they live (e.g. *j'habite à Paris/au pays de Galles/à la campagne*), to talk about the times of school subjects (e.g. *à onze heures, j'ai géographie*), to describe food flavours and sandwich fillings (e.g. *un sandwich au fromage, une glace à la vanille*), and to refer to mealtimes (e.g. *au petit déjeuner*). Students should also remember it from pages 12–13 of *Équipe nouvelle 2* Unit 1: *Quand je vais au collège/à une boum*, etc.
This focus on the different uses of *à* creates an opportunity to build students' awareness of phrases that cannot be translated word for word and therefore prepares them for the *Guide pratique* section on non-literal translations.

Refer students to the grammar section on page 135 of the Students' Book for further information on *à*.

W18 Page 18 of the *Encore* and *En plus* Workbooks provides further practice of *à* and could be used at this point.

2 En forme!

Follow-up activities:
- **OHT 6A** could be used at this point together with overlay **6C** for further practice of *j'ai mal* + *à* + parts of the body. In preparation for the following activities, photocopy the captions from **6C** onto acetate and cut them up.
- Place **OHT 6A** on the OHP. Point at a picture and say *Tu as mal au/à l'/à la/aux* + corresponding part of body. If what you say matches the picture, a student comes out, chooses the correct caption, and places it beside the picture. If what you say doesn't match the picture, students must say the correct version, e.g. *Non, j'ai mal au/à l'/à la/aux* + name of appropriate body part.
- Place **OHT 6A** on the OHP. Number the pictures 1–9 at random. Allow students to look at them for 30 seconds then switch off the OHP. Ask them in pairs to recall the order: *1 = J'ai mal à la jambe, 2 = J'ai mal …*, etc. Switch the OHP back on to check, erase the numbers and renumber the pictures in a different order, then repeat the activity.

Presentation
- Prior to working on activity **3a** of the Students' Book, introduce the *avoir* phrases from the *Expressions-clés* using **Flashcards 126–134**. You could also use **Flashcard 88** to represent *j'ai soif* and **Flashcard 135** for *j'ai faim*.
- First, introduce each expression (apart from *je tousse*) with *j'ai …*, showing the relevant flashcards.
- Then, distribute the flashcards around the class. Say the expressions again and ask the student with the appropriate card to lift it high before passing it on to someone who doesn't have a card. You could ask students to be the callers this time.
- Next, ask students holding the cards to say the phrases they represent in the style of the card, e.g. *j'ai soif* as if they are really parched.
- Finally, show a card and ask the whole class to "act" it out.

- **OHTs 7A** and **7B** could also be used to present and practise the 11 phrases. You may wish to photocopy the overlay **7B** on to acetate and cut it up so that students can play matching games.
- For further practice, play Three-in-a Row using **OHT 7A**, perhaps with you versus the class. The aim is to name three phrases in a row ahead of your opponent, crossing the pictures out on the acetate as they are mentioned. The bottom right-hand square on the OHT is blank: here, for revision, you could ask students to supply an expression using *j'ai mal au/à l'/à la/aux …*
- For other suggestions, see the Presentation section in the teacher's notes for the previous spread (page 58).

AT 1.2 | **AT 3.2** **3a** *Lis et écoute.*
Students read the speech bubbles for the different fairy tale characters while listening to the recording.

CD 1, track 27 / Cassette 1, side 2 — page 23, activité 3a

Blanche-Neige:
– Miam miam! J'ai faim! Oh là là, j'ai mal au ventre. Beurk! J'ai envie de vomir!

La Belle au bois dormant:
– Aïe! Mon doigt! Brrrrrrr! J'ai froid et … aaaahhhh! J'ai envie de dormir!

Dracula:
– Oh! J'ai très mal aux dents! Et j'ai soif!

Le grand méchant loup:
– Pff, j'ai chaud! 39 degrés! J'ai de la fièvre! Et ma gorge! Hum hum hum, je tousse! Oh non, j'ai la grippe! Je n'ai pas faim! Zut alors!

Jacques et le haricot magique:
– Oh, mes yeux! Aïe, mon nez! Atchoum! Atchoum! Oh là là, j'ai le rhume des foins!

AT 4.2 **3b** *Recopie les phrases avec les bonnes Expressions-clés.*
Students copy out the speech bubbles, filling in the missing phrases with the help of the *Expressions-clés*.

Answers: see transcript above

AT 2.2 **3c** *Dis les phrases, de mémoire!*
Students look back at the incomplete speech bubbles in the Students' Book and read them aloud, attempting to fill in the missing phrases from memory. Point out that the exclamations and the pictures should act as clues to help them.

AT 2.3 **3d** *Imagine les conversations chez le médecin. Joue-les avec un(e) partenaire.*
Referring again to the pictures and speech bubbles in activity **3a**, students work with a partner to create and perform conversations between each character and a doctor.

C22 | **C24** Feuilles 22 *Écoute Encore* and 24 *Parle Encore* provide additional practice of *j'ai mal* plus parts of the body and could be completed at this point.

W15 Additional reading and writing practice of the language of this spread is provided on page 15 of the *Encore* and *En plus* Workbooks.

Guide pratique

This section focuses on non-literal translations and launches **8W8**. When considering the different *avoir* expressions, remind students of *Tu as quel âge? J'ai … ans* (How old are you? I am … years old) from Unit 1. You might also like to point out that *je tousse* can be translated either as "I cough" or as "I have a cough": another example of how it is not always possible to translate word for word between French and English.

1 Students give the English equivalents of the French *avoir* expressions.

Answers: a It hurts! b I am 13 years old. c I am cold. d I am thirsty.

2 Students translate some additional common phrases from French into English.

Answers: a It is hot. b Is there a cinema? c It is raining. d How are you? e I'm very well. f What are you like?/ Describe yourself.

C33 Feuille 33 *Guide pratique 2* could be used at this point. It focuses on using a dictionary to find idioms and non-literal meanings.

C28 Feuille 28 *Lis et écris En plus 1* could also be used here. It provides additional practice of the language of this spread and reinforces the idea that it is not always possible to translate literally between one language and another.

Challenge!

AT 4.2 **A** *Choisis un personnage en secret. Écris ce qui ne va pas. Ton/Ta partenaire devine qui tu es.*
Students secretly choose one of the fairy tale characters and describe, in writing, what is wrong with them. Their partner tries to work out which character they have chosen by asking questions about their ailments.

AT 4.2 **B** *Invente le plus possible d'excuses pour ne pas aller à l'école un matin!*
Students invent as many excuses as possible for not being able to go to school. Suggest that they start with *Je ne vais pas à l'école ce matin parce que …*, then add a list of ailments as long as possible. Challenge them to memorize and say as many as possible in a single go.

AT 4.3 **C** *Écris une conversation entre Pinocchio et un médecin!*
Students invent a conversation between Pinocchio and his doctor. Before students begin this activity, remind them of the story of Pinocchio by brainstorming either in groups or as a whole class. (Pinocchio begins life as a wooden boy and goes through various changes as a result of his behaviour, e.g. long nose, pointed donkey ears and tail, is swallowed by a whale, and eventually becomes a real boy at the end of the story.)

2 En forme!

Planning Page

2.3 C'est la forme! pages 24–25

Objectives
- Say what is good or bad for your health
- Understand and give basic advice on healthy living (using the imperative) (**8L1 – L**)
- Say you agree/disagree
- Revise negatives (**7S5**)

Resources
Students' Book, pages 24–25
CD 1, track 28; CD 3, tracks 8–9
Cassette 1, side 2; cassette 4, side 1
Encore/En plus Workbooks, pages 16 and 19
OHTs 8A and 8B
Flashcards 61–78; 79–87; 142–148
Copymaster 23

Key language
C'est bon/mauvais pour la santé.
manger des fruits/des bonbons
boire de l'eau
aller au collège à pied
aller au lit tard
faire du sport
fumer
Je suis d'accord. Je ne suis pas d'accord.

Programme of Study reference
1b, 1c, 2a, 2c, 2d, 2e, 2f, 3b, 3c, 3e, 4a, 5a, 5c, 5d, 5e, 5f, 5i

Starters
- *À vos marques*, page 24.
- Play a "Health Shoot-out" game as follows using phrases learned on the spread. Two students stand up. Student A says either *C'est bon pour la santé* or *Ce n'est pas bon pour la santé*; then, without any hesitation whatsoever, student B must say something to match. For example: student A: *C'est bon pour la santé*; student B: *Aller au lit tôt*; student A: *Ce n'est pas bon pour la santé*; student B: *Manger des bonbons*. If B is unable to say a phrase, or if he/she hesitates for a moment, B must sit down and another student takes over.
- Say a range of phrases, healthy and unhealthy suggestions, taken from the "road signs" idea on pages 24–25 of the Students' Book. On mini-whiteboards, students draw a symbol for each expression: a circle if it is a suggestion to do something healthy, a triangle if it is something unhealthy, e.g. if you say *Mange des bonbons* students should draw a triangle.

ICT suggestions
- Students could use clip art and interesting fonts to create posters or calendars for display in the classroom (see Creative activities).

Creative activities
- In pairs, students create a poster giving healthy advice. They draw symbols and write captions, either using the "road signs" idea from page 24 of the Students' Book or thinking of a different way to make the message of the poster as visual as possible.
- Students create a calendar (monthly) giving health advice ideally suitable for the time of year.

Plenaries
- *Challenge!* page 25.
- Use **OHTs 8A** and **8B** to play a memory game. Place both OHTs together on the OHP and give students time to study them. Then remove **8B** and ask students to remember the location of each piece of advice. Check by placing **OHT 8B** back on the OHP.
- Play Noughts and Crosses using **OHTs 8A** and **8B** together.
- Say or write one word from the lesson; students in pairs say a question or answer containing that word.

Homework suggestions
- Students write a paragraph about what they do to be healthy, using the first person singular.
- Using the language learned so far, students write a short dialogue between two famous sports personalities of their choice, discussing health issues. They could then act out their script with a partner in the next lesson.

2.3 C'est la forme!

pages 24–25

À vos marques

AT 3.1/2

Quiz-santé! Lis les mots et fais deux listes.
Students complete this mini-quiz on healthy eating. They sort the words provided into two lists: foods they eat often and foods they don't eat often (you may need to explain the meaning of *souvent*). When they have finished, provide them with the following information so that they can assess their responses to the quiz:
Plus de bleu et d'orange: Attention! Tu ne manges pas toujours bien. Ce n'est pas bon pour la santé!
Plus de vert: C'est bien, tu manges des choses qui sont bonnes pour la santé.

Follow-up activity: Students could add more food items to those given in *À vos marques* and discuss each one: *C'est bon ou ce n'est pas bon pour la santé?*

Presentation

▶ Do some further preparatory work and at the same time revise how to form negatives (7S5) using **Flashcards 79–87** (drinks) or any available pictures of food, e.g. pictures cut from magazines. Ask students to discuss the food and drink items using *j'aime bien, je n'aime pas* and *c'est bon/ce n'est pas bon pour la santé*. Remind them to use link words, e.g. *Le coca, ce n'est pas bon pour la santé mais j'aime bien ça! Les épinards, c'est bon pour la santé mais je n'aime pas ça. Le lait, c'est bon pour la santé et j'aime ça! Les chips, ce n'est pas bon pour la santé et je n'aime pas ça.*

▶ Continue the revision of negatives (7S5) by asking students to recall previous contexts in which they have used negative expressions. Then draw students' attention to the *Expressions-clés* and ask them to turn each of the positive phrases into a negative and each negative phrase into a positive. Changing phrase g (*Fais du sport*) into a negative will also reinforce the fact that *du, de la, de l'* and *des* change to *de* in a negative sentence.

AT 3.2 **1a** *Lis les conseils de santé dans Expressions-clés. Relie-les aux panneaux.*
Students match the *Expressions-clés* to the numbered signs. Encourage them to look for clues, e.g. cognates (*sport*, etc.).

Answers: 1 h; 2 c; 3 g; 4 d; 5 f; 6 e; 7 a; 8 b

AT 1.2 **1b** *Écoute et vérifie.*
Students listen to the recording to check their answers. At the same time, place **OHT 8B** on the OHP and ask students to come out and point to each symbol as it is mentioned on the recording.

CD 1, track 28
Cassette 1, side 2

page 24, activité 1b

1 – Ne fume pas, ce n'est pas bon pour la santé.
2 – Mange des fruits, c'est bon pour la santé.
3 – Fais du sport! C'est bon pour la santé.
4 – Ne mange pas de bonbons. C'est mauvais pour la santé.
5 – Ne va pas au lit trop tard. C'est mauvais pour la santé.
6 – Va au collège à pied! C'est bon pour la santé.
7 – Bois de l'eau! C'est bon pour la santé.
8 – Ne bois pas de sodas. C'est mauvais pour la santé.

AT 2.2 **1c** *Jeu de mime. A mime un panneau, B dit le conseil. Ensuite, changez de rôles.*
Students take turns to perform mimes for the signs. Their partner guesses the corresponding advice from the *Expressions-clés*.

Follow-up activities:
▶ Place **OHT 8B** on the OHP and place a blank acetate on top. Ask students to come out and draw a circle around each symbol they think is good for the health and a triangle (danger sign) around each symbol they think is bad for the health. Then add on **OHT 8A** so that students can check their answers.
▶ Make a copy of **OHT 8A** (the circles and triangles) and cut it up. Place them on **OHT 8B** in the wrong place. Ask students to say whether they agree or disagree, using negatives, e.g. place a circle over smoking and say *Fumer, c'est bon pour la santé!* Students say *Non, je ne suis pas d'accord. Ce n'est pas bon pour la santé.*

Zoom grammaire

This section focuses on the imperative (*tu* and *vous* forms) and launches 8L1.

1 Students categorize each phrase according to whether it is a piece of advice or an instruction.

Answers: Advice: Ne mangez pas de chocolat! Mange des fruits! Fais de l'exercice! Faites du vélo! Bois beaucoup d'eau!
Instructions: Répétez! Ne touche pas! Écoute! Levez la main! Baissez les bras! Discutez en classe! Ne bougez pas!

2 Students now look at the verb endings and consider why there is a difference. They list the phrases according to whether they are in the *tu* or *vous* form.

Answers: The *tu* forms are: Mange des fruits! Fais de l'exercice! Bois beaucoup d'eau! Ne touche pas! Écoute!
The *vous* forms are: Ne mangez pas de chocolat! Faites du vélo! Répétez! Levez la main! Baissez les bras! Discutez en classe! Ne bougez pas!

3 Students consider the negative imperatives. They should notice not only that *ne … pas* is placed around the verb but also that *du* becomes *de*.

Refer students to the grammar section on the imperative on page 143 of the Students' Book.

2 En forme!

W19 Additional practice of the imperative is provided on page 19 of the *Encore* and *En plus* Workbooks.

AT 4.2 **2a** *Trouve d'autres conseils. Dessine des panneaux.*
Students design additional signs representing other healthy lifestyle tips. They write the corresponding advice for each new sign. You may want to focus on the *Zoom grammaire* section on the imperative before doing this activity (see notes above).
To support students, use flashcards as prompts, e.g. **Flashcards 61–78** (sports and leisure activities), **Flashcards 142–148** (means of transport). Ask students to make up advice based on the flashcards, e.g. *Ne va pas au collège en voiture, va au collège à pied ou à vélo. C'est bon pour la santé.*

AT 2.3 **2b** *Discute tes nouveaux conseils avec un(e) partenaire. Il/Elle est d'accord ou pas?*
Students discuss their new healthy lifestyle signs from activity **2a** with a partner.

C23 Feuille 23 *Écoute En plus* provides further practice of the language of this spread and could be completed at this point.

W16 Page 16 of the *Encore* and *En plus* Workbooks could also be used here for additional reading and writing practice.

Challenge!

AT 3.2 **A** *Écris correctement les conseils. Traduis.*
AT 4.2 Students separate out the words and the sentences, copy out the advice correctly and translate it into English.

Answers: Bois de l'eau! Ne bois pas de sodas! Ne mange pas de bonbons! Va au collège à pied et ne va pas au lit trop tard! = Drink water! Don't drink fizzy drinks! Don't eat sweets! Walk to school and don't go to bed too late!

AT 4.3 **B** *Choisis cinq conseils pour Matthieu et écris-lui un e-mail.*
Students write an e-mail to Matthieu, giving him five pieces of advice.

AT 2.3/4 **C** *Écris des questions et interviewe un(e) partenaire: il/elle est en forme? Donne des conseils!*
AT 4.2 Students write a series of questions to ask their partner, to find out whether they are healthy or not. They offer various pieces of advice, depending on their partner's answers. To ensure that students use a reasonable level of accuracy and range of language in the interviews, each interviewee should be allowed to see the questions in advance and have a few minutes to mentally prepare his/her answers.

Planning Page

2.4 Mission-santé
pages 26–27

Objectives
- Understand a text describing what someone did to be healthy and use it as a source for own writing (**8T6 – L**)
- Use the perfect tense (**8W5, 8S7 – R**) (**7S5**)
- Revise accents and pronunciation (**8S8 – L**)

Resources
Students' Book, pages 26–27
CD 1, tracks 29–31; CD 3, tracks 12–14
Cassette 1, side 2; cassette 4, side 1
Encore/En plus Workbooks, page 17
OHTs 9, 10A and 10B
Copymasters 20, 21, 25, 27, 29, 31 and 34

Key language
Qu'est-ce que tu as fait?
j'ai pris, j'ai mangé, je n'ai pas mangé, j'ai bu, je n'ai pas bu, j'ai fait, je suis allé(e), je ne suis pas allé(e)

Programme of Study reference
1a, 1b, 1c, 2a, 2b, 2c, 2d, 2f, 2g, 2h, 2i, 3a, 3b, 3c, 3e, 4a, 4c, 4d, 5a, 5c, 5d, 5e, 5f, 5i

Starters
- *À vos marques*, page 26.
- Copymaster 20 *À vos marques*, activity 2.
- Recap on the homework suggestion for the previous spread (see page 64 of this book) by asking students in pairs to perform their dialogues between two famous sports personalities.
- Play "*Passé/Présent* Shoot-out". Two students stand up. You say a sentence in either the present or the perfect tense, e.g. *J'ai mangé des fruits*. The first student to say the correct tense (e.g. *passé*) wins; the other student sits down and is replaced by someone else.
- Throw a die: the number shown indicates how many things you want your students to say about their diet during the previous week. For example, if you throw a two, a student has to say two things, e.g. *J'ai mangé des pommes et j'ai bu du lait*.

ICT suggestions
- Using PowerPoint®, students prepare a text or diary about how healthy they were during the previous week, similar to Natacha's diary on page 26 of the Students' Book. They replace some of the words with pictures, e.g. scanned drawings, clip art. As they give their presentation, the class provide the missing words.
- Working in pairs, students prepare a poster using attractive fonts, clip art, etc. to present the *Mission-santé* objectives. Ask them to add five objectives to those already listed (see page 26), using previously learned language and *ne … pas*.

Creative activities
- In groups, students prepare the cards for a game of Dominoes. Each card is divided into two halves, with the beginning of a sentence on one half and a drawing on the other half:

| 🚲 | J'ai bu | 🥛 | J'ai mangé | 🍎 | Je n'ai pas fait de |

Make sure students realize that a sentence begun on one card must be finished off on another card, e.g. if they make a card with the phrase *J'ai bu* on it, there must be a corresponding card showing a picture of a type of drink, so that the two cards can be "matched" to create a complete sentence.
Once students have completed their cards, they exchange them with another group and play Dominoes using the other group's cards, saying the phrases aloud as they match them up.
- In groups, students imagine they work for an advertising agency. They have to advertise one product that is excellent for the health (e.g. a new brand of yoghurt) and one product that isn't very good for the health (e.g. a new chocolate bar). They imagine a short scene, either a TV or a radio advertisement, in which they try to persuade the public to buy it, using as much as possible of the language they have learned so far in this unit.

Plenaries
- *Challenge!* page 27.
- Copymaster 21 *Challenge!* activity 2.
- Use **OHT 9** and a blank acetate. Black out some words of your own choice on the blank overlay, depending on what you would like to concentrate on, e.g. all perfect tense verbs, past participles, time phrases, names of food items, etc. Ask students to read out the text, filling in the gaps. Remove the acetate so that they can check their responses.
- Hold a class discussion to summarize the different ways to understand and adapt a text, based on **OHT 9**.

Homework suggestions
- Students write a paragraph summarizing how healthy or unhealthy they were during the previous week. If they prefer, they can invent; in that case, tell them they have to use the following words (one point per word each time it is used): *le chocolat, le champagne, les baskets, la grand-mère*.
- Students work in pairs for this activity. Student A imagines and writes the diary entries of a health freak, e.g. Rosemary Conley; student B invents the diary entries of an anti-health activist, e.g. Michael Moore. Each student then reads their partner's diary and presents it to the rest of the class, e.g. *Lundi, Rosemary a mangé du poisson et des fruits. Michael Moore a mangé des hamburgers et des frites*.

2 En forme!

2.4 Mission-santé
pages 26–27

À vos marques

AT 3.2 *Lis et explique en anglais les sept objectifs de Mission-santé. Ils sont possibles pour toi?*
Students explain in English the seven goals listed in the *Mission-santé* leaflet. They predict how many they think they will be able to achieve this week. Encourage students to respond using *Pour moi, c'est possible parce que …* and *Pour moi, ce n'est pas possible parce que …*

Answers: 1 eat a good breakfast; 2 eat five portions of fruit and vegetables; 3 drink a litre of water; 4 do an hour of physical activity; 5 don't eat sweets between meals; 6 don't drink fizzy drinks; 7 don't go to bed later than 10 o'clock

AT 1.4/5
AT 3.4/5 *1a Écoute et lis le journal "Mission-santé" de Natacha. Relie les objectifs aux jours de la semaine.*
Students read the text of Natacha's diary while listening to the recording. They match each objective to the day of the week on which she achieved it.

Answers: 1 lundi; 2 dimanche; 3 samedi; 4 mardi; 5 jeudi; 6 vendredi; 7 mercredi

---

CD 1, track 29   page 26, activité 1a
Cassette 1, side 2

J'ai atteint tous les objectifs de Mission-santé! Voici mon journal de la semaine!
<u>lundi</u>
Ce matin, j'ai pris un bon petit déjeuner: j'ai mangé une banane, une orange et des céréales et j'ai bu un verre d'eau et un chocolat chaud. C'était bon.
<u>mardi</u>
Aujourd'hui, je ne suis pas allée au collège en bus. J'ai marché 15 minutes le matin et 15 minutes le soir. En plus, pendant les récrés, j'ai fait de l'exercice! J'ai marché dans la cour du collège avec Juliette. C'est de l'activité physique. Super! C'était facile!
<u>mercredi</u>
Ce soir, j'ai fait mes devoirs, j'ai joué sur ma console, j'ai surfé sur Internet et je ne suis pas allée au lit tard: je suis allée au lit à 21 h 30. Hmm … C'était un peu tôt!
<u>jeudi</u>
Je n'ai pas mangé de biscuits, ni de pains au chocolat, ni de barres chocolatées pendant les récrés! J'ai mangé une pomme. Hmm … Pas de sucreries entre les repas: ce n'était pas facile! J'adore les pains au chocolat!!!
<u>vendredi</u>
Je n'ai pas bu de soda au collège, ni à la maison! Cet après-midi, au goûter, je n'ai pas pris de limonade, j'ai bu du lait. C'était bien.
<u>samedi</u>
Cet après-midi, j'ai bu une bouteille d'eau minérale (un litre et demi). Beurk! Je n'aime pas l'eau! C'était difficile.
<u>dimanche</u>
Au petit déjeuner, j'ai mangé une banane. À midi, j'ai mangé du poulet avec des haricots verts et une salade de fruits. Cet après-midi, j'ai bu un jus d'orange et j'ai mangé des fruits secs. Voilà, mes cinq portions de fruits et légumes! Alors ce soir, j'ai mangé une pizza … C'était ma récompense!

AT 3.4/5 *1b Relis et trouve dans le texte …*
Students search Natacha's diary for the food and drink items. Ask them to come out to the OHP and circle the words on **OHT 9**.

Answers: six aliments: céréales, biscuits, pains au chocolat, barres chocolatées, poulet, pizza; six boissons: eau/eau minérale, chocolat chaud, soda, limonade, lait, jus d'orange; six fruits et légumes: banane, orange, pomme, salade de fruits, des fruits secs, haricots verts

1c Trouve …
Students search the text for the French equivalents of the English phrases. Again, they could come out to the OHP and circle or underline the words in the text on **OHT 9**.

Answers: a j'ai marché; b la cour; c de barres chocolatées; d des haricots verts; e des fruits secs; f récompense

AT 2.3/4 *2 Relis bien le texte. Tu es Natacha. Ton/Ta partenaire t'interviewe. Réponds de mémoire, puis change de rôle.*
In pairs, students take turns to ask and answer questions about Natacha's diary, with one student playing the part of Natacha and the other that of the interviewer. The student answering the questions should try to do so from memory, with the book closed. The interviewer could award points for correct answers. At this stage, you may want to focus on the *Zoom grammaire* on the perfect tense (see below).

AT 4.4/5 *3 À toi de faire la mission-santé! Écris un journal. (Voir Guide pratique.)*
This activity should be completed over the course of a week. Challenge students to take part in the health challenge and write a diary of their successes (or failures!), using Natacha's text as a model. See also the notes on the *Guide pratique* section below.

Zoom grammaire

This section focuses on the *passé composé* and reinforces **8W5** and **8S7**.
Before starting this section, you may need to revise the present tense of *avoir* and *être* with students to promote confidence, fluency and accuracy later on. Write up the present tense of both verbs on the board or OHP with gaps and ask students to fill them in to complete the paradigms. Alternatively, say a verb and a pronoun and students write on mini-whiteboards the conjugated form, e.g. you say *avoir* and *il*, and students should write *il a*.

1 Students search Natacha's diary for the past participles of the infinitives given.

Answers: allée, joué, marché, pris, bu, fait

2 Students rewrite the sentences, using the correct forms of *avoir* and replacing the infinitives with past participles.

En forme! 2

Answers: a J'ai regardé la télévision. b Tu as fait du sport? c Il a mangé des bonbons. d Elle a joué sur sa console. e Vous avez fait du surf hier? f Elles ont bu du lait.

3 Students consider any differences between the perfect tense of *aller* and the other perfect tense verbs here.

Answers: they should notice not only that *être* is used instead of *avoir* but also that the feminine form has an extra "e" on the past participle

If appropriate, ask students to look for another type of past tense in Natacha's diary: *c'était/ce n'était pas*. The Students' Book doesn't mention the imperfect tense at this stage, although the *Guide pratique* section does ask students to work out the meaning of *c'était*. (*C'était* will appear again in Unit 5 in the context of describing a past holiday).

Refer students to the grammar section on page 142 of the Students' Book for further information on the perfect tense.

Follow-up activities:
▶ Use **OHT 10A** with overlay **10B** to highlight differences between the present tense and the perfect tense.
▶ Divide the class into two teams and place **OHT 10A** on the OHP. Students from one team say a verb in the infinitive; students from the other team must fill in the OHT to score points. They then swap roles.

C31 Additional practice of the perfect tense is provided on Feuille 31 *Grammaire 2*.

Guide pratique

This section launches **8T6**. It gives students practice in how to use context to understand a text and how to use an existing text to help write their own.

1 Referring back to Natacha's diary, students use context to work out the English equivalents of some French phrases.

Answers: a for an afternoon snack; b during break times; c it was

2 Students note down all the time phrases used in Natacha's diary. They will be able to recycle these phrases when they write their own diary in activity **3**.

Answers: ce matin, aujourd'hui, le matin, le soir, pendant les récrés, ce soir, tard, à 21 h 30, tôt, entre les repas, cet après-midi, au petit déjeuner, à midi

Follow-up activity: To reinforce negatives (**7S5**), ask students to form the negative of some phrases from Natacha's diary (e.g. *j'ai fait, j'ai pris*) and to turn some of the negative phrases (e.g. *je ne suis pas allé(e)*) into positive statements.

Ça se dit comme ça!

This section focuses on French accents and on hearing the difference between present and past tense forms and launches **8S8**.

1 Students read out the list of words and pick out the ones whose vowel sounds change because of the accents. Draw their attention to the *-aï-* sound in *maïs*: students should remember this sound from the exclamation *aïe!* used on pages 20–21. The list of words is recorded so that students can check their pronunciation.

Answers: the vowel sounds change in 7, 8 and 9

CD 1, track 30 page 27, Ça se dit comme ça! activité 1
Cassette 1, side 2

1 – la … là
2 – ou … où
3 – mer … mère
4 – secret … secrète
5 – il … île
6 – route … août
7 – mange … mangé
8 – rose … rosée
9 – mais … maïs
10 – sur … sûr

2 Students listen and indicate whether each item is in the present or the perfect tense.

Answers: present tense: 2, 3, 6; perfect tense: 1, 4, 5

CD 1, track 31 page 27, Ça se dit comme ça! activité 2
Cassette 1, side 2

1 – J'ai mangé du poisson et du riz.
2 – Je mange du céleri.
3 – Il regarde un film à la télé.
4 – Il a regardé un film à la télé.
5 – Tu as fait du foot aujourd'hui?
6 – Oui, je fais du foot tous les mardis.

Follow-up activity: Look at the English meanings of the words in activity **1** above, in particular of the words whose spellings have minor differences but whose meanings are completely different. Challenge students to find similar examples in English, e.g. "their" and "there", "where" and "wear", "here" and "hear", etc.

C34 Activities 4–6 of Feuille 34 *Ça se dit comme ça!* provide further practice of these pronunciation points and could be used at this point.

2 En forme!

C25 **C27** **C29** Feuille 25 *Parle En plus*, Feuille 27 *Lis et écris Encore 2* and Feuille 29 *Lis et écris En plus 2* could also be used here. They all provide further practice of the language of this spread.

W17 Additional reading and writing practice is also provided on page 17 of the *Encore* and *En plus* Workbooks.

Challenge!

AT 4.3 **A** *Résume ce que dit Natacha des sept objectifs de Mission-santé.*
Students write a brief summary of Natacha's diary, saying what she did each day to achieve her goals, e.g. *Lundi, j'ai pris un bon petit déjeuner. Mardi, j'ai …* They could refer back to the original list of *Mission-santé* objectives on page 26, changing each infinitive into the first person singular form of the perfect tense.

AT 4.4/5 **B** *Raconte un week-end "santé" ou le contraire.*
Students write a paragraph about a healthy weekend or an unhealthy one. Remind them of the ideas and phrases used when discussing healthy/unhealthy options on the previous spread.

AT 2.4/5 **C** *Décris ta semaine. Tu as atteint trois objectifs? Ton/Ta partenaire dit si c'est vrai ou faux et dit pourquoi. Ensuite, changez de rôles.*
Students need to have completed activity **3** before they can do this task. Working in pairs, they take turns to tell their partner three objectives they have achieved over the previous week. They may tell the truth or they may give false information, and the partner tries to guess when they are bluffing. To ensure that students achieve a good level of accuracy and range of language, they should show each other their three goals prior to the activity so that they have time to prepare a response to each statement.

En forme! 2

2.5 La belle équipe, épisode 2

pages 28–29

Objectives
- Develop listening and reading skills via a soap story based on the language of the unit (**8L2 – R**)
- Develop ability to recognize and use features that add authenticity and expression to written texts (**8T2 – R**)

Resources
Students' Book, pages 28–29
CD 1, track 32
Cassette 0, side 0

Programme of Study reference
1a, 1c, 2a, 2b, 2g, 2h, 2i, 3b, 3c, 3e, 4a, 4d, 5d, 5e, 5g, 5i

For general information on introducing and exploiting the soap story, refer to page 19 of the Introduction.

This episode begins where the previous episode ended: Juliette, Matthieu and Natacha have been successful in the auditions! However, when they announce the good news to Arnaud, he doesn't seem very enthusiastic. Matthieu accuses him of being jealous, both boys become angry, and the two girls have to calm the situation down. A few days later, Matthieu develops a temperature. During a rehearsal, he becomes so ill that Natacha telephones the doctor: it turns out that he has appendicitis and must go to hospital. Without Matthieu, the friends won't be able to rehearse for the talent competition … which is in two weeks' time! What are they going to do?!

AT 1.4 **1a** *Écoute et regarde les photos!*
The continuation of the soap episode reinforces **8L2** and **8T2**. Ask students to try to predict what might happen in the next instalment.

CD 1, track 32 — page 28, La belle équipe, épisode 2
Cassette 1, side 2

1 – Juliette, Matthieu et Natacha … vous êtes sélectionnés pour le Concours! Félicitations!
 – Ouais! Génial!
 – Oh là là … je rêve!
 – Vite, on va voir Arnaud!
2 – Salut, Arnaud! On est sélectionnés! On s'appelle "les Pieds-Nus"!
 – Ah? Bravo.
 – Tu n'es pas très enthousiaste!
 – Pff … il est jaloux!
3 – Moi? Jaloux? D'un clown comme toi?
 – Un clown, moi? Répète!
 – OK! Ça va, ça va!
4 Quelques jours plus tard …
 – Brrr! J'ai froid et j'ai mal au ventre.
 – Tu as un petit rhume … Va à la pharmacie!
 – Tu as de la fièvre! Va chez le médecin ce soir.
 – Mais non, ce soir, il y a la répétition des Pieds-Nus!
 – Alors bois beaucoup d'eau et mange des kiwis, pour les vitamines.
 – Oui, docteur Natacha!
5 Plus tard, chez Arnaud …
 – Matthieu, c'est à toi! Matthieu?
 – Euh … J'ai très mal et j'ai envie de vomir!
 – Tu n'as pas mangé assez de kiwis!
 – Arrête, Juliette! C'est sérieux. J'appelle le médecin!
6 – Mon garçon, c'est une mauvaise appendicite. Il faut opérer tout de suite.
 – Mais docteur … Non! Je … les Pieds-Nus … le concours au théâtre!
 – Va d'abord à l'hôpital. Ta santé, c'est plus important que le théâtre!
7 – Pauvre Matthieu …
 – Les répétitions, sans Matthieu, ce n'est pas possible!
 – C'est la cata! Et le concours, c'est dans deux semaines!
À suivre …

AT 1.4 **1b** *Écoute et lis. Trouve …*
AT 3.4 Give students a few minutes to read the text in silence. They then search the text for the French equivalents of the English expressions.

Answers: a félicitations!; b sélectionnés; c enthousiaste; d comme toi; e une appendicite; f opérer; g tout de suite; h les répétitions

1c *Lis les textes. Trouve les phrases.*
Students search the text again and note down the sentences in which each piece of information is expressed.

Answers: a Vous êtes sélectionnés pour le Concours! b Tu n'es pas très enthousiaste! c Moi? Jaloux? D'un clown comme toi? d Tu as un petit rhume … Va à la pharmacie! Tu as de la fièvre! Va chez le médecin ce soir. e J'ai très mal et j'ai envie de vomir! f Mon garçon, c'est une mauvaise appendicite. Il faut opérer tout de suite. g C'est la cata! Et le concours, c'est dans deux semaines!

2a *Écoute bien l'intonation et décide à qui correspond chaque mot.*
Students listen again to the story, focusing on intonation to identify the moods of the different speakers.

Answers: <u>happy/enthusiastic</u>: (in frame 1) Matthieu, Natacha and Juliette, (in frame 2) Juliette; <u>angry</u>: (in frame 3) Arnaud and Matthieu; <u>ill</u>: (in frames 4 and 5) Matthieu; <u>worried</u>: (in frame 4) Juliette and Natacha, (in frame 5) Natacha

2b *Répète et imite l'intonation!*
Students listen again and copy the intonation.

2c *Réécoute et répète ces petits mots très français! C'est quoi en anglais?*
Play the recording again, pausing to allow students to repeat the exclamations.

2 En forme!

Answers: ouais!: yeah!; *vite!*: quick!; *moi?*: me?; *euh …*: er …; *alors*: so/in that case; *oh là là!*: wow!; *pff!*: any suitable expression of scorn, e.g. hmf!, bah!; *OK, ça va!*: OK/all right, that's enough/that'll do!; *mais non!*: no way!

Super-challenge!   page 30

This extension page is intended to stretch more able students who are confident with the core language of the unit. It combines language from the unit with unfamiliar language and develops grammar points introduced in the main body of the unit. It can be used flexibly either as part of a teacher-led lesson or as alternative independent class and homework material.

Objectives

▶ Develop the use of plural forms of perfect tense verbs
▶ Research and write about a famous French sports personality (**8C2 – L**)

Resources

Students' Book, page 30
Encore/En plus Workbooks, page 20

Programme of Study reference

1b, 1c, 2c, 2h, 2i, 3c, 3d, 3e, 4a, 4c, 4d, 5d, 5e, 5f, 5g, 5i

AT 3.4/5

1 *Lis le texte et trouve …*
This magazine-style article focuses on the fitness regime of a team of cyclists taking part in the *Tour de France*. Students search the text for specific items of vocabulary.

Answers: quatre sports: le cyclisme, le footing, la musculation, le ski (the text also mentions *la piscine*, which implies *la natation*); seize aliments: de la viande, du jambon, des œufs, du fromage, du pain, des fruits (frais), des tartines, de la confiture, des carottes, du poulet, du poisson grillé, des pâtes, du riz, des sucreries, des tartelettes de fruits, des gâteaux de riz; trois boissons: du jus de fruits, des sodas, de l'eau

2 *Traduis les cinq questions en anglais.*
Students look back at the text and pick out the five questions asked by the interviewer. They translate the questions into English.

Answers: What did you have for breakfast? What did you eat yesterday evening? How much water did you drink during the race? Which sports did you do before the race? Did you go skiing?/You didn't go skiing, did you?

AT 4.3

3 *Écris trois choses sur les cyclistes que tu savais et trois choses qui te surprennent.*
Students write down three things from the article that they already knew about the cyclists and three things that they find surprising.

AT 4.4/5

Follow-up activity: Students research the training programme and diet of a famous French sports personality. They could produce a magazine article about it, based around an interview, in the same style as the text in the Students' Book. This activity launches **8C2**.

Zoom grammaire

This grammar section looks at the perfect tense in more detail, and focuses particularly on the plural forms.

1 Students first search the text for three present tense verbs.

Answers: Le cyclisme <u>est</u> un sport difficile. Bien manger, c'<u>est</u> important. Les coureurs <u>ont</u> beaucoup de muscles et d'énergie.

2 Students indicate which tense is used throughout the rest of the article.

Answer: the perfect tense

3 Students list all the plural verb forms used in the article.

Answers: nous avons parlé/mangé/bu/fait; nous (ne) sommes (pas) allés; vous avez pris/mangé/bu/fait; vous n'êtes pas allés; ils/elles/certains coureurs/d'autres ont mangé/pris/bu/fait; certaines équipes sont allées

4 Students search the text for an alternative to *nous*.

Answers: on a bu; they should notice that *avoir* is in the third person singular

5 Students write additional sentences in the perfect tense using the table as a guide.

Refer students to the grammar section on the perfect tense on page 142 of the Students' Book.

W20 Page 20 of the *Encore* and *En plus* Workbooks could be used at this point.

Vocabulaire   page 31

This page provides a summary of the key language covered in this unit. It could be used as a handy reference for students as they work through the unit. Alternatively, students could use its clear French–English format with language organized thematically when learning vocabulary.

C18 Feuille 18 *Vocabulaire* also contains a summary of the key language of the unit and could be given to students at this point for revision purposes. See page 7 of the Introduction for ideas on how to use this copymaster.

W21 Page 21 of the *Encore* and *En plus* Workbooks also provides a summary of the key language of the unit.

En forme! 2

Podium
page 32

The *Podium* page provides students with an end-of-unit checklist of learning objectives in French and English. At the foot of the page are activities at three levels of difficulty (bronze, silver and gold) to extend the work of the unit. Encourage students to select an activity at the most appropriate level.

C19 Feuille 19 *Podium* could also be used at this point. This worksheet contains activities to help students keep track of their progress. See page 7 of the Introduction for ideas on how to use it to help self- and peer-assessment.

W22 Page 22 of the *Encore* and *En plus* Workbooks also provides an end-of-unit checklist in French and English with activities to help students keep track of their progress.

Encore Unité 2
pages 98–99

Objectives
These reinforcement pages are intended for those students requiring further practice of core language from the unit. They can be used by students who finish other activities quickly or as alternative class and homework material.

Resources
Students' Book, pages 98–99
CD 1, tracks 33–34
Cassette 1, side 2

Programme of Study reference
1a, 1c, 2a, 2b, 2c, 2d, 2h, 2i, 3e, 4a, 5a, 5c, 5d, 5e, 5f, 5i

AT 3.1 **1** *Relie et écris sept parties du corps.*
AT 4.1 Students match the two halves of each word to find seven parts of the body.

Answers: pouce, gorge, visage, oreilles, épaule, genou, tête

AT 3.2 **2a** *Lis les bulles et trouve les mots qui manquent dans la boîte.*
Students use the words provided to fill in the gaps in the cartoon story.

Answers: see transcript below

AT 1.2 **2b** *Écoute et vérifie.*
Students listen to the recording to check their answers.

CD 1, track 33
Cassette 1, side 2
page 98, activité 2b

1 – Ça ne va pas?
 – Oh non! J'ai mal à la tête.
2 – Et j'ai mal au ventre.
3 – Tu as chaud. Tu as de la fièvre?
4 – Oui et j'ai très soif.
5 – Oh! Et j'ai envie de vomir!
6 – Aaaaah! Alors, salut!

AT 2.2 **2c** *Joue la conversation avec un(e) partenaire.*
Students perform the conversation with a partner.

AT 1.3 **3a** *Écoute les trois conversations chez le médecin. Note les symptômes et les conseils.*
AT 4.2 Students listen to the three conversations at the doctor's. They note down each person's symptoms and the advice they are given.

Answers: 1 (Matthieu) très mal au ventre, envie de vomir, ne mange pas et va aux urgences; 2 très mal aux dents, mal aux yeux, prends un antidouleur et ne mange pas; 3 très mal à la tête, chaud et froid, bois de l'eau et va au lit

CD 1, track 34
Cassette 1, side 2
page 99, activité 3a

1 – Bonsoir, docteur.
 – Bonsoir, Matthieu. Qu'est-ce qui ne va pas?
 – J'ai très mal au ventre.
 – Tu as envie de vomir?
 – Oui, un peu.
 – Hum … Ne mange pas et va aux urgences!
2 – Bonjour, docteur.
 – Bonjour. Qu'est-ce qui ne va pas?
 – J'ai très mal aux dents.
 – Tu as mal aux yeux?
 – Oui, un peu.
 – Hmm … Prends un antidouleur et ne mange pas!
3 – Bonjour, docteur.
 – Bonjour. Qu'est-ce qui ne va pas?
 – J'ai très mal à la tête.
 – Tu as chaud?
 – Ben … J'ai chaud et j'ai froid.
 – Hum … Bois de l'eau et va au lit.

AT 2.3 **3b** *À deux, inventez des conversations chez le médecin (comme celle de Matthieu). Choisissez des symptômes et des conseils dans la liste.*
Students work in pairs to invent and act out conversations with a doctor, using the lists of symptoms and advice provided.

AT 3.3 **4a** *Lis les mots 1–4 de parents pour l'école. Réponds aux questions en anglais.*
Students read the sick notes written by parents and answer comprehension questions in English.

73

2 En forme!

Answers: a she has flu, a headache and a temperature; b a dentist; c number 1; d drink plenty of water, don't eat too much chocolate, eat fruit and vegetables instead

AT 4.2/3 **4b** *Écris le mot pour Matthieu.*
Referring back to their answers for activity **3a**, students write a sick note for Matthieu.

Possible answer: Matthieu ne va pas à l'école aujourd'hui parce qu'il a mal au ventre et il a envie de vomir. Il ne mange pas et il va aux urgences.

AT 4.2/3 **4c** *Invente un mot pour toi!*
Students write a sick note for themselves.

En plus Unité 2 pages 110–111

Objectives
These extension pages are intended for more able students who are confident with the core language of the unit. They can be used by students who finish other activities quickly or as alternative class and homework material.

Resources
Students' Book, pages 110–111

Programme of Study reference
1c, 2c, 2d, 2h, 3e, 4c, 5a, 5c, 5d, 5e, 5f, 5g, 5i

AT 4.2 **1** *Révise les noms d'aliments de l'unité 2. Fais deux listes.*
Students revise food vocabulary by writing what they did and didn't eat yesterday.

AT 3.3 **2a** *Lis l'article (p. 110) et choisis le bon titre anglais.*
Students read the article *Santé-Junior* and select an appropriate English title.

Answer: b Eat your way to good health!

AT 2.3 **2b** *Est-ce que tu as bien mangé hier? Explique pourquoi à ton/ta partenaire.*
Referring to their lists in activity **1** and to the advice given in the article, students take turns to explain to their partner whether their diet yesterday was healthy or unhealthy, giving reasons.

AT 4.3 **2c** *Écris des conseils pour le déjeuner et le dîner pour l'article.*
Students write two additional sections for the article, providing tips for a healthy lunch and evening meal.

AT 2.3/4 **2d** *Discute avec ton/ta partenaire. Vous êtes d'accord? Pas d'accord?*
Students discuss their meal suggestions (activity **2c**) with a partner.

AT 2.3 **3a** *A pose les questions du test (à droite) et conseille un sport à B. Changez de rôle.*
AT 3.3 Students work in pairs, taking turns to ask each other the questions from the sports quiz and give appropriate advice.

AT 4.3/4 **3b** *Ajoute d'autres questions et d'autres sports au mini-test.*
Students invent additional questions and advice to add to the quiz, incorporating different types of sport. This could be done as a whole-class activity, in small groups or in pairs.

Point lecture pages 122–123

These pages are intended to encourage independent reading. Students should attempt them once they are confident with the core language of the unit. They can be used by students who finish other activities quickly or as alternative class and homework material.

Objectives
▶ Learn some French idioms (**8C5 – L**)
▶ Develop reading for pleasure via song lyrics (**8C4 – R**)

Resources
Students' Book, pages 122–123
CD 1, tracks 35–36
Cassette 1, side 2

Programme of Study reference
1a, 1c, 2a, 2b, 2h, 3b, 3c, 3e, 4a, 5a, 5d, 5e, 5f, 5g, 5i

AT 1.2 **1a** *Écoute et lis! Quels mots décrivent Charlie?*
AT 3.2 Students read the Charlie cartoon while listening to the recording. They select appropriate words to describe Charlie.

Answers: stupide, sportif

CD 1, track 35 page 122, activité 1
Cassette 1, side 2

– Le vélo, c'est super pour la forme! … Regardez! Sans les mains! … Regardez! Sans les pieds! … Regardez! Sans les yeux!
– Regardez! Sans les dents!
– Ha ha ha!

AT 1.2 **1b** *Réécoute. À deux, lisez l'histoire.*
AT 2.2 After listening again to the recording, students read it with a partner, focusing on intonation and trying to sound as authentic as possible.

AT 3.2 **2a** *Regarde les dessins 1–4 et complète ces expressions françaises avec les bons mots.*
AT 4.2 The pictures represent various idioms. Students select words from the box to complete each caption. This activity launches **8C5**.

Answers: 1 pied; 2 yeux, tête; 3 gorge; 4 cheveux

AT 3.2 **2b** *C'est quoi en anglais?*
This activity focuses on non-literal translations. Students choose English expressions that are equivalent to the French.

Answers: c'est le pied!: it's great!; *coûter les yeux de la tête*: it costs an arm and a leg; *avoir un chat dans la gorge*: to have a frog in one's throat; *couper les cheveux en quatre*: to split hairs

AT 1.4 **3a** *Écoute la chanson et numérote les dessins dans l'ordre mentionné.*
This song reinforces **8C4**. Students listen and number the pictures in the order in which they are mentioned.

Answers: a, b, c, e, d, l, f, i, h, g, j, k

CD 1, track 36   page 123, activité 3
Cassette 1, side 2

Ouille, aïe, oh là là!
Tous les matins
au petit déjeuner,
j'entends Maman
me répéter:
"Ne bois pas ci,
ne bois pas ça,
bois du jus de fruits,
pas du coca!"

Ouille, aïe, oh là là!
Vive le milk-shake et le coca!

L'après-midi
à la cantine,
moi, j'ai envie
de grosses tartines.
Mais pour la forme
on nous le dit:
mangez des pommes
et des kiwis!

Ouille, aïe, oh là là!
Vive les tartines au chocolat!

Je fais du yoga
j'ai mal au dos.
Je fais du judo,
j'ai mal aux bras.
Un sport génial
pour la santé,
c'est le football
à la télé!

Ouille, aïe, oh là là!
Vive la télé et le sofa!

Ouille, aïe, oh là là!
Vive le milk-shake et le coca!
Vive les tartines au chocolat!
Vive la télé et le sofa!

3b *Réécoute et chante!*
Students listen again and join in with the song.

AT 3.3 **3c** *Arrange les morceaux de phrases suivants pour faire un nouveau couplet!*
Students rearrange the phrases to come up with an additional verse for the song.

Answers: Le soir au dîner, / Papa me dit: / "Fais attention / à ta santé. / Pas de télé / ni de sortie! / Mange léger / et va au lit!"

AT 4.3/4 **3d** *À toi d'inventer un autre couplet!*
Students write their own extra verse for the song.

Copymasters

Feuille 20 À vos marques

There are two starter activities on this copymaster. Activity 1 could be used either with pages 20–21 of the Students' Book or as revision of parts of the body before beginning pages 22–23. Activity 2 uses the perfect tense so could be completed with pages 26–27.

1 *Continue les listes logiques.*
Students complete each sequence using an appropriate body part. Accept any answers that can be justified. As a follow-up activity, students could create their own lists for a partner to solve, e.g. all feminine, all masculine or all plural words.

Answers: 1 mains (les pieds sont au bout des jambes, les mains sont au bout des bras); 2 bouche (tout est sur la tête); 3 dents (les doigts sont sur la main, les dents sont dans la bouche); 4 le nez, les nez (ne change pas au pluriel); 5 le ventre (suite de parties du corps uniques)

2 *Découpe les débuts et les fins de phrases. Arrange-les pour faire (a) huit choses bonnes pour la santé, (b) huit choses mauvaises pour la santé, et puis (c) huit choses que tu as faites cette semaine!*
Students match up the sentence halves to make eight healthy things, eight unhealthy things and eight things that they have done this week.

Answers: <u>Healthy</u>: J'ai mangé des pommes. Je n'ai pas mangé de chips. J'ai bu du jus de fruits frais. Je n'ai pas bu de Coca-Cola. J'ai joué au tennis et au basket. Je n'ai pas joué à la PlayStation. Je suis allé(e) au centre sportif. Je ne suis pas allé(e) au lit tard.
<u>Unhealthy</u>: J'ai mangé des chips. Je n'ai pas mangé de pommes. J'ai bu du Coca-Cola. Je n'ai pas bu de jus de fruits frais. J'ai joué à la PlayStation. Je n'ai pas joué au tennis et au basket. Je suis allé(e) au lit tard. Je ne suis pas allé(e) au centre sportif.

2 En forme!

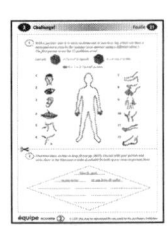

Feuille 21 Challenge!

There are two plenary activities on this copymaster. Activity 1 could be used with pages 22–23 of the Students' Book; activity 2 could be used with pages 26–27.

1 This is a dice game to practise *j'ai mal …* Students take turns to roll the dice and to say a phrase corresponding to the numbers they have thrown, e.g. 4 = *J'ai mal aux dents*; 2 + 7 = 9 = *J'ai mal au ventre*. The winner is the first person to correctly say all 12 ailments. This game could be developed into a conversation, with students asking and answering the question *Qu'est-ce qui ne va pas?* or *Tu as mal où?*

2 Students note down nine tips on how to keep fit. They could refer back to pages 26–27 of the Students' Book or to Feuille 20 *À vos marques* if they are short of inspiration, but do encourage them to come up with their own ideas. After discussion with a partner, students write their suggestions into the shape on the copymaster: the idea behind the diamond shape is that it enables them to rank their ideas as most important (at the top), of equal importance (in the middle), of least importance (at the bottom), etc. Encourage them to continue their discussion, e.g. by talking about what they themselves did last week to keep fit: *Je n'ai pas fumé*, etc.

Feuille 22 Écoute Encore

This copymaster practises *j'ai mal …* plus parts of the body and could be used with pages 22–23 of the Students' Book.

AT 1.2

1a *Écoute les neuf conversations chez le médecin et numérote les dessins.*
Students listen to the conversations and select a picture to represent each one.

Answers: toothache: 2; headache: 4; stomach ache: 1; sore throat: 8; earache: 3; sore feet: 6; sore eyes: 9; sore nose: 7; sore back: 5

AT 4.2 **1b** *Réécoute et complète les phrases.*
Students listen again and fill in the missing phrases in the captions.

Answers: see transcript below

CD 3, track 7 Feuille 22, activité 1
Cassette 4, side 1

1 – Qu'est-ce qui ne va pas?
  – Nous avons mal au ventre.
2 – Qu'est-ce qui ne va pas?
  – Ils ont mal aux dents.
3 – Qu'est-ce qui ne va pas?
  – Moi, j'ai mal à l'oreille.
4 – Qu'est-ce qui ne va pas?
  – Elle a mal à la tête.
5 – Qu'est-ce qui ne va pas?
  – Elles ont mal au dos.
6 – Qu'est-ce qui ne va pas?
  – Il a mal aux pieds.
7 – Qu'est-ce qui ne va pas? Vous avez mal au nez?
8 – Qu'est-ce qui ne va pas? Tu as mal à la gorge?
9 – Qu'est-ce qui ne va pas?
  – On a mal aux yeux.

Feuille 23 Écoute En plus

This copymaster could be completed after working on pages 24–25 of the Students' Book.

AT 1.3

1a *Écoute et numérote les conseils de Claire et de Manon dans l'ordre où tu les entends.*
Students listen to the two girls giving advice to their friend, who is ill. They number the pieces of advice in the order in which they are mentioned.

Answers: 1 a; 2 e; 3 c; 4 d; 5 b; 6 g; 7 h; 8 f

AT 1.3
AT 4.3

1b *Réécoute. Écris les trois conseils pour lesquels Claire et Manon sont d'accord.*
Students listen again and note down the three pieces of advice on which the two girls agree.

Answers: mange des fruits, des légumes et des pâtes; ne mange pas de chocolat; ne va pas au lit trop tard

CD 3, track 8 Feuille 23, activité 1
Cassette 4, side 1

– Oh là là … Ça ne va pas. Je ne suis pas très en forme …
– Ah, qu'est-ce qui ne va pas?
– Je ne sais pas … J'ai un peu mal au ventre …
– Ah, alors bois un coca. C'est bon quand tu as mal au ventre.
– Ah non, je ne suis pas d'accord! Ne bois pas de sodas, ce n'est pas bon du tout pour la santé. Surtout mange des fruits et des légumes … et des pâtes, pour avoir de l'énergie! Tu n'es pas d'accord, Manon?
– Si si! C'est vrai, je suis d'accord, les fruits, les légumes, les pâtes, tout ça, c'est bon pour la santé …
– Euh … oui, mais …
– Oui, et ne mange pas de chocolat. Le chocolat, c'est mauvais quand on a mal au ventre.
– Oui, c'est vrai, je suis d'accord avec ça.
– Et fais du sport! Va au collège à pied et va à la piscine!
– Non! Là, je ne suis pas d'accord. Ne fais pas de sport si tu as mal au ventre. Par contre, ne va pas au lit trop tard. Ça, c'est important.
– Oui, oui, bon, c'est vrai. Et puis, surtout surtout surtout, …
– Oh! oh! oh! Écoutez toutes les deux!! Je bois de l'eau, je mange des fruits, je mange des légumes, je mange des pâtes, je fais du sport, je ne vais pas au lit tard …
– OK, OK!
– Ne t'énerve pas, *keep cool*!
– Nous, on veut juste te donner des conseils … Si tu veux être en bonne santé, il faut savoir quoi faire …

En forme! 2

AT 1.3 **2a** *Écoute Yann et sa mère. Qu'est-ce qui ne va pas?*
Students listen and note down what is wrong with Yann.

Answers: mal au ventre, mal à la tête, mal aux jambes, envie de dormir, envie de vomir

CD 3, track 9   Feuille 23, activité 2a
Cassette 4, side 1

– Yann! Yann! Il est huit heures! Vite, lève-toi!
– Oh non, maman, ça ne va pas …
– Qu'est-ce qui ne va pas?
– J'ai … J'ai mal au ventre …
– Hmmm, mal au ventre, hein? Tu as mal au ventre tous les lundi matins!
– Non, vraiment maman! J'ai très mal au ventre et j'ai mal à la tête!
– Hmmm, mal à la tête, hein? Trop de PlayStation! Allez, debout!
– Maman! Je ne suis pas en forme, c'est vrai! J'ai mal aux jambes!
– Ah, tu as mal aux jambes? Tu as un test d'éducation physique au collège? Aujourd'hui?? C'est ça, non?!!
– Non, maman, je ne suis vraiment pas bien! J'ai envie de dormir …
– Ah oui, tu regardes la télé trop tard le soir, allez debout …
– Maman, j'ai envie de vomir …
– Oh non, Yann! Tu es malade! Pauvre chéri! Il faut dire quand ça ne va pas! Mon pauvre chéri!

AT 4.3 **2b** *Écris des conseils pour Yann.*
Students write down what they would advise Yann to do.

Possible answers: Bois de l'eau, c'est bon pour la santé. Va au lit. Prends un antidouleur. Appelle le médecin.

Feuille 24 Parle Encore

This copymaster can be used with pages 22–23 of the Students' Book.

AT 2.2 **1a** *Tu es une des personnes malades. Réponds aux questions de ton/ta partenaire.*
1b *Changez de rôle.*
Students work in pairs. Partner A pretends to be one of the characters pictured; partner B must find out who they are by asking questions about their ailments. They then swap roles.

AT 2.2 **2** *Joue au morpion.*
Students play Noughts and Crosses using the illustrated grid. If they are able to correctly say a phrase representing one of the pictures, they draw their nought or their cross on the grid. The winner is the first student to achieve a straight line of noughts or crosses.

Feuille 25 Parle En plus

This copymaster can be used with pages 26–27 of the Students' Book.

AT 2.4/5 **1** *Hier, Victor et Anya ont fait la mission santé. Partenaire A pose des questions sur Anya et partenaire B répond. Prends des notes et donne un point par objectif atteint.*
2 *Partenaire B pose des questions sur Victor et partenaire A répond. Comparez. Qui a le mieux atteint les sept objectifs?*
Students ask each other questions to find out how successful Victor and Anya were in the health challenge. Photocopy and cut up the copymaster so that students cannot see their partner's details.

Feuille 26 Lis et écris Encore 1

This copymaster provides basic practice of the vocabulary for parts of the body and could be used with pages 20–21 of the Students' Book.

AT 3.1 **1** *Regarde les dessins. Entoure les noms dans la grille.*
Students search the grid for the French words for parts of the body.

Answers:

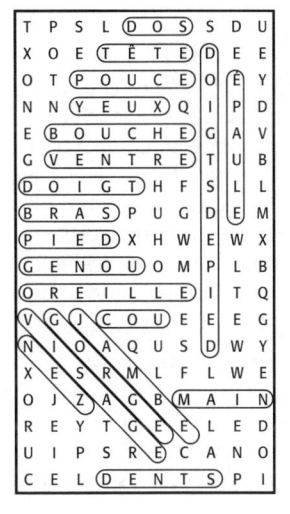

```
T P S L D O S S D U
X O E T Ê T E D E E
O T P O U C E O Ê Y
N N Y E U X Q I P D
E B O U C H E G A V
G V E N T R E T U B
D O I G T H F S L E
B R A S P U G C E X
P I E D X H W E W X
G E N O U O M P L B
O R E I L L E H T Q
V G J C O U E E G C
N I O A Q U S D W Y
X E S R M L F L W E
O J Z A G B M A I N
R E Y T G E L E D
U I P S R E C A N O
C E L D E N T S P I
```

AT 4.1 **2** *Écris le nom sous chaque dessin. N'oublie pas l'article: le, la, l' ou les.*
Students label each illustration with the correct French word, including the article *le*, *la*, *l'* or *les*.

Answers: la tête; la gorge; la main; la jambe; la bouche; le cou; le bras; le dos; les yeux; le genou; le nez; le ventre; le visage; le pied; le doigt; les doigts de pied; l'épaule; l'oreille; les dents; le pouce

2 En forme!

AT 3.3

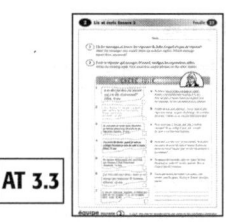

Feuille 27 Lis et écris Encore 2

This copymaster could be used towards the end of pages 26–27 of the Students' Book.

1 Lis les messages et trouve les réponses de Julie. Lequel n'a pas de réponse?
Students match the young people's letters with their corresponding replies from the agony aunt. They indicate which letter has no reply.

Answers: 1 d; 2 b; 3 e; 5 a; 6 f; 7 c; there is no reply to message 4

AT 4.3/4

2 Écris la réponse qui manque. D'abord, souligne les expressions utiles.
Students write their own reply to message 4. To help them, suggest that they first underline the phrases they think will be useful to them for their own text.

Possible answer: Va au lit plus tôt! Dors plus tard le matin si possible. Ne bois pas de café, ce n'est pas bon pour la santé. Mange des fruits, comme les kiwis, les oranges et les fraises pour les vitamines.

Feuille 28 Lis et écris En plus 1

This copymaster could be used with pages 22–23 of the Students' Book.

AT 3.2
AT 4.3

1 Tu es en France avec une amie qui ne parle pas français. Elle va chez le médecin. Traduis pour le médecin et ton amie!
Students imagine they are helping an English friend to explain her symptoms to a French doctor. This translation exercise extends students by requiring them to switch between the first and third persons of the verb. It also reinforces the idea that it is not always possible to translate literally between one language and another.

Answers: 1 Elle a mal à la tête, elle a mal au ventre et elle a envie de vomir. 2 Non, elle n'a pas chaud, elle a très froid. 3 *Do you have a sore throat?* Oui, elle a mal à la gorge et elle tousse beaucoup. 4 *Do you have a temperature?* Oui, elle a de la fièvre et elle a mal aux yeux. 5 *Are you thirsty?* Oui, elle a très soif. 6 *You have flu. Here is some medicine.* Merci et au revoir!

Feuille 29 Lis et écris En plus 2

This copymaster could be used with pages 26–27 of the Students' Book. It provides an opportunity for further work on **8T6**, which was launched via the *Guide pratique* on pages 26–27.

AT 3.4/5

1 Lis le texte une fois. C'est quoi? Coche.
Students read once through the text and tick the correct option to indicate what type of text it is.

Answer: health advice for the start of the new school year

2 À deux, écrivez les mots que vous ne connaissez pas. Cherchez-en un seul dans le dictionnaire. Devinez le sens des autres.
Students make a note of the words from the text that they don't understand. They may look up one word only in a dictionary and must try to deduce the others.

3 Relis le texte. Réponds en anglais.
Students answer questions in English about the text.

Answers: 1 They should get up early and have a good breakfast, e.g. fruit or fruit juice, wholemeal bread or cereal, plus some dairy produce, and they should remember to brush their teeth. 2 If they're not having a hot meal, they should have sandwiches made with wholemeal bread, with cheese or lean meat, plus raw vegetables and fruit. They should drink plenty of water instead of fizzy drinks. 3 They shouldn't smoke. 4 They should do 30 minutes to an hour of moderate activity each day after school, with more intensive exercise twice a week. 5 Go to bed early.

AT 4.4/5

4 Tu suis les conseils ou pas? Explique en adaptant les mots du texte et en ajoutant des détails.
Students explain, in writing, whether they themselves follow this advice.

Follow-up activity: For extra grammar practice, students could rewrite the text using the second person singular form of the imperative, e.g. *Le matin, lève-toi tôt et prends le repas le plus important de la journée …*

Feuille 30 Grammaire 1

This copymaster focuses on gender, plurals and adjective agreement and should accompany the *Zoom grammaire* on page 21 of the Students' Book.

1 Lis les phrases. Les mots en gras sont-ils masculins ou féminins, singuliers ou pluriels? Pourquoi? Écris sur une feuille.
Students decide whether the bold words in each sentence are masculine, feminine, singular or plural. They note down the clues that led them to each decision.

Answers: (clues to each answer are given in brackets): 2 *tapis* is masculine singular (*le*), *chambre* is feminine singular (*ta*); 3 *sweats* is masculine plural (*beaux, -s* ending on *sweats*), *magasin* is masculine singular (*son*); 4 *cousins* is masculine plural (*des, -s* ending on *cousins*, *irlandais* is masculine); 5 *Madame Guimenez* is feminine singular (*-e* ending on *française*, *Madame* is a feminine word), *mari* is masculine singular (*son*); 6 *gants* is masculine plural (*-s* ending on *gants*, *noirs* shows masculine/plural agreement)

2 Entoure le(s) bon(s) mot(s) dans chaque phrase.
Students use their knowledge of genders and adjective agreement to work out what the correct words are in each sentence.

Answers: 1 le chocolat; 2 son amie; 3 un pantalon; 4 mes sœurs; 5 ma mère; 6 un short

3 *Complète les phrases avec les adjectifs de la boîte.*
Students select adjectives to complete each sentence.

Answers: 1 grande; 2 français, écossaise; 3 noir, verte; 4 petites, courts; 5 droit

4 *Complète les phrases. Attention aux accords!*
Students complete the sentences. They must work out for themselves the correct form of the words, using their knowledge of gender and agreement.

Answers: 1 tes; 2 blonds; 3 mon; 4 filles; 5 généreuse; 6 blanches

Feuille 31 Grammaire 2

This copymaster focuses on the perfect tense and should be done after the *Zoom grammaire* on page 27 of the Students' Book.

1 Students select the correct phrases to complete five sentences about the perfect tense.

Answers: 1 a; 2 b; 3 b; 4 a; 5 b

2a *Souligne les participes passés.*
Students select all the past participles from the panel of words.

Answers: marché, allé, mangé, allée, joué, pris, fait, bu

2b *Écris une phrase avec chaque participe passé.*
Students write one sentence for each past participle they found in **2a**.

2c *Écris l'infinitif des verbes soulignés dans l' activité 2a sur une feuille.*
Students write the infinitives of the verbs from **2a** on a separate sheet of paper.

Answers: marcher, aller, manger, aller, jouer, prendre, faire, boire

3 *Sur une feuille, fais le plus possible de phrases au passé composé avec les mots dans la boîte.*
Students construct sentences in the perfect tense using the words from the box.

Feuille 32 Guide pratique 1

This copymaster accompanies the *Guide pratique* on page 21 of the Students' Book. It focuses on words that have more than one dictionary definition.

1 *Choisis la bonne phrase en anglais. Vérifie dans un dictionnaire.*
Students read the French sentences and choose the most appropriate English translation of each. They look up the words in a dictionary to check their answers.

Answers: 1 b; 2 b; 3 b; 4 b

2 *Traduis en anglais. Cherche les mots soulignés dans le dictionnaire.*
Students look up the underlined words in a dictionary and translate the sentences into English.

Answers: 1 He's eating a peach. 2 He goes fishing on Saturdays. 3 He goes/climbs into the peach tree. 4 He doesn't like fishing. 5 He likes fishing at sea.

Feuille 33 Guide pratique 2

This copymaster focuses on non-literal translations and idioms. It could be used with the *Guide pratique* on page 23 of the Students' Book.

1a *Lis ces expressions idiomatiques françaises. Quel mot chercher dans le dictionnaire? Souligne.*
In each French idiom, students underline the word they would look up in a dictionary in order to find the meaning of the phrase. The answers may vary depending on which dictionary you use for this activity.

Answers: 1 bras; 2 main; 3 poche; 4 poche; 5 pied; 6 casser; 7 fourmi; 8 œil

1b *Cherche dans le dictionnaire et traduis en anglais.*
Students look up the idioms from **1a** in a dictionary and translate them into English.

Answers: 1 Dad has a lot of influence. 2 You'd swear by it. 3 He has bags under his eyes. 4 He doesn't miss a thing/He has eyes in the back of his head. 5 He's as fit as a fiddle. 6 She gets on my nerves/annoys me. 7 She has pins and needles in her leg. 8 He's glaring at his dog.

2 *Traduis en français, avec l'aide d'un dictionnaire!*
Students use a dictionary to find the French equivalents of the English phrases.

Answers: 1 J'ai assez à faire. 2 C'est le directeur. 3 Elle fait une gaffe! 4 J'improvise!

Feuille 34 Ça se dit comme ça!

Activities 1–3 focus on the differences in intonation between questions, statements and exclamations, and could be used with the *Ça se dit comme ça!* section on page 20 of the Students' Book. Activities 4–6 focus on accents and could be used with *Ça se dit comme ça!* on page 27.

1 *Écoute et coche la bonne colonne.*
Students listen and indicate whether each item is a question, an exclamation or a statement.

Answers: questions: 3, 4, 7; exclamations: 2, 6, 8; statements: 1, 5, 9

2 En forme!

CD 3, track 10
Cassette 4, side 1
Feuille 34, activité 1

1 – Juliette est assez grande et mince.
2 – Juliette est assez grande et mince!!
3 – Juliette est assez grande et mince?
4 – Elle met des jupes courtes pour aller au collège?
5 – Elle met des jupes courtes pour aller au collège.
6 – Elle met des jupes courtes pour aller au collège!!!
7 – Stéphane a très mal à la tête?
8 – Stéphane a très mal à la tête!!!
9 – Stéphane a très mal à la tête.

2 *Écoute et ajoute la ponctuation: ?, ! ou .*
Students listen and add the correct punctuation to the end of each phrase.

Answers: 1 question; 2 exclamation; 3 statement; 4 statement; 5 exclamation; 6 question

CD 3, track 11
Cassette 4, side 1
Feuille 34, activité 2

1 – Ça ne va pas, Matthieu?
2 – Elle s'appelle Natacha aussi!
3 – Elle habite à Dieppe.
4 – Son père habite au Canada.
5 – Tu détestes le look habillé!
6 – Il met un short pour aller au collège?

3 *Choisis une intonation pour ces exemples. Lis-les. Ton/Ta partenaire devine.*
Students look at the six sentences and decide whether each one is going to be a statement, an exclamation or a question. They then read out the sentences to their partner, who should be able to tell, by focusing on the intonation, what each one is supposed to be.

4 *Écoute et coche.*
Students are given a list of phrases where certain words look similar, one of the main differences being the accents. They listen and indicate which phrases are used on the recording.

Answers: see transcript below

CD 3, track 12
Cassette 4, side 1
Feuille 34, activité 4

1 – j'ai mangé
2 – je suis aux halles
3 – bien joué!
4 – il arrose
5 – tu es arrivé où?
6 – Julia habite ici

5 *Ajoute les accents. Souligne les mots quand l'accent change la prononciation. Écoute et vérifie.*
Students add the missing accents and underline the words whose pronunciation is changed by the accents. They listen to the recording to check.

Answers: see correct accents in the transcript below

CD 3, track 13
Cassette 4, side 1
Feuille 34, activité 5

1 – Je suis allée chez toi.
2 – C'est un hôtel.
3 – Elle habite où?
4 – Elle a un bébé.
5 – Tu aimes les vêtements habillés?
6 – Je préfère le look décontracté.
7 – J'ai mal à la tête.

6 *Lis les mots. Écoute et vérifie.*
Students practise pronouncing the accented words then listen to check.

CD 3, track 14
Cassette 4, side 1
Feuille 34, activité 6

– fête des mères … l'Île de Ré … pâté … À toi! … château … Tu vas où?

Encore Workbook

Page 14 (2.1)

Use with pages 20–21 of the Students' Book.

AT 3.1 **1a** *C'est quelle partie du corps? Note les numéros.*
Students match the numbered parts of the monster's body to the correct items in the vocabulary list.

Answers: a 1; b 6; c 4; d 3; e 2; f 5; g 9; h 12; i 10; j 11; k 7; l 8; m 14; n 13

AT 4.1 **1b** *Recopie les mots au bon endroit.*
Students then label the monster's body, using the words from activity **1a**.

AT 4.1 **2** *Dessine un monstre à la page 23 et écris le nom des parties du corps.*
Students draw and label their own monster.

Page 15 (2.2)

Use with pages 22–23 of the Students' Book.

AT 3.2
AT 4.2 **1** *Complète les bulles.*
Students select appropriate phrases to label the drawings representing various ailments.

Answers: a J'ai soif! b J'ai mal au ventre. c J'ai chaud. d J'ai froid. e J'ai mal aux pieds. f J'ai envie de dormir. g J'ai mal à la tête. h J'ai mal à l'oreille.

Page 16 (2.3)

Use with pages 24–25 of the Students' Book.

AT 3.2 **1** *Lis les conseils. Tu es d'accord ou pas d'accord?*
Students read the advice and tick or cross each item to show whether they agree or disagree with it.

Answers: the following captions should be ticked: Bois de l'eau! Ne va pas au lit trop tard! Mange des fruits! Va à l'école à pied! Ne mange pas de bonbons! Fais du sport!

AT 4.2 **2a** *Écris d'autres conseils.*
Students use the pictures as prompts to write some additional advice for a healthy lifestyle.

Possible answers: a Mange des oranges. b Ne mange pas de chips. c Mange des légumes/carottes. d Ne mange pas de pizza. e Ne bois pas de sodas. f Fais du jogging/sport.

AT 3.2 **2b** *Ton/Ta partenaire lit et dit "d'accord" ou "pas d'accord".*
Students show their partner what they have written in activity **2a**. The partner indicates whether or not they agree by saying *d'accord* or *pas d'accord* for each item. This open-ended activity could form the basis of oral work in which students discuss their ideas in pairs.

Page 17 (2.4)

Use with pages 26–27 of the Students' Book.

AT 3.3/4 **1** *Lis le journal de Juliette. Souligne les huit autres verbes au passé composé.*
Students search Juliette's diary for eight perfect tense verbs.

Answers: j'ai pris, j'ai mangé, j'ai bu, je suis allée, je n'ai pas mangé, je n'ai pas regardé, j'ai fait, j'ai marché

AT 4.3/4 **2** *Lis les notes de Juliette et complète son journal pour le dimanche.*
Students use the notes provided to complete Juliette's diary entry for Sunday.

Possible answers: Dimanche matin, j'ai pris un bon petit déjeuner. J'ai mangé des céréales et j'ai bu un jus de pomme. Après, j'ai fait mes devoirs.
Dimanche après-midi, je suis allée à la piscine avec Natacha. J'ai nagé pendant deux heures. Après, j'ai mangé une pomme.
Dimanche soir, j'ai regardé un film a la télé. Je suis allée au lit à neuf heures.

Page 18 Grammaire

Use with pages 22–23 of the Students' Book. Activity 1 practises *à* in the context of the unit (i.e. with *j'ai mal*); activity 2 recycles other uses of *au/à l'/à la/aux*.

1 *Complète les phrases avec "à la", "à l'", "au" ou "aux".*
Students fill in the gaps using *à la, à l', au* or *aux*.

Answers: a à la; b au; c aux; d à l'; e aux; f au; g aux

2 *Barre la mauvaise forme de la préposition "à".*
In each sentence, students cross out the incorrect form of *à*.

Answers: the correct forms are: a au; b à la; c à la; d à la; e à l'; f à la; g à l'; h aux; i à; j au

Page 19 Méli-mélo

This page focuses on the imperative and could therefore be used with pages 24–25 of the Students' Book.

1 *Barre le mauvais verbe dans les phrases du prof.*
Students cross out the incorrect verb in each sentence.

Answers: the correct forms are: a lève; b faites; c n'écris; d mangez; e discutez; f écrivez; g répétez; h fais

2 *Complète les verbes du prof et écris les verbes dans la grille.*
Students add the correct imperative ending to each verb then use these to fill in the crossword grid.

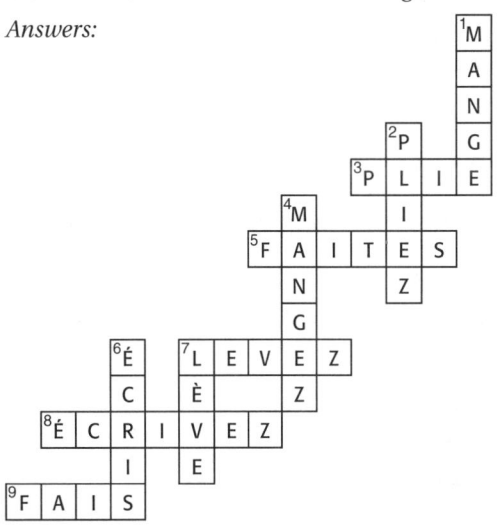

Answers:

Page 20 Challenge!

Use with page 30 of the Students' Book.

AT 3.3/4 **1** *Lis le texte A sur le voyage d'Annie et réponds aux questions pour elle à la page 23.*
Students answer questions in French on Annie's text.

Answers: 2 J'ai mangé trois repas par jour. 3 J'ai mangé du pain, du fromage, du lait, des biscuits et des olives.
4 Je suis allée à l'école. 5 J'ai fait un pique-nique rapide, j'ai mangé de la viande froide et des fruits. 6 Je n'ai pas bu de vin.

AT 3.3/4 **2** *Lis le texte B sur le voyage de Thomas. Complète ce résumé avec les participes passés dans la boîte.*
Students complete a summary of Thomas's text using the past participles given in the box.

Answers: Il est <u>allé</u> dans une famille pauvre. Il n'a pas <u>mangé</u>, mais il a beaucoup <u>travaillé</u>! L'après-midi, il a <u>fait</u> une sieste et après, il a <u>mangé</u> des galettes et il a <u>bu</u> de l'eau. Il a encore <u>travaillé</u>. Le soir, il a <u>mangé</u> des céréales, mais il n' a pas <u>bu</u> de cacao.

2 En forme!

En plus Workbook

Page 14 (2.1)
Use with pages 20–21 of the Students' Book.

AT 4.1   **1** *C'est quelle partie du corps? Écris les noms.*
Students label the monster's body. Suggest that they refer to the Students' Book if they need support with the vocabulary.

Answers: 1 la tête; 2 les yeux; 3 le nez; 4 les oreilles; 5 la bouche/les dents; 6 le cou; 7 les épaules; 8 le bras; 9 la main; 10 le doigt; 11 le dos; 12 le ventre; 13 la jambe; 14 le pied

AT 4.1   **2a** *Dessine un monstre à la page 23. Écris le nom des parties du corps.*
Students draw and label their own monster.

AT 2.3   **2b** *Décris ton monstre à ton/ta partenaire. Il/Elle dessine. Comparez!*
Students take turns to describe their monster to a partner, who draws it.

Page 15 (2.2)
Use with pages 22–23 of the Students' Book.

AT 3.2   **1** *Écris la bonne phrase de la liste sous les dessins.*
AT 4.2   Students select appropriate phrases to label the drawings representing various ailments.

Answers: a J'ai soif! b J'ai mal au ventre. c J'ai mal à la tête. d J'ai froid. e J'ai mal aux pieds. f J'ai envie de dormir.

AT 4.2   **2** *Écris une phrase pour chaque dessin.*
Students write a caption for each drawing.

Answers: J'ai chaud. J'ai mal à l'oreille.

Page 16 (2.3)
Use with pages 24–25 of the Students' Book.

AT 4.2   **1a** *Écris les conseils sur les dessins. Ils ne sont pas tous bons!*
Students write the advice represented by each picture. Point out that not all the advice is good!

Answers: a Fume! b Bois de l'eau! c Ne va pas au lit trop tard! d Mange des fruits! e Bois du soda! f Va à l'école à pied! g Ne mange pas de bonbons! h Fais du sport!

1b *Tu es d'accord ou pas d'accord?*
Students then compare their answers from activity **1a** with those of a partner and discuss whether they agree or disagree with the advice, ticking or crossing each picture as appropriate. For example: student A: *Bois de l'eau: c'est bon pour la santé*; student B: *Oui, je suis d'accord.*

AT 4.2   **2a** *Regarde les dessins. Écris d'autres conseils à la page 23.*
Students use the pictures as prompts to write some additional advice for a healthy lifestyle.

Possible answers: a Mange des oranges. b Ne mange pas de chips. c Mange des légumes/carottes. d Ne mange pas de pizza. e Ne bois pas de sodas. f Fais du jogging/sport.

AT 3.2   **2b** *Ton/Ta partenaire lit tes conseils et dit "d'accord" ou "pas d'accord".*
Students show their partner what they have written in activity **2a**. The partner indicates whether or not they agree by saying *d'accord* or *pas d'accord* for each item. This open-ended activity could form the basis of oral work in which students discuss their ideas in pairs.

Page 17 (2.4)
Use with pages 26–27 of the Students' Book.

AT 3.3/4   **1** *Lis le journal de Juliette. Complète avec les verbes au passé composé à droite.*
Students fill in the gaps in Juliette's text using the past participles given.

Answers: j'ai fait, j'ai pris, j'ai mangé, j'ai bu, je suis allée, je n'ai pas mangé, je n'ai pas regardé, j'ai fait, j'ai marché

AT 4.4   **2** *Lis les notes de Juliette et complète son journal pour le dimanche.*
Students use the notes provided to complete Juliette's diary entry for Sunday.

Possible answers: Dimanche matin, j'ai pris un bon petit déjeuner. J'ai mangé des céréales et j'ai bu un jus de pomme. Après, j'ai fait mes devoirs.
Dimanche après-midi, je suis allée à la piscine avec Natacha. J'ai nagé/J'ai fait de la natation pendant deux heures. Après, j'ai mangé une pomme.
Dimanche soir, j'ai regardé un film à la télé. Je ne suis pas allée au lit tard.

Page 18 Grammaire
Use with pages 22–23 of the Students' Book. Activity 1 practises *à* in the context of the unit (i.e. with *j'ai mal*); activity 2 recycles other uses of *au/à l'/à la/aux*.

1 *Barre la mauvaise forme de "à".*
Students cross out the incorrect forms of *à*.

Answers: the correct forms are: a à la; b au; c aux; d à l'; e aux; f au; g à la; h aux

2 *Complète avec la forme correcte de la préposition "à".*
In each sentence, students fill in the correct form of *à*.

Answers: a au; b à la; c au; d à la; e à l'; f aux; g à l'; h aux; i à; j au

3 *Traduis ces phrases en français.*
Students translate the sentences into French.

Answers: a Je prends le petit déjeuner à huit heures. b Elle va à l'école/au collège? c Il aime parler aux enfants. d J'ai mal à la jambe.

Page 19 Méli-mélo

This page focuses on the imperative, genders and plurals. It should be used towards the end of the unit, with or after pages 24–25 of the Students' Book.

1 *Complète les verbes dans les phrases du prof. Utilise le contexte pour t'aider!*
Students add the correct imperative endings, using clues within each sentence to help them decide whether to use the *tu* or the *vous* form.

Answers: a écris; b fais; c lève; d faites; e mangez; f levez; g plie; h écrivez; i pliez; j mange

2 *Écris les verbes à la bonne personne de l'impératif dans les bulles du prof.*
Students write the correct imperative form of each verb.

Answers: a écoute; b pliez; c levez; d mange; e fais; f écrivez

3 *Complète les réponses du fermier avec des pluriels. Vérifie dans le dictionnaire.*
Students fill in the correct plurals in each sentence.

Answers: a petites fermes; b beaux chevaux; c choux verts; d jolis veaux; e grands prix; f journaux locaux

4 *À la page 23, adapte la description dans la bulle pour ces personnes: (a) ta sœur (b) tes deux grands frères (c) tes deux petites sœurs.*
Students adapt the description, focusing on genders, agreements and verb forms.

Answers: a J'ai une sœur. Elle est très sympa et très marrante, mais elle est aussi patiente, sérieuse et travailleuse. Elle est grande et belle. Elle n'est pas grosse. Elle est rousse.
b J'ai deux grands frères. Ils sont très sympa et très marrants, mais ils sont aussi patients, sérieux et travailleurs. Ils sont grands et beaux. Ils ne sont pas gros. Ils sont roux.
c J'ai deux petites sœurs. Elles sont très sympa et très marrantes, mais elles sont aussi patientes, sérieuses et travailleuses. Elles sont grandes et belles. Elles ne sont pas grosses. Elles sont rousses.

Page 20 Super-challenge!

Use with page 30 of the Students' Book.

1 *Lis les deux textes. Quel texte est écrit par Annie? Et par Thomas? Pourquoi?*
Students look at the two texts and decide which one has been written by Annie and which by Thomas. They explain how they were able to work this out.

Answers: *Chez les Romains* is Annie's text; the clue lies in the opening words *Je suis allée*, where the past participle ends in the feminine *-e*. *Chez les Aztèques* uses the masculine form *je suis allé* so must have been written by Thomas.

2 *Relis. Souligne en rouge les verbes au présent. Souligne en bleu les verbes au passé composé.*
Students read the text again. They underline the present tense verbs in red and the perfect tense verbs in blue.

Answers:
Chez les Romains: present tense verbs: (une famille) habite, les enfants mangent, ils prennent, les Romains mangent, ils boivent, les filles romaines ne boivent pas, les familles pauvres prennent, les riches préfèrent; perfect tense verbs: je suis allée, j'ai mangé, j'ai pris, j'ai fait, j'ai mangé, j'ai bu, j'ai pris, j'ai mangé, je n'ai pas bu
Chez les Aztèques: present tense verbs: les enfants travaillent, les familles richent mangent … et boivent, ce n'est pas; perfect tense verbs: je suis allé, je n'ai pas beaucoup mangé, je suis allé, j'ai fait, j'ai mangé, j'ai bu, j'ai encore travaillé, je n'ai pas beaucoup mangé, je n'ai pas aimé, je n'ai pas bu

AT 3.4/5

3 *Réponds aux questions sur Annie à la page 23.*
Students answer questions in French about Annie.

Answers: b Le matin, elle a mangé du pain et du fromage. Elle a bu du lait. c Le midi, elle a mangé un pique-nique à l'école. d Elle a mangé le dîner après l'école vers 15 heures.

AT 4.4/5

4 *Résume le texte de Thomas en 60 mots à la page 23. Utilise "il".*
Students summarize Thomas's text in French, in about 60 words.

Révisions Unités 1–2

This revision spread provides consolidation and further practice of language from Units 1–2. You can take students through the activities as a whole class, or they can work independently or in pairs. The activities should help students prepare for the assessment for Units 1–2.

Resources
Students' Book, pages 33–34
CD 1, tracks 37–38
Cassette 1, side 2

AT 3.2 **1a** *Relie les questions et les réponses. Quelle est la question qui manque?*
Students match up the questions and answers and supply the missing question.

Answers: 1 b; 2 i; 3 f; 4 c; 5 e; 6 a; 7 h; 8 g; 9 d Qu'est-ce qui ne va pas?/Ça va?

AT 2.2/3 **1b** *Joue au morpion avec un(e) partenaire. Pour gagner, réponds aux questions pour toi. Invente une question pour le numéro 9!*
Students play Noughts and Crosses using the questions from **1a**. In order to "win" a square, they must supply their own details in answer to the question. They make up their own question for number 9.

AT 1.3 **2** *Écoute. Qui parle a–d?*
Students listen to the conversations about clothes and match the speakers to the pictures.

Answers: 1 c; 2 d; 3 b; 4 a

CD 1, track 37 page 33, activité 2
Cassette 1, side 2

1 – C'est quoi, ta tenue préférée?
 – Moi, j'aime mon jean, mon sweat jaune et mes bottes.
 – Tu aimes le look décontracté?
 – Oui, c'est ça! Le look décontracté, c'est pratique.
2 – Toi, aussi, tu aimes le look décontracté?
 – Non, moi, je préfère le look sport.
 – C'est quoi, ta tenue préférée?
 – Ma tenue préférée. C'est un short, un tee-shirt et des baskets.
3 – C'est quoi, ta tenue préférée?
 – Ma tenue préférée? C'est une jupe rouge, une chemise blanche et une veste noire.
 – Avec des bottes.
 – Non, avec des chaussures noires.
 – Tu aimes le look habillé, c'est ça?
 – Oui, c'est ça!
4 – C'est quoi, ta tenue préférée?
 – Ça dépend. Je mets un jean ou un petit pantalon gris, avec un sweat ou un pull. Je mets toujours mes grosses chaussures noires.
 – Tu aimes le look décontracté?
 – Oui, le look décontracté, c'est sympa.

AT 4.3 **3** *Invente un uniforme d'été et d'hiver pour tes profs. Écris des explications.*
Students invent and describe a school uniform for summer and winter for their own teachers.

AT 3.3/4 **4a** *Lis l'e-mail de Khalida. Choisis la bonne réponse.*
Students read Khalida's e-mail and select the correct answer to each question.

Answers: 1 b; 2 a; 3 a; 4 a; 5 b; 6 b

AT 4.3 **4b** *Écris les réponses aux questions.*
Students write full answers to the questions in **4a**.

Answers: 1 Sammy est anglais. 2 Il est grand et blond. 3 Elle met une robe et des sandales. 4 Elle a mangé du poulet avec des légumes et elle a bu du lait. 5 Elle a chaud, mal au ventre et elle a envie de vomir. 6 Elle va au lit.

AT 1.3/4 **5** *Écoute les cinq conversations et note les problèmes. Il y a un ou plusieurs symptômes. Choisis un conseil pour chaque personne.*
Students listen to the five conversations and note down each person's symptoms. They select an appropriate piece of advice for each person.

Answers: 2 mal au pied: c; 3 rhume des foins: e; 4 mal à la tête: d; 5 froid, chaud, mal à la tête, de la fièvre, mal à la gorge, je tousse, mal au ventre, envie de vomir, la grippe: a

---

CD 1, track 38 page 34, activité 5
Cassette 1, side 2

1 – Oh là là, ça ne va pas.
 – Qu'est-ce qui ne va pas?
 – C'est ma sœur.
 – Qu'est-ce qu'elle a, ta sœur? Elle est malade?
 – Elle dit qu'elle a de la fièvre.
 – Elle a la grippe?
 – Non non, mais elle a très très mal aux dents.
2 – Oh, ça ne va pas …
 – Qu'est-ce qui ne va pas?
 – J'ai eu un accident, là, en sortant du bus. Je me suis fait mal, très mal!
 – Un accident?
 – Oui, je suis tombé … Aïeeeeeeeeee! Mon pied! J'ai mal au pied!
 – Montre … Oh là là! C'est horrible! Ton pied! Il est peut-être cassé!
3 – Atchoum … Atchoum …
 – Tu as un rhume?
 – Non, pas vraiment … Atchoum … Atchoum …
 – Tu tousses?
 – Non, pas vraiment. En fait, j'ai commencé à éternuer au début du printemps. J'ai toujours mal au nez comme ça au printemps et en été, quand il fait chaud!
 – Mais alors, c'est peut-être le rhume des foins.
4 – Oh là là, j'ai mal à la tête.
 – Bois un jus d'orange, c'est très bon quand on a mal à la tête. C'est plein de vitamine C.
 – J'ai déjà bu trois grands verres de jus d'orange.
 – Mange des kiwis, c'est bon aussi.

– J'ai mangé quatre kiwis!
– Et tu as toujours mal?
– Ben oui, j'ai de plus en plus mal! …
5 – Brrr …
– Ça ne va pas?
– Non, j'ai froid, j'ai chaud et j'ai mal à la tête …
– Oh! Tu as de la fièvre?
– Oui, je crois. Hier aussi, j'avais de la fièvre. Et j'ai mal à la gorge …
– Tu tousses?
– Oui, je tousse … Aïe, mon ventre! J'ai mal au ventre quand je tousse … et j'ai envie de vomir …
– Moi, je crois que tu as la grippe …

Contrôle Unités 1–2

For general comments on assessment, see page 22 of the Introduction.

Resources
Copymasters 103–110
CD 3, tracks 43–48
Cassette 1, side 2

Feuille 103   Écoute Encore

AT 1.2 1 *Écoute le défilé de mode. Retrouve le nom des mannequins.*
Students listen to the fashion show commentary and match the models' names to their outfits.

Answers: 1 Amélie; 2 Sidonie; 3 Christian; 4 Alain; 5 Emma

Mark scheme: 1 mark for each = 5 marks

Assessment criteria: Students who achieve 4 or 5 marks show evidence of performance at AT 1.2.

CD 3, track 43   Feuille 103, activité 1
Cassette 1, side 2

– Voici Christian. Il a un short, un sweat, une casquette et des baskets … Maintenant, c'est Alain. Il a un pantalon, un tee-shirt et des chaussures … Ah, voici Amélie. Elle a un blouson, un pull, un jean et des bottes … Nous avons maintenant Emma. Elle a une jupe, une chemise, une veste et des sandales … Et voilà Sidonie. Elle a une robe et … une cravate … hmmm. Bizarre!

AT 1.3 2 *Écoute deux jeunes chez le médecin. Qu'est-ce qui ne va pas? Coche.*
Students listen to the two conversations at the doctor's and tick the pictures to indicate each person's symptoms.

Answers: Antoine: headache, sore throat, cough, high temperature; Lucien: stomach ache, feeling sick, sore neck, headache

Mark scheme: 1 mark for each correct tick = 8 marks

Assessment criteria: Students who achieve 7–8 marks show evidence of performance at AT 1.3.

CD 3, track 44   Feuille 103, activité 2
Cassette 1, side 2

– Alors, Antoine, qu'est-ce qui ne va pas aujourd'hui?
– J'ai mal à la tête, docteur, et j'ai très mal à la gorge.
– Tu tousses?
– Euh oui, je tousse un peu.
– D'accord. Et est-ce que tu as de la fièvre?
– Oui, j'ai de la fièvre. J'ai pris ma température et j'ai 39 …

– Bien, maintenant c'est Lucien, c'est ça?
– Oui, docteur.
– Qu'est-ce qui ne va pas?
– J'ai mal au ventre, docteur, très mal au ventre.
– Ah bon? Tu as envie de vomir?
– Oui, j'ai envie de vomir. Et j'ai très mal au cou et à la tête.
– Hmmm, tu as mal au cou et à la tête … Et le dos? Tu as mal au dos?
– Non, je n'ai pas mal au dos …

AT 1.4 3 *Écoute ta correspondante se présenter. Note les détails.*
Students listen to Anya speaking about herself and note down in French the details of what she says.

Answers: âge: 14; nationalité: française; description: grande, mince, brune; santé: rhume, tousse; vêtements: jean, tee-shirt (rouge), blouson (bleu), casquette, baskets

Mark scheme: 1 mark for each correct answer = 12 marks

Assessment criteria: Students who achieve 9 marks or more show evidence of performance at AT 1.4.

CD 3, track 45   Feuille 103, activité 3
Cassette 1, side 2

– Salut! Je suis ta nouvelle correspondante! Je m'appelle Anya Moulin, j'épelle, c'est A-N-Y-A M-O-U-L-I-N. J'ai 14 ans. Je suis française, mais ma mère est algérienne. Je suis grande, mince et brune. En ce moment, j'ai un rhume et je tousse beaucoup! Pour venir chez toi, je vais porter ma tenue préférée: un jean … un tee-shirt rouge … un blouson bleu … une casquette … et … des baskets. Voilà. À bientôt!

Feuille 104   Écoute En plus

AT 1.3 1 *Écoute le défilé de mode. Dessine le vêtement qui manque sur chacun.*
Students listen to the fashion show commentary while studying the pictures of the models: an item of clothing is missing from each model. They first need to work out which picture represents each person; they then draw the missing items of clothing on the pictures.

Answers: 1 red boots; 2 tie; 3 white cap; 4 black shoes; 5 blue sandals

Mark scheme: 1 mark for each correct item = 5 marks

Assessment criteria: Students who score 4 or 5 marks show evidence of performance at AT 1.3.

CD 3, track 46   Feuille 104, activité 1
Cassette 1, side 2

– Voici Christian, qui aujourd'hui porte un short bleu, un sweat vert, une casquette blanche et des baskets blanches … Maintenant, c'est Alain. Il a un pantalon noir, un tee-shirt bleu et des chaussures noires … Ah, voici Amélie, qui porte un blouson rouge, un pull blanc, un jean bleu et des bottes rouges … Nous avons maintenant Emma qui a une jupe verte, une chemise verte, une veste bleue et des sandales bleues … Et voilà Sidonie. Elle a une robe longue et … une cravate … hmm. Bizarre …

Contrôle Unités 1–2

AT 1.4 **2** *Marque quatre choses qui ne vont pas pour Martin [M] et quatre choses pour Guillaume [G].*
Students listen to the two conversations at the doctor's and indicate each person's symptoms.

Answers: Martin: sore throat, cough, fever, hay fever; Guillaume: sore head, sore neck, feeling sleepy, sore eyes

Mark scheme: 1 mark for each correct symptom = 8 marks

Assessment criteria: Students who achieve 7–8 marks show evidence of performance at AT 1.4.

CD 3, track 47   **Feuille 104, activité 2**
Cassette 1, side 2

– Alors Martin, qu'est-ce qui ne va pas aujourd'hui?
– Je tousse un peu. Et quand je tousse, j'ai mal à la gorge! Atchoum! Atchoum! Et puis, j'ai un peu de fièvre … c'est grave, non?

– Bien, maintenant c'est Guillaume, c'est ça?
– Oui, docteur.
– Qu'est-ce qui ne va pas?
– J'ai mal à la tête, docteur, très mal à la tête. Et aux yeux aussi, mal, mal aux yeux. Et j'ai très mal au cou.
– Hmmm, tu as mal à la tête, aux yeux, au cou, … hmmm, je n'aime pas ça …
– Et j'ai envie de dormir, j'ai très envie de dormir, mais j'ai trop mal à la tête …
– Allez, vite à l'hôpital, c'est urgent! J'appelle une ambulance.

AT 1.4/5 **3** *Écoute ta nouvelle correspondante. Réponds sur une feuille.*
Students listen to Malika talking about herself and note down in French the details of what she says.

Answers: 1 Malika Poulain; 2 15; 3 française; 4 fille unique; 5 petite, mince et blonde (2 marks); 6 tousse, mal aux yeux (half mark each = 1 mark); 7 beaucoup de sport, mange beaucoup de fruits/légumes (half mark each = 1 mark); 8 frites, coca (half mark each = 1 mark); 9 short, tee-shirt, casquette, baskets (half mark each = 2 marks); 10 le look sport

Mark scheme: 1 mark per correct response unless otherwise indicated above = 12 marks

Assessment criteria: Students who achieve 10 marks or more show evidence of performance at AT 1.5; students who achieve 5–9 marks show evidence of performance at AT 1.4.

CD 3, track 48   **Feuille 104, activité 3**
Cassette 1, side 2

– Salut! Je suis ta nouvelle correspondante! Je m'appelle Malika Poulain, j'épelle, c'est M-A-L-I-K-A P-O-U-L-A-I-N. J'ai 15 ans. Mon anniversaire, c'est le 15 mars. Je suis française, mais ma mère est marocaine. Je suis fille unique. Je suis petite, mince et blonde.

Ah là là! En ce moment, j'ai un rhume des foins, alors, je tousse beaucoup et j'ai mal aux yeux! Mon nez et mes yeux sont tout rouges!
Mais, en général, je suis très en forme. Je fais beaucoup de sport et je mange beaucoup de fruits et légumes. Hier, par contre, je suis allée au Macdo avec une copine et j'ai mangé des frites et bu du coca. Tu aimes ça, toi? Moi, je déteste!
Pour venir chez toi, je vais porter ma tenue préférée: un short, un tee-shirt, une casquette et des baskets. J'adore le look sport. Voilà. À bientôt!

Feuille 105   Parle Encore

Students work in pairs for these activities. Give the top half of the sheet to one student and the bottom half to their partner.

AT 2.2 **1a/1b** Students take turns to tell each other what they wear to a party.

Mark scheme: 1 mark for each correct garment mentioned = 5 marks

Assessment criteria: Students who are able to mention 4 or 5 appropriate garments show evidence of performance at AT 2.2.

AT 2.3 **2a/2b** Students take turns to tell each other what is wrong with them, using the pictures as prompts.

Mark scheme: 1 mark for each correct part of the body, 1 mark for each correct use of *au/à l'/à la/aux* = 10 marks

Assessment criteria: Students who achieve 8 or more marks show evidence of performance at AT 2.3.

AT 2.4/5 **3a/3b** Students interview each other using the questions supplied.

Mark scheme: 2 marks for each correct response (1 mark for content, 1 mark for accuracy of language) = 10 marks

Assessment criteria: Students who demonstrate ability to express themselves in the past tense and who achieve 8 or more marks are beginning to show evidence of performance at AT 2.5; students who achieve 5–7 marks show evidence of performance at AT 2.4.

Feuille 106   Parle En plus

Students work in pairs for these activities. Give the top half of the sheet to one student and the bottom half to their partner.

AT 2.3 **1a** *Ton/Ta partenaire a cinq problèmes de santé. Pose cinq questions et coche.*
1b *Choisis cinq "problèmes". Réponds oui/non à ton/ta partenaire.*
Each student chooses five ailments from those pictured, but hides them from their partner. They then take turns to question each other to find out each other's ailments.

Contrôle Unités 1–2

Mark scheme: 1 mark for each correct question = 5 marks

Assessment criteria: Students who correctly ask 4 or 5 questions show evidence of performance at AT 2.3.

AT 2.4/5 **2a** *Pose les questions de la fiche à ton/ta partenaire. Note ses réponses.*
2b *Regarde les détails. Imagine que tu es David/Daisy (Ravi/Aïsha). Réponds aux questions de ton/ta partenaire.*
Each student is given information in English about one of the characters (David/Daisy or Ravi/Aïsha). They play the role of their character, answering their partner's questions.

Mark scheme: 4 marks for question 1; 2 marks for question 2; 6 marks for question 3 (3 marks for content, 3 marks for accurate use of the perfect tense) = 12 marks

Assessment criteria: Students who achieve 10 or more marks and who are able to use the perfect tense correctly are beginning to show signs of performance at AT 2.5; students who achieve 5–9 marks show evidence of performance at AT 2.4.

Feuille 107   Lis Encore

AT 3.2 **1** *Choisis une phrase pour chaque personne.*
Students match the descriptions of appearance and clothing to the pictures.

Answers: 1 c; 2 d; 3 a; 4 e

Mark scheme: 2 marks for each correct choice = 8 marks

Assessment criteria: Students who achieve 6 marks or more show evidence of performance at AT 3.2.

AT 3.3 **2** *Lis la carte et souligne les bons mots.*
Students read Constantin's letter about how he ended up in hospital. They then circle the correct phrase in each statement to give a summary of the main points.

Answers: 1 Constantin, à l'hôpital; 2 au genou, au pied; 3 chez le médecin; 4 sa jambe; 5 n'est pas content, des repas

Mark scheme: 1 mark per correct choice = 8 marks

Assessment criteria: Students who achieve 6 marks or more show evidence of performance at AT 3.3.

AT 3.4/5 **3** *Relis la carte et réponds en anglais.*
Students read the letter again and answer comprehension questions in English.

Answers: 1 yesterday; 2 car accident; 3 outside school; 4 she has a headache and a sore back; 5 he says you don't eat very well in hospital; 6 he thinks he's caught a cold; 7 some crisps and his blue pullover

Mark scheme: 1 mark per correct answer = 9 marks

Assessment criteria: Students who achieve 8 or 9 marks are beginning to show evidence of performance at AT 3.5; students who achieve 4–7 marks show evidence of performance at AT 3.4.

Feuille 108   Lis En plus

AT 3.3 **1a** *Choisis une phrase pour chaque personne.*
Students match the descriptions of clothing to the pictures. One description does not have a corresponding picture.

Answers: 1 b; 2 a; 3 d

1b *Dessine la tenue de la quatrième personne.*
Students draw the clothes that feature in description c.

Answers: black trousers, white shirt, black tie

Mark scheme: 2 marks for each correct answer in 1a, 2 marks for 1b = 8 marks

Assessment criteria: Students who achieve 7 or 8 marks show evidence of performance at AT 3.3.

AT 3.4 **2** *Lis le journal de Khalida. Écris les mots qui manquent sur une feuille.*
Students read Khalida's diary and note down the missing words.

Answers: 1 allée; 2 ventre; 3 vomir; 4 parce que; 5 forme; 6 légumes; 7 bois; 8 sodas/coca; 9 mets; 10 look

Mark scheme: 1 mark for each word = 10 marks

Assessment criteria: Students who achieve 8 marks or more show evidence of performance at AT 3.4.

AT 3.4/5 **3** *Réponds aux questions en anglais sur une feuille.*
Students answer questions in English on Khalida's diary.

Answers: 1 a boy in Khalida's class at school; 2 tall, blond, good-looking and very nice; 3 stomach ache and feeling sick so went to bed; 4 healthy food, e.g. vegetables with meat or fish, lots of fruit; 5 because her mother said it helps when you have stomach ache and feel sick; 6 going to the cinema with Sammy; 7 her short skirt, T-shirt and red trainers because it's practical and comfortable

Mark scheme: 1 mark for each correct answer = 7 marks

Assessment criteria: Students who achieve 6 or 7 marks are beginning to show evidence of performance at AT 3.5; students who achieve 4–5 marks show evidence of performance at AT 3.4.

Feuille 109   Écris Encore

AT 4.2 **1** *Complète chaque phrase avec quatre vêtements.*
Students complete the sentences with appropriate items of clothing.

Mark scheme: 1 mark for each correctly spelt item of clothing = 8 marks

Assessment criteria: Students who achieve 6 marks or more show evidence of performance at AT 4.2.

AT 4.3/4 **2** *Adapte l'e-mail de Sophie pour parler de toi.*
Students write a paragraph about themselves, using the text provided as a model. They replace Sophie's details with their own.

Contrôle Unités 1–2

Mark scheme: first six sentences: 1 mark for each piece of information correctly substituted; final sentence: 2 marks; total = 8 marks

Assessment criteria: Students who achieve 7 or 8 marks show evidence of performance at AT 4.4; students who achieve 4–6 marks show evidence of performance at AT 4.3.

AT 4.4/5

3 *Réponds aux questions.*
Students provide written answers to questions about their eating habits and any sports they do.

Mark scheme: 3 marks per pair of answers (1 mark for a, 1 mark for b, 1 mark for spelling and accuracy of language) = 9 marks

Assessment criteria: Students who demonstrate ability to express themselves in the past tense and who achieve 7 or more marks are beginning to show evidence of performance at AT 4.5; students who achieve 4–6 marks show evidence of performance at AT 4.4.

Feuille 110 Écris En plus

AT 4.3

1 *Complète les phrases et décris au moins deux symptômes dans chacune.*
Students complete the sentences, giving at least two symptoms for each ailment.

Possible answers: accept any appropriate symptoms

Mark scheme: 1 mark for each symptom = 4 marks

Assessment criteria: Students who achieve 4 marks show evidence of performance at AT 4.3.

AT 4.4

2 *Qu'est-ce que tu as fait le week-end dernier pour être en forme? Regarde les dessins et écris un paragraphe (utilise et/mais/parce que).*
Students write a paragraph in the perfect tense to describe the activities shown in the pictures.

Possible answer: Le week-end dernier, j'ai fait de l'exercice/du sport, mais je ne suis pas allé(e) à la piscine parce que je n'aime pas la natation. J'ai mangé des fruits et des légumes parce que c'est bon pour la santé, et j'ai bu un litre d'eau. Par contre, je n'ai pas bu de sodas et je n'ai pas mangé de pizza ou de frites parce que ce n'est pas bon pour la santé.

Mark scheme: 1 mark for describing each picture, plus 3 extra marks for use of connectives = 9 marks

Assessment criteria: Students who achieve 7 marks or more show evidence of performance at AT 4.4.

AT 4.4/5

3 *Lis le message de Mehdi. Écris une réponse sur une feuille. Regarde les notes.*
Students write a few paragraphs giving information about themselves, their lifestyle, health, fitness, etc., what they did last weekend, and their favourite style of clothing. Draw their attention to the guidance on mark allocation provided on the sheet.

Mark scheme: 2 marks for personal details, 4 marks for fitness, 4 marks for what they did last weekend, 2 marks for favourite style of clothes = 12 marks

Assessment criteria: Students who demonstrate ability to express themselves in the past tense and who achieve 9 marks or more show evidence of performance at AT 4.5; students who achieve 5–8 marks show evidence of performance at AT 4.4.

Unit 3 Overview grid

Pages/Contexts/ Cultural focus	Objectives	Grammar	Skills and Pronunciation	Key language	Framework	PoS	AT level
36–37 **3.1 Sélection télé** TV programmes Opinions	Name different types of TV programme; say what types of TV programme you like/dislike; use connectives to give more detailed answers; understand feedback on work		Using connectives Expressing opinions	*un documentaire, un film, un dessin animé (les dessins animés), un feuilleton, un jeu (les jeux), une émission sportive (les émissions sportives), une émission pour la jeunesse, une série, la météo, les informations* *J'adore/J'aime (bien)/Je préfère/Je n'aime pas/Je déteste (regarder) … C'est génial/intéressant/drôle. Ce n'est pas mal. Ce n'est pas marrant. C'est nul/débile.* *et, mais, parce que, comme, aussi, par contre*	8W1, 8W3 – L 8W2 – R	1c, 2a, 2c, 2d, 2f, 2g, 2i, 3b, 3c, 3e, 4a, 4c, 4d, 5a, 5b, 5c, 5d, 5e, 5f, 5i	1.2–3, 2.2–4, 3.1, 4.2–4
38–39 **3.2 On va au cinéma?** Types of film The 24-hour clock	Name different types of film; say what film you are going to see at the cinema; revise telling the time and learn the 24-hour clock; say what time a film is on	*aller* + infinitive	Silent endings and pronounced endings	*Qu'est-ce que tu vas voir au cinéma? Je vais voir … C'est un film d'aventure, un film policier, un film de science-fiction, un film d'horreur, un western, une comédie, un film romantique, un dessin animé. C'est à quelle heure? C'est à 20 h 30.*	8W6 – L 8W5, 8S7 – R	1a, 1b, 1c, 2a, 2b, 2c, 2d, 2f, 2h, 3b, 3c, 3d, 3e, 4a, 4c, 4d, 5a, 5c, 5d, 5e, 5f, 5i	1.2–3, 2.2–3, 3.3, 4.2–4
40–41 **3.3 On organise un rendez-vous** Invitations Arranging to meet	Ask someone if they'd like to do something; say that you would like to do something; arrange a time to meet; arrange a place to meet	*vouloir*	Listening for gist and detail	*Tu veux aller au cinéma/au parc/à la piscine/à la plage/à la patinoire/en ville? Tu veux faire du vélo/nager/danser? Oui, je veux bien. On se retrouve à quelle heure? À cinq heures. On se retrouve où? Chez moi/toi. Au parc/Au café/À la piscine. Devant la bibliothèque.*	8S3, 8L3 – L	1b, 1c, 2a, 2c, 2d, 2f, 2g, 2h, 2i, 3a, 3b, 3c, 3d, 3e, 4a, 5a, 5c, 5d, 5e, 5f, 5i	1.2–3, 2.2–3, 3.3, 4.3–4
42–43 **3.4 Que d'excuses!** Using the telephone Declining an invitation and giving excuses	Understand and give telephone numbers; make a telephone call; decline an invitation using *pouvoir*; give excuses for not going out using *devoir*; take part in unscripted exchanges	*pouvoir, devoir, vouloir*		*C'est quoi, le numéro de téléphone? C'est le 04 34 56 78 91. Allô. C'est Matthieu? Oui, c'est Matthieu. Est-ce que je peux parler à Arnaud, s'il te plaît/s'il vous plaît? Oui, attends/attendez. Ne quittez/quittez pas. Tu veux venir chez moi/aller au cinéma? Je ne peux pas. Je dois faire mes devoirs/aller voir ma grand-mère/promener mon frère/garder le chien/ranger ma chambre.*	8L5, 8C3 – L	1a, 1b, 1c, 2a, 2b, 2c, 2d, 2e, 2f, 2g, 2h, 3a, 3b, 3c, 3d, 3e, 4a, 4c, 4d, 5a, 5b, 5d, 5e, 5f, 5i	1.2–3, 2.2–4, 3.2–3, 4.2–4
44–45 **3.5 La belle équipe, épisode 3** Soap story	Develop listening and reading skills via a soap story based on the language of the unit					1a, 1c, 2a, 2b, 2g, 2h, 2i, 3b, 3c, 3e, 4a, 4d, 5a, 5d, 5e, 5g, 5i	1.4, 2.4, 3.4, 4.2–3
46 **Super-challenge!** Arrangements to meet	Develop the use of the modal verbs *vouloir, pouvoir* and *devoir*	*pouvoir, devoir, vouloir* (plural forms)				1b, 1c, 2a, 2c, 2d, 2h, 3b, 3c, 3d, 3e, 4a, 5d, 5e, 5i	1.3, 3.3

ÉQUIPE NOUVELLE 2 UNIT 3 MEDIUM TERM PLAN

About this unit: In this unit students work in the context of free time and leisure, including watching television, going out and going to the cinema. They learn to name and describe different types of programme and film, state and justify preferences, give, accept and refuse invitations. At the same time, they develop their ability to build sentences using a range of connectives, modal verbs and verbs in different tenses, especially the future with *aller*, as well as improving their understanding of question types and their sensitivity to intonation. The unit features young people's attitudes to the media and also provides opportunities to research information about French film stars and popular French television programmes. Progress at word level is developed via the language of opinions and exceptions to sound–spelling rules.

Framework objectives (launch)	Teaching and learning	Week-by-week overview (assuming 6 weeks' work or 10–12.5 hours)
8W1: adding abstract words	Express opinions.	**Week 1** Introduction to unit objectives. Name types of TV programme. Say what types of TV programme you like/dislike. Express opinions. Use connectives to give more detailed answers. Understand feedback on work.
8W3: words about progress	Understand feedback on oral and written work.	
8W6: sound–spelling exceptions	Pronunciation with telling the time: when to pronounce the endings of numbers and when not to pronounce them, e.g. *dix-neuf heures dix en dix minutes*.	**Week 2** Name different types of film. Say what film you are going to see at the cinema, using *aller* + infinitive. Revise telling the time and learn the 24-hour clock. Say what time a film is on. Learn about silent endings and pronounced endings.
8S3: modal verbs	How to recognize and use *vouloir*, *pouvoir*, *devoir*. Recognize similarities in construction in *vouloir* and *pouvoir*.	
8L3: relaying gist and detail	Understand the gist and detail of answerphone messages confirming time and place to meet.	**Week 3** Ask someone if they'd like to do something, using *vouloir* + infinitive. Accept an invitation and say that you would like to do something. Arrange a time and place to meet. Develop skills in listening for gist and detail.
8L5: unscripted speech	Develop classroom language. Ask for help and information using *pouvoir*: *Est-ce que tu peux me passer un stylo, s'il te plaît? Est-ce que vous pouvez répéter cela, s'il vous plaît?*	
8C3: daily life and young people	Make a telephone call in France: telephone numbers read out in pairs (*cinquante-trois, quarante-sept*, etc.) compared with English where read out as individual numbers (five, three, four, seven, etc.). French regional dialling codes.	**Week 4** Understand and give telephone numbers. Make a telephone call. Decline an invitation using *pouvoir*. Give excuses for not going out using *devoir*.
Framework objectives (reinforce)	**Teaching and learning**	
8W2: connectives	Use of connectives to give more detailed answers.	**Week 5** Develop listening and reading skills via a soap episode.
8W5: verb tenses	Near future using *aller* + infinitive.	
8S7: present, past and future	Near future using *aller* + infinitive.	**Week 6** *Super-challenge!* for more able students. Recycle language of the unit via *Encore*, *En plus* and *Point lecture* pages. Students check progress via the *Podium* self-assessment checklist in the Students' Book and on Feuille 36.
8C2: famous people	Students research and write about a famous French film star on the *Point lecture* page.	
	Teaching and learning (additional)	
	TV programmes. Language of opinions. Types of film. Revise numbers. Telling the time and 24-hour clock. Revise activities, places to visit. Meeting places. Excuses not to go out.	

3 On se relaxe!

Unit objectives
Contexts: TV and cinema; going out
Grammar: *aller* + infinitive; modal verbs: *vouloir, pouvoir, devoir*
Language learning: using connectives; listening for gist and detail
Pronunciation: sound–spelling exceptions
Cultural focus: TV channels; the 24-hour clock

Assessment opportunities
Listening: Students' Book, page 37, activity 3a; Students' Book, page 112, *En plus*, activity 1
Speaking: Students' Book, page 40, activity 1c; Students' Book, page 112, *En plus*, activity 3

This opening page introduces the main themes of the unit, including the 24-hour clock. You might decide to teach the 24-hour clock now rather than later in the unit so that students can discuss programme times and feed back answers as fully as possible.

AT 3.3 **1** *Lis le programme de télé. Recopie et complète la grille.*
Students scan the extract from a French TV guide and fill in the grid, giving programme titles, times and channels. You may wish to explain the word *divertissement*, which appears twice (see TF1 and France 2), although students don't actually need to understand the word in order to complete the activity.

Answers: a 20.05; b Des chiffres et des lettres, France 2; c Questions pour un champion; d 18.00, France 2; e Canal +

2 *Tu reconnais des émissions? C'est quoi en anglais?*
Students consider whether there are any programmes they recognize, and give their English titles. Encourage them to use clues such as cognates to deduce the programme titles.

Some possible answers: La Ferme Célébrités (The Farm); Des chiffres et des lettres (Countdown); Urgences (ER); Questions pour un champion (A Question of Sport)

3 *En anglais, compare avec un programme de télé chez toi.*
In this quick activity in English, students compare the extracts with a UK TV guide, looking at types of programme, different channels, use of the 24-hour clock, etc.

Follow-up activity: You could provide students with the following information about French TV channels:
▶ There are six main TV channels in France: France 2, France 3 and La Cinquième/Arte are state-owned but still carry advertising; TF1 and M6 are private channels; Canal + is a pay channel.
▶ Those living in certain regions can also receive Télé-Monte-Carlo (TMC) or Radio-Télé-Luxembourg (RTL).
▶ In addition, there are numerous satellite and cable channels. See additional information about cable channels given on the Unit 3 *Point lecture* page (page 124 of the Students' Book).

On se relaxe! 3

Planning Page

3.1 Sélection télé — pages 36–37

Objectives

- Name different types of TV programme
- Say what types of TV programme you like/dislike (**8W1 – L**)
- Use connectives to give more detailed answers (**8W2 – R**)
- Understand feedback on work (**8W3 – L**)

Resources

Students' Book, pages 36–37
CD 1, tracks 39–40; CD 3, tracks 15 and 17
Cassette 2, side 1; cassette 4, side 1
Encore/En plus Workbooks, page 24
OHTs 11, 12A and 12B
Copymasters 37, 39, 40 and 50

Key language

un documentaire, un film, un dessin animé (les dessins animés), un feuilleton, un jeu (les jeux), une émission sportive (les émissions sportives), une émission pour la jeunesse, une série, la météo, les informations
J'adore/J'aime (bien)/Je préfère/Je n'aime pas/Je déteste (regarder) …
C'est génial/intéressant/drôle. Ce n'est pas mal. Ce n'est pas marrant. C'est nul/débile.
et, mais, parce que
comme, aussi, par contre

Programme of Study reference

1c, 2a, 2c, 2d, 2f, 2g, 2i, 3b, 3c, 3e, 4a, 4c, 4d, 5a, 5b, 5c, 5d, 5e, 5f, 5i

Starters

- *À vos marques*, page 36.
- Copymaster 37 *À vos marques*: activities 1a–1c could be used after the *Guide pratique* section on connectives.
- Whole-class game: students agree an action to represent each TV programme, e.g. clapping for *un jeu*; say aloud the names of the programmes and ask students to perform the corresponding actions. Anyone who does the wrong action or is too slow sits down and is out of the game.
- A copy of the transcript for activity **1b** could be given to students while working on the connectives on this spread. Ask them to underline in different colours the different types of programme, opinions and connectives.

ICT suggestions

- Students use desktop publishing, clip art and interesting fonts to design a poster about their favourite TV programme.
- Students write up their results from the survey in activity **4**, using ICT to present their findings effectively.
- Students word-process a first draft of their texts for the *Challenge!* activities. They then ask a partner or the teacher to read and comment on their work, before preparing their final draft.

Creative activities

- Students devise a rap of the TV programmes and opinions to aid vocabulary learning.
- Students make crosswords using actual titles of programmes as clues and the corresponding French words for programme types as the solutions, e.g. the solution to the clue *The Simpsons* would be *un dessin animé*.
- Students record or video themselves giving a short oral presentation (as in the speech bubble in the *Guide pratique* box on Students' Book page 37) about their TV likes and dislikes. This could be prepared for homework in advance and students could listen to or watch the recordings afterwards to decide on the best one.

Plenaries

- *Challenge!* page 37.
- Students summarize what they have learned in the lesson in their own words, working first with a partner, then joining with another two students before reporting back to the class.
- Students play Word Tennis, following a model on the board or OHP, e.g.
  A: *J'aime …*
  B: *… les documentaires parce que …*
  A: *… c'est super!*
  B: *Je n'aime pas …*
- Students have 30 seconds to write as many types of TV programme as they can. They then check their list with a partner, scoring a point for every programme spelt correctly and a bonus point if they have listed a programme that is not on their partner's list. The same activity could be used with opinions.

Homework suggestions

- Students learn vocabulary and key expressions (meaning, pronunciation, gender and spelling) and make a game to test themselves or a partner.
- Students prepare a short oral presentation (as in the speech bubble in the *Guide pratique* box on Students' Book page 37) on their TV likes and dislikes.
- Students could interview family members or friends (in English or in French) about their TV likes and dislikes and write up their findings, e.g. *Mon père aime les informations parce que c'est intéressant.*
- *Encore/En plus* Workbooks, page 24.

3 On se relaxe!

3.1 Sélection télé — pages 36–37

À vos marques

Parle de la télé pendant deux minutes.
In this quick starter activity, students talk about likes and dislikes of TV programmes. The use of English programme titles helps to get them interested in the topic. The activity also revises simple opinions; if appropriate, brainstorm different ways of giving positive and negative opinions before students begin.

AT 3.1 **1a** *Regarde les photos et les Mots-clés. C'est quel genre d'émission?*
Students study the photos and indicate which type of TV programme is represented by each. Encourage them to use clues such as cognates to deduce the answers or to look up words in the glossary if necessary.

Answers: 1 un jeu; 2 un documentaire; 3 une émission sportive; 4 un dessin animé; 5 un feuilleton; 6 les informations; 7 la météo; 8 une émission pour la jeunesse; 9 un film; 10 une série

AT 1.2 **1b** *Écoute et vérifie.*
Students listen to check their answers. This recording reminds them not only of different ways of expressing opinions but also of the connective *parce que* from Unit 1. The *Guide pratique* on page 37 focuses more closely on this and the other connectives featured in the recording, e.g. *par contre, mais, aussi, comme.*

CD 1, track 39 page 36, activité 1b
Cassette 2, side 1

1 – C'est un jeu. J'aime bien les jeux parce que c'est drôle, les jeux.
2 – C'est un documentaire. C'est intéressant, les documentaires. J'aime surtout les documentaires sur les animaux.
3 – C'est une émission sportive. Moi, j'adore faire du sport et j'adore les émissions sportives.
4 – C'est un dessin animé. Je n'aime pas les dessins animés parce que c'est débile.
5 – C'est un feuilleton. J'adore les feuilletons! Par contre, je n'aime pas les documentaires. C'est nul.
6 – C'est les informations. Je n'aime pas ça, mais c'est important.
7 – C'est la météo. Ce n'est pas marrant, mais c'est utile.
8 – C'est une émission pour la jeunesse. J'aime bien regarder les émissions pour la jeunesse parce que c'est drôle!
9 – C'est un film. J'adore regarder les films à la télé et au cinéma.
10 – C'est une série. J'aime les séries, comme *Urgences* et *Friends*, parce que c'est génial.

Follow-up activities:
▶ A copy of this transcript could be given to students at a later stage (perhaps as a starter activity while working on this spread). Ask them to underline in different colours the different types of programme, opinions and connectives.
▶ If appropriate, you could work on the *Guide pratique* section on connectives at this point. **OHT 11** could then be used as it gives students the opportunity to practise asking someone what type of TV programme they like/dislike. First, establish with the class what type of TV programme each picture represents. Explain that the pictures in the left-hand column represent what the girl is asking and that the pictures in the right-hand column show the boy's responses. Point to each of the pictures in turn and ask students to imagine the conversation between the girl and boy, e.g. Girl: *Tu aimes les films?* Boy: *Oui, j'aime les films, mais j'adore les documentaires.* Students could add opinions, if appropriate, at relevant points in the conversation. The right-hand column could be covered up for students to give their own responses to the girl's questions.

AT 2.3/4 **2** *Parle encore de la télé!*
This is an extension of the *À vos marques* activity. Students now express their opinions in more detail, giving reasons. To encourage them to stay on task for the activity, set a time limit and ask them to count how many programmes they manage to discuss in the time.

AT 1.3 **3a** *Écoute. Note les émissions qu'ils aiment et les émissions qu'ils n'aiment pas.*
Students listen to the teenagers discussing TV programmes and indicate their likes and dislikes. Instead of noting down the words, students could simply give the numbers of the corresponding photos from page 36.

Answers: <u>Arnaud</u>: aime les émissions sportives et les dessins animés, n'aime pas les jeux; <u>Natacha</u>: n'aime pas la télé (ou le cinéma); <u>Matthieu</u>: aime les informations et la météo, n'aime pas les émissions pour la jeunesse; <u>Juliette</u>: aime les dessins animés et les films, n'aime pas les émissions sportives; <u>Max</u>: aime les jeux et les feuilletons, n'aime pas les documentaires; <u>Roxanne</u>: aime les jeux et les émissions pour la jeunesse, n'aime pas les documentaires

AT 1.3 / AT 4.3 **3b** *Réécoute et écris une bulle pour chaque personne. Utilise les Mots-clés.*
Students listen again and use their notes to write a speech bubble about each teenager's likes and dislikes. If appropriate, this could be a group writing activity, in which each group member writes a single speech bubble for one teenager only; or students could work in pairs to write all the speech bubbles. The first person singular could be used here in contrast to the third person, which will be required in *Challenge!* activity **C**.

Answers: see transcript below

CD 1, track 40 page 37, activité 3 et Guide pratique
Cassette 2, side 1

– Arnaud, tu aimes regarder la télévision?
– Oui, j'adore les émissions sportives. C'est génial! J'aime aussi les dessins animés … Par contre, je déteste les jeux parce que c'est nul!

– Et toi, Natacha?
– Moi, je déteste la télé et le cinéma!
– Quoi!?

– Salut, Matthieu. Qu'est-ce que tu aimes regarder à la télé?
– J'aime bien regarder les informations … et j'aime aussi la météo. C'est pas mal. Par contre, je n'aime pas les émissions pour la jeunesse parce que c'est débile.

– Juliette, qu'est-ce que tu aimes?
– Moi, à la télé, j'adore les dessins animés, comme *Looney Tunes*. C'est drôle! J'aime aussi regarder les films.
– Et les émissions sportives?
– Ah non, les émissions sportives, c'est pas marrant. Je n'aime pas beaucoup ça.

– Et toi, Max?
– J'aime regarder les jeux, comme *Le Bigdil*, mais je préfère les feuilletons. J'adore les feuilletons … Ils sont super … mais par contre je n'aime pas les documentaires.

– Roxanne, qu'est-ce que tu préfères?
– J'adore les jeux.
– Les jeux, et …
– Et j'aime bien aussi les émissions pour la jeunesse, mais je n'aime pas les documentaires. Les documentaires sont toujours nuls!

AT 2.3 **4** *Sondage. Choisis cinq genres d'émission et pose la question "Tu aimes …?" Note les réponses et les points.*
Students take part in a class survey on opinions of TV programmes, following the note-taking system suggested in the Students' Book. Although the instruction suggests that they limit their survey to five different types of programme, more able students could cover the full range. Encourage them to include as much detail as possible in their answers.

Guide pratique

This skills section looks at the use of connectives to link ideas, express opinions and add variety and interest to spoken and written work. It launches **8W1** (adding abstract words) and reinforces **8W2** (using connectives).

1 Students find all the connectives used in the speech bubble.

Answers: J'aime la météo <u>parce que</u> c'est intéressant. <u>Par contre</u>, je n'aime pas les dessins animés <u>parce que</u> c'est nul. J'adore <u>aussi</u> les feuilletons, <u>comme</u> *EastEnders*, <u>parce que</u> c'est intéressant.

2 Students listen again to the recording for activity **3** and raise their hand each time they hear a connective.

CD 1, track 40 page 37, activité 3 et Guide pratique
Cassette 2, side 1
as activity **3** above

Follow-up activities:
▶ **OHTs 12A** and **12B** could be used for further practice of connectives. **OHT 12A** provides a core text; **OHT 12B** provides a variety of overlays, either words or pictures, for use with the core text.
▶ The OHTs could be used for a whole-class speaking activity, all repeating together, or with an individual student giving a response, before the pictures/words are changed and another student responds. It is important to focus on pronunciation as students read the text.
▶ Students could write their own paragraph of text by filling in the gaps. The level of this task may be varied depending on which overlays from **12B** are used: choose the pictures to increase the difficulty and the words to make the task easier.

C39 **C40** Further listening practice on TV programmes is provided in activity 1 on Feuille 39 *Écoute Encore* and activity 1 on Feuille 40 *Écoute En plus*. Both these activities could be used while working on this spread.

W24 Additional reading and writing practice of the language of this spread is provided on page 24 of the *Encore* and *En plus* Workbooks.

C50 At some point during work on this spread, launch Framework objective **8W3** (understanding words about progress) via Feuille 50 *Guide pratique 2*. This copymaster also creates an opportunity to develop the use of French for everyday classroom events.

Challenge!

AT 4.2 **A** *Fais deux listes: (1) les émissions que tu aimes (2) les émissions que tu n'aimes pas.*
Students list the TV programmes they like and dislike.

AT 4.3 **B** *Écris un exemple pour chaque genre d'émission et donne ton opinion.*
Students express their opinions of the different types of TV programme. Encourage them to write in as much detail as possible, using a range of opinions and connectives, and point out that they will be marked on the quality of their language.

AT 4.4 **C** *Écris environ 80 mots sur "La télé et ma classe".*
Students use the survey results (activity **4**) as the basis of a written report on their class's opinions. This activity requires them to use third person singular and plural verb forms. Encourage them to write in as much detail as possible, using a wide variety of connectives and opinions, and point out that they will be marked on the quality of their language.

3 On se relaxe!

Planning Page

3.2 On va au cinéma?   pages 38–39

Objectives

- Name different types of film
- Say what film you are going to see at the cinema (**8W5, 8S7 – R**)
- Revise telling the time and learn the 24-hour clock
- Say what time a film is on
- Develop awareness of sound–spelling exceptions (**8W6 – L**)

Resources

Students' Book, pages 38–39
CD 1, tracks 41–42; CD 3, tracks 18 and 23–24
Cassette 2, side 1; cassette 4, side 1
Encore/En plus Workbooks, page 25
OHTs 13A and 13B; *Équipe nouvelle 1* OHT 18
Flashcards 135–141
Copymasters 40, 43, 45, 47 and 51

Key language

Qu'est-ce que tu vas voir au cinéma? Je vais voir …
C'est un film d'aventure, un film policier, un film de science-fiction, un film d'horreur, un western, une comédie, un film romantique, un dessin animé.
C'est à quelle heure? C'est à 20 h 30.

Programme of Study reference

1a, 1b, 1c, 2a, 2b, 2c, 2d, 2f, 2h, 3b, 3c, 3d, 3e, 4a, 4c, 4d, 5a, 5c, 5d, 5e, 5f, 5i

Starters

- *À vos marques*, page 38.
- Write a variety of digital 24-hour clock times on the board or OHP and ask *Le film commence à quelle heure?*
- Write a range of 24-hour clock times on the board, focusing on ones that might be easily confused by students, e.g. 16.40 and 06.40, 15.05 and 15.50. Divide the class into two teams and invite a volunteer from each team to come to the front. Say a time in French and award a point to the student who first touches the correct time. If appropriate, one of the students in the class could give the times, but the student must have good pronunciation and a clear voice.
- After the *Zoom grammaire* activity, play this game. Students prepare two signs, one saying *présent* and one saying *futur*. Say some simple sentences (as in activity **1** of the *Zoom grammaire* section) and students hold up the appropriate sign to identify whether the sentence describes an action in the present or the future.

ICT suggestions

- Students word-process a short message (using the texts in activity **3** as a model), describing a film they would like to see at the weekend. The messages could then be displayed or circulated around the class for students to try to guess who wrote each message. You could provide some cinema listings from a local newspaper as prompts for this activity.
- Students work in pairs to prepare a short PowerPoint® presentation to show that they understand how to refer to the future using *aller* + infinitive.

Creative activities

- Students draw pictures or collect images from magazines or the Internet to create a poster advertising a film. If needed, provide a model text for students to adapt or expand, e.g. *Au cinéma Odéon ce week-end/ Shrek 2/un dessin animé/le film commence à …/C'est amusant! Un film pour toute la famille!*

Plenaries

- *Challenge!* page 39.
- Students carry out a survey in class, asking *Qu'est-ce que tu vas voir au cinéma le week-end prochain?*, and collate the responses in graphic or text form.
- Give students one minute to list as many activities as possible (real or imaginary) that they are going to do next weekend, e.g. *Je vais faire du foot*. This gives them the opportunity to recycle previously learned language with a new grammar focus. One point could be given for every correct sentence, with a bonus point available if students think of an activity that no one else has on their list. This activity could be adapted to students working in pairs and using the *on/nous* form of the verb instead.
- Play Hot Seat for five minutes at the end of a lesson. One student sits in the "hot seat" at the front of the class and answers questions until they make a mistake; a new volunteer then comes to the hot seat. Vary the questions according to the ability of individual students, e.g. *Comment dit-on "a cartoon" en français? Qu'est-ce que tu vas voir au cinema le week-end prochain et pourquoi?* The winner is the student in the hot seat at the end of the five minutes or when the bell rings for the end of the lesson.

Homework suggestions

- Students learn the different genres of film (meaning, pronunciation, spelling).
- Students devise a wordsearch on films (and TV programmes from the previous spread, if appropriate) for another student to complete the following lesson.
- Students prepare an annotated poster of local cinema listings from the newspaper or Internet. The film listings could be stuck in the middle of an A4 piece of paper and annotated with a variety of language, e.g. *C'est un film de science-fiction. Le film commence à dix-huit heures trente. J'adore* Shrek 2 *parce que c'est amusant*. If appropriate, the posters could be sent to a partner school or penfriend.
- *Encore/En plus* Workbooks, page 25.

On se relaxe! ③

3.2 On va au cinéma? pages 38–39

À vos marques

AT 2.2 *Il est quelle heure?*
AT 4.2 This starter activity to revise time could be done either orally or in writing. If appropriate, reuse **OHT 18** (clock face) from the *Équipe nouvelle 1* OHTs.

Answers: a il est trois heures et demie; b il est six heures vingt; c il est cinq heures moins le quart; d il est huit heures et quart; e il est midi/minuit dix; f il est trois heures moins dix; g il est onze heures et demie; h il est deux heures moins le quart

Presentation

Use **Flashcards 135–141** at this stage to present the different film types. See page 17 of the Introduction for ideas on how to present and practise language using flashcards and OHTs.

AT 1.2/3 **1a** *Écoute les huit conversations. C'est quel genre de film?*
Students listen to the conversations and indicate the type of film (listed in the *Mots-clés*) mentioned in each one.

Answers: 1 b; 2 g; 3 c; 4 e; 5 f; 6 a; 7 h; 8 d

1b *Réécoute. Le film est à quelle heure?*
Students listen again and note down the time of each film.

Answers: 1 20.30; 2 19.20; 3 18.40; 4 21.15; 5 17.00; 6 20.10; 7 17.30; 8 23.00

CD 1, track 41 page 38, activité 1
Cassette 2, side 1

1 – Qu'est-ce que tu vas voir?
 – Ce soir, je vais voir un film policier.
 – C'est à quelle heure?
 – C'est à vingt heures trente.
2 – Le week-end prochain, je vais aller au cinéma.
 – Qu'est-ce que tu vas voir?
 – Je vais voir un film romantique. Je suis très romantique!
 – C'est à quelle heure?
 – Le film commence à dix-neuf heures vingt.
3 – Je vais voir un film de science-fiction ce soir à dix-huit heures quarante.
4 – J'adore les westerns parce que c'est intéressant. Il y a un western ce soir à vingt et une heures quinze.
5 – Tu aimes les comédies? Moi, j'adore ça et je vais voir une comédie ce soir à dix-sept heures.
6 – Il y a un bon film d'aventure au cinéma ce soir à vingt heures dix. On y va?
7 – On va aller au cinéma pour voir un dessin animé à dix-sept heures trente. Tu veux venir?
8 – Super! J'adore les films d'horreur et Dracula passe au cinéma ce soir. Ça commence à vingt-trois heures!

Point culture

This panel draws attention to the fact that the 24-hour clock is used more frequently in French than in English. As an example of this, refer students back to the TV guide on page 35. Point out that train timetables (not only in France but also in the UK and other countries) tend to use the 24-hour clock, so it is important to be able to use it.

Follow-up activities:
Use **OHTs 13A** and **13B** to practise the different film types and times. The following ideas may be helpful:

▶ Revise the names of the different film types, perhaps using the layout of **OHT 13A** as a Noughts and Crosses grid (with a blank OHT overlay for you to mark the noughts and crosses for each team).
▶ Then turn off the OHP and cover three pictures with sticky notes; turn the OHP back on again. Students identify which films are hidden. If appropriate, students could be encouraged to give an opinion about the missing films.
▶ Place overlay **13B** onto **13A** for question-and-answer work on what time a particular film starts.

AT 2.3 **2** *Écris en secret cinq films et cinq heures. Discute avec un(e) partenaire en utilisant les Expressions-clés et note les réponses.*
Students choose five films from the recording in activities **1a** and **1b**. With a partner, they take turns to ask and answer questions about which films they are going to see and what time the films begin. This activity could be extended to include real cinema listings: it does not matter if these are in English because the main purpose of the activity is to name film types in French and give 24-hour clock times.

Zoom grammaire

This section focuses on *aller* plus the infinitive to express the future. It provides another opportunity to reinforce **8W5** and **8S7**.

1 Students indicate whether each sentence is in the present or the future.

Answers: a present; b future; c future; d present; e future

2 Students fill in the gaps in the sentences using the correct form of *aller*.

Answers: a vais; b allons; c va; d allez; e vas; f vont

Refer students to the grammar section on page 144 of the Students' Book for further information on *aller* + infinitive.

C47 Feuille 47 *Grammaire 1* provides additional practice of *aller* + infinitive and could be used at this point.

AT 3.3 **3** *C'est quel film? Lis les messages.*
Students match the films to the captions.

Answers: a Nuit des Vampires; b La Dimension Finale; c Flics Extra; d Flics Extra

3 On se relaxe!

C40 Activity 2 on Feuille 40 *Écoute En plus* provides further listening practice on the 24-hour clock and could be used at this point.

C43
C45 Feuille 43 *Lis et écris Encore 1* and Feuille 45 *Lis et écris En plus 1* could also be used here for additional reading and writing practice on the topic of films.

W25 Further reading and writing activities are provided on page 25 of the *Encore* and *En plus* Workbooks.

Ça se dit comme ça!

This section focuses on word endings that are sometimes silent and sometimes pronounced. It launches **8W6** (sound–spelling exceptions).

1 Students listen to the recording and follow the text in the Students' Book. Make sure they understand that the final consonant of words ending in *-x* or *-s* is pronounced only if the following word begins with a vowel or mute *h*.

🎧 **CD 1, track 42**   page 39, Ça se dit comme ça! activité 1
Cassette 2, side 1

a – Le film commence à dix heures.
b – Tu as dix billets pour le film?
c – Le train part dans trois minutes.
d – Les trois amis vont aller au cinéma.

C51 Feuille 51 *Ça se dit comme ça!* provides further practice of this pronunciation point and could be used here.

Challenge!

AT 4.2/3 **A** *Qu'est-ce que tu vas voir au cinéma le week-end prochain?*
Students imagine what they are going to see at the cinema next weekend. They write a few sentences giving the film title, type of film and what time it begins.

AT 4.3 **B** *Écris un message (comme dans l'activité 3) pour inviter un(e) ami(e) au cinéma le week-end prochain.*
Students write a message similar to those in activity **3**, inviting someone to the cinema next weekend.

AT 4.3/4 **C** *Réponds à ce message.*
Students write a reply to a message, expressing and justifying their opinions on types of film and saying what they are going to see at the cinema next weekend. Encourage them to include a wide range of connectives and opinions.

On se relaxe! 3

Planning Page

3.3 On organise un rendez-vous

pages 40–41

Objectives

- Ask someone if they'd like to do something (**8S3 – L**)
- Say that you would like to do something
- Arrange a time to meet (**8L3 – L**)
- Arrange a place to meet

Resources

Students' Book, pages 40–41
CD 1, tracks 43–44; CD 3, tracks 16 and 20
Cassette 2, side 1; cassette 4, side 1
Encore/En plus Workbooks, page 26
OHTs 14A and 14B
Flashcards 61–78
Copymasters 38, 39, 41, 44 and 49

Key language

Tu veux aller au cinéma/au parc/à la piscine/à la plage/à la patinoire/en ville?
Tu veux faire du vélo/nager/danser?
Oui, je veux bien.
On se retrouve à quelle heure?
À cinq heures.
On se retrouve où?
Chez moi/toi.
Au parc/Au café/À la piscine.
Devant la bibliothèque.

Programme of Study reference

1b, 1c, 2a, 2c, 2d, 2f, 2g, 2h, 2i, 3a, 3b, 3c, 3d, 3e, 4a, 5a, 5c, 5d, 5e, 5f, 5i

Starters

- *À vos marques*, page 40.
- Present a dialogue (like the one in activity **1c** on Students' Book page 40) in jumbled form, either on the board or on cut up strips of paper, for students to reorder.
- Give the name of a place in the town and ask students to say or write as interesting a sentence as possible including the word, e.g. *piscine – je vais aller à la piscine le week-end prochain parce que c'est amusant*.
- Students perform their extended conversations (see plenary suggestion below) and the rest of the class award marks for fluency, pronunciation, how well the conversation has been learned, etc.

ICT suggestions

- Students word-process short messages inviting someone out (as on Students' Book page 41). These could be displayed in class for students to read and vote for the activity they would most like to do. The winner is the student who has the most friends to go out with!

Creative activities

- Students extend the title of the spread to "*On organise un rendez-vous à* (name of nearest town)". They design a poster showing all the places to visit accompanied by the relevant questions, e.g. *Tu veux aller en ville? Tu veux aller au parc?*

Plenaries

- *Challenge!* page 41.
- Copymaster 38 *Challenge!* activities 1a and 1b.
- Discuss how short sentences can be improved by the use of simple connectives, e.g. *Je veux aller au parc – Je veux aller au parc le week-end prochain parce que j'adore faire du foot et c'est amusant.*
- With a partner, students write up and learn (for homework) an extended conversation planning social activities for the weekend. The conversations could be performed as a starter activity the following lesson.

Homework suggestions

- Students learn the spellings and genders of places in the town.
- Students learn the extended conversation they have written (see plenary suggestion above), ready to perform the following lesson.
- *Encore/En plus* Workbooks, page 26.

3 On se relaxe!

3.3 On organise un rendez-vous

pages 40–41

À vos marques

AT 2.2 *Jeu de mémoire: les activités du week-end.*
Students play a memory game to practise leisure activities. Student A says an activity; student B repeats A's activity and adds another; student C repeats A's and B's activities and adds a third; and so on. If they need help remembering the vocabulary for leisure activities, use **Flashcards 61–78** or OHT pictures as support.

AT 1.2 **1a** *Écoute les conversations. C'est quelle photo? Attention! Il y a huit photos et sept conversations.*
Students listen to the recording and match each conversation to a photo. The *Guide pratique* section on listening for gist and detail (see notes below) could either be done now, before activity 1a, or later in the spread.

Answers: 1 a; 2 h; 3 b; 4 d; 5 e; 6 c; 7 f

AT 1.3 **1b** *Réécoute. Recopie et complète la grille. Regarde les Expressions-clés.*
Students listen again and note down details of the times and meeting places. After focusing on the 24-hour clock on the previous spread, students now have an opportunity to revise the 12-hour clock.

Answers:

photo	heure	rendez-vous
a	6 h	parc
b	7 h 30	devant le cinéma
c	5 h 30	chez toi
d	8 h	devant la patinoire
e	8 h 30	club des jeunes
f	10 h	chez moi
g	no conversation for this photo	
h	7 h	au café

CD 1, track 43   page 40, activité 1
Cassette 2, side 1

1 – Tu veux faire du vélo ce soir?
 – Oui, super! On se retrouve à quelle heure?
 – À six heures au parc?
 – D'accord.
2 – Tu veux aller au café?
 – Bonne idée!
 – On se retrouve au café?
 – Oui, à quelle heure?
 – À sept heures?
 – D'accord.
3 – On va au cinéma?
 – Oui, d'accord. On se retrouve à quelle heure?
 – À sept heures et demie.
 – On se retrouve où?
 – Devant le cinéma.
 – D'accord.
4 – Tu veux aller à la patinoire?
 – Oui, je veux bien. On se retrouve à quelle heure?
 – À huit heures devant la patinoire?
 – À huit heures? D'accord.
5 – On va danser ce soir, non?
 – Oui, on se retrouve à quelle heure?
 – À huit heures et demie, au club des jeunes?
 – Oui, d'accord.
6 – On va à la piscine?
 – OK. J'aime nager. On se retrouve à quelle heure?
 – À cinq heures et demie. Ça va?
 – Oui, ça va. Et on se retrouve où?
 – Chez toi!
7 – Tu veux aller à la plage?
 – Non, ça ne me dit rien.
 – Mais on peut faire de la voile!
 – Bon, d'accord. On se retrouve à quelle heure?
 – À dix heures. Et on se retrouve où?
 – Chez moi?
 – D'accord.

AT 2.3 **1c** *Organise des rendez-vous avec un(e) partenaire. Utilise les détails de l'activité 1b.*
Working in pairs, students use the details from the grid in activity **1b** to recreate the conversations, suggesting activities together with a time and a place to meet.

Follow-up activities:
▶ Use **OHTs 14A** and **14B** to provide extended practice (without written support) of the role-play conversation. The small pictures on **14B** should be cut up and placed in the empty speech bubbles on **14A** as cues to create a variety of conversations.
▶ Students could practise a conversation in pairs before a volunteer pair is chosen to perform the conversation to the class. With a less able group, only a few picture cues should be changed each time; but with a more able group of students, all the cues could be changed after each conversation.
▶ The picture cues could also be used as the stimulus for students to write up an extended conversation arranging a date with someone.

AT 3.3 **2a** *Lis ces messages et note les détails.*
Students read the messages and make a note of the main details.

Answers:

	Activité	Heure	Où
a	café	4 h	chez Quentin
b	piscine	7 h 30 ce soir	piscine
c	cinéma (film policier, commence 7 h 30)	7 h ce soir	chez Amélie
d	patinoire	7 h 15 ce soir	au café

On se relaxe! 3

AT 3.3 **2b** *Qui …?*
Students look back at the messages in **2a**. They indicate who is being referred to in each question a–d.

Answers: a Christelle (message b); b Lise (message c); c Jeanne (message d); d Quentin (message a)

AT 1.3 **2c** *Écoute les trois personnes qui laissent des messages. C'est qui?*
Students listen to three messages left on an answerphone. Referring again to activity **2a**, they indicate who has left each message.

Answers: 1 Lise; 2 Christelle; 3 Jeanne

🎧 **CD 1, track 44**   page 41, activité 2c
Cassette 2, side 1

1 – Allô, Amélie. Ici Lise. Dis-moi, tu veux aller au cinéma ce soir? Je sais que tu aimes les films policiers. Je viens chez toi à sept heures. Ça va? Au revoir.
2 – Salut! Tu veux aller à la piscine ce soir? À sept heures ou à sept heures et demie, comme tu veux.
3 – Allô. Je voudrais laisser un message pour Bastien. Tu veux faire du sport ce soir? Moi, je veux aller à la patinoire. On se retrouve au café à sept heures et quart. D'accord?

Guide pratique

This section gives students tips on how to improve their listening skills. It focuses on listening for gist and detail (launching **8L3**), predicting the sort of language that is likely to occur, and looking out for any clues that might help with understanding.

1 Students are asked what details they might need to focus on if listening to arrangements for a date.

Answers: details about the planned activity, exact time and place to meet, any admission fees/prices, etc.

2 Students are asked to predict what language they are likely to hear if listening to *la météo*.

Answer: weather forecast: encourage students to come up with as many weather expressions as possible

C49 Activity 1 on Feuille 49 *Guide pratique 1* could be used at this point. It provides additional guidance and practice on listening for gist and detail. (Activities 2 and 3 on Feuille 49 also focus on listening for gist and detail, but they include telephone numbers so would be more appropriate for use with pages 42–43 of the Students' Book.)

Zoom grammaire

This grammar section launches **8S3**. It focuses on the first, second and third person singular forms of the modal verb *vouloir*.

1 Students complete the sentences using the correct form of *vouloir*.

Answers: a veux; b veux; c veut; d veut; e veux; f veut

Refer students to the grammar section on page 144 of the Students' Book for further information on *vouloir*.

C39 Activity 2 on Feuille 39 *Écoute Encore* provides further listening practice on the language of this spread and could be used at this point.

C41 C44 Feuille 41 *Parle Encore* and Feuille 44 *Lis et écris Encore 2* could also be used here. Feuille 41 focuses on *vouloir/aller* + infinitive in the context of arranging what to watch on TV. Feuille 44 practises invitations and arrangements to meet, and also revises TV vocabulary together with opinions and connectives.

W26 Page 26 of the *Encore* and *En plus* Workbooks provides additional practice on written invitations and could also be used at this point.

Challenge!

AT 4.3 **A** *Invite un(e) ami(e) au cinéma. Adapte le message c de l'activité 2a.*
Students write a short message inviting a friend to the cinema, using message c in activity **2a** as a model. If appropriate, model with students exactly what they can adapt: the names of the people, the type of film, the two times, the meeting place.

AT 4.3/4 **B** *Qu'est-ce que tu veux faire ce week-end? Écris un message pour inviter un(e) ami(e) à sortir avec toi!*
In this more open-ended activity, students come up with their own choice of activity and write an invitation to a friend. Encourage them to include as much detail as possible, including opinions. Brainstorm with them alternative places/activities that they already know from *Équipe nouvelle 1*, e.g. *au zoo, au parc, au centre sportif, à la plage*.

C *Prépare une activité de grammaire pour ton/ta partenaire sur les verbes "aller" et "vouloir" + infinitif. Prépare une feuille de réponses et corrige.*
Students devise a grammar activity on *aller* and *vouloir* for their partner to complete. Encourage them to think about the different types of activity that they could use, e.g. gap-fill tasks, matching verb forms to subject pronouns, etc.
When correcting their partner's work, students could use the expressions from Feuille 50 *Guide pratique 2* (which they will have completed when working on pages 36–37 of the Students' Book). This provides an opportunity for further work on Framework objective **8W3** (understanding and giving feedback on work).

3 On se relaxe!

Planning Page

3.4 Que d'excuses! pages 42–43

Objectives
▶ Understand and give telephone numbers (**8C3 – L**)
▶ Make a telephone call
▶ Decline an invitation using *pouvoir*
▶ Give excuses for not going out using *devoir* (**8S3**)
▶ Take part in unscripted exchanges (**8L5 – L**)

Resources
Students' Book, pages 42–43
CD 1, tracks 45–47; CD 3, tracks 19 and 21–22
Cassette 2, side 1; cassette 4, side 1
Encore/En plus Workbooks, pages 27–29
OHT 15
Copymasters 37, 38, 40, 42, 46, 48 and 49

Key language
C'est quoi, le numéro de téléphone?
C'est le 04 34 56 78 91.
Allô. C'est Matthieu?
Oui, c'est Matthieu.
Est-ce que je peux parler à Arnaud, s'il te plaît/s'il vous plaît?
Oui, attends/attendez. Ne quitte/quittez pas.
Tu veux venir chez moi/aller au cinéma?
Je ne peux pas. Je dois faire mes devoirs/aller voir ma grand-mère/garder mon frère/promener le chien/ranger ma chambre.

Programme of Study reference
1a, 1b, 1c, 2a, 2b, 2c, 2d, 2e, 2f, 2g, 2h, 3a, 3b, 3c, 3d, 3e, 4a, 4c, 4d, 5a, 5b, 5d, 5e, 5f, 5i

Starters
▶ *À vos marques*, page 42.
▶ Copymaster 37 *À vos marques*, activities 2a and 2b.
▶ Play a game of Buzz with the class. Select a number (e.g. three) and students count around the class, saying "Buzz" every time the number (or a multiple of the number) appears, e.g. *Un, deux, buzz, quatre, cinq, buzz, … onze, buzz* (12 is multiple of three), *buzz* (13 contains the number three). This is an excellent numeracy revision activity.
If appropriate, students could play the game in small groups; the winning group is the one to reach the highest number without making a mistake.
Instead of using the English word "Buzz" while playing this game, you could substitute an appropriate French word, e.g. *truc, tralala, blablabla, baratin, patati patata, merci, au revoir*. You may decide on a different word each time you play the game, depending on the needs of the class or any particular language or pronunciation points you wish to practise.

▶ Present sequences of numbers on the board or OHP; students continue the sequence. Students could devise the beginning of a sequence for others in the class to continue.

ICT suggestions
▶ Students prepare a useful list of local telephone numbers for a French visitor to the area, as on page 42 of the Students' Book. They may have to search the Internet to find the necessary information or they could use a local telephone directory.

Creative activities
▶ Students make crossword puzzles to practise numbers, with figures for clues (e.g. 15, 20) and the solutions to be numbers written in words (e.g. *quinze, vingt*) inside the crossword grid.

Plenaries
▶ *Challenge!* page 43.
▶ Copymaster 38 *Challenge!* activities 2a and 2b.
▶ Play *Qui est le champion de maths?* Give a sum in French, e.g. 34 + 57, and students compete to work out the solution. The winner is the first student to call out the correct answer in French.
▶ Call out some imaginary telephone numbers for students to note down (on mini-whiteboards, if possible) and show. Students win a point for each telephone number they are able to note down correctly. This game can be made easier or more challenging by varying the complexity of the numbers and the speed at which you say the numbers.

Homework suggestions
▶ Students learn the key phrases for talking on the telephone and giving excuses.
▶ Students devise a game to practise the verbs *vouloir, pouvoir* and *devoir*. Allow them to play the game with a partner the following lesson and to evaluate how useful the game was to aid learning.
▶ If appropriate, students could telephone another student in the class to arrange a date, give excuses, etc., and report back the following lesson. It will be interesting for students to see how much more complicated it is to have a conversation in French with someone you can't see!
▶ *Encore/En plus* Workbooks, page 27.

On se relaxe! 3

3.4 Que d'excuses! pages 42–43

Presentation

Before beginning work on this spread, it might be a good idea to plan some activities to practise high numbers. See suggestions on the Planning Page.

À vos marques

AT 2.2 *Choisis cinq numéros en secret. Compare avec un(e) partenaire. Vous avez choisi des numéros différents?*
Working in pairs, each student chooses five numbers from the lottery ticket. They then discuss and compare their choices. The purpose of this activity is to give students a chance to revise and practise the numbers before the main activities of the spread begin.

AT 1.3 **1a** *Lis les "Numéros utiles" et écoute. Où est-ce qu'on téléphone?*
Students listen to the recording and study the list of useful Dieppe telephone numbers. They note down where each person is telephoning.
Before doing this activity, launch **8C3** by making sure students know how to say French telephone numbers. Point out that they are said in pairs rather than as individual numbers, e.g. 02 35 53 91 46 is said as *zéro deux, trente-cinq, cinquante-trois, quatre-vingt-onze, quarante-six*, not as "zero two three five five three …", etc. Explain that the first two numbers designate an area of France (e.g. 01 is the dialling code for the Paris area; 02 is the dialling code for north-west France, where Dieppe is situated), and the next two numbers refer to a specific place within that area, e.g. 35 is the code for Dieppe.

Answers: 1 Taxis; 2 Hôpital; 3 Cinéma Rex; 4 Office de tourisme; 5 Pompiers; 6 SNCF gare principale

---

CD 1, track 45 **page 42, activité 1a**
Cassette 2, side 1

1 – C'est quoi, le numéro de téléphone?
 – C'est le 02 35 84 20 05.
 – Pardon?
 – C'est le 02 35 84 20 05.
2 – C'est quoi, le numéro de téléphone?
 – C'est le 02 35 06 76 76.
 – Pardon? Est-ce que vous pouvez répéter cela, s'il vous plaît?
 – C'est le 02 35 06 76 76.
 – Merci!
3 – C'est quoi, le numéro de téléphone?
 – C'est le 02 35 84 22 74.
 – Pardon? Est-ce que tu peux répéter cela, s'il te plaît?
 – C'est le 02 35 84 22 74.
4 – C'est quoi, le numéro de téléphone?
 – C'est le 02 35 84 11 77.
 – Pardon?
 – C'est le 02 35 84 11 77.
5 – C'est quoi, le numéro de téléphone?
 – C'est le 02 35 84 33 00.
 – Pardon? Est-ce que vous pouvez répéter cela, s'il vous plaît?
 – C'est le 02 35 84 33 00.
6 – C'est quoi, le numéro de téléphone?
 – C'est le 02 35 06 69 33.
 – Pardon?
 – C'est le 02 35 06 69 33.

AT 1.2
AT 2.2 **1b** *A lit un des "Numéros utiles" à haute voix. B note le numéro (livre fermé!) et puis vérifie le numéro (livre ouvert!). Ensuite, changez de rôles.*
Students work in pairs to practise reading aloud and noting down the numbers from the list of Dieppe telephone numbers. Encourage them to ask for clarification where necessary by using unscripted phrases, e.g. *Pardon?*, *Est-ce que tu peux répéter cela, s'il te plaît?* This launches Framework objective **8L5** (taking part in unscripted exchanges).

Follow-up activities:
▶ Continue the launch of **8L5** by focusing on classroom expressions to use on a regular basis.
▶ Write the following expressions on the board or OHP and ask students if they can work out what they mean in English: *Est-ce que vous pouvez répéter cela, s'il vous plaît? Vous pouvez parler plus lentement, s'il vous plaît? Est-ce que je peux aller aux toilettes, s'il vous plaît? Est-ce que je peux emprunter un stylo, s'il vous plaît?* This activity also continues the launch of **8S3** (modal verbs): point out to students that modal verbs can form the basis of some very useful classroom phrases.
▶ Brainstorm other classroom expressions that students use spontaneously, referring back if necessary to pages 10–11 of *Équipe nouvelle 1* Students' Book.
▶ Students could word-process a prompt sheet to stick into their exercise books to remind themselves of all the useful phrases they know to help them communicate in French, e.g. *Pardon? Tu peux/Vous pouvez parler moins vite, s'il te plaît/s'il vous plaît?*

AT 1.3
AT 3.3 **2a** *Écoute et lis la conversation téléphonique entre Matthieu et Juliette (à droite).*
Students listen to the telephone conversation between Matthieu and Juliette while following the text in the Students' Book.

CD 1, track 46 **page 42, activité 2a**
Cassette 2, side 1

– C'est quoi le numéro de téléphone? Ah voilà! 02 35 11 98 52.
– Allô.
– Allô, Juliette?
– Non, c'est sa grand-mère.
– Est-ce que je peux parler à Juliette, s'il vous plaît?
– Oui, attends. Ne quitte pas.

– Allô, c'est Juliette.
– Salut, Juliette. C'est Matthieu. Tu veux venir chez moi ce soir?
– Ce soir? Je ne peux pas. Je dois faire mes devoirs.

3 On se relaxe!

– Demain soir alors?
– Non, je dois aller à une répétition des Pieds-Nus.
– Ah, non. Zut!
– Désolée, Matthieu. Au revoir.

AT 3.3 **2b** *Relis la conversation. Trouve …*
Students read the telephone conversation again, searching for the French equivalents of the English expressions.

Answers: a Est-ce que je peux parler à Juliette, s'il vous plaît? b Oui, attends. Ne quitte pas. c Je ne peux pas. d Je dois faire mes devoirs.

AT 2.3
AT 3.3 **2c** *À trois, jouez la conversation.*
Working in groups of three, students read the conversation aloud, changing roles so that they each have a chance to perform the different parts. Allow them to listen to the recording again so that they can focus on pronunciation and intonation. You could use old telephones or mobile phones as props, if available, to make the activity more interesting and authentic. More able students could try to learn the conversation by heart.

AT 1.3 **3a** *Écoute. Mets les excuses dans l'ordre.*
Each picture represents a different excuse: students listen and match the phrases (from the *Expressions-clés*) to the pictures. Students could write out a phrase for each picture. Refer back to Juliette's two excuses in activity **2a** (*Je dois faire mes devoirs. Je dois aller à une répétition des Pieds-Nus*).

Answers: 1 e; 2 c; 3 a; 4 b; 5 d

CD 1, track 47
Cassette 2, side 1
page 43, activité 3a

1 – Je fais de l'escalade tous les samedis. Tu veux venir?
– Tous les samedis? Euh … non, je ne peux pas. Je dois ranger ma chambre.
2 – Tu veux faire de l'escalade avec moi samedi prochain?
– De l'escalade? Euh … non, je ne peux pas. Je dois garder mon frère samedi matin.
3 – J'adore faire de l'escalade le samedi matin. Tu veux venir avec moi?
– Euh … non. Je dois faire mes devoirs.
4 – Tu aimes l'escalade? Je fais de l'escalade samedi matin. Tu veux venir?
– Euh … Je ne peux pas. Je dois aller voir ma grand-mère.
5 – Je fais de l'escalade tous les samedis. Tu veux venir?
– Pardon?
– Tu veux faire de l'escalade samedi matin?
– Euh … non, je ne peux pas. Je dois promener le chien.

Follow-up activities:
▶ **OHT 15** could be used at this point to provide additional practice of asking questions and giving excuses. The OHT can be used as a whole sheet, by placing a pen to point to one of the places and another pen to point to an excuse, to prompt students to invent short conversations, e.g.
A: *Tu veux aller au café?*
B: *Non, je ne peux pas. Je dois promener le chien.*
The final smiley face represents *Oui, je veux bien!*
▶ Alternatively, **OHT 15** can be cut up and a selection of the pictures used each time to act as a cue for a short conversation, e.g. the picture of the café plus the question mark with the dog excuse underneath.

AT 2.2/3 **3b** *A propose une activité. B refuse!*
In pairs, students practise suggesting activities and declining. They could perform their conversations while the class listen and note down key details, e.g. date and time of the activities, excuses, etc.

Zoom grammaire
This section continues the launch of **8S3**, focusing on the modal verbs *pouvoir*, *devoir* and *vouloir*.

1 Using their knowledge of the conjugation of *vouloir* (from the previous spread) together with the work they have already done on this spread, students attempt to work out the first, second and third person singular forms of *pouvoir* and *devoir*.

Answers: je peux, tu peux, il/elle/on peut; je dois, tu dois, il/elle/on doit

2 Students unjumble the sentences.

Answers: a Tu veux aller en ville? b Tu peux promener le chien? c Sophie veut aller au café. d Tu dois faire tes devoirs.

Refer students to the grammar section on page 144 of the Students' Book for further information on modal verbs.

C48 Feuille 48 *Grammaire 2* provides additional practice of *vouloir*, *pouvoir* and *devoir* and could be used at this point.

W28
W29 Pages 28 and 29 of the *Encore* and *En plus* Workbooks could also be used here. Both pages focus on modal verbs, and page 29 incorporates *aller* + infinitive too.

C40 Additional listening practice on invitations and excuses is provided in activities 3a and 3b on Feuille 40 *Écoute En plus*.

C49 Listening practice on telephone numbers and invitations, with a specific focus on listening for gist and detail, is provided in activities 2 and 3 of Feuille 49 *Guide pratique 1*. Both these activities could be used at this point, together with activity 1 if not already used with the previous spread.

C42 Feuille 42 *Parle En plus* provides further practice of arranging activities, planning when and where to meet, etc. If used towards the end of this spread, it will enable students to draw on the full range of language learned during Unit 3.

On se relaxe! 3

C46 Feuille 46 *Lis et écris En plus 2* incorporates all the vocabulary and grammar points of the unit, so could be used either towards the end of this spread or later in the unit.

W27 Extra reading and writing practice on giving excuses is provided on page 27 of the *Encore* and *En plus* Workbooks.

Challenge!

AT 3.2
AT 4.2 **A** *Recopie et complète ces phrases. Traduis en anglais.* Students copy out and complete the sentences, replacing the pictures with suitable phrases. They translate the sentences into English.

Answers: 1 Je ne peux pas faire du football. Je dois faire mes devoirs. *I can't play football. I have to do my homework.* 2 Je ne peux pas promener le chien. Je dois ranger ma chambre. *I can't take the dog for a walk. I have to tidy my room.* 3 Je ne peux pas aller au cinéma. Je dois aller voir ma grand-mère. *I can't go to the cinema. I have to visit my grandmother.*

AT 4.3/4 **B** *Adapte la conversation téléphonique, activité 2a, page 42. Change les noms, l'activité proposée et les excuses.* Students adapt the telephone conversation from activity **2a**, changing the names, the telephone number, activities and excuses. Students could perform their conversations and, if possible, record them for peer-assessment. They will need to agree beforehand what they are going to focus their assessment on, e.g. pronunciation, expression, intonation and/or number of adaptations.

AT 2.4
AT 4.4 **C** *Tu veux faire de l'escalade? Non? Invente d'autres excuses!* Students make a list of as many excuses as possible (sensible or amusing!) to avoid going climbing. Opinions could also be added, e.g. *... parce que je dois faire du shopping. C'est fatigant!* Students could be encouraged to check each other's work and make further suggestions. This activity is intended to encourage students to recycle language learned in other contexts.
The activity could also be a speaking activity with students working in a small group, taking it in turns to give an excuse. How many different excuses can the students think of?

3 On se relaxe!

3.5 La belle équipe, épisode 3

pages 44–45

Objectives

▶ Develop listening and reading skills via a soap story based on the language of the unit (**8L2**)

Resources

Students' Book, pages 44–45
CD 1, track 48
Cassette 2, side 1

Programme of Study reference

1a, 1c, 2a, 2b, 2g, 2h, 2i, 3b, 3c, 3e, 4a, 4d, 5a, 5d, 5e, 5g, 5i

For general information on introducing and exploiting the soap story, refer to page 19 of the Introduction.

At the beginning of this episode, Matthieu announces that he won't be able to take part in rehearsals for the talent competition because he needs to recover from his operation. This is a major setback for the Pieds-Nus because they can't rehearse without him.
Juliette tries to coax Arnaud into taking Matthieu's place, but he still won't help out, saying that he is too shy. The following day, she tries again, and yet again Arnaud refuses. Juliette now becomes frustrated with him and says she is going to visit Matthieu, whereupon Arnaud has a fit of jealousy and tries to persuade her to go sailing with him instead. Juliette agrees … but only if Arnaud will stand in for Matthieu at rehearsals! What will he do?

AT 1.4 **1** *Écoute et lis. À ton avis, qu'est-ce qu'Arnaud va faire ensuite?*
AT 3.4 Students listen to the recording and follow the text in the Students' Book. Ask them to try to predict what Arnaud's reaction will be. Each episode of the soap story provides opportunities for students to use various strategies to understand the text (picture clues, contextual clues, intonation of the speakers, etc.), enabling further reinforcement of **8L2**.

CD 1, track 48 page 44, La belle équipe, épisode 3
Cassette 2, side 1

1 – Allô! Ici, Natacha. Est-ce que je peux parler à Matthieu?
 – Salut, Natacha. C'est moi!
 – Ah, Matthieu, comment ça va?
 – Bof! Je dois rester une semaine au lit après l'opération. C'est nul!
 – Quoi? Mais alors, tu ne peux pas venir aux répétitions des Pieds-Nus?
 – Non, je ne peux pas bouger.
2 – Sans Matthieu, qu'est-ce qu'on peut faire? On doit avoir un garçon pour les Pieds-Nus.
 – Dis, Juliette! Tu aimes bien Arnaud … et il t'aime bien aussi, non?!
 – Ah bon? Tu penses? Peut-être …
 – Demande-lui de venir aux répétitions!
 – Hummm … Je peux essayer.
3 Plus tard …
 – Tu aimes bien la musique, Arnaud? Tu veux jouer avec les Pieds-Nus?
 – Juliette, j'adore écouter de la musique et regarder les émissions de musique à la télé. Mais je suis trop timide!
 – Mais Arnaud, sans toi, c'est fini pour les Pieds-Nus.
 – Ce n'est pas mon problème!
4 – Alors, il vient?
 – Pas de succès pour le moment!
 – Allez, Juliette! Tu dois réussir!
5 Le lendemain …
 – Tu es libre ce soir, Arnaud?
 – Libre? Euh … Je fais de la voile jusqu'à six heures.
 – On a une répétition à sept heures. Tu peux venir alors?
 – Ah non! Encore les Pieds-Nus! Ce soir, je dois garder ma petite sœur.
 – Toujours des excuses! Tu es nul! Salut! Je vais chez Matthieu.
6 – Chez Matthieu? Pourquoi? Reste! Tu veux faire de la voile avec moi? C'est super, la voile!
 – Je reste si tu viens à la répétition!
 – Quoi? …
7 – Allez, Arnaud, fais ça pour Matthieu, pour Natacha. Arnaud, fais ça pour moi …!
À suivre …

2 *Trouve dans le texte …*
Students search the text for the French equivalents of the English phrases.

Answers: a après l'opération; b je ne peux pas bouger; c peut-être; d je peux essayer; e tu dois réussir; f fais ça pour moi

3a *Vrai ou faux?*
Students answer some true/false questions on the text.

Answers: a faux; b vrai; c faux; d vrai; e faux; f vrai

AT 4.2/3 **3b** *Corrige les phrases fausses.*
Students correct the false statements from **3a**.

Answers: a Matthieu ne peut pas aller aux répétitions des Pieds-Nus. Il doit rester une semaine au lit. c Arnaud ne veut pas jouer avec les Pieds-Nus. e Arnaud doit garder sa petite sœur.

AT 2.4 **4** *À quatre, jouez l'épisode.*
AT 3.4 Students act out the episode in groups. More able students could attempt to learn their character's part by heart.
If possible, allow students to record themselves on video so that they can later watch each other's performances and judge them according to agreed criteria, e.g. filming quality, pronunciation, acting skill.

On se relaxe! 3

Follow-up activities:

▶ Students work in pairs to word-process a summary of the episode in exactly 40 words. The limited word count encourages them to really think about their choice of vocabulary, etc.

▶ Alternatively, ask students to write a "photo brief" for each scene in this episode, e.g. Photo 1: *Matthieu est malade. Il est dans don lit. Il parle avec Natacha au téléphone.*

▶ Because we are now half way through the soap story (this was the third episode and there are six in total), it might be a good idea to ask students to recap on events up to this point. They could work in small groups to write 10 simple sentences to summarize the story so far.

▶ Students reread the soap and, working with a partner, identify new language they have learned in the unit.

▶ Students identify all the phrases in the soap story that use the verbs *pouvoir*, *vouloir* and *devoir*. Play the recording and ask students to stand up each time they hear a part of one of these verbs.

Super-challenge! page 46

This extension page is intended to stretch more able students who are confident with the core language of the unit. It combines language from the unit with unfamiliar language and develops grammar points introduced in the main body of the unit. It can be used flexibly either as part of a teacher-led lesson or as alternative independent class and homework material.

Objectives

▶ Develop the use of the modal verbs *vouloir*, *pouvoir* and *devoir*

Resources

Students' Book, page 46
CD 1, track 49
Cassette 2, side 1
Encore/En plus Workbooks, page 30

Programme of Study reference

1b, 1c, 2a, 2c, 2d, 2h, 3b, 3c, 3d, 3e, 4a, 5d, 5e, 5i

AT 3.3 **1a** *Relie les conversations.*
Students use their knowledge of previously learned language together with inference skills to work out which speech bubbles (1–6 and a–f) go together.

Answers: 1 c; 2 d; 3 a; 4 f; 5 b; 6 e

AT 1.3 **1b** *Écoute et vérifie.*
Students listen to check their answers.

CD 1, track 49 page 46, activité 1b
Cassette 2, side 1

1 – Tu veux aller à la piscine avec moi samedi soir? Je peux te retrouver à l'arrêt de bus à six heures et demie.

– Non, je ne peux pas, je dois aller chez ma grand-mère vers sept heures.

2 – Nous devons aller en ville demain matin. Tu veux venir? Nous pouvons prendre le bus à dix heures et demie.

– Oui, bonne idée! Je veux acheter un cadeau d'anniversaire pour ma sœur.

3 – Qu'est-ce que vous voulez manger ce soir?

– On peut aller au Macdo! On veut manger un burger-frites!

4 – Paul peut mettre sa casquette bleue pour aller à la discothèque, non?

– Non, il veut porter une tenue habillée! Il doit trouver sa cravate rouge!

5 – Luc et Cédric peuvent aller à la patinoire?

– Non, ils doivent faire leurs devoirs et puis, après, ils veulent faire du vélo au parc.

6 – Comme devoirs ce soir, vous devez compléter l'exercice 2 – et vous pouvez aussi lire la page 32.

– Oh non! Je ne peux pas faire ça. C'est trop difficile!

Zoom grammaire

This grammar section looks at *vouloir*, *pouvoir* and *devoir* in more detail. Students should notice that, although these verbs are irregular, they do follow similar patterns. It is important to remind students that modal verbs are followed by an infinitive: to illustrate this point, they could add infinitives to each of the verb forms listed in the conjugation table.

1a Students look back at the conversations at the top of the page, focusing on the different forms of *vouloir*, *pouvoir* and *devoir*. This should help them to fill in the conjugation table for these verbs. They can check their answers by referring to pages 140–141 of the Students' Book.

1b Not all the verb forms for the conjugation table appear in the speech bubbles, so students will need to work these out for themselves. For example, they should be able to work out *nous voulons* from *vous voulez* and *nous pouvons*.

2 Students copy and complete the English sentences giving information about modal verbs.

Answers: a an infinitive; b *vouloir*, an infinitive; c *devoir*, an infinitive, must/have to

3 Students translate the sentences into French.

Answers: a Je dois ranger ma chambre. b Tu peux aller au cinéma ce soir? c Nous voulons/On veut faire du patinage/aller à la patinoire. d Elle doit promener le chien. e Matthieu et Arnaud peuvent aller à la piscine. f Je veux aller au club des jeunes, mais je dois faire mes devoirs!

Refer students to the grammar section on modal verbs on page 144 of the Students' Book.

W30 Page 30 of the *Encore* and *En plus* Workbooks could be used at this point.

3 On se relaxe!

Vocabulaire *page 47*

This page provides a summary of the key language covered in this unit. It could be used as a handy reference for students as they work through the unit. Alternatively, students could use its clear French–English format with language organized thematically when learning vocabulary.

C35 Feuille 35 *Vocabulaire* also contains a summary of the key language of the unit and could be given to students at this point for revision purposes. See page 7 of the Introduction for ideas on how to use this copymaster.

W31 Page 31 of the *Encore* and *En plus* Workbooks also provides a summary of the key language of the unit.

Podium *page 48*

The *Podium* page provides students with an end-of-unit checklist of learning objectives in French and English. At the foot of the page are activities at three levels of difficulty (bronze, silver and gold) to extend the work of the unit. Encourage students to select an activity at the most appropriate level.

C36 Feuille 36 *Podium* could also be used at this point. This worksheet contains activities to help students keep track of their progress. See page 7 of the Introduction for ideas on how to use it to help self- and peer-assessment.

W32 Page 32 of the *Encore* and *En plus* Workbooks also provides an end-of-unit checklist in French and English with activities to help students keep track of their progress.

Encore Unité 3 *pages 100–101*

Objectives
These reinforcement pages are intended for those students requiring further practice of core language from the unit. They can be used by students who finish other activities quickly or as alternative class and homework material.

Resources
Students' Book, pages 100–101
CD 1, track 50
Cassette 2, side 1

Programme of Study reference
1c, 2a, 2c, 2d, 2h, 2i, 3e, 4a, 5a, 5c, 5d, 5e, 5f, 5i

AT 1.3 **1a** *Écoute les six conversations. Les numéros dans la liste sont bons ou non?*
Students compare the telephone numbers given on the recording with those listed in the Students' Book. They indicate which numbers in the list are incorrect.
The extensive number practice provided in these first few activities may well prove useful for all students, including those who would usually tend to work on the *En plus* pages.

Answers: 1 correct; 2 incorrect; 3 correct; 4 incorrect; 5 correct; 6 incorrect

AT 1.3 **1b** *Réécoute. Recopie et corrige les numéros qui sont faux.*
Students listen again and correct the wrong numbers.

Answers: Pariscope: 01 41 34 73 **22**; musée Claude-Monet: 0**5** 32 51 28 21; club des jeunes: 03 80 08 **33** 25

CD 1, track 50 **page 100, activité 1**
Cassette 2, side 1

1 – C'est quoi, le numéro de téléphone du Grand Café Capucines à Paris?
  – Le Grand Café Capucines à Paris … voyons … c'est le 01 43 12 19 00.
  – 01 43 12 19 00. Très bien. Merci.
2 – Je vais téléphoner à Pariscope. C'est quoi, le numéro de téléphone?
  – Pour Pariscope, c'est le 01 41 34 73 22, je crois.
  – 01 41 34 73 22?
  – Oui, je crois.
3 – C'est quoi, le numéro de téléphone de la tour Eiffel?
  – La tour Eiffel … Un instant … c'est le 01 44 11 23 23.
  – Attendez, attendez … 01 44 11 …
  – 23 23.
  – D'accord.
4 – Nathalie! C'est quoi, le numéro de téléphone du musée Claude-Monet?
  – Euh … c'est le 05 32 51 28 21.
  – 05 32 51 28 21, OK, merci beaucoup.
5 – Vous allez téléphoner au parc floral?
  – Oui, mais je n'ai pas le numéro. C'est quoi?
  – Pour le parc floral, c'est le 04 72 45 69 18.
  – Vous pouvez répéter, s'il vous plaît?
  – Bien sûr, c'est le 04 72 45 69 18.
6 – C'est quoi, le numéro de téléphone du club des jeunes?
  – C'est le 03 80 08 33 25.
  – Je vais le noter … 03 80 08 33 25.

AT 2.2/3 **1c** *A choisit un dessin et demande le numéro. B donne le numéro.*
In pairs, students practise asking for and giving the telephone numbers listed.

AT 4.2/3 **2a** *Qu'est-ce que tu vas faire le week-end prochain? Écris une liste de dix activités.*
Students write a list of 10 activities that they are going to do next weekend.

On se relaxe! **3**

AT 2.2/3 **2b** *Compare avec un(e) partenaire. Puis comparez avec la classe. Qui gagne?*
Students compare their list from activity **2a** with a partner. They score two points for an activity that their partner hasn't listed, but only one point for an activity that appears on both their lists. They then compare their lists with the rest of the class, and points are awarded in the same way until one pair emerges as the overall winner. This activity emphasizes the use of the infinitive.

AT 4.2/3 **3** *Écris les conversations.*
Students write conversations following the picture prompts. They could then read aloud their conversations in pairs.

Answers: a Tu veux regarder un documentaire ce soir? Non, je dois faire mes devoirs. b Tu veux regarder une émission sportive? Non, je dois promener le chien. c Tu veux regarder les dessins animés ce soir? Non, je dois aller voir ma grand-mère. d Tu veux regarder un jeu? Non, je dois ranger ma chambre. e Tu veux regarder la météo? Non, je dois garder mon (petit) frère.

AT 3.3 **4a** *Lis les bulles. Relie les images à la bonne personne.*
Students read about four people's plans for the coming weekend. They match each person to the appropriate pictures.

Answers: Bastien: b; Janila: a, d; Noémie: c, f; David: e, g

AT 3.3 **4b** *Tu veux passer le week-end avec qui? Pourquoi?*
AT 4.3 Referring back to the speech bubbles in **4a**, students explain who they would like to spend the weekend with, and why.

En plus Unité 3   pages 112–113

Objectives
These extension pages are intended for more able students who are confident with the core language of the unit. They can be used by students who finish other activities quickly or as alternative class and homework material.

Resources
Students' Book, pages 112–113
CD 1, track 51
Cassette 2, side 1

Programme of Study reference
1c, 2a, 2c, 2d, 2h, 2i, 2j, 3b, 3c, 3e, 4a, 4c, 4d, 5a, 5c, 5d, 5e, 5f, 5i

AT 1.3 **1** *Écoute l'annonce. Trouve les six erreurs.*
Students listen to the recording while studying the film listings in the Students' Book. They find the six mistakes made on the recording.

Answers: mistakes are underlined in the transcript below; the corrections are: *Astérix et les Indiens*: un dessin animé; *Grease*: à dix-neuf heures cinq; *Chacun cherche son chat*: le 26 avril; *Harry Potter*: à vingt et une heures dix; *Fargo*: à vingt heures vingt-cinq; *Star Trek*: à dix-neuf heures

CD 1, track 51   page 112, activité 1
Cassette 2, side 1

Astérix et les Indiens, <u>un western</u>, c'est le 20 avril à dix-sept heures quarante-cinq.
Grease, une comédie musicale, c'est le 22 avril à <u>dix-neuf heures</u>.
Chacun cherche son chat, une comédie, c'est le <u>25</u> avril à vingt heures quinze.
Harry Potter, un film d'aventure avec Daniel Radcliffe, c'est le 29 avril à <u>dix-neuf</u> heures dix.
Fargo, un film policier, c'est le premier mai à vingt heures <u>trente-cinq</u>.
Star Trek, un film de science-fiction, c'est le 3 mai à <u>vingt et une heures</u>.

AT 2.3/4 **2** *A choisit un film (à droite). B devine le film choisi. Puis changez de rôles.*
AT 3.3/4 Working in pairs, each student chooses a film from the cinema listings, keeping it secret from their partner. The partner works out which film they have chosen by asking questions about the type of film, what time it begins, etc.

AT 2.3-5 **3** *Avec un(e) partenaire, prépare une conversation sur les projets pour le week-end prochain. Utilise les questions et les connecteurs de la liste.*
AT 4.3-5 Students work in pairs to make up a conversation about their plans for next weekend. Although a few words and phrases are provided as prompts, this is primarily an open-ended activity designed to help students to initiate and develop conversations. Students will perform at a variety of levels depending on the length and complexity of their exchanges, range of language used, etc. This activity might be appropriate for peer-assessment.

AT 3.5 **4a** *Lis la lettre et mets les illustrations dans le bon ordre.*
Students read the letter and note down the pictures in the order in which they are mentioned in the text.

Answers: c, g, h, b, d, f, a, e

4b *Cherche et note les verbes au futur: une partie du verbe "aller" + infinitif. Il y en a combien? Compare avec un(e) partenaire.*
Students search the text for parts of *aller* + infinitive, then compare their answers with a partner.

Answers: Qu'est-ce que <u>tu vas faire</u> …? Moi, <u>je vais faire</u> beaucoup de choses! … <u>je vais faire</u> mes devoirs … <u>nous allons manger</u> une glace … <u>je vais passer</u> mon samedi soir au centre sportif … <u>on va faire</u> de la natation … <u>Ça va être</u> amusant! Dimanche matin, <u>je vais promener</u> le chien et <u>acheter</u> des croissants … À midi, <u>je vais manger</u> au restaurant … <u>Je vais lui donner</u> une cravate … Plus tard, <u>je vais faire</u> de la voile … Dimanche soir, <u>je vais aller</u> chez Alika et <u>on va regarder</u> un peu la télévision … <u>Ça va être</u> un week-end sympa! <u>Tu vas passer</u> un bon week-end?

109

3 On se relaxe!

Follow-up activity: Students could search the text for modal verbs + infinitive.

AT 4.5 **4c** *Écris une réponse à Conrad (80–100 mots).*
Students write about their own plans for the coming weekend. If appropriate, this could be a paired writing task, with students drafting and redrafting their work on the computer. Model a possible response to Conrad first with students before letting them work independently.

Point lecture   pages 124–125

These pages are intended to encourage independent reading. Students should attempt them once they are confident with the core language of the unit. They can be used by students who finish other activities quickly or as alternative class and homework material.

Objectives
- Develop reading for information and pleasure via texts on cinema and TV
- Research and write about a famous French film star (**8C2 – R**)

Resources
Students' Book, pages 124–125

Programme of Study reference
1c, 2g, 2h, 2i, 3b, 3c, 3d, 3e, 4a, 4c, 4d, 5d, 5e, 5g, 5i

AT 3.3 **1** *Lis l'annonce et réponds aux questions.*
Students answer questions about the cinema advertisement.
Answers: a Cinéma Jean Renoir; b 1 quai Bérigny, Dieppe; c 02 35 82 04 43; d non; e 20 h 30; f 22 h 45; g Le retour du jedi; h oui; i non

AT 3.4 **2** *Lis l'article sur les chaînes du câble. Note les points importants en anglais et compare avec un(e) partenaire.*
Students read the article about cable TV and note down in English what they consider to be the main points. They compare their notes with those of a partner.
Possible answers: MTV: American music channel; in English; shows video clips and concerts. Canal J: for children aged 2–14; shows cartoons, series and films for young people. Eurosport: shows sport 24 hours a day, big events as well as sports that don't usually get much TV coverage. Other channels: lots of film channels such as Ciné premier.

AT 3.4/5 **3a** *Quels sont les quatre acteurs/actrices et les quatre films mentionnés?*
This page is based on the young people's website www.momes.net. Students read some comments from the site and pick out the names of four actors and four films.
Answers: les acteurs/actrices: Johnny Depp, Guillaume Lemay-Thivierge, Jennifer Aniston, Trévor Morgan; les films: Le Matou, Jurassic Park 3, Napoléon en Australie, Darkman, Billy Elliott, La Cure

AT 3.4/5 **3b** *Qui …?*
Students answer additional questions on the texts.
Answers: a Émilie; b Matthieu; c Barbara; d Albane; e Clara; f Trévor Morgan

Follow-up activity: To reinforce Framework objective **8C2**, ask students to research a favourite film star or film and to write a short text in the same style as the young people's texts on page 125 of the Students' Book. Encourage them to visit the site www.momes.net and to click on the link to "cinéma" (as instructed in the article heading on page 125) in order to read additional comments by young people about films and film stars.

Copymasters

Feuille 37 À vos marques
There are two starter activities on this copymaster.
The top half of the sheet focuses on connectives and is intended for use with pages 36–37 of the Students' Book. It shows students how the use of connectives can help to make their writing more interesting.
The bottom half of the sheet focuses on modal verbs + infinitive and can be used with pages 42–43 of the Students' Book.

1a *Utilise les connecteurs (et, aussi, comme, mais, parce que, par contre) et écris un paragraphe plus intéressant.*
Students rewrite the paragraph about TV viewing preferences, using connectives to link sentences and make the text more interesting to read. They could work in pairs on this activity.
Possible answer: J'adore les films <u>parce que</u> c'est super! <u>Par contre</u>, je n'aime pas les informations <u>parce que</u> c'est nul! J'adore les feuilletons <u>comme</u> Coronation Street <u>parce que</u> c'est génial. J'aime <u>aussi</u> la météo <u>parce que</u> c'est intéressant, <u>mais</u> je préfère la série Friends <u>parce que</u> c'est drôle.

1b *Compte tes points. Tu as combien de points pour ton paragraphe?*
Students score points for each connective used, following the points system provided on the copymaster.

1c *Tu peux réécrire le paragraphe pour avoir plus de points? Compare avec ton/ta partenaire.*
Students redraft their paragraph, trying to increase their score.

Follow-up activity: Students could make up their own paragraph of text about their TV viewing preferences, trying to score as many points as possible. This could be a class competition.

On se relaxe! 3

2a *Relie les questions et les réponses.*
Students match the questions and answers.

Answers: 1 e; 2 f; 3 c; 4 b; 5 d; 6 a

2b *Écris une réponse différente pour chaque question. Compare avec ton/ta partenaire.*
Students write their own response to each question. Encourage more able students to use connectives, opinions, etc. to make their answers as varied as possible. They then compare with a partner and select their best response to share with the rest of the class. Sharing good work helps to raise standards.

Feuille 38 Challenge!

There are two plenary activities on this copymaster.
Activities 1a and 1b focus on *vouloir* and could be used towards the end of pages 40–41 of the Students' Book. It is a good idea to provide extra practice of *vouloir* at this point before *pouvoir* and *devoir* are introduced on the following spread.
Activities 2a and 2b practise *devoir* + infinitive so should be used towards the end of pages 42–43.

1a *Écris cinq phrases avec les mots et les dessins qui sont dans les cercles.*
Students write five sentences using the words and pictures supplied. Point out that only two forms of *vouloir* are required for all these pronouns/subjects (thereby demonstrating to students that the verb *vouloir* is not so difficult after all!), and that the pronunciation of *veux* and *veut* is the same. Activities 1a and 1b could be adapted for use with *pouvoir* and *devoir* once these two verbs have been taught on the following spread.

Some possible answers: Je veux faire de la natation/aller à la piscine. Tu veux aller au café? Thomas/Elle/Mon copain/On veut regarder la télé/faire du vélo/aller au cinéma/faire du surf.

1b *Donne les phrases à ton/ta partenaire qui note l'anglais pour chaque phrase.*
Students exchange their five sentences with a partner, who translates them into English.

2a *Tu veux faire tes devoirs? Non?! Imagine dix excuses.*
Students make up 10 excuses for not doing their homework, using *devoir* + infinitive. The reason why 10 excuses are required is to encourage students to go beyond those given on page 43 of the Students' Book. Less able students could work in pairs to invent the excuses then compare with another pair of students in activity **2b**; the number of excuses could also be reduced for less able students.

2b *Compare avec ton/ta partenaire. Qui trouve les meilleures excuses?*
Students compare their excuses from **2a** with a partner.

Feuille 39 Écoute Encore

Activity 1 provides further practice of TV programmes and could be used with pages 36–37 of the Students' Book. Activity 2 focuses on making arrangements to meet; it could be used with pages 40–41 of the Students' Book.

AT 1.3/4

1 *Écoute. La famille Leroy regarde beaucoup la télévision. Qui aime quoi?*
Students listen to the interviews about TV viewing preferences and tick or cross the grid to show each person's likes and dislikes.

Answers: <u>Mme Leroy</u>: likes soaps and the news, dislikes sport; <u>M. Leroy</u>: likes documentaries and sport, dislikes films; <u>Clémence</u>: likes game shows and soaps, dislikes documentaries; <u>Guy</u>: likes films and the weather forecast, dislikes children's programmes; <u>Sylviane</u>: likes game shows and children's programmes, dislikes soaps

CD 3, track 15   Feuille 39, activité 1
Cassette 4, side 1

– Madame Leroy, vous aimez regarder la télévision?
– Oui.
– Qu'est-ce que vous aimez regarder?
– J'aime beaucoup les feuilletons.
– Les feuilletons français?
– Oui … et j'aime aussi regarder les informations. Je regarde les informations tous les soirs.
– Vous regardez les émissions sportives?
– Non, je n'aime pas le sport, je ne regarde pas les émissions sportives.

– Monsieur Leroy, vous aimez regarder la télévision?
– Ah oui, oui … beaucoup.
– Qu'est-ce que vous regardez?
– J'aime beaucoup les documentaires.
– Les documentaires?
– Oui … et les émissions sportives. J'adore le sport, les matchs de foot ou de rugby.
– Et les films?
– Oh non, les films, non, je n'aime pas spécialement les films.

– Clémence, tu aimes la télévision?
– Oui. C'est génial.
– Qu'est-ce que tu regardes?
– J'adore les jeux.
– Les jeux …
– Oui … c'est drôle les jeux. J'aime bien.
– Et tu regardes les feuilletons?
– Oui, bien sûr! J'adore les feuilletons.
– Il y a des émissions que tu n'aimes pas?
– Non, j'aime tout! Sauf les documentaires.
– Tu n'aimes pas les documentaires?
– Non, je déteste les documentaires.

3 On se relaxe!

– Guy, tu aimes regarder la télévision?
– Oui, c'est intéressant.
– Qu'est-ce que tu regardes?
– J'aime beaucoup les films.
– Oui …
– Euh … et j'aime aussi regarder la météo. Je regarde la météo tous les jours.
– Tu aimes les émissions pour la jeunesse?
– Ah non, je n'aime pas les émissions pour enfants. Ce n'est pas marrant.

– Sylviane, tu regardes souvent la télévision?
– Oui. Je regarde la télé tous les jours, surtout le week-end.
– Qu'est-ce que tu aimes regarder?
– J'adore les jeux, et j'aime toutes les émissions pour la jeunesse.
– Et les feuilletons?
– Non, je déteste les feuilletons.

AT 1.2/3 2 *Écoute. Relie l'activité, l'heure et l'endroit où les jeunes se retrouvent.*
Students listen to the conversations. For each one, they indicate the proposed activity together with the meeting time and place.

Answers: 1 10.00 e; 2 2.30 c; 3 11.30 a; 4 3.30 b; 5 7.00 d

CD 3, track 16   Feuille 39, activité 2
Cassette 4, side 1

1 – Tu veux faire du vélo?
 – Du vélo? Oui, je veux bien. À quelle heure?
 – À dix heures?
 – Oui, d'accord. À dix heures. On se retrouve devant le parc?
 – Devant le parc? Bonne idée. À plus tard!
2 – Élodie, tu veux aller à la plage?
 – À la plage? Oui, super!
 – On se retrouve à quelle heure?
 – À deux heures et demie.
 – À deux heures et demie? D'accord! On se retrouve où?
 – Chez moi?
 – Oui, chez toi. Bonne idée! À plus tard, Élodie!
3 – Tu veux aller à la piscine?
 – Oui, j'adore ça!
 – On se retrouve à la piscine à onze heures et demie?
 – À la piscine à onze heures et demie? D'accord!
4 – Tu veux faire de la voile cet après-midi?
 – Oui, je veux bien.
 – On se retrouve à trois heures et demie. Ça va?
 – Oui, à trois heures et demie, ça va. On se retrouve où?
 – À la plage?
 – À la plage? Bonne idée!
5 – Tu veux aller au cinéma ce soir, Benjamin?
 – Oui. C'est une bonne idée d'aller au cinéma! On se retrouve chez moi à sept heures?
 – À sept heures chez toi. D'accord.

Feuille 40 Écoute En plus

Activity 1 provides further listening practice on TV programmes and could be completed with pages 36–37 of the Students' Book. Activity 2 also focuses on TV programmes but incorporates the 24-hour clock, so it should be completed with pages 38–39. Activities 3a and 3b focus on invitations/excuses and could be used with pages 42–43 of the Students' Book.

AT 1.4 1 *Écoute.*
Students listen to Antoine and Nathalie discussing what to watch on TV. Make sure they have read and understood the three questions before listening to the recording, so that they know what to listen out for.

Answers: 1 a; 2 b; 3 Cartoon Factory

CD 3, track 17   Feuille 40, activité 1
Cassette 4, side 1

– Qu'est-ce que tu veux regarder?
– J'aime bien les émissions sportives.
– Il y a la Formule 1.
– Sur quelle chaîne?
– TF1.
– À quelle heure?
– C'est à 13 h 15 …
– Ah, c'est intéressant. Je veux bien regarder la Formule 1.
– Ah non, ce n'est pas marrant. Oh regarde, il y a un bon film.
– C'est quoi, le film?
– *Nord et Sud*, sur M6. C'est à 13 h 15.
– Ah non, je ne veux pas regarder ce film.
– Alors, on peut sortir. On va en ville?
– D'accord.
– On peut regarder la télé ce soir. Il y a *Cartoon Factory* à 19 heures. C'est génial. J'adore les dessins animés. Et toi?
– Oui, c'est drôle, *Cartoon Factory*. Alors, ce soir on regarde *Cartoon Factory*.
– Oui.

AT 1.4 2 *Changements de programme. Écoute l'annonce et écris les heures.*
Students listen to the details of rescheduled TV programmes and write in the missing times.

Answers: L'enfer blanc: 13 h 20; Les veinards: 16 h 45; Astérix et Cléopâtre: 18 h 30; Notre belle famille: 20 h

CD 3, track 18   Feuille 40, activité 2
Cassette 4, side 1

Suite à cette transmission en direct, il y a des changements au programme de l'après-midi … *L'enfer blanc* commence maintenant à 13 heures 20, *Opération cosinus* commence à 15 heures, notre film *Les veinards* va commencer à 16 heures 45, et le dessin animé avec

On se relaxe! 3

Astérix, *Astérix et Cléopâtre*, va maintenant commencer à 18 heures 30. Et pour terminer, vous pouvez voir la série *Notre belle famille* à 20 heures.

AT 1.4 **3a** *Écoute. Gisèle invite des copains à une boum. Note les excuses sur une feuille. C'est quand, la boum?*
Students listen and note down each person's excuse for not coming to the party. They also note down the time of the party.

Answers: Julien: devoirs; Isabelle: ranger sa chambre; Nicolas: devoirs; Sophie: garder son frère; Anne-Laure: cinéma; Benjamin: grand-mère; la boum est samedi soir

CD 3, track 19 **Feuille 40, activité 3a**
Cassette 4, side 1

– Allô.
– Allô, Julien. Ici Gisèle. Il y a une boum chez moi samedi soir. Tu veux venir?
– Samedi soir? Euh … Je ne peux pas.
– Pourquoi?
– Euh … Je dois faire mes devoirs.
– Tes devoirs? Ah bon. Au revoir!

– Allô.
– Isabelle? C'est Gisèle. Il y a une boum chez moi samedi soir. Tu veux venir?
– Samedi soir? Désolée, je dois ranger ma chambre.
– Tu dois ranger ta chambre samedi soir? Oh ma pauvre! Bon, ben … à bientôt!
– Merci pour l'invitation. Au revoir.

– Allô.
– Salut, Nicolas! Ici Gisèle. Tu veux venir à ma boum samedi soir?
– Euh, non. Je ne peux pas.
– Qu'est-ce que tu fais samedi soir?
– Euh … Je dois faire mes devoirs.
– Tu fais tes devoirs samedi soir? Comme Julien? Incroyable!

– Allô.
– Bonjour, Sophie. Il y a une boum chez moi samedi soir. Tu veux venir?
– J'adore les boums, mais je ne peux pas. Je suis désolée, mais samedi soir je dois garder mon frère.
– Ton frère, il a quel âge?
– Il a trois ans.
– Dommage, il est trop jeune pour venir. Bon, au revoir.

– Allô.
– Anne-Laure?
– Allô, oui.
– C'est moi, Gisèle. Il y a une boum chez moi samedi soir. Tu veux venir?
– Samedi soir, je ne peux pas. Je vais au cinéma avec Nicolas.
– Avec Nicolas? Bon, au revoir.

– Allô.
– Benjamin, tu veux venir à une boum chez moi samedi soir?
– Oui, je veux bien, mais je dois aller voir ma grand-mère.
– Ah non!
– Mais je peux venir chez toi après. D'accord?
– Oui, super! À samedi!
– À samedi! Au revoir.

3b *Qui ne dit pas la vérité? Pourquoi?*
Based on what they have heard for activity **3a**, students decide which person is not telling the truth.

Answers: Nicolas, because he is going to the cinema with Anne-Laure

Feuille 41 Parle Encore

Although the activities on this copymaster are set within the context of TV programmes (taught on pages 36–37), they provide opportunities to practise *vouloir/aller* + infinitive. It might therefore be more appropriate to use the copymaster with pages 40–41 of the Students' Book, after the *Zoom grammaire* on *vouloir*.

1 Students choose their preferred programmes from the TV listings and note them in the *Moi* column of the grid provided.

AT 2.3/4 **2** Working in pairs, students explain to each other their preferred programmes and give reasons for their choices. Encourage them to use a range of opinions and connectives. Students note down their partner's choices in the *Partenaire* column of the grid.

AT 2.4 **3** Students now negotiate to agree on TV programmes they would both be happy to watch. They complete the *Choix final* column.

Feuille 42 Parle En plus

This copymaster should be used towards the end of pages 42–43 of the Students' Book, enabling students to draw on the full range of language learned during Unit 3.

AT 3.3/4 **1** *Lis la conversation avec ton/ta partenaire. Souligne tous les verbes et les infinitifs.*
Working in pairs, students read the conversation. They underline all the verbs that are followed by infinitives. Make sure that students understand the meanings of the underlined phrases before they move on to activity **2**.

Answers:
A: Qu'est-ce que <u>tu vas faire</u> samedi matin?
B: <u>Je vais jouer</u> au tennis avec Jason. <u>Tu veux aller</u> au café samedi après-midi?
A: <u>Je ne peux pas aller</u> au café parce que <u>je dois aller</u> en ville avec Stéphanie.

3 On se relaxe!

B: <u>Tu veux aller</u> au cinéma samedi soir?
A: Oui, je veux bien. À quelle heure?
B: À sept heures et demie. Et on se retrouve où?
A: Chez moi?
B: Bon. On se retrouve à sept heures et demie chez toi et <u>on va aller</u> au cinéma.
A: D'accord.

AT 2.5 **2** *Organise un week-end intéressant avec tes ami(e)s. Utilise la conversation de l'activité 1 comme exemple.*
This is an open-ended activity in which students circulate around the class, trying to agree on/arrange activities with a variety of people. The conversation in activity 1 serves as a useful model, while the pictures provide a few ideas. Agree on some ground rules beforehand, e.g. students must not use English, they may not arrange more than one activity with the same person. This activity will be quite straightforward initially because students will be "free", but it will become increasingly complicated as they plan more and more activities for the weekend and are forced to negotiate, make excuses, etc.

Feuille 43 Lis et écris Encore 1
This copymaster provides further practice of types of film and could be used with pages 38–39 of the Students' Book.

AT 3.1 **1** *Regarde les symboles. C'est quelle sorte de film? Choisis.*
Students choose the correct caption for each picture.

Answers: 1 un western; 2 un film d'horreur; 3 un dessin animé; 4 un film policier; 5 une comédie; 6 un film de science-fiction

AT 4.2/3 **2** *Écris les conversations.*
Students follow the model provided to write a question and answer for each picture.

Answers: 1 Tu veux voir le film policier ce soir? Non, je veux voir le film de science-fiction. 2 Tu veux voir le dessin animé ce soir? Non, je veux voir le film romantique. 3 Tu veux voir le film d'horreur ce soir? Non, je veux voir la comédie. 4 Tu veux voir le film de science-fiction ce soir? Non, je veux voir le film policier.

AT 3.3 **3** *Dans la lettre, souligne les trois erreurs.*
Students read the film advertisement then underline the three errors in the letter.

Answers: the errors are: lundi (the film is not shown on Mondays); un film de science-fiction (it's a detective film); quatorze heures trente (should be 14 h 35)

Feuille 44 Lis et écris Encore 2
This copymaster practises invitations and arranging to meet, together with TV vocabulary, opinions and connectives. It could be used with pages 40–41 of the Students' Book.

AT 3.3 **1a** *Complète les messages avec les mots de la boîte.*
Students fill in the gaps in the invitations using the words provided.

Answers: 1 piscine; 2 vélo, heures; 3 chez moi; 4 après-midi, devant

AT 4.3 **1b** *Choisis le message b, c ou d et écris une réponse sur une feuille.*
Students write their own reply to message b, c or d, adapting the model provided.

AT 3.3 **2a** *Fais ce petit jeu-test. Entoure tes réponses.*
Students complete the mini-quiz on television viewing habits.

AT 4.3/4 **2b** *Tu aimes la télévision? Copie et complète ces phrases sur une feuille.*
Students expand the phrases provided to write a paragraph about their own TV preferences.

Feuille 45 Lis et écris En plus 1
This copymaster provides reading practice on the topic of films and could be used with pages 38–39 of the Students' Book.

AT 3.4 **1a** *Lis le résumé des films et trouve le bon titre pour chaque genre de film.*
Students read the cinema guide and find a film title for each of the film types listed.

Answers: 1 un dessin animé: *Les Simpson*; 2 un film romantique: *Quatre jours à Paris*; 3 un film d'horreur: *Le cimetière oublié*; 4 un film policier: *Enquête interdite*; 5 une comédie: *Qui est qui?*

AT 4.3 **1b** *Tu veux regarder quel film? Pourquoi?*
Students explain which film they would prefer to see, giving reasons for their choice.

AT 3.4 **2** *Réponds aux questions.*
Students answer questions in French on the cinema listings.

Answers: 1 non, on va au Cinévog Saint-Lazare; 2 non (mardi et mercredi); 3 à 17 h; 4 on téléphone au 01 40 30 30 31; 5 il perd tout son argent/il n'a pas d'argent; 6 un chien; 7 elle préfère Daniel

Feuille 46 Lis et écris En plus 2
This copymaster incorporates all the vocabulary and grammar points of the unit, so should be used towards the end of the unit, either with or after pages 42–43 of the Students' Book.

AT 3.5 **1a** *Lis la lettre. Vrai ou faux?*
Students answer true false questions on the letter.

Answers: 1 faux; 2 vrai; 3 faux; 4 faux; 5 vrai; 6 faux; 7 vrai; 8 vrai; 9 faux

On se relaxe! 3

AT 3.5 / **AT 4.3**

1b *Corrige les phrases fausses.*
Students correct the false answers from activity **1a**.

Answers: 1 Angus est britannique. 3 Henri ne parle pas bien anglais. 4 Henri aime surtout les dessins animés. 6 Il a vu un film policier. 7 C'est un film de science-fiction. 9 Henri n'aime pas faire ses devoirs.

2a *Souligne toutes les questions qu'Henri pose dans sa lettre.*
Students underline all the questions in Henri's letter.

Answers: Ça va? Qu'est-ce que tu fais le week-end? Tu aimes regarder la télé aussi? Qu'est-ce que tu préfères regarder à la télé? Tu aimes aller au cinéma? Qu'est-ce que tu aimes voir comme films? Pourquoi? Qu'est-ce que tu vas faire le week-end prochain? Tu veux me rendre visite l'année prochaine?

AT 4.5

2b *Écris sur une feuille la réponse d'Angus à Henri. N'oublie pas les opinions et les connecteurs!*
Students write a reply to Henri. Encourage them to redraft their work after comparing with a partner. If necessary, refer them back to the *Guide pratique* section on page 95 of *Équipe nouvelle 1* Students' Book for advice on checking for errors.

Feuille 47 Grammaire 1

This copymaster focuses on *aller* + infinitive to express the future and should be used with pages 38–39 of the Students' Book.

1 *Choisis le bon verbe pour compléter le poème.*
Students select the correct verb forms to complete each line of the poem. This activity focuses on recognition and use of the infinitive.

Answers: aller, venir, visiter, aller, inviter, faire, sortir, venir

2 *Qu'est-ce qu'ils vont faire?*
In response to the picture prompts, students write a sentence to say what the people are going to do.

Answers: 1 Max va faire du ski. 2 Anne va aller au café. 3 Romain va faire du football. 4 Catherine va regarder la télé. 5 Jean et Marc vont faire de la natation. 6 Juliette et Claire vont faire du vélo.

3 *Qu'est-ce que tu vas faire ce week-end? (Choisis six activités.)*
Students write six sentences to say what they themselves are going to do next weekend.

Feuille 48 Grammaire 2

This copymaster focuses on *vouloir*, *pouvoir* and *devoir*, and should be used with pages 42–43 of the Students' Book.

1 *Réécris les phrases dans le bon ordre.*
Students rewrite the sentences using correct word order.

Answers: 1 Tu veux faire du skate? 2 On peut aller en ville. 3 Je dois garder mon frère.

2 *Écris une question, une suggestion et une excuse pour les illustrations.*
Students write three sentences for each picture: one sentence using *vouloir*, one using *pouvoir*, and the third using *devoir*.

Answers: 1 Tu veux aller à la piscine? On peut aller à la piscine. Je dois aller à la piscine. 2 Tu veux regarder la télé? On peut regarder la télé. Je dois regarder la télé. 3 Tu veux faire du football? On peut faire du football. Je dois faire du football.

3 *Complète les phrases.*
Students complete the sentences using the correct form of an appropriate modal verb.

Answers: 1 Tu <u>peux</u>/<u>veux</u> sortir ce soir? Non, je <u>dois</u> rester à la maison. 2 Anne <u>veut</u> acheter un jean. Mais elle ne <u>peut</u> pas. Elle n'a pas d'argent. 3 Les enfants <u>doivent</u> faire les devoirs. Mais ils ne <u>veulent</u> pas parce qu'ils <u>veulent</u> jouer au foot dans le parc! 4 Tu <u>dois</u> ranger ta chambre? Oui, mais je <u>veux</u> aller au cinéma avec toi!

Feuille 49 Guide pratique 1

This copymaster focuses on listening for gist and detail. Activity 1 could be used with the *Guide pratique* on page 41 of the Students' Book; activities 2 and 3 practise telephone numbers so should be used with pages 42–43.

1 *Écoute les six émissions de télé. C'est quel genre d'émission?*
Students follow the advice given in the Flashback panel to work out the different types of TV programme represented on the recording. Before beginning this activity, remind students of the different types of TV programme and ask them to consider any clues or sound effects they might hear that would help them to work out their answers. Stress that they are listening for gist only, so there is no need to focus on trying to understand any detail.

Answers: 1 un documentaire; 2 la météo; 3 les informations; 4 une émission sportive; 5 une émission pour la jeunesse; 6 un jeu

---

CD 3, track 20   Feuille 49, activité 1
Cassette 4, side 1

1 – Aujourd'hui on va en Afrique pour observer les animaux sauvages – des lions, des éléphants, des girafes …
2 – Soleil dans le nord de la France, mais pluie et orages dans le sud.
3 – Aujourd'hui, grave accident sur l'autoroute A1. Trois cars et un camion …
4 – Bienvenue au stade de France pour le match de foot entre Marseille et Paris Saint-Germain …

3 On se relaxe!

5 – Un, deux, trois, nous irons au bois; quatre, cinq, six …
6 – Et à la fin du jeu, l'équipe bleue a cinq points et l'équipe rouge a six points. Félicitations à l'équipe rouge! …

2 *Écoute et note les numéros de téléphone de Natacha, Arnaud, Matthieu et Juliette.*
Students listen and note down the telephone numbers, referring to the guidance in the Flashback panel.
Answers: Natacha: 02 35 24 67 39; Arnaud: 02 35 40 18 77; Matthieu: 02 35 61 51 62; Juliette: 02 35 11 98 52

CD 3, track 21 Feuille 49, activité 2
Cassette 4, side 1

– C'est quoi, ton numéro de téléphone, Natacha?
– Mon numéro de téléphone, c'est le 02 35 24 67 39.
– 02 35 24 67 39, c'est ça?
– Oui, c'est ça.

– C'est quoi, ton numéro de téléphone, Arnaud?
– Mon numéro de téléphone, c'est le 02 35 40 18 77.
– 02 35 40 18 77, c'est ça?
– Oui, c'est ça.

– C'est quoi, ton numéro de téléphone, Matthieu?
– Mon numéro de téléphone, c'est le 02 35 61 51 62.
– 02 35 61 51 62, c'est ça?
– Oui, c'est ça.

– C'est quoi, ton numéro de téléphone, Juliette?
– Mon numéro de téléphone, c'est le 02 35 11 98 52.
– 02 35 11 98 52, c'est ça?
– Oui, c'est ça.

3 *Écoute et réponds aux questions 1–5.*
Students listen to the conversation in which Antoine and Nathalie are arranging to go to the cinema. They answer questions, first on the gist of the conversation then on specific details.
Answers: 1 c; 2 b; 3 02 45 72 15 93; 4 cinq euros pour les moins de 15 ans; 5 à 18 h 45 devant le cinéma

CD 3, track 22 Feuille 49, activité 3
Cassette 4, side 1

– Salut Nathalie! Tu veux sortir ce soir?
– Oui, je veux bien. On va où?
– Il y a un bon film de science-fiction au cinéma.
– D'accord. Le film est à quelle heure?
– Je ne sais pas. On doit téléphoner.
– C'est quoi le numéro de téléphone?
– C'est le 02 45 72 15 93.
– Le 02 45 72 15 93?
– Oui, c'est ça.
– Je vais téléphoner …
– Bonjour. Ici Cinéma Rex. Pour connaître les horaires des films de ce soir, tapez 1…
– Alors, le film est à 19 h 00. Ça coûte 5 euros pour les moins de 15 ans.
– On se retrouve où et quand?
– À 18 h 45 devant le cinéma?
– 18 h 45 devant le cinéma. Très bien. À tout à l'heure.

Feuille 50 Guide pratique 2

This copymaster focuses on understanding feedback on work and launches Framework objective **8W3**. The sentences in activity 2 practise the connectives *parce que* and *mais*, so you might find it appropriate to use the copymaster as a follow-up to the *Guide pratique* on connectives on page 37 of the Students' Book.

1 *Remplis les cercles avec les phrases 1–8.*
Students allocate the phrases to the correct circle, depending on whether they are things they need "to do" or things they need "to take note of".
Answers: à faire: attention aux accents, vérifie dans ton dictionnaire, vérifie ton orthographe; à noter: beaucoup mieux, bon travail, travail très soigné, le "s" ne se prononce pas, bon effort

2 *Complète les phrases avec les mots de la boîte.*
Students complete each sentence (*C'est beaucoup mieux parce que …* and *C'est beaucoup mieux mais …*) using the phrases provided.
Answers: C'est beaucoup mieux parce que … tu as fait beaucoup d'effort, tu as utilisé des mots intéressants, tu as parlé sans hésiter. C'est beaucoup mieux mais … tu peux aussi vérifier l'orthographe, tu peux ajouter des adjectifs, tu peux donner un peu plus de détails.

Feuille 51 Ça se dit comme ça!

This copymaster focuses on sound–spelling exceptions in the pronunciation of numbers. It should be used with the *Ça se dit comme ça!* panel on page 39 of the Students' Book. There will be further work on liaison in Unit 5 on Feuille 85.

1 *Écoute et répète ces phrases. Fais attention à la prononciation des numéros!*
Students listen to the recording and repeat the phrases, following the text on the copymaster.

CD 3, track 23 Feuille 51, activité 1
Cassette 4, side 1

– Un, deux, trois, quatre, cinq, six … j'ai six oranges!
– Vite! Le train part dans six minutes!
– Le film commence à deux heures. On y va?
– Deux billets pour le film *Harry Potter*, s'il vous plaît.
– Je vais jouer au foot avec mes trois amis.
– J'adore les trois lions au zoo.

On se relaxe! 3

2a *Lis les phrases et souligne où il y a une liaison. Compare avec ton/ta partenaire.*
Students read the sentences and underline the numbers where the endings are pronounced.

Answers: see transcript

2b *Lis les phrases à haute voix. Écoute et vérifie.*
Students read the sentences aloud then listen to the recording to check their pronunciation.

CD 3, track 24 Feuille 51, activité 2b
Cassette 4, side 1

1 – J'ai <u>deux</u> amis en France.
2 – J'ai deux chiens et <u>un</u> hamster.
3 – J'ai mangé <u>trois</u> oranges et une pomme aujourd'hui.
4 – Tu as trois minutes pour arriver au collège!
5 – Le film commence à <u>dix</u> heures.
6 – Au cinéma Rex, il y a dix films tous les week-ends.
7 – Dans ma trousse, j'ai six crayons et une règle.
8 – Les <u>six</u> enfants veulent jouer dans le parc.

Encore Workbook

Page 24 (3.1)
Use with pages 36–37 of the Students' Book.

AT 4.1 **1** *Complète.*
Students fill in the missing vowels to complete the types of TV programme.

Answers: a les films; b les jeux; c les documentaires; d la météo; e les informations; f les dessins animés; g les feuilletons; h les émissions sportives; i les émissions pour la jeunesse

AT 3.1 **2** *Vrai ou faux?*
Students answer true/false questions on Bruno's TV preferences.

Answers: a vrai; b faux; c faux

AT 4.2/3 **3** *Et toi? Complète.*
Students complete the sentences to give their own TV viewing preferences.

Page 25 (3.2)
Use with pages 38–39 of the Students' Book.

AT 4.1 **1a** *Utilise le code pour trouver les films qu'ils préfèrent.*
Students use the code to work out each person's favourite type of film.

Answers: Anne: les comédies; Mustapha: les films policiers; Nadia: les dessins animés; Nicolas: les films d'horreur

AT 4.2 **1b** *Écris une phrase pour chaque personne.*
Students write a sentence to express each person's preferences.

Answers: Anne aime les comédies. Mustapha aime les films policiers. Nadia aime les dessins animés. Nicolas aime les films d'horreur.

AT 4.2 **2** *Et toi? Qu'est-ce que tu aimes comme film?*
Students express in writing their own film preferences.

Page 26 (3.3)
Use with pages 40–41 of the Students' Book.

AT 3.3 **1** *Lis les messages et complète la grille.*
Students read the invitations and fill in the details in the grid provided.

Answers:

	destination	heure	où
Martin	cinéma	mercredi, 2 h 15	café
Alice	piscine	demain, 10 h	piscine
Thomas	plage	samedi, 3 h 30	chez Thomas
Fatiha	en ville	lundi, 9 h 15	cinéma

AT 4.2 **2** *Recopie et complète les messages.*
Students copy and complete the messages, replacing the pictures with words.

Answers: 1 Tu veux aller à la patinoire samedi soir? On se retrouve à huit heures au café. À bientôt. 2 Tu veux faire du vélo jeudi soir? Si oui, on se retrouve devant le cinéma à sept heures et quart!

AT 4.3 **3** *Invite un copain/une copine à sortir. Écris un message à la page 33.*
Students write their own invitation, specifying a proposed activity together with a meeting place and time.

Page 27 (3.4)
Use with pages 42–43 of the Students' Book.

AT 4.2/3 **1** *Écris une excuse pour chaque invitation.*
Students give written excuses in response to the picture prompts, choosing from the phrases provided.

Answers: b Je ne peux pas. Vendredi, je dois ranger ma chambre. c Je ne peux pas. Jeudi, je dois garder mon petit frère. d Je ne peux pas. Mardi, je dois promener le chien. e Je ne peux pas. Samedi matin, je dois faire du shopping. f Je ne peux pas. Mercredi, je dois faire mes devoirs.

AT 3.2 **2** *Suis la bonne route pour trouver l'excuse de Dracula.*
Students follow a route through the clouds to find a sentence expressing what Dracula has to do.

Answer: Je dois aller à la piscine.

3 On se relaxe!

Page 28 Grammaire

Use with pages 42–43 of the Students' Book.

1 *Relie.*
Students match the French verb forms to their English equivalents.

Answers: 1 d; 2 a; 3 c; 4 e; 5 f; 6 b

2 *Complète.*
Students fill in the gaps in the message using the correct verb forms.

Answers: veux, peux, peut, veux, peut, veut

3 *Complète.*
Students choose an infinitive from the box to complete each sentence.

Answers: a aller; b sortir; c voir; d regarder

Page 29 Méli-mélo

This page pulls together and mixes much of the language and grammar of the whole unit, focusing on *vouloir*, *pouvoir*, *devoir* and *aller* + infinitive. It should therefore be used towards the end of the unit, either with or after pages 42–43.

1 *Choisis le bon verbe pour traduire les phrases en anglais.*
Students fill in the gap in each sentence using the correct form of *pouvoir*, *vouloir* or *devoir*.

Answers: a ne peux pas; b dois; c veux; d peux; e veux; f ne veux pas

2 *Écris la bonne forme du verbe entre parenthèses.*
Students complete the sentences by filling in the correct forms of *vouloir*, *pouvoir*, *devoir* or *aller*.

Answers: a vas; b veut; c doit; d va; e vais; f dois; g peut; h veux

Page 30 Challenge!

Use with page 46 of the Students' Book.

[AT 3.3/4] **1** *Réponds aux questions en anglais.*
Students answer questions in English on Nathan's arrangements for Saturday afternoon.

Answers: a He wants to see his friends. b Going to the beach, going to the swimming pool, going ice skating. c Nicolas has to go to a wedding, Florentin has to help mother to tidy the house, Rebecca doesn't like ice skating/has to do homework. d To a party at Benjamin's house. e Nicolas, Florentin and Rebecca are all at the party.

2 *Complète le résumé avec les verbes de la boîte.*
Students complete a summary of the text in French, using the verb forms provided in the box.

Answers: veut, peut, doit, peut, va, veut, veut, veut, veut

En plus Workbook

Page 24 (3.1)

Use with pages 36–37 of the Students' Book.

[AT 4.1] **1a** *Complète le nom des émissions.*
Students fill in the missing vowels to complete the types of TV programme.

Answers: les films; les jeux; les documentaires; la météo; les informations; les dessins animés; les feuilletons; les émissions sportives; les émissions pour la jeunesse

[AT 3.3] **1b** *Lis la bulle de Bruno. Dessine ☺ ou ☹.*
Students read about Bruno's TV preferences. They draw an appropriate symbol beside each programme type to indicate Bruno's opinion.

Answers: Bruno likes the weather, game shows, sports programmes, soaps, cartoons, the news; he dislikes films, children's programmes, documentaries

1c *Et toi? Dessine ☺ ou ☹ pour toi.*
Students draw symbols to indicate their own TV preferences.

[AT 4.3/4] **2** *Écris une bulle pour toi à la page 33.*
Students write about their TV preferences. Encourage them to use a range of connectives and to express a variety of opinions.

Page 25 (3.2)

Use with pages 38–39 of the Students' Book.

[AT 4.1] **1a** *Utilise le code pour trouver les films qu'ils préfèrent.*
Students use the code to work out each person's favourite type of film.

Answers: Nadia: les dessins animés; Mustapha: les films d'horreur

[AT 4.2] **1b** *Écris une phrase pour chaque personne.*
Students write a sentence to express each person's preferences.

Answers: Nadia aime les dessins animés. Mustapha aime les films d'horreur.

[AT 4.3/4] **1c** *Et toi? Tu aimes quel genre de film? Écris des phrases à la page 33.*
Students express their own opinions of different types of film.

[AT 3.3/4] **2** *Lis le message et réponds aux questions en anglais.*
Students read the message giving details of different films and answer questions in English.

Answers: a Sunday afternoon; b in town; c horror films; d she doesn't like them very much; e at 10 past 3 (15.10); f at 20 past 5 (17.20)

Page 26 (3.3)

Use with pages 40–41 of the Students' Book.

AT 3.3 **1** *Lis les messages et complète la grille.*
Students read the invitations and fill in the details in the grid provided.

Answers:

	destination	heure	où
Martin	cinéma	mercredi, 2 h 15	café
Alice	piscine	demain, 10 h	piscine
Thomas	plage	samedi, 3 h 30	chez Thomas
Fatiha	en ville	lundi, 9 h 15	cinéma

AT 4.3 **2** *Recopie et complète les deux messages ci-dessous.*
Students copy and complete the messages, replacing the pictures with words.

Answers: 1 Tu veux aller à la patinoire samedi soir? On se retrouve à huit/vingt heures au café. À bientôt. 2 Tu veux faire du vélo jeudi soir? Si oui, on se retrouve devant le cinéma à sept heures et quart/à dix-neuf heures quinze!

AT 4.3 **3** *Invite un copain/une copine à sortir. Écris un message à la page 33.*
Students write their own invitation, specifying a proposed activity together with a meeting place and time.

Page 27 (3.4)

Use with pages 42–43 of the Students' Book.

AT 4.3 **1** *Écris une excuse pour chaque invitation.*
Students give written excuses in response to the picture prompts.

Answers: b Je ne peux pas. Vendredi, je dois ranger ma chambre. c Je ne peux pas. Dimanche, je dois aller voir ma grand-mère. d Je ne peux pas. Jeudi, je dois garder mon petit frère. e Je ne peux pas. Mardi, je dois promener le chien. f Je ne peux pas. Samedi matin, je dois faire du shopping/les courses. g Je ne peux pas. Mercredi après-midi, je dois faire mes devoirs.

AT 3.2 **2** *Suis la bonne route pour trouver la réponse de Dracula. Complète sa bulle.*
Students follow a route through the clouds to find Dracula's response to the invitation.

Answer: Je ne peux pas aller à la plage parce que je dois aller au lit tôt.

Page 28 Grammaire

Use with pages 42–43 of the Students' Book.

1 *Traduis en français.*
Students translate the English verb forms into French.

Answers: a je veux; b ils/elles veulent; c il veut; d je peux; e tu peux; f on peut/nous pouvons

2 *Complète avec la bonne forme du verbe.*
Students fill in the gaps in the message using the correct verb forms.

Answers: veux, peux, peut, veux, peuvent, veut

3 *Complète avec des verbes à l'infinitif.*
Students choose infinitives from the box to complete each sentence.

Answers: a aller, payer; b sortir, venir; c voir, acheter; d rester, regarder

Page 29 Méli-mélo

This page pulls together and mixes much of the language and grammar of the whole unit, focusing on *vouloir*, *pouvoir*, *devoir* and *aller* + infinitive. It should therefore be used towards the end of the unit, either with or after pages 42–43.

1 *Complète les phrases avec le bon verbe.*
Students fill in the gap in each sentence using the correct form of *pouvoir*, *vouloir*, *devoir* or *aller*.

Answers: a vas; b veut; c doit; d vont/peuvent; e vais; f devons; g peuvent/vont; h voulez

2 *Écris "devoir", "pouvoir" ou "vouloir" à la bonne forme pour faire des phrases vraies pour toi.*
Students complete the sentences to express information about their own lifestyle, adding the correct positive or negative forms of *devoir*, *pouvoir* or *vouloir*.

3 *Lis l'e-mail de Katya. Réponds à ses questions. Utilise le futur (aller + infinitif) et devoir/vouloir/pouvoir + infinitif. Marque un point par verbe utilisé!*
Students write a reply to the e-mail, trying to use modal verbs and *aller* + infinitive as often as possible. They score a point for each correct use of the verbs.

Page 30 Super-challenge!

Use with page 46 of the Students' Book.

AT 3.4 **1** *Coche le meilleur résumé de l'histoire.*
Students tick the sentence that best summarizes the story.

Answer: c

2 *C'est qui A, B, C, D et E?*
In these sentences, the people's names have been replaced by the letters A, B, C, D and E. Students look back at the text and work out who is represented by each letter.

Answers: A: Rebecca; B: Florentin; C: Nicolas; D: Nathan; E: Benjamin

AT 4.4/5 **3** *La même histoire arrive à Isabelle. Adapte le texte et raconte son histoire avec des éléments de la boîte à la page 33. (Environ 150 mots.)*
Students write a similar text to tell Isabelle's story. They are provided with a few sentences to set the scene together with a panel of phrases as prompts.

Unit 4 Overview grid

National Curriculum

Pages/Contexts/ Cultural focus	Objectives	Grammar	Skills and Pronunciation	Key language	Framework	PoS	AT level
50–51 **4.1 Elle joue au foot, il joue du piano** Sports and musical instruments Football in France	Revise sports; say what sports you play; say what musical instruments you play or would like to play; say how often you do activities; find out about football in France	*jouer à* *jouer de* Different meanings of common words	Time expressions	*jouer au tennis, au ping-pong,* etc. *faire du football, de la voile, de l'équitation,* etc. *le clavier, le piano, le violon, la batterie, la flûte, la guitare* *Tu joues de quel instrument? Je joue du clavier/du piano/du violon/de la batterie/de la flûte/de la guitare. Je ne joue pas d'instrument. Quand? de temps en temps, tous les jours, souvent, une/deux/trois fois par jour/semaine/mois, le lundi, le mardi,* etc., *ne … jamais*	8S5, 8T1, 8T3 – L 8W1, 8S2, 8C3 – R	1b, 1c, 2a, 2c, 2d, 2f, 2h, 2i, 3a, 3b, 3c, 3e, 4a, 4c, 4d, 5a, 5d, 5e, 5f, 5i	1.3, 2.2–4, 3.3, 4.2–4
52–53 **4.2 Ma journée** Daily routine	Talk about your daily routine; ask someone about their daily routine; describe someone else's daily routine; write a longer description	Reflexive verbs	Writing a longer description	*je me réveille, je me lève, je me lave, je m'habille, je prends le petit déjeuner, je me brosse les dents, je me couche À quelle heure est-ce que tu …? à + time*	8T5 – L 8W2, 8W5, 8S1, 8S7 – R	1a, 1b, 1c, 2a, 2b, 2c, 2d, 2f, 2h, 2i, 2j, 3b, 3c, 3e, 4a, 4d, 5a, 5d, 5e, 5f, 5i	1.3, 2.2–4, 3.3, 4.2–4
54–55 **4.3 À la maison** Household chores (present tense)	Name different household chores; say what you do/don't do on a regular basis; use verb tables; improve your speaking skills	Using verb tables	Sounding French	*faire son lit, faire le ménage, faire la cuisine, faire les courses, faire la vaisselle, ranger sa chambre, mettre le couvert*	8T7 – L 8W4, 8S3, 8L1, 8L5 – R	1b, 1c, 2a, 2b, 2c, 2d, 2f, 2g, 3b, 3c, 3d, 3e, 4a, 4d, 5a, 5c, 5d, 5e, 5f, 5i	1.3, 2.2–4, 3.2, 4.2–4
56–57 **4.4 J'ai donné un coup de main!** Household chores (past tense)	Say what you have/haven't done to help at home; use the negative with the past tense; adapt a text	Use of the negative with the perfect tense	Adapting a text	*Qu'est-ce que tu as fait? lundi/hier/ce week-end/le week-end dernier j'ai fait la cuisine/la vaisselle/le lit/ le ménage/les courses, j'ai mis le couvert, j'ai rangé ma chambre je n'ai pas fait la cuisine, tu n'as pas fait ton lit, ils n'ont pas fait les courses*	8S6 – L 8S1 – R	1b, 1c, 2a, 2c, 2d, 2f, 2h, 2i, 2j, 3c, 3e, 4a, 4d, 5a, 5c, 5d, 5e, 5f, 5i	1.3–4, 2.2–5, 3.4–5, 4.2–5
58–59 **4.5 La belle équipe, épisode 4** Soap story	Develop listening and reading skills via a soap story based on the language of the unit					1a, 1c, 2a, 2b, 2g, 2h, 2i, 3b, 3c, 3e, 4a, 4d, 5a, 5d, 5e, 5g, 5i	1.4, 2.4, 3.4
60 **Super-challenge!** Young people's attitudes and lifestyles	Understand some comments about teenagers; use reflexives in the negative; develop awareness of sound–spelling exceptions; agree/disagree with other people's opinions	Plural forms of reflexive verbs Negatives with reflexive verbs	*-ent* endings (silent or pronounced)		8W6, 8S1, 8C3 – R	1a, 1b, 1c, 2a, 2b, 2f, 2g, 3c, 3d, 3e, 4a, 4d, 5a, 5c, 5d, 5e, 5i	1.4, 3.3, 4.3

About this unit: In this unit students work in the context of daily routine and helping in the home. They learn to describe their daily routine, to ask about routines of teenagers, and to describe what they do (or do not do) to help at home. Whilst working in these contexts, students learn to understand and use reflexive verbs in the present tense. They also consolidate and extend their knowledge of modal verbs and the use of the *passé composé* (including negatives with *ne … pas* and *ne … jamais*). The unit also provides opportunities for extended dialogues, for unscripted speech, for personalizing a model letter and for looking at the impact of vocabulary in a text. Progress at word level is developed by working on abstract expressions of time, connectives in continuous text and exceptions to sound–spelling rules.

Week-by-week overview (assuming 6 weeks' work or 10–12.5 hours)

Week 1 Introduction to unit objectives. Revise sports. Say what sports you play. Say what musical instruments you play or would like to play. Say how often you do activities. Find about football in France.

Week 2 Talk about your daily routine. Ask someone about their daily routine. Describe someone else's daily routine. Write a longer description.

Week 3 Name different household chores. Say what you do/don't do on a regular basis. Use verb tables. Improve your speaking skills.

Week 4 Say what you have/haven't done to help at home. Use the negative with the past tense. Adapt a text.

Week 5 Develop listening and reading skills via a soap episode.

Week 6 *Super-challenge!* for more able students. Recycle language of the unit via *Encore*, *En plus* and *Point lecture* pages. Students check progress via the *Podium* self-assessment checklist in the Students' Book and on Feuille 53. Use the *Révisions* and *Contrôles* sections for formal assessment of student progress.

Framework objectives (launch)

	Teaching and learning
8S5: negative forms and words	Revision of *ne … pas*; *ne … jamais*. Negatives in the perfect tense.
8S6: substituting and adding	Adapt a longer text.
8T1: meanings in context	*Jouer à* and *jouer de*.
8T3: language and text types	Before working on sports you play/don't play, predict what content/language might occur.
8T5: writing continuous text	Write a continuous text using connectives and time markers.
8T7: checking inflections and word order	Use verb tables to check pronoun and verb agreements.

Framework objectives (reinforce)

	Teaching and learning
8W1: adding abstract words	Expressions of time to describe frequency.
8W2: connectives	Use connectives to write a continuous text.
8W4: word endings	Use verb tables to conjugate verbs in the present tense.
8W5: verb tenses	Present tense of reflexive verbs; compare present and perfect tenses in a text about what Arnaud did last weekend.
8W6: sound–spelling exceptions	*Couchent* (not sounded) and *adolescents* (sounded) on *Super-challenge!* page.
8W8: non-literal meanings	Develop awareness of non-literal translations via the song on the *Point lecture* page, e.g. *sous la pluie* = in the rain, *au soleil* = in the sunshine.
8S1: word, phrase and clause sequencing	Word order of reflexive verbs in the present tense with positive and negative expressions; word order of negative expressions in the perfect tense.
8S2: connectives in extended sentences	Use expressions of time to build complex sentences.
8S3: modal verbs	Use of modals + infinitive to talk about helping around the house (page 54, activities 1a and 1b). Use of modal verbs in the soap story.
8S7: present, past and future	Present tense of reflexive verbs; compare present and perfect tenses in a text about what Arnaud did last weekend.
8L1: listening for subtleties	How to sound French 2: hesitation techniques.
8L5: unscripted speech	How to sound French 2.
8C3: daily life and young people	Football in France. Young people's attitudes and lifestyles (on the *Super-challenge!* page).

Teaching and learning (additional)

Revise sports. Musical instruments. Daily routine expressions. Household chores.

4 Tous les jours

Unit objectives

Contexts: leisure activities; daily routine
Grammar: *jouer à, jouer de*; revision of present tense verbs; revision of negatives; present tense of reflexive verbs (including negatives); different meanings of common words; verb tables; perfect tense with the negative
Language learning: expressions of time; using connectives and time markers in writing; how to sound French; adapting a text
Pronunciation: silent ending *-ent* in present tense verb forms
Cultural focus: football in France; young people's daily routine; teenagers' relations with their parents

Assessment opportunities

Reading: Students' Book, page 51, activity 2c; Students' Book, page 127, *Point lecture*, activity 2b
Writing: Students' Book, page 57, *Guide pratique*, activity 1; Students' Book, page 57, *Challenge!* activity A or B

This opening page revises vocabulary for sports and leisure activities. In preparation for work on the next spread, draw students' attention to the phrase *jouer au foot* (so far students may have used only *faire du foot*). The word *ping-pong* is new, but students should be able to deduce its meaning from the sound effects on the recording.

AT 1.2 **1a** *Écoute et regarde les photos. Quelle activité n'est pas mentionnée?*
Students listen to the recording while looking at the pictures representing leisure activities in Dieppe. They select the picture/activity that isn't mentioned on the recording.

Answer: le tennis

CD 2, track 1 page 49, activité 1a
Cassette 2, side 2

– Au Club Vacances, je joue au foot.
– Moi, je préfère regarder des vidéos.
– J'aime bien aller à la pêche.
– Moi, j'aime aller à la piscine, faire de la natation.
– Moi, je vais à la plage faire du surf. J'adore faire du surf!
– Au Club Vacances, je fais de l'équitation.
– Je fais de la voile.
– J'aime jouer au ping-pong. On joue?
– D'accord!

AT 4.1/2 **1b** *Fais une liste des neuf activités.*
Students list the nine activities shown in the photos. Depending on students' ability, they could either list the nouns only, or infinitive phrases (e.g. *jouer au ping-pong*), or you could ask them to write a statement in the first person singular for each activity (e.g. *je fais de la natation*).

Answers: a des vidéos; b la natation; c le football; d la pêche; e la voile; f l'équitation; g le tennis; h le ping-pong; i le surf

AT 2.2/3 **1c** *A pose une question pour chacune des neuf activités, B répond.*
Before beginning this task, each student estimates how many activities their partner does. They then ask each other questions to find out. Whose estimate was the most accurate?

AT 2.2/3 **1d** *Remue-méninges. À deux, pensez à d'autres sports et activités pour ajouter à votre liste.*
AT 4.1/2 In pairs, students brainstorm additional sports and leisure activities. This encourages them to recall appropriate language from Part 1 of the course and to use dictionaries or the glossary at the back of the book to look up new vocabulary. Pairs could feed back to the class while you record the information on the board or OHP. This could be a competition, with pairs competing to see who draws up the longest list within a set time.

Planning Page

Tous les jours **4**

4.1 Elle joue au foot, il joue du piano

pages 50–51

Objectives

- Revise sports (**8T1, 8T3 – L**)
- Say what sports you play
- Say what musical instruments you play or would like to play
- Say how often you do activities (**8S5 – L**) (**8W1, 8S2 – R**)
- Find out about football in France (**8C3 – R**)

Resources

Students' Book, pages 50–51
CD 2, track 2
Cassette 2, side 2
Encore/En plus Workbooks, page 34
OHTs 16A, 16B and 16C
Flashcards 61–69
Copymasters 54, 55 and 60

Key language

jouer au tennis, au ping-pong, au football, au hockey, etc.
faire du football, du judo, de la voile, de la natation, de l'équitation, etc.
le clavier, le piano, le violon, la batterie, la flûte, la guitare
Tu joues de quel instrument?
Je joue du clavier/du piano/du violon/de la batterie/de la flûte/de la guitare.
Je ne joue pas d'instrument.
Quand?
de temps en temps, tous les jours, souvent
une/deux/trois fois par jour/semaine/mois
le lundi, le mardi, etc.
ne … jamais

Programme of Study reference

1b, 1c, 2a, 2c, 2d, 2f, 2h, 2i, 3a, 3b, 3c, 3e, 4a, 4c, 4d, 5a, 5d, 5e, 5f, 5i

Starters

- *À vos marques*, page 50.
- Copymaster 54 *À vos marques*, activities 1a and 1b.
- Revise the alphabet and sports/leisure activities with a quick oral game. Divide the class into two teams and say, for example, *Je cherche une activité qui commence par la lettre N*. The first student to suggest a suitable activity (e.g. *la natation*) wins a point for their team. The first team to achieve five points wins. (Variation: ask for *une activité qui finit par la lettre …*)
- Play Kim's game using **Flashcards 61–69**. Stick the cards to the board with putty adhesive. Three volunteers come to the front of the class and turn their backs while you remove two or three cards. Which volunteer is the first to name the missing cards?

ICT suggestions

- Students use clip art and interesting fonts to create posters for display in the classroom to remind themselves of the vocabulary for activities and/or the time expressions from pages 50–51.
- To reinforce the language of pages 50–51, students type out the texts of *Planète musique* (about Florence, Claude and Justin). They then delete every fifth or sixth word, replacing it with XXX. Can they key the words back in accurately without referring to the Students' Book?
- Students use the Internet to do some research, perhaps for homework, on a French footballer or on football in France in general. Useful websites:
www.fff.fr
www.football.fr
www.sport-en-france.com/football
www.planetefootball.com
There are many other websites if students use a search engine (e.g. www.yahoo.fr or www.google.fr).

Creative activities

- Students cut pictures from newspapers or magazines, or use clip art, to create a frieze of people doing different sports and/or playing musical instruments. They write a speech bubble for each, explaining what they are doing, when, how often and where they play.
- Students devise crossword puzzles to swap with a partner, using words and expressions from the *Mots-* and *Expressions-clés*.

Plenaries

- *Challenge!* page 51.
- Copymaster 55 *Challenge!* activity 1.
- Using examples from the phrases on pages 50–51, reflect on the importance of learning the gender of nouns (e.g. to be able to construct accurate sentences when combining with *à* or *de*). If appropriate, extend to other reasons why learning gender is important (e.g. in order to make adjective agreements, choose the correct possessive pronoun, etc.).

Homework suggestions

- Students learn vocabulary and key expressions (meaning, pronunciation and spelling, with special emphasis on gender of nouns).
- *Encore/En plus* Workbooks, page 34.
- Make a photocopy of **OHT 16A** for each student. They write a suitable sentence in each speech bubble. To make this activity more challenging, ask students to include a different time expression in each.
- Students use the Internet or the library to find out more about a French footballer, or about other sports that are popular in France. They write details in English, but could include any useful French words or expressions they encounter.

4 Tous les jours

4.1 Elle joue au foot, il joue du piano
pages 50–51

Presentation

▶ Before beginning work on this spread, and before students open their books, write up the spread heading (*Elle joue au foot, il joue du piano*) on the board or OHP and ask students to predict what language is likely to be covered here. This encourages them to associate different aspects of language with different contexts and text types, and launches **8T3**.

▶ This spread, with its focus on *jouer à* and *jouer de*, provides an opportunity for the launch of **8T1** (meanings in context). You could do this either at the beginning of work on the spread or in conjunction with the *Zoom grammaire* section.

Point out to students that they have met these two very common words *à* (*au/à l'/à la/aux*) and *de* (*du/de l'/de la/des*) in many different contexts and that their meanings tend to change depending on the context. Ask students to come up with as many different uses of *à* and *de* as they can, and write up their suggestions on the board or OHP together with the English meanings. For example: *du chocolat* (some chocolate, any chocolate), *à neuf heures* (at nine o'clock), *à Paris* (in/to Paris), *il va au cinéma* (he's going to the cinema), *au petit déjeuner* (for/at breakfast). Include some examples where the words *à* and *de* are omitted in English, e.g. *faire du foot* (to play football), *un sandwich au fromage* (a cheese sandwich).

▶ Use **Flashcards 61–69** to present/revise the names of sports if necessary. For instance, you could write the names of the sports on the board or OHP as a numbered list. When you show a card, students have to give the corresponding number. Then show each card in turn, covered with a blank sheet of paper. Gradually reveal the picture. How quickly can students name the sport pictured?

À vos marques

AT 2.2 *Jeu de mémoire: jouez à deux ou à trois.*

▶ Students play a memory game to practise the sports vocabulary, using the grid of picture prompts provided. Student A begins by saying they play one of the sports; student B repeats A's sentence, adding a second sport; student C repeats B's sentence and adds a third sport; and so on. Depending on students' ability, you may need to brainstorm the sports beforehand and write phrases up on the board or OHP.

▶ If this type of starter activity with a memory element proves too difficult, students could simply use the picture prompts to help them name or write a list of the nine activities.

▶ Alternatively, students could use the grid to play Noughts and Crosses: they must name the activity or say a sentence (e.g. *je joue au foot*) in order to "win" the square.

AT 4.2/3 **1a** *Tu fais les activités illustrées à droite? Tous les jours? De temps en temps? Jamais? Écris neuf phrases.*

Students write sentences stating how often they do the sports featured in the *À vos marques* grid. It would be useful to work on the *Guide pratique* panel on time expressions before beginning this activity: see notes below.

Follow-up activity: Students could go on to write similar sentences about the activities they brainstormed on the previous page (Students' Book page 49, activity **1d**).

AT 2.3 **1b** *Et ton/ta partenaire? Pose des questions.*

In pairs, students question each other on their responses to activity **1a**, asking whether they do the activities and, if so, how often. They could record each other's answers and then either feed back to the class or write a report in the third person singular, e.g. *Lucy ne joue jamais au tennis*, etc.

Guide pratique

This section reinforces **8W1** and **8S2** through its focus on the use of time expressions to make spoken or written work more detailed. Students are also introduced to the negative *ne … jamais*, which launches **8S5**.

1 Students match the English time expressions to the *Expressions-clés*.

Answers: every day: *tous les jours*; now and again: *de temps en temps*; never: *ne … jamais*; often: *souvent*; once a day: *une fois par jour*; twice a month: *deux fois par mois*; three times a week: *trois fois par semaine*

2 Students add a suitable time expression to each sentence. Before students begin this activity, point out that *ne … jamais* works in exactly the same way as *ne … pas*, i.e. it goes around the verb, *du/de l'/de la/des* change to *de* after it. (With more able students, you could also introduce *ne … plus*.) Make sure students are aware that some of the phrases (e.g. *tous les jours, de temps en temps*) can go either at the beginning or at the end of a sentence.

Follow-up activity: Use **OHT 16A** with overlays **16B** and **16C** for further practice of the time expressions with sports vocabulary.

Point culture

This section provides information on French football and the French national football team. It provides an opportunity to reinforce **8C3**. Football fans may be keen to do some research, perhaps for homework, on a French footballer or on football in France in general. Useful websites:
www.fff.fr
www.football.fr
www.sport-en-france.com/football
www.planetefootball.com
There are many other websites if students use a search engine (e.g. www.yahoo.fr or www.google.fr).
Some students may prefer to find out about a different sport.

Tous les jours 4

Presentation

▶ On the board or OHP, write the English names of the six musical instruments featured: drums, flute, guitar, keyboard, piano, violin. Students must match them to the *Mots-clés* at the top of page 51. Four are cognates so should cause no problem, although it is important to stress the correct pronunciation. Can students work out the other two? (For example: *batterie* – *battre* = to beat = drums.)

▶ Mime playing one of the instruments; the class have to say which one. Then students work in pairs, taking turns to mime and guess the name of the instrument being played.

AT 1.3 **2a** *Écoute. On joue de quels instruments dans le collège de Florence?*
Prepare for this activity by asking students to list the musical instruments from the *Mots-clés*. They then listen to the recording and tick the instruments mentioned.

Answers: le piano, la guitare, le violon, le clavier, la flûte

---

CD 2, track 2   page 51, activité 2a
Cassette 2, side 2

– Florence, tu joues de quel instrument au collège?
– Moi, je joue du piano.
– Et toi, tu joues de quel instrument?
– Euh … moi, je ne joue pas d'instrument.
– Ah, bon. Et toi?
– Je joue de la guitare.
– Et toi?
– Moi aussi, de la guitare.
– Moi, je joue du violon.
– Et toi, tu joues de quel instrument?
– Moi, je joue du clavier.
– Et moi, je joue de la flûte.

Follow-up activity: Ask students to find out and list the instruments that are played in your own school. They could present their findings as an illustrated chart.

AT 2.3 **2b** *Et dans ton collège? A écrit trois instruments en secret. B devine.*
Working in pairs, each student notes down three instruments and keeps them hidden from their partner. The partner asks questions to work out what they have written down. Who can guess their partner's instruments in the fewest guesses?

AT 3.3 **2c** *Lis l'article à droite. Vrai ou faux?*
Students answer true/false questions on the article.

Answers: a faux; b faux; c faux; d faux; e vrai

Follow-up activity: Students correct the false statements in activity **2c**.

Answers: a Florence joue du piano. b Elle joue tous les jours. c Claude joue tous les jours. d Il va au club des jeunes le samedi.

Zoom grammaire

This section focuses on when to use *jouer à* and when to use *jouer de*.

1 Students write sentences using *jouer à* and *jouer de*.

Answers: a Anne joue au football et au tennis, et elle joue du piano et de la flûte. b Bruno joue au rugby, de la batterie, du violon, et il joue au golf.

Refer students to the grammar section on page 144 of the Students' Book for further information on *jouer à* and *jouer de*.

C60 Feuille 60 *Lis et écris Encore 1* provides further practice of the language of this spread and could be used at this point.

W34 Page 34 of the *Encore* and *En plus* Workbooks provides further practice and could also be used here.

Challenge!

AT 4.2/3 **A** *Fais des phrases.*
Students make sentences using the jumbled words provided.

AT 4.3/4 **B** *Réponds aux questions.*
Students write their own answers to the questions about sports and musical instruments. Before they begin, direct them towards appropriate sentences from this spread that they could adapt.
The third question (*Tu voudrais jouer d'un instrument?*) has been included in order to offer students who don't play a musical instrument the opportunity to say what they would like to play. Students have already met *Je voudrais* + noun in *Équipe nouvelle 1* (in Unit 5 in the context of saying what they would like to eat and drink), but you may need to explain the structure *Je voudrais* + infinitive. Ask students whether they can think of any other instances where they would use a verb followed by an infinitive (e.g. *Je vais* + infinitive to refer to the future, *J'aime* + infinitive to refer to something they like doing).

AT 2.3/4 **C** *Avec un(e) partenaire, imagine une interview avec Florence, Claude ou Justin.*
Working in pairs, students make up an interview with one of the characters from this spread. They could use the questions from *Challenge!* activity **B**. Before students begin this activity, make sure they are clear about the format of the questions.

4 Tous les jours

Planning Page

4.2 Ma journée
pages 52–53

Objectives
- Talk about your daily routine (8W5, 8S1, 8S7 – R)
- Ask someone about their daily routine
- Describe someone else's daily routine
- Write a longer description (8T5 – L) (8W2 – R)

Resources
Students' Book, pages 52–53
CD 2, tracks 3–4; CD 3, tracks 25 and 28
Cassette 2, side 2; cassette 4, side 2
Encore/En plus Workbooks, pages 35 and 38
OHTs 17A and 17B
Copymasters 56, 57, 61, 64 and 66

Key language
je me réveille, je me lève, je me lave, je m'habille, je prends le petit déjeuner, je me brosse les dents, je me couche
À quelle heure est-ce que tu …?
à + time

Programme of Study reference
1a, 1b, 1c, 2a, 2b, 2c, 2d, 2f, 2h, 2i, 2j, 3b, 3c, 3e, 4a, 4d, 5a, 5d, 5e, 5f, 5i

Starters
- *À vos marques*, page 52.
- Copymaster 61 *Lis et écris Encore 2*, activities 1a and 1b.
- *Encore/En plus* Workbooks, page 35, activity 1.
- Students draw simple symbols to represent each of the *Expressions-clés*. They could either write their own captions for the symbols or swap with a partner who guesses what the symbols represent and fills in the captions.

ICT suggestions
- Students word-process (and illustrate with clip art if there is time) the questions and their answers for activity 2b on page 52. They could ask a partner to read and check their work before printing out.
- Students do a PowerPoint® presentation to explain the present tense of reflexive verbs (see *Zoom grammaire*, page 53).

Creative activities
- Students work in pairs to recreate an interview with Pierre Rousseau, recording or videoing their performance if possible.
- Students make two sets of cards, the first set with the seven daily routine expressions written on, and the second with pictures illustrating the seven expressions. They can use the finished cards to play games such as Word–Picture Snap or Pelmanism.

Plenaries
- *Challenge!* page 53.
- Tell students a series of statements – some true, some false – about your daily routine, including details of time and rooms of the house. The class decide which statements are true.
- As a follow-up to the *Guide pratique* on page 53, divide the class into two teams. They take turns to come to the board or OHP to extend a sentence, e.g. *Mon frère se lève*, attempting to make it as long as possible.
- Students tell their partner one important thing they have learned during the lesson. Allow time for each pair to feed back to the rest of the class.

Homework suggestions
- Copymaster 61 *Lis et écris Encore 2*.
- Copymaster 66 *Guide pratique 1*.
- *Encore/En plus* Workbooks, page 35.

Tous les jours **4**

4.2 Ma journée
pages 52–53

À vos marques
Trouve l'intrus et dis pourquoi.
This activity revises sports and musical instruments from the previous spread, and reintroduces days of the week and meals/times of day from Part 1 of the course. Students find the odd-one-out in each set of words. Accept alternative answers to those given below if students can justify them.

Answers: a *la semaine* because it is the only word that isn't a sport, or *l'équitation* because all the other words begin with *la*; b *une chemise* because it is not a musical instrument, or *violon* because all the other words have seven letters; c *regarder* because it is a verb and all the other words are days of the week, or *jeudi* because all the other words have eight letters; d *le petit déjeuner* because it is a meal and all the others are times of day

Presentation
▶ Before starting work on this spread, you may like to revise telling the time and rooms of the house.
▶ To revise the time, you could provide a list of times written as figures, e.g. 11.30, to be matched with a list of times written as words, e.g. *onze heures trente*.
▶ To revise the rooms of the house, you could add a further odd-one-out line to the *À vos marques* activity: *une cuisine, une salle de bains, une chambre, un collège*. Once students have identified the odd-word-out and explained how they made their choice, ask them to brainstorm to recall other rooms they have met.

AT 1.3
AT 3.3
1a *Regarde les dessins. Écoute et lis.*
Before playing the recording, set the scene by looking at the photo of Juliette talking to Matthieu: what are they talking about? (They are discussing whether Juliette has time to fit a quick exercise session into her daily routine.) Students listen and follow the text in the Students' Book. Ask them to consider how Juliette might be able to find time for a quick exercise session either in the morning or the evening, e.g. by getting out of bed as soon as she wakes, by going to bed a little later.

CD 2, track 3   page 52, activité 1a
Cassette 2, side 2

– Tu fais des exercices le matin?
– Non, je n'ai pas le temps!
– Dix minutes … ce n'est pas beaucoup!
– Oui, mais … écoute … Pendant la semaine, je me réveille à six heures trente. À six heures quarante-cinq, je me lève … et puis, je me lave.
À six heures cinquante-cinq, je m'habille.
À sept heures, je prends le petit déjeuner.
Ensuite, je me brosse les dents.
– Le soir, alors! Fais des exercices le soir. Tu te couches à quelle heure?
– Le soir, je me couche à neuf heures trente.

AT 1.3
AT 3.3
1b *Écoute Juliette. C'est quel dessin? Note l'heure.*
Students listen to Juliette describing her daily routine again, but this time the details are in a different order. Students listen and indicate the letter of each picture as it is mentioned. They then note down the time of each activity.

Answers: 1 a: 6.30; 2 f: 7.20; 3 e: 7.00; 4 d: 6.55; 5 b: 6.45; 6 c: 6.45; 7 g: 9.30

CD 2, track 4   page 52, activité 1b
Cassette 2, side 2

– Salut! Qu'est-ce que je fais le matin? Eh bien …
1 – Je me réveille à six heures trente.
2 – Je me brosse les dents dans la salle de bains à sept heures vingt.
3 – Je prends mon petit déjeuner dans la cuisine à sept heures.
4 – Je m'habille dans ma chambre à six heures cinquante-cinq.
5 – Je me lève à six heures quarante-cinq.
6 – À six heures quarante-cinq, je me lave dans la salle de bains.
7 – Le soir, je me couche à neuf heures trente.

Follow-up activity:
▶ **OHTs 17A** and **17B** could be used at this point to consolidate the vocabulary for describing daily routine together with the present tense of reflexive verbs. Cut up the word bricks from **17B** and keep them stored in an envelope.
▶ Place **17A** on the OHP and point to one of the pictures. Have the bricks needed to build the caption for that picture in jumbled order at the bottom of the screen. For example, for the first picture (girl waking up) you will need *réveille, me, je*. Ask students to construct a caption. Repeat with the other pictures until all the captions are complete.
▶ Although the word bricks include first, second and third person singular forms, you could at this stage use the first and second person bricks only, saving the *il* and *elle* forms until you have worked on the *Zoom grammaire* panel (see notes below).

AT 4.2/3
2a *Réponds aux questions à droite pour Juliette.*
To help students familiarize themselves with questions using the *tu* form of reflexive verbs, ask them to copy out each question first and then write Juliette's answer beside it. Most of the questions can be answered by referring to the captions in the Students' Book; however, in order to answer question 6, students will need to refer to their answers from activity **1b**.

Answers: 1 Je me réveille à six heures trente. 2 Je me lève à six heures quarante-cinq. 3 Je m'habille à six heures cinquante-cinq. 4 Je prends le petit déjeuner à sept heures. 5 Je me lave à six heures quarante-cinq. 6 Je me brosse les dents à sept heures vingt. 7 Je me couche à neuf heures trente.

127

4 Tous les jours

AT 4.2/3 — **2b** *Recopie et complète le questionnaire pour toi.*
Students copy out the questionnaire again and complete it with their own information. To support less able students, you could prepare for this activity by using **OHT 17A**. Make an overlay by drawing a small clock face to go with each picture. This could be used to elicit statements such as: *Je me réveille à 7 h 10.*

AT 4.3/4 — **2c** *Utilise tes réponses pour écrire une description de ta journée. (Lis d'abord Guide pratique, p. 53.)*
Students now expand their answers to the questionnaire (activity **2b**) to write a longer description of their daily routine. They need to have worked on the *Guide pratique* panel (see notes below) before doing this activity.

AT 2.3/4 — **2d** *Interviewe ton/ta partenaire. Pose les questions du questionnaire.*
In pairs, students ask each other the questions from the questionnaire and make a note of their partner's answers.

Guide pratique

This section launches **8T5** and reinforces **8W2**. It provides tips on how to produce a longer, more detailed piece of written work. Refer students back to the connectives used in Juliette's account of her daily routine (*et puis, ensuite*) and ask them to suggest others that they've met previously. Students then follow the advice to produce more detailed versions of the three sentences given.

C66 — Feuille 66 *Guide pratique 1* could be used at this point. It provides further guidance and practice of writing a longer description.

AT 3.3 — **3a** *Relie les descriptions aux illustrations à droite.*
You may prefer to work on the *Zoom grammaire* section (see notes below) before beginning this activity, which introduces the third person singular of reflexive verbs together with a wider range of these verbs (*il se prépare*: literally "he prepares himself"; *il se repose*: literally "he rests himself"; *il s'entraîne*: literally "he trains himself"). Students match each caption to a picture on the storyboard. They should be able to use contextual clues or picture clues to understand the text, even though some of the vocabulary is new and they won't be able to understand every word. Reinforce the literal translations of reflexive verbs.

Answers: 1 d; 2 b; 3 e; 4 f; 5 c; 6 a

Follow-up activity: You could work as a whole class, or students could work in pairs, to arrange the statements into chronological order to give an account of the footballer's day. Once this is done, read out the correct sequence so that students can check their answers and familiarize themselves with the pronunciation of the new vocabulary. Then ask questions on the text, e.g. *Qu'est-ce qu'il fait de 10 heures à 11 heures?*; students respond by reading out the corresponding statement a–f.

AT 2.2/3 — **3b** *A décrit une illustration. B donne le numéro.*
Working in pairs, students take turns to read out a caption and their partner gives the number of the corresponding picture. More able students could try to experiment a little with the language by varying the captions, e.g. instead of reading out caption b, they could substitute *Il met sa tenue de football.*

Zoom grammaire

This grammar section reinforces **8W5**, **8S1** and **8S7** by looking at the first, second and third person singular forms of reflexive verbs.
Focus on the way the reflexive pronoun changes the literal meaning of the phrases: *Je me lave* = "I wash" or literally "wash myself". Further develop this concept by showing how other known verbs could be made reflexive, e.g. *regarder: je me regarde dans le miroir* = "I look at myself in the mirror". You could extend this even further by showing how a reflexive verb can be made non-reflexive, e.g. *je couche le bébé, je lave la voiture.*

1 Students copy out the sentences, adding in the missing reflexive pronouns.

Answers: a me; b se; c te; d se

Refer students to the grammar section on page 143 of the Students' Book for further information on this grammar point. Note also that the *Point lecture* song lyrics on page 126 of the Students' Book provide further practice of the present tense of reflexive verbs.

W38 — Page 38 of the *Encore* Workbook could be used at this point: it focuses on the first, second and third person singular forms of reflexive verbs.

C64 / **W38** — Feuille 64 *Grammaire 1* and page 38 of the *En plus* Workbook also focus on reflexive verbs. However, they incorporate both singular and plural forms, whereas the *Zoom grammaire* section on this spread deals only with the first, second and third person singular. You may therefore prefer to save this copymaster and the *En plus* Workbook page until the *Super-challenge!* page (page 60 of the Students' Book), where plural forms of reflexive verbs are taught.

Follow-up activities:
OHTs **17A** and **17B** can be used for further practice with reflexive verb forms. For example:
▶ Using **17A** only, point to a picture and ask: *Qu'est-ce qu'elle fait?*
▶ Using only the word bricks from **17B**, make sentences with the reflexive pronouns missing. Students fill the gaps with the correct pronouns.
▶ Using only the word bricks from **17B** again, mime an action and ask a student to come out to the OHP and select and position the correct bricks to describe what you are doing. Once they understand how the activity works, students can take turns to perform the mimes in

your place. For less able groups, restrict the choice of bricks available so that students concentrate on the accurate sequencing of the words. With more able groups, you could jumble the bricks from several sentences.

C56 / **C57** Activity 1 on Feuille 56 *Écoute Encore* provides further practice of daily routine vocabulary and could be used at this point. Activity 1 on Feuille 57 *Écoute En plus* could also be used: it provides practice of daily routine vocabulary together with the 12-hour clock.

C61 Additional reading and writing practice of daily routine vocabulary is provided on Feuille 61 *Lis et écris Encore 2*.

W35 Page 35 of the *Encore* and *En plus* Workbooks also provides reading and writing practice using the language of this spread.

Challenge!

AT 4.2/3 **A** *Réponds au questionnaire, p. 52, pour Pierre Rousseau. (Invente les détails qui ne sont pas donnés.)*
Referring back to the questionnaire on page 52, students give Pierre Rousseau's answers to the questions, using the first person singular of the verbs and inventing any details that aren't supplied.

AT 4.4 **B** *Décris la matinée de Juliette (voir p. 52).*
Students produce a written description of Juliette's routine, referring back to page 52 and changing the first person verbs into the third person singular. As a follow-up, they could imagine a similar description of Charlie le chat's routine, working on what they know of his character.

AT 4.4 **C** *Écris une description plus détaillée des 24 heures de Pierre Rousseau.*
Students expand the details of Pierre Rousseau's day into a longer, more detailed description in the third person singular. Refer them back to the *Guide pratique* for some suggestions on writing a longer account.

4 Tous les jours

Planning Page

4.3 À la maison
pages 54–55

Objectives
- Name different household chores
- Say what you do/don't do on a regular basis (**8S3 – R**)
- Use verb tables (**8T7 – L**) (**8W4 – R**)
- Improve your speaking skills (**8L1, 8L5 – R**)

Resources
Students' Book, pages 54–55
CD 2, tracks 5–7; CD 3, track 28
Cassette 2, side 2; cassette 4, side 2
Encore/En plus Workbooks, page 36
OHT 18A
Copymasters 54, 57 and 63

Key language
faire son lit, faire le ménage, faire la cuisine, faire les courses, faire la vaisselle, ranger sa chambre, mettre le couvert

Programme of Study reference
1b, 1c, 2a, 2b, 2c, 2d, 2f, 2g, 3b, 3c, 3d, 3e, 4a, 4d, 5a, 5c, 5d, 5e, 5f, 5i

Starters
- *À vos marques*, page 54.
- Copymaster 54 *À vos marques*, activities 2a and 2b.
- Make a memory chain around the class (or in groups of three or four):
  A: *Je range ma chambre.*
  B: *Je range ma chambre et je fais la vaisselle.*
  C: *Je range ma chambre, je fais la vaisselle et je fais le ménage*, etc.
- Provide students with a list of infinitives and subject pronouns (e.g. *être/elles, avoir/nous, venir/vous, prendre/je, manger/nous, devoir/tu, pouvoir/on*) and ask them to use the verb tables at the back of the Students' Book to locate the correct present tense form to go with the subject pronoun given. For example, *être/elles: sont.*

ICT suggestions
- Students word-process a dossier of the language learned so far in this unit.
- Students prepare a PowerPoint® presentation showing which chores the class like and dislike most (see activity **1c**).

Creative activities
- Students work in pairs or small groups to devise a rap using the *Expressions-clés* (they could mime as they rap: *Je fais mon lit*, etc.). Alternatively, they could set the phrases to a well-known tune, e.g. to the tune of "She'll be coming round the mountain":
  Faire son lit, faire le ménage, faire la cuisine,
  Faire les courses, faire la vaisselle, ranger sa chambre,
  Faire son lit, mettre le couvert,
  Mettre le couvert
  Mettre le couvert
  Faire son lit, mettre le couvert, faire son lit.
- Students write out the seven key expressions as anagrams for their partner to work out.

Plenaries
- *Challenge!* page 55.
- Say a single word from the lesson. In pairs, students must think of a question and answer containing the word.
- Students suggest strategies for learning and remembering the *Expressions-clés*.
- Show **OHT 18A** and ask students to provide a caption for each picture.

Homework suggestions
- Copymaster 63 *Lis et écris En plus 2*.
- *Encore/En plus* Workbooks, page 36.
- Students' Book, page 54, activity 1c.
- Students write a short text setting out their resolutions for helping out at home, e.g. *Je vais faire mon lit tous les jours*, etc.

Tous les jours **4**

4.3 À la maison
pages 54–55

À vos marques

AT 3.2
AT 4.2 *Écris les phrases pour Dracula.*
To revise the language of the previous spread, students rewrite the speech bubble to give a description of Dracula's routine, separating out the words and adding punctuation.

Answers: Je me réveille tous les jours à minuit. Je me couche le matin à six heures. Je me brosse les dents une fois par jour.

AT 1.3
AT 3.2 **1a** *Écoute et note les suggestions.*
Students listen to the young people talking about different ways of helping around the house. They note down the letters of the pictures corresponding to each person's suggestions.
Revise modal verbs (from Unit 3) and reinforce Framework objective **8S3** by drawing students' attention to the use of *on peut* + infinitive used throughout the recording (see also activity **1b** below). If appropriate, point out *Tu sais faire la cuisine?* in the interview with Thomas and explain that this follows exactly the same pattern (i.e. verb followed by infinitive) as *pouvoir*, *vouloir* and *devoir*.

Answers: Martin: e; Nathalie: c; Antoine: a; Flore: d; Thomas: b; Kristelle: f, g

---

🎧 **CD 2, track 5** page 54, activité 1a
Cassette 2, side 2

– Martin, qu'est-ce qu'on peut faire pour aider à la maison?
– Euh, pour aider, on peut faire son lit. Je fais mon lit tous les matins.

– Nathalie, qu'est-ce qu'on peut faire pour aider à la maison?
– On peut faire le ménage. Par exemple, j'ai fait le ménage ce week-end.

– Qu'est-ce qu'on peut faire pour aider à la maison, Antoine?
– On peut ranger sa chambre.
– Tu ranges ta chambre?
– Oui, mais je n'aime pas ça.

– Flore, qu'est-ce qu'on peut faire pour aider à la maison?
– Euh, par exemple, on peut faire les courses. Moi, je vais souvent au supermarché pour faire les courses.

– Thomas, qu'est-ce qu'on peut faire pour aider à la maison?
– On peut faire la cuisine.
– Tu sais faire la cuisine?
– Oui, j'aime beaucoup faire la cuisine.

– Qu'est-ce qu'on peut faire pour aider à la maison, Kristelle?
– On peut mettre le couvert, ou bien on peut faire la vaisselle. Ça aide.

AT 2.2 **1b** *A mime une tâche. B devine.*
Working in pairs, students take turns to mime one of the tasks for their partner to guess. Students could give their answers using infinitives (as in the model provided); or you could ask them to use the first and second person singular, e.g. Partner A: *Tu fais le ménage?* Partner B: *Non, je fais mon lit.*
Alternatively, you could take this opportunity to further reinforce Framework objective **8S3** (modal verbs) by asking students to use *on peut ...*, following the same pattern as in the recording for activity **1a**. For example: Partner A: *On peut faire le ménage?* Partner B: *Non, on peut faire son lit.* Encourage more able students to use a variety of modals, e.g. Partner A: *Tu dois/veux faire la cuisine?* Partner B: *Non, je dois/veux faire les courses.*

AT 4.2 **1c** *Fais une liste des tâches. 1 = la plus agréable, 7 = la moins agréable.*
Students list the tasks in order of preference, ranging from the least unpleasant to the most unpleasant. Or they could list the tasks and allocate points to reflect the usefulness of each task, e.g. do they think tidying one's room is more useful than setting the table?

Follow-up activity: Students could compare their lists from activity **1c** with a partner and discuss their choices: Partner A: *Faire la vaisselle, c'est la moins agréable.* Partner B: *Non, je ne suis pas d'accord ...*

AT 1.3 **2** *Écoute Matthieu. Trouve le dessin (p. 54) qui ne va pas.*
Students listen and make a note of the letters (from the pictures on page 54) of the chores that Matthieu says he does and doesn't do.

Answers: chores done: e, c, d; chores not done: a

🎧 **CD 2, track 6** page 55, activité 2
Cassette 2, side 2

– Dis, Matthieu, tu fais ton lit?
– Oui! Normalement, je fais mon lit le matin.
– Tous les jours?
– Oui.
– Ouah! Bravo! Et ... Tu fais le ménage?
– Oui, de temps en temps je fais le ménage.
– Tu fais les courses aussi?
– Oui, je fais les courses. Pas de problème!
– Bravo! Génial! Et tu ranges ta chambre?
– Ma chambre? Euh ... ben ...
– Ah ah ... tu ne ranges pas ta chambre???
– Ben ..., ça dépend!

AT 2.3/4 **3** *Interviewe ton/ta partenaire.*
In pairs, students interview each other to find out what they do to help around the house.

C57 Activity 2 on Feuille 57 *Écoute En plus* provides additional listening practice on household chores in the present tense, together with expressions of frequency, and could be used at this point.

4 Tous les jours

C63 Feuille 63 *Lis et écris En plus 2* could also be used here. It practises household chores in the present tense, together with daily routine.

W36 Additional reading and writing practice of the language of this spread is provided on page 36 of the *Encore* and *En plus* Workbooks.

Guide pratique

This section reinforces **8L1** and **8L5**. It provides tips on how to sound more authentic when speaking French by adding in hesitation words.

1 Students listen to the recording and note down how many times they hear the hesitation words.

Answers: euh: 4; bof: 1; ben: 3; tu sais: 1

CD 2, track 7 page 55, Guide pratique, activité 1
Cassette 2, side 2

– Pendant la semaine … euh … je me réveille vers sept heures, mais … euh … le week-end … ben … je reste un peu plus longtemps au lit. Le ménage? Bof! Euh …tu sais … je ne fais jamais mon lit … mais … ben … euh … je fais le ménage une ou deux fois par semaine … Bon, ben, voilà!

---

2 Students work in pairs to tell each other about their daily routine and what they do to help at home, using the prompts provided and incorporating some of the French hesitation words.

Zoom grammaire

This grammar section gives guidance on how to use verb tables, thereby launching **8T7** and reinforcing **8W4**.

1 Students use the verb tables in the back of the Students' Book to find the present tense forms of the verbs given.

Answers: a tu es; b on porte; c Juliette et Natacha veulent; d nous buvons; e mes parents sont; f vous mangez; g Juliette et Arnaud vont; h ils prennent; i la grand-mère danse

2 Students find the perfect tense of the verbs given.

Answers: a j'ai eu; b elle a fait; c mon frère et moi avons eu; d les profs ont fait; e tu as mis

Refer students to the verb tables on pages 139–141 of the Students' Book and the section on the perfect tense on page 142.

Follow-up activity: For extra practice on using verb tables, give students some additional phrases to complete for homework, requiring them to supply the correct form not only of the verbs but also of the possessive adjectives. For example, provide them with phrases such as "Je (ranger sa chambre)" or "Tu (faire son lit)?" and ask them to put the verbs and the possessive adjectives into the correct form (*Je range ma chambre. Tu fais ton lit?*).

Challenge!

AT 4.2/3 **A** *Qu'est-ce que tu fais pour aider à la maison? Écris sept phrases.*
Students write sentences stating what they do to help at home.

AT 4.4 **B** *Écris un paragraphe pour expliquer ce que chaque membre de ta famille fait à la maison. C'est juste?*
Students write a longer text explaining what the different members of their family do to help at home. They comment on whether or not this is fair.

AT 2.3/4 **C** *À deux, imaginez une interview avec une personne très travailleuse (ou très paresseuse).*
AT 4.3/4 Students work in pairs to invent an interview with either a very hard-working person or a very lazy person. Pairs could learn their interviews and perform them to the class. Encourage them to incorporate some of the French hesitation words from the *Guide pratique* section.

Planning Page

4.4 J'ai donné un coup de main

pages 56–57

Objectives

- Say what you have/haven't done to help at home
- Use the negative with the past tense (8S1 – R) (8S5)
- Adapt a text (8S6 – L)

Resources

Students' Book, pages 56–57
CD 2, tracks 8–9; CD 3, tracks 26–27 and 30
Cassette 2, side 2; cassette 4, side 2
Encore/En plus Workbooks, pages 37 and 39
OHTs 18A and 18B, 19A, 19B and 19C
Copymasters 55, 56, 57, 58, 59, 62, 65 and 67

Key language

Qu'est-ce que tu as fait?
lundi/hier/ce week-end/le week-end dernier, …
j'ai fait la cuisine, j'ai fait la vaisselle, j'ai fait mon lit, j'ai fait le ménage, j'ai fait les courses, j'ai mis le couvert, j'ai rangé ma chambre
je n'ai pas fait la cuisine, tu n'as pas fait ton lit, ils n'ont pas fait les courses

Programme of Study reference

1b, 1c, 2a, 2c, 2d, 2f, 2h, 2i, 2j, 3c, 3e, 4a, 4d, 5a, 5c, 5d, 5e, 5f, 5i

Starters

- *À vos marques*, page 56.
- Show **OHT 18A**. Point to a picture and make a statement, e.g. *Elle a fait les courses*. If it is true, students stand. If it is false, they remain seated.
- Write some jumbled sentences on the board or OHP for students to rearrange, e.g. *ménage / mon / ce / pas / fait / week-end / père / n' / a / le = Ce week-end, mon père n'a pas fait le ménage.*
- Students reread Arnaud's letter and write five comprehension questions (or true/false statements) to swap with a partner.

ICT suggestions

- Students make a bar chart, pie chart or graph to show the results of their class survey (see *Challenge!* activity **C**).
- Students word-process their adaptation of Arnaud's letter, using colour to highlight the parts they have changed.

Creative activities

- Students draw a cartoon strip or write a dialogue using as many of the *Expressions-clés* from the unit as possible.
- Students play a game of *Qui suis-je?* One student is blindfolded. Another student is nominated to stand behind the blindfolded student and say what they did/didn't do to help at home last weekend, disguising their voice, e.g. by making it gruff or squeaky. How quickly can the blindfolded person guess who is speaking?

Plenaries

- *Challenge!* page 57.
- Copymaster 55 *Challenge!* activity 2.
- Students change a list of positive perfect tense statements into negative sentences. They check their partner's work to make sure that they have both understood and correctly applied the rule.
- In pairs, students write as many different negative perfect tense sentences as they can in two minutes.
- Students discuss in pairs elements of the unit so far that they feel confident about and others they are less confident about. Allow time for feedback to clear up any concerns.

Homework suggestions

- *Encore/En plus* Workbooks, pages 37 and 39.
- Copymaster 62 *Lis et écris En plus 1*.
- Copymaster 65 *Grammaire 2*, activities 1 or 3.
- Copymaster 67 *Guide pratique 2*.

4 Tous les jours

4.4 J'ai donné un coup de main

pages 56–57

À vos marques

Trouve dans la lettre d'Arnaud …
To revise known language, students search Arnaud's letter for various details.

Answers: les pièces: la cuisine, ma chambre, la salle à manger; les tâches ménagères: faire la vaisselle, faire les courses, faire son lit, ranger sa chambre; quelque chose à manger: du poulet, des frites; les verbes au présent: je me lève, je déteste ça, je suis nul, je me couche, c'est mon passe-temps préféré, j'aime bien le week-end; les verbes au passé composé: tu m'as posé des questions, ce que j'ai fait le week-end dernier, j'ai mangé dans la cuisine, j'ai fait la vaisselle, j'ai fait les courses, j'ai fait mon lit, je n'ai pas rangé ma chambre, j'ai retrouvé mes amis, on a joué au ping-pong, je n'ai pas gagné, j'ai écouté mes CD, j'ai regardé un film, je suis allé à la plage, j'ai fait de la voile, on a mangé, j'ai promené le chien, j'ai fait mes devoirs, qu'est-ce que tu as fait le week-end dernier?

AT 3.4/5
1a *Lis la lettre. Arnaud a passé un bon week-end?*
Students decide whether they think Arnaud has enjoyed his weekend.

Answer: yes

AT 2.4/5
1b *Donne à ton/ta partenaire trois raisons pour ta réponse à l'activité 1a.*
Students tell their partner three reasons for their answer to activity **1a**.

Possible answers: parce qu'il a retrouvé ses amis au club des jeunes, parce qu'il a écouté ses CD/regardé un film d'horreur, parce qu'il a fait de la voile (c'était génial)

AT 1.3/4
AT 3.4/5
2 *Écoute la mère d'Arnaud. Elle parle d'Arnaud, mais elle fait des erreurs. Vrai ou faux?*
This activity focuses on the detail of Arnaud's letter. Students listen to Arnaud's mother and compare what she says with the details given in the letter. They pick out what is true and what is false in what she says.
Before listening, students list numbers 1–8; as they listen, they tick or cross each number to indicate true or false. You will need to keep pausing the recording so that students have time to check the information given in the letter. You could use **OHT 19A** when checking answers, to highlight the relevant part of the letter.

Answers: 1 true; 2 false (il a pris son petit déjeuner dans la cuisine); 3 false (il a fait la vaisselle); 4 false (il n'a pas rangé sa chambre); 5 false (samedi après-midi, il est allé au club des jeunes/samedi soir, il a écouté des CD et il a regardé la télé); 6 false (dimanche matin, il est allé à la plage et il a fait de la voile); 7 true; 8 false (il a fait ses devoirs)

CD 2, track 8 page 56, activité 2
Cassette 2, side 2

1 – Arnaud se lève à neuf heures le week-end.
2 – Samedi matin, il a pris son petit déjeuner dans la salle à manger.
3 – Il n'a pas fait la vaisselle!
4 – Il a rangé sa chambre, mais il n'aime pas ça!
5 – Samedi soir, il est allé au club des jeunes.
6 – Dimanche matin, il a regardé un film à la télé.
7 – Après le déjeuner, il a promené le chien.
8 – Il n'a pas fait ses devoirs.

Follow-up activities:
▶ Students write true/false statements about Arnaud's letter and exchange with a partner.
▶ Ask students some comprehension questions on the letter, in either English or French.

Guide pratique

This section launches **8S6** through its focus on how to adapt a text. Students adapt Arnaud's letter to write about their own weekend, following the advice given. You could use **OHTs 19A**, **19B** and **19C** to work on the letter with students.

C67 Feuille 67 *Guide pratique 2* provides additional guidance and practice on how to adapt a model text; it could be used at this point.

Zoom grammaire

This grammar section focuses on how to make negative statements in the perfect tense. It continues the launch of **8S5** and provides another opportunity to reinforce **8S1**. Before starting work on this section, you could use **OHTs 18A** and **18B**. For example, draw a cross beside one of the pictures on **18A** and use the cut-out bricks to build a caption. Repeat this for one or two other pictures. Then ask a volunteer to come to the front and choose a picture. He/She then constructs a caption for the picture using the word bricks.

1a After looking at the pictures and captions showing how the negative is formed with perfect tense verbs, students rewrite the speech bubble, making all the statements negative.

Answers: see transcript below

1b Students listen to the recording to check their answers.

CD 2, track 9 page 57, Zoom grammaire, activité 1b
Cassette 2, side 2

– Ce matin, je <u>n'ai pas fait</u> mon lit et je <u>n'ai pas rangé</u> ma chambre. Marion <u>n'a pas mis</u> le couvert pour le petit déjeuner et elle <u>n'a pas préparé</u> le café. Mes parents

Tous les jours 4

n'ont pas fait les courses l'après-midi, et ils n'ont pas fait le ménage. Papa n'a pas fait la cuisine à sept heures et Marie et moi, nous n'avons pas fait la vaisselle.

AT 2.2-4
AT 4.2-5

C *Les filles font plus de travail à la maison que les garçons? Fais un sondage dans ta classe. Interviewe tes camarades de classe et présente les résultats.*
Students carry out a survey to find out what the boys and girls in their class did last week to help at home. They write a report on their findings or present them graphically.

Refer students to the grammar section on page 145 of the Students' Book for further information on this grammar point.

C65 Feuille 65 *Grammaire 2* focuses on negative and positive statements in the perfect tense and could be used at this point.

C56
C57 Activities 2 and 3 on Feuille 56 *Écoute Encore* provide further listening practice on household chores using the perfect tense, and could be used at this point. Activity 3 on Feuille 57 *Écoute En plus* could also be used: it focuses on household chores in the perfect tense, including negatives, but also incorporates other language, e.g. leisure activities.

C58
C59 Further speaking practice using the language of this spread is provided on Feuille 58 *Parle Encore* and Feuille 59 *Parle En plus*.

C62 Feuille 62 *Lis et écris En plus 1* could also be used at this point. It practises the vocabulary for household chores with the perfect tense, including negatives.

W37 Page 37 of the *Encore* and *En plus* Workbooks provides additional practice of household chores with the perfect tense, including negatives.

W39 Much of the language and vocabulary of this unit is pulled together on page 39 of the *Encore* and *En plus* Workbooks, which could be used with this spread or at any point from now on.

AT 4.3/4

Challenge!

A *Écris ce que Martin et Nathalie ont fait pour aider à la maison samedi dernier.*
Students write what Martin and Nathalie did last weekend, using the pictures as prompts. They could go on to write additional sentences to say what each person didn't do.

Answers: Martin: J'ai fait la vaisselle, j'ai fait la cuisine et j'ai fait les courses. Nathalie: J'ai fait mon lit, j'ai mis le couvert et j'ai fait le ménage.

AT 4.4/5

B *Explique ce que tu as fait et n'as pas fait pour aider à la maison le week-end dernier.*
Students write an account of what they did and didn't do last weekend to help at home.

4 Tous les jours

4.5 La belle équipe, épisode 4

pages 58–59

Objectives

▶ Develop listening and reading skills via a soap story based on the language of the unit (**8L2, 8L6, 8S3**)

Resources

Students' Book, pages 58–59
CD 2, track 10
Cassette 2, side 2

Programme of Study reference

1a, 1c, 2a, 2b, 2g, 2h, 2i, 3b, 3c, 3e, 4a, 4d, 5a, 5d, 5e, 5g, 5i

For general information on introducing and exploiting the soap story, refer to page 19 of the Introduction.

At the beginning of this episode, Natacha and Juliette are relieved and overjoyed that Arnaud has finally agreed to help the Pieds-Nus by standing in for Matthieu at rehearsals. Juliette thinks they should rehearse every day, while Arnaud thinks once a week will be enough. To Arnaud's horror, they finally agree to meet at least three times a week.

The three friends then visit Matthieu, who is still recovering from his operation and has to spend most of his time confined to bed. He tells them his new daily routine. Matthieu seems particularly interested in the amount of time Arnaud has been spending with Natacha and Juliette: is he jealous?

Later, at rehearsals, the two girls are dismayed to find that Arnaud's singing is truly dreadful: he can't sing a note! Could this be the end of the road for the Pieds-Nus?

AT 1.4
AT 3.4

1a *Écoute et lis. Quel est le problème?*
Students listen to the recording and follow the text in the Students' Book. Encourage them to use various strategies to help with understanding, e.g. using the pictures as clues, deducing meaning from context, intonation of the speakers, etc. This provides another opportunity for work on **8L2** (media listening skills).

Answer: Arnaud can't sing

CD 2, track 10 page 58, La belle équipe, épisode 4
Cassette 2, side 2

1 – Alors, tu as parlé à Arnaud? Qu'est-ce qu'il a dit?
  – Il a dit "oui".
  – Ouf! Génial!
  – Il vient au club des jeunes ce soir à sept heures. Tu peux venir aussi?
  – Oui, pas de problème! À ce soir!
2 Le soir, au club des jeunes …
  – Les répétitions sont hyper-importantes. On se retrouve tous les jours?
  – Ah non! Tu exagères! Une fois par semaine, ça suffit!
  – Non, ça ne suffit pas. Trois fois par semaine … minimum!
  – Quoi??? Trois fois par semaine!
  – S'il te plaît, Arnaud. Sois sympa.
3 – Alors, on se retrouve le mercredi à deux heures, le vendredi à cinq heures et le dimanche à onze heures. Tu as noté, Arnaud?
  – Oui, oui, c'est noté!
  – Et maintenant, on va chez Matthieu. Sa mère dit qu'il s'ennuie. Tu viens avec nous, Arnaud?
  – Oui, bonne idée.
4 Plus tard, dans la chambre de Matthieu …
  – Ça va, Matthieu?
  – Pff! C'est nul!
  – Tu dois rester au lit?
  – Oui! Je me réveille le matin à six heures pour les médicaments, je me lève à sept heures, je me lave, je prends mon petit déjeuner, mais je ne m'habille pas parce que je dois retourner au lit à neuf heures!
5 – Alors, Juliette a fait de la voile avec toi?
  – Oui, elle est assez bonne.
  – Et tu vois Natacha tous les jours pour les répétitions?
  – Ben … trois fois par semaine … Mais, tu es jaloux ou quoi?
6 C'est la première répétition …
  – Tu commences là … Ensuite, c'est Natacha … et puis, c'est moi. Tu comprends?
  – Oui, pas de problème! À vos ordres, chef!!
  – Allez, on commence!
  – *Je joue de la guitare, tu joues de la batterie, mais qui joue du clavier? …*
7 – C'est atroce! Ça fait mal aux oreilles! Natacha, qu'est-ce qu'on va faire?
À suivre …

1b *Trouve dans le texte …*
Students search the text for the French equivalents of the English phrases.

Answers: a qu'est-ce qu'il a dit?; b pas de problème; c à ce soir; d une fois par semaine, ça suffit; e sois sympa; f tu es jaloux ou quoi?; g à vos ordres, chef; h qu'est-ce qu'on va faire?

2a *Réécoute le début de l'épisode. Écoute bien l'intonation des personnages. Qu'est-ce qu'ils pensent?*
Students listen again to the beginning of the recording (frames 1 and 2). Can they work out the mood of the speakers by focusing on their tone of voice?

2b *Répète les phrases de l'image 2 et imite l'intonation!*
Students listen to the recording for frame 2, repeating and imitating the intonation. This provides an opportunity for further work on **8L6** (expression in speech), which will be formally reinforced in Unit 5.

3 *Relie et recopie les phrases.*
Before students begin this activity, ask them some simple comprehension questions (e.g. true/false, multiple choice) to check their understanding of the text. Students

Tous les jours 4

then go on to match the beginnings and endings of the sentences, before copying them out to provide a summary in French of the soap episode. They could work on this in pairs, or it could be done orally as a whole-class activity.

The soap story provides another opportunity to recap on modal verbs (**8S3**): see *pouvoir* and *devoir* used in frames 1 and 4, and *vouloir* and *devoir* in the sentence halves in activity 3.

Answers: a 3; b 1; c 5; d 4; e 6; f 2

AT 2.4
AT 3.4
4 *En groupes de quatre, jouez l'épisode.*
Students act out the episode in groups.

Super-challenge! page 60

This extension page is intended to stretch more able students who are confident with the core language of the unit. It combines language from the unit with unfamiliar language and develops grammar points introduced in the main body of the unit. It can be used flexibly either as part of a teacher-led lesson or as alternative independent class and homework material.

Objectives

▶ Understand some comments about teenagers (**8C3 – R**)
▶ Use reflexives in the negative (**8S1 – R**) (**8S5**)
▶ Develop awareness of sound–spelling exceptions (**8W6 – R**)
▶ Agree/Disagree with other people's opinions

Resources

Students' Book, page 60
CD 2, tracks 11–14; CD 3, tracks 31–32
Cassette 2, side 2; cassette 4, side 2
Encore/En plus Workbooks, page 40
En plus Workbook, page 38
Copymasters 64 and 68

Programme of Study reference

1a, 1b, 1c, 2a, 2b, 2f, 2g, 3c, 3d, 3e, 4a, 4d, 5a, 5c, 5d, 5e, 5i

AT 3.3
1a *Lis les opinions. Cherche les mots que tu ne connais pas dans le glossaire. Tu es d'accord?*
This page focuses on some controversial comments about teenagers' daily lives and attitudes, thereby reinforcing **8C3**. It also introduces the plural forms of reflexive verbs. By looking at the use of negatives with reflexive verbs, it continues the launch of **8S5** and provides another opportunity to reinforce **8S1**.
Students read the comments a–h, looking up any unknown words in a glossary, then say whether they agree or disagree. This provides an opportunity to revise *je suis/ne suis pas d'accord* and could be done orally as a whole-class activity or with students working in pairs.
Once students have had a chance to comment orally, they could copy out each speech bubble and write their own opinion beside it. More able students could give a reason for their opinion, e.g. *Ils se couchent tard: Je ne suis pas d'accord parce que je me couche à neuf heures et demie tous les jours.*

AT 1.4
1b *Écoute les interviews. Note les opinions dans l'ordre mentionné.*
Students listen to the interviews. The speakers' opinions correspond to those expressed in activity **1a**. Students listen and note down the letters of the speech bubbles in the order in which they are mentioned.

Answers: a, d, e, b, g, h, c, f

CD 2, track 11 page 60, activité 1b
Cassette 2, side 2

– Les adolescents ... ils sont sympa?
– Sympa, non ... ils ne sont pas sympa.
– Ah non? Ils ne sont pas sympa? C'est vrai?
– Et, vous savez ... ils se ressemblent tous.
– Ils se ressemblent tous? Mais non! C'est vrai, ça? ...

– Et ils sont fainéants ... Le week-end, par exemple, ils ne se lèvent pas avant midi.
– Ils ne se lèvent pas avant midi. Oh là là! C'est vrai? Pourquoi?
– Ben, ils se couchent tard.
– Ils se couchent tard ... Tous?

– Et puis, au collège, ils ne travaillent pas. Ils ne s'intéressent pas au travail scolaire.
– Vous croyez? Ils ne s'intéressent pas au travail scolaire?
– Ben, en général.
– Ils s'intéressent à quoi, alors?
– Oh là là, je ne sais pas, moi. Ils s'ennuient toujours. Ils ont l'air de s'ennuyer quand on les voit ...
– Alors, les adolescents s'ennuient?
– Ils s'ennuient, oui.

– Le plus grand problème, c'est la discipline. Ils ne respectent pas la discipline.
– C'est important, la discipline?
– Oui, bien sûr, la discipline c'est important.
– Et ils ne respectent pas la discipline?
– Non. Les adolescents n'écoutent pas leurs parents ...
– Non?
– Et ils se disputent avec leurs frères et sœurs.
– Ils se disputent?
– Oui. C'est un grand problème, vous savez ...

AT 1.4
AT 4.3
1c *Continue les contradictions de Matthieu. Ensuite, écoute et vérifie.*
The *Zoom grammaire* (see notes below) should be completed before students begin this activity, because it practises the use of negatives with reflexive verbs. Referring back to the speech bubbles in activity **1a**, students make all the positive statements negative and

137

4 Tous les jours

the negative statements positive. They then listen to the recording to check their answers.

Answers: a Ils sont sympa. b Ils ne se couchent pas tard. c Ils respectent la discipline. d Ils ne se ressemblent pas tous. e Le week-end, ils se lèvent avant midi. f Ils ne se disputent pas avec leurs frères et sœurs. g Ils s'intéressent au travail scolaire. h Ils ne s'ennuient pas toujours.

CD 2, track 12 page 60, activité 1c
Cassette 2, side 2

– En general, les adolescents sont sympa. Ils ne se couchent pas tard. Ils respectent la discipline. Et ils ne se ressemblent pas tous. Je ne suis pas d'accord. Le week-end, ils se lèvent bien avant midi. Ils ne se disputent pas avec leurs frères et sœurs. Enfin, pas toujours … Ils s'intéressent au travail scolaire. Ils ne s'ennuient pas toujours. Enfin, c'est mon opinion.

Ça se dit comme ça!

This pronunciation section focuses on the silent *-ent* ending and reinforces **8W6** on sound–spelling exceptions. All the examples given here involve reflexive verbs, so it is worth stressing that this applies to all verbs, not only reflexives.

1 Students look at the three verbs given and say how they would pronounce the *-ent* ending. They listen to the recording to check their answer. Point out that, although the spelling is different, the pronunciation of the singular and plural forms (both the pronouns and the verb) is exactly the same in forms such as *il regarde/ils regardent, il se lève/ils se lèvent, elle se couche/elles se couchent*, etc.

Answer: it is not pronounced

CD 2, track 13 page 60, Ça se dit comme ça! activité 1
Cassette 2, side 2

– ils se lèvent
– elles se couchent tard
– ils se disputent

2 Students practise reading aloud the three phrases given, then listen to the recording to check their pronunciation.

CD 2, track 14 page 60, Ça se dit comme ça! activité 2
Cassette 2, side 2

a – ils se ressemblent tous
b – elles s'ennuient
c – ils ne s'intéressent pas au travail scolaire

Follow-up activity: Point out to students that the *-ent* ending does not always remain silent. Can they find a word on the *Super-challenge!* page where the *-ent* is pronounced? (See the word *adolescents* in the sub-heading.) Can they think of any other words where it is pronounced? They might remember *souvent* or *instrument* (both introduced on page 50), *immédiatement* (used in the *Guide pratique* panel on page 53), or *normalement* (from Arnaud's letter on page 56), or of course *comment*.

You could write up on the board or OHP a list of phrases containing words ending in *-ent* (e.g. *il est violent, généralement ils mettent des baskets, en ce moment*) and ask students to indicate those where the ending is pronounced and those where it remains silent. Can they tell you the rule?

C68 Feuille 68 *Ça se dit comme ça!* could be used here. It provides additional guidance and practice on silent endings.

Zoom grammaire

This grammar section focuses on the plural forms of reflexive verbs and the use of negatives (**8S5**) with reflexive verbs.

1 Students complete each sentence using the correct form of the verb in brackets.

Answers: a je me lève; b vous vous couchez; c les enfants se réveillent; d nous nous habillons, nous nous lavons

2 Students search the speech bubbles for two examples of negative reflexives.

Answers: Le week-end, ils ne se lèvent pas avant midi. Ils ne s'intéressent pas au travail scolaire.

3 Students fill in the missing words to complete the rule about negative reflexives.

Answer: Put *ne* before the reflexive pronoun and put *pas* after the verb.

4 Students make the positive sentences negative.

Answers: a Je ne me lève pas tard. b Tu ne te couches pas avant midi? d Natacha ne s'intéresse pas au sport. d Elles ne se réveillent pas à six heures.

5 Finally, students say whether the comments a–h are justified in relation to themselves. This requires them to change the third person singular forms used in the speech bubbles into the first person singular, and of course to change the sentences from positive to negative or vice versa, as appropriate. Point out that comment d requires a further amendment: *Je ressemble/ne me ressemble pas aux autres.*

Tous les jours 4

Follow-up activity: Students could work in groups or pairs to think up their own list, inventing new, positive opinions. For example: *Ils s'intéressent toujours aux cours de français. Ils aident toujours le professeur. Ils ne parlent jamais en classe.*

Refer students to the two grammar sections on pages 143 (reflexive verbs) and 145 (negatives + reflexive verbs) of the Students' Book.

C64 / W38 Feuille 64 *Grammaire 1* and page 38 of the *En plus* Workbook focus on the first, second and third person singular and plural forms of reflexive verbs. If not already used with the *Zoom grammaire* section on page 53 of the Students' Book, they could be used at this point.

W40 Page 40 of the *Encore* and *En plus* Workbooks could also be used here.

Vocabulaire   page 61

This page provides a summary of the key language covered in this unit. It could be used as a handy reference for students as they work through the unit. Alternatively, students could use its clear French–English format with language organized thematically when learning vocabulary.

C52 Feuille 52 *Vocabulaire* also contains a summary of the key language of the unit and could be given to students at this point for revision purposes. See page 7 of the Introduction for ideas on how to use this copymaster.

W41 Page 41 of the *Encore* and *En plus* Workbooks also provides a summary of the key language of the unit.

Podium   page 62

The *Podium* page provides students with an end-of-unit checklist of learning objectives in French and English. At the foot of the page are activities at three levels of difficulty (bronze, silver and gold) to extend the work of the unit. Encourage students to select an activity at the most appropriate level.

C53 Feuille 53 *Podium* could also be used at this point. This worksheet contains activities to help students keep track of their progress. See page 7 of the Introduction for ideas on how to use it to help self- and peer-assessment.

W42 Page 42 of the *Encore* and *En plus* Workbooks also provides an end-of-unit checklist in French and English with activities to help students keep track of their progress.

Encore Unité 4   pages 102–103

Objectives

These reinforcement pages are intended for those students requiring further practice of core language from the unit. They can be used by students who finish other activities quickly or as alternative class and homework material.

Resources

Students' Book, pages 102–103
CD 2, tracks 15–16
Cassette 2, side 2

Programme of Study reference

1c, 2a, 2g, 2i, 3a, 3b, 3c, 3e, 4a, 5a, 5d, 5e, 5i

AT 3.2 **1a** *Regarde les dessins. Relie chaque phrase à la bonne personne.*
Students match each sentence to a musical instrument and find the name of the person who plays that instrument.

Answers: a Anne; b Luc; c Marc; d Léa; e Noé; f Lise

AT 3.2 **1b** *Regarde le programme du club de musique. Qui joue …?*
Students study the weekly schedule for the music club and answer questions on how often the young people play their instruments.

Answers: a Lise; b Luc, Marc, Noé; c Anne; d Léa

AT 4.2 **1c** *Écris une phrase pour chaque jeune.*
Students write a sentence for each person, saying how often they play their instruments.

Answers: Luc: Je joue du piano deux fois par semaine. Noé: Je joue du violon deux fois par semaine. Marc: Je joue du clavier deux fois par semaine. Léa: Je joue de la guitare cinq fois par semaine. Lise: Je joue de la flûte une fois par semaine. Anne: Je joue de la batterie trois fois par semaine.

AT 2.2 **1d** *Test de mémoire à deux: A lit une phrase, B dit vrai ou faux sans regarder sa liste.*
In pairs, students take turns to read out sentences from their lists (from activity **1c**). The partner says whether it is true or false, without looking at their own list or at the Students' Book.

AT 1.2 **2a** *Regarde les photos-mystère. Écoute. C'est quelle photo?*
Students look at the "mystery photos" while listening to the recording. They indicate which photo is represented by each statement. If they would find this too difficult, they could predict each statement first (either in pairs or as a whole class) and then listen to the recording to check their answers.

Answers: 1 e; 2 c; 3 g; 4 f; 5 h; 6 b; 7 a; 8 i; 9 d

4 Tous les jours

CD 2, track 15
Cassette 2, side 2
page 102, activité 2a

1 – Je me couche.
2 – Je prends mon petit déjeuner.
3 – Je me lave.
4 – Je joue au football.
5 – Je joue de la guitare.
6 – Je me brosse les dents.
7 – Je me réveille.
8 – Je fais la vaisselle.
9 – Je m'habille.

AT 2.2/3

2b *Joue au morpion avec un(e) partenaire.*
Students play Noughts and Crosses in pairs, using the grid of "mystery photos".
In order to place their counter and "win" the square, they must correctly say a sentence in the first person singular to represent that particular square, e.g. *Je m'habille*. Alternatively, they could ask a question using the *tu* form, e.g. *Tu t'habilles?*, or give a statement in the third person singular, e.g. *Il s'habille*. To increase the difficulty of this activity, ask students to include a time or place (or both) in each sentence, e.g. *À huit heures, je m'habille dans ma chambre*.
Either before or after this oral activity, students could write out the list of nine statements.

AT 1.2 **3a** *Écoute. C'est samedi ou dimanche?*
Students study the two pictures of the household before listening to the recording. Make sure they understand all the vocabulary (e.g. *papy, mamie*), and ask them to think in advance about what each person is doing and therefore predict the language they are likely to hear.
Answers: 1 dimanche; 2 samedi; 3 dimanche; 4 samedi; 5 samedi; 6 dimanche

CD 2, track 16
Cassette 2, side 2
page 103, activité 3a

1 – Anne a rangé sa chambre.
2 – Paul a fait la vaisselle.
3 – Mamie a fait les courses.
4 – Papy a mis le couvert dans la salle à manger.
5 – Maman a fait son lit.
6 – Papa a fait la cuisine.

AT 2.3 **3b** *À tour de rôle, dis ce que tu as fait. Ton/Ta partenaire dit qui tu es.*
Referring again to the household pictures, students in pairs take turns to choose a person and say what they did on a specific day. The partner works out which person they have chosen.

AT 4.3 **3c** *Choisis un jour: samedi ou dimanche. Écris qui a fait quoi.*
Students choose either Saturday or Sunday and write down what the people did on that day. They could either give the activities only, e.g. *Papy a mis le couvert*, or they could include names of rooms, e.g. *Papy a mis le couvert dans la salle à manger*.
Possible answers: Samedi, Anne a fait le ménage (dans la salle de bains). Maman a fait son lit (dans sa/la chambre). Papy a mis le couvert (dans la salle à manger). Mamie a fait la cuisine (dans la cuisine). Paul a fait la vaisselle (dans la cuisine). Papa a fait les courses.
Dimanche, Anne a rangé sa chambre. Paul a fait son lit. Maman a fait le ménage (dans la salle à manger). Papa a fait la cuisine (dans la cuisine). Papy a fait la vaisselle (dans la cuisine). Mamie a fait les courses.

En plus Unité 4
pages 114–115

Objectives
These extension pages are intended for more able students who are confident with the core language of the unit. They can be used by students who finish other activities quickly or as alternative class and homework material.

Resources
Students' Book, pages 114–115
CD 2, tracks 17–19
Cassette 2, side 2

Programme of Study reference
1c, 2a, 2c, 2f, 2h, 2i, 3e, 4a, 4d, 5a, 5d, 5e, 5f, 5i

AT 1.4 **1a** *Écoute l'interview. Recopie et complète la fiche.*
Students listen to the interview with Laurent Dury and note down the details that are missing from his *fiche*.
Answers: Âge: 30 ans; Métier: compositeur, écrit la musique des chansons d'*Équipe*; Famille: célibataire, une copine; Passions: la musique, la littérature, les chiens

CD 2, track 17
Cassette 2, side 2
page 114, activité 1a

– Tu t'appelles comment?
– Je m'appelle Laurent Dury.
– Tu as quel âge, Laurent?
– J'ai 30 ans.
– Oui. Et tu habites où?
– Alors, j'habite à Londres depuis 1996.
– Qu'est-ce que tu fais comme métier?
– Eh bien, je suis compositeur. J'ai écrit la musique des chansons d'*Équipe*!
– Oui, c'est super! Tu es marié, Laurent?
– Ah non … Je suis célibataire, mais j'ai une copine en France!
– Ah d'accord! Et tu as des passions, Laurent?

Tous les jours 4

– Oh oui, ma grande passion, c'est la musique, bien sûr! J'aime aussi la littérature et j'adore les chiens!

Follow-up activity: Students could, for homework, produce a *fiche* for a favourite musician, film or sports star, which could later be used as the stimulus for oral work.

AT 1.3
AT 3.4
1b *Lis "Ma journée typique". Écoute les questions et réponds pour Laurent. Puis, écoute ses réponses pour vérifier.*
Students read Laurent's account of a typical day in the text *Ma journée typique*. They then listen to the recorded questions and answer on behalf of Laurent, either orally or in writing, using the information given in the text. There is a pause after each question on the recording to allow time for students to give their answers orally.

Answers: see transcript below

CD 2, track 18 page 114, activité 1b
Cassette 2, side 2

– Tu te lèves à quelle heure?
– Je me lève à 8 h 00.
– Qu'est-ce que tu fais d'abord?
– Je me prépare et je prends mon petit déjeuner.
– Tu te mets à ton ordinateur à quelle heure?
– Je me mets à mon ordinateur à 8 h 30 et je compose.
– Tu t'arrêtes à quelle heure pour déjeuner?
– Je m'arrête pour déjeuner à 13 h 00.
– Qu'est-ce que tu fais l'après-midi?
– Je vais à des rendez-vous. Je me repose ou je me promène en ville ou dans un parc.
– Est-ce que tu travailles l'après-midi?
– Je me remets à l'ordinateur à 16 heures et je travaille encore trois heures.
– Qu'est-ce que tu fais le soir?
– Je dîne à la maison et je regarde la télé ou je vais chez des amis, et … de temps en temps au concert de musique classique.

AT 3.4
AT 4.3
1c *Lis "Mes débuts". Réponds aux questions à droite.*
Students read Laurent's account of his early days as a musician and give written answers to the questions.

Answers: 1 J'ai commencé la musique à 10 ans. 2 Je joue de l'orgue, du piano, du clavier et un peu de la guitare. 3 J'ai fait des études de musique, j'ai été prof de musique et j'ai joué dans des groupes. 4 Je suis venu à Londres pour faire de la musique pour le multimédia.

AT 4.3-5
2 *Prends de bonnes résolutions. Écris une liste.*
Responding to the picture prompts representing household chores, students use *aller* + infinitive to write about their resolutions for the future. They have not yet used *aller* + infinitive in this context. Instead of writing a straightforward list, encourage them to include time expressions and connectives, together with some opinions.

Model answer: Je vais ranger ma chambre et faire le ménage dans ma chambre une fois par semaine, et je vais faire mon lit tous les jours. Je vais faire la cuisine souvent parce que j'aime ça, et je vais faire les courses de temps en temps. Je vais mettre le couvert tous les jours. Deux ou trois fois par semaine, je vais faire la vaisselle aussi, mais je déteste ça!

AT 1.4
3 *Lis les questions a–e. Écoute Marie. Réponds aux questions.*
Students listen to the conversation between Marie and her mother and note down answers to the questions in French. Instead of doing this as an individual task, you could complete it as a whole-class oral activity.

Answers: a non; b non; c non; d elle a fait la vaisselle; e elle a fait le ménage

CD 2, track 19 page 115, activité 3
Cassette 2, side 2

– Marie, qu'est-ce que tu as fait toute la journée?
– Euh … j'ai regardé des vidéos.
– Tu as regardé des vidéos? Tu n'as pas fait les courses?
– Euh non, je n'ai pas fait les courses.
– Et le dîner? Tu n'as pas fait la cuisine?
– Euh non, je n'ai pas encore fait la cuisine.
– Tu n'as pas mis le couvert dans la salle à manger?
– Euh non, je n'ai pas mis le couvert … Non.
– Tu es impossible! Bon, je vais préparer le dîner.

– Après le repas …
– Alors Marie, tu as fait la vaisselle, j'espère?
– Oui, maman, j'ai fait la vaisselle.
– Et tu as fait le ménage dans le salon?
– Oui, maman, j'ai fait le ménage.
– Hmmmph!
– Et maintenant je suis fatiguée, je me couche.

AT 2.3-5
4 *Jeu de rôle.*
Students work in pairs to invent and perform a role-play, similar to the conversation in activity **3**. Encourage them to be creative and to use hesitation techniques (from the *Guide pratique* on page 55) to add authenticity and expression to their performances.

4 Tous les jours

Point lecture
pages 126–127

These pages are intended to encourage independent reading. Students should attempt them once they are confident with the core language of the unit. They can be used by students who finish other activities quickly or as alternative class and homework material.

Objectives
- Develop reading for information and pleasure via song lyrics and magazine-style problem page letters
- Develop awareness of non-literal translations (**8W8 – R**)

Resources
Students' Book, pages 126–127
CD 2, track 20
Cassette 2, side 2

Programme of Study reference
1a, 1c, 2a, 2b, 2g, 2h, 2i, 3b, 3c, 3d, 3e, 4a, 4c, 4d, 5d, 5e, 5f, 5g, 5i

AT 1.4/5 **1a** *Écoute la chanson. Donne ton opinion.*
Students listen initially with their books closed in order to react to the style of music, etc. To revise numbers 0–20, the Students' Book asks them to give the song a mark out of 20; but if you wish to practise higher numbers you could ask them to award it a percentage instead.
You could then play the song again with students following the lyrics in their books. Has their initial reaction changed now that they have seen the lyrics? Would they change their marks?

CD 2, track 20
Cassette 2, side 2
page 126, activité 1

Refrain:
Tu <u>te lèves</u> le matin
Et le monde <u>se réveille</u>
Et tu brilles
Et la vie
Est plus belle.
Bonjour, bonjour le soleil,
Tu <u>te lèves</u> et le monde <u>se réveille</u>.

Au soleil, sous la pluie,
On <u>s'amuse</u>, on <u>s'ennuie</u>.
À midi, à minuit,
C'est normal, c'est la vie.
Refrain

Je <u>me lève</u>, je <u>m'habille</u>,
Au collège, c'est lundi.
Vivement samedi!
C'est normal, c'est la vie.
Refrain

Je <u>me couche</u> chaque soir,
Je <u>m'endors</u>, tôt ou tard,
Doucement, sans cauchemars,
C'est normal, c'est comme ça.
Refrain

AT 3.4 **1b** *Réécoute et lis. Recopie la chanson, en remplaçant les chiffres par les verbes de la boîte.*
Students listen again, following the lyrics in the Students' Book. They copy out the song, filling in the gaps using the words provided.

Answers: see underlining in transcript above

1c *Choisis la bonne traduction, a ou b, pour ces extraits de la chanson.*
Students choose the correct English translations for some of the phrases from the song. This activity draws attention to the fact that literal translations from one language to another are not always possible and provides an opportunity to reinforce Framework objective **8W8**.

Answers: 1 b; 2 b; 3 b; 4 a

1d *Réécoute et chante.*
Students join in with the song.

AT 3.4 **2a** *Lis l'article et trouve …*
Students search the magazine-style problem page letters for the French equivalents of the English phrases.

Answers: a mes parents sont très sévères; b même le week-end; c tu es d'accord?; d tu te lèves à quelle heure le matin?; e elle a beaucoup de travail au collège; f je prépare le dîner; g écris un planning avec toutes les tâches ménagères; h partagez le travail

2b *Réponds aux questions en anglais.*
Students answer comprehension questions in English on Olivier's letter.

Answers: a in a small flat; b his mother and sister; c she's a teacher; d he does the shopping, does the housework/cleans up and cooks the evening meal; e nothing; f draw up a rota with all the household chores on it and share the work between Olivier, his mother and his sister

2c *Discute de la lettre de Sophie et de sa réponse avec un(e) partenaire. Écris un résumé en anglais.*
In pairs, students discuss Sophie's letter and Valérie's reply. They write a summary in English.

Answers: Sophie is 13, lives in Clermont-Ferrand, and has very strict parents who insist that she goes to bed every evening at eight o'clock, even at weekends. Valérie thinks this might be rather unreasonable, but at the same time she wonders what time Sophie gets up in the morning (she might be thinking that if Sophie tends to sleep in late every morning, this might be the reason why her parents make her go to bed early). Valérie suggests two things: that Sophie asks permission to go to bed later at weekends; that Sophie's parents talk to a teacher or to the parents of Sophie's friends, to find out what time other teenagers of Sophie's age go to bed.

AT 4.4/5

2d *Écris une lettre à Valérie. Choisis un des problèmes suivants.*
Students choose one of the problems listed and write a letter asking for Valérie's advice. Students could exchange their letters with a partner, who pretends to be Valérie and writes a reply: this would provide practice of the imperative and modal verbs.

Copymasters

Feuille 54 À vos marques

There are two starter activities on this copymaster.
The top half of the sheet focuses on *jouer à* and *faire de* and can be used with pages 50–51 of the Students' Book. The bottom half of the sheet emphasizes the spelling of key vocabulary for household chores and can be used with pages 54–55 of the Students' Book.

1a *Déchiffre et écris le message de Charlie.*
Students decipher the mirror-writing and write out a correct version of Charlie's text about the sports he does. Students could be set a time limit for doing this, or they could compete to see who can work it out first. Have available a couple of small mirrors if you think less able students might need them.

Answers: Le samedi, je joue au foot et je fais de l'équitation. Le dimanche, je vais à la pêche. Génial!

1b *Coche les activités de Charlie.*
Students tick the activities that Charlie mentions.

Answers: 1, 4, 6

2a *Écris les voyelles pour compléter le message de Cendrillon.*
Students fill in the missing vowels to complete Cinderella's text about the household chores she does.

Answers: Ah là là! Tous les jours, je fais le ménage, je range ma chambre, je fais les courses, je fais la cuisine, je mets le couvert et je fais la vaisselle. C'est nul!

2b *Et toi, tu fais quelles tâches?*
Students write their own text about household chores.

Feuille 55 Challenge!

There are two plenary activities on this copymaster.
Activity 1 focuses on *jouer à* and *faire de*, and could be used with pages 50–51 of the Students' Book. Activity 2 could be used towards the end of or after pages 56–57. It incorporates much of the language of the unit and highlights verb forms in both the perfect and the present tense.

1 *Écris les activités de la liste sur le diagramme.*
Students are given two spider diagrams to complete: in one diagram, they fill in all the activities that go with *jouer à*; in the other, they fill in the activities that go with *faire de*. Fast finishers could write a sentence for each phrase on the reverse of the sheet, e.g. *je joue au foot, je joue au ping-pong*, etc., or this could be done for homework.

Answers: jouer à: foot, ping-pong, tennis, hockey, golf; faire de: foot, natation, surf, équitation, voile, judo

2 *Prends un élément dans chaque colonne. Tu peux faire combien de phrases logiques en trois minutes?*
Students are given three minutes to make as many logical sentences as they can, using the columns of words provided. If some students have difficulty distinguishing the perfect and the present tense verb forms, you could cross out the present tense options to avoid confusion. Instead of using this as a plenary activity in class, you might prefer to set it for homework: some students will enjoy trying to come up with hundreds of sentences!

Feuille 56 Écoute Encore

Activity 1 provides further practice of daily routine vocabulary and could be used with pages 52–53 of the Students' Book. Activities 2 and 3 practise household chores in the perfect tense so should be used with pages 56–57.

AT 1.2

1 *Écoute. Qui parle? Numérote les dessins dans l'ordre.*
Students listen to the statements about daily routine and number the pictures in the order in which they are mentioned.

Answers: a 3; b 2; c 4; d 1; e 5

CD 3, track 25   **Feuille 56, activité 1**
Cassette 4, side 2

1 – Mathilde prend son petit déjeuner.
2 – Aurélie se lave.
3 – Alex se brosse les dents.
4 – Jojo se réveille.
5 – Omar s'habille.

AT 1.2

2 *Écoute et choisis le bon symbole.*
Students listen to the young people saying what they have done to help at home. They indicate their understanding by circling one of the two symbols.

Answers: a cooking; b washing up; c setting the table; d tidying bedroom; e shopping; f washing up

4 Tous les jours

CD 3, track 26
Cassette 4, side 2
Feuille 56, activité 2

a – Tu as fait la cuisine aujourd'hui, Karima?
– Oui. J'ai fait la cuisine: j'ai préparé le dîner.
b – Et toi, Antoine, qu'est-ce que tu as fait?
– Moi, j'ai fait la vaisselle.
– Tu aimes faire la vaisselle?
– Non!
c – Nathalie, qu'est-ce que tu as fait pour aider à la maison?
– J'ai mis le couvert ce soir.
– Tu as mis le couvert?
– Oui, avant le dîner.
d – Martin, tu as rangé ta chambre?
– Ma chambre? Oui, j'ai rangé ma chambre ce week-end.
e – Julie, qu'est-ce que tu as fait pour aider à la maison?
– J'ai fait les courses samedi matin.
f – Et toi, Nicolas, qu'est-ce que tu as fait?
– Moi, j'ai fait la vaisselle.
– C'est tout?
– Oui, j'ai fait la vaisselle, c'est tout. C'est déjà pas mal.

AT 1.3/4 3 *Écoute et coche la grille.*
Students listen and tick the grid to show what the young people did last weekend to help at home. The completed grid could later be used as a stimulus for students to write sentences in the third person using the perfect tense (perhaps for homework).

Answers: Luc: made his bed, tidied his room; Farida: made her bed, went shopping; Max: set the table, washed the dishes; Charlotte: did the cooking and hoovering; Kévin: went shopping, tidied his room; Céline: washed up (twice), made her bed

CD 3, track 27
Cassette 4, side 2
Feuille 56, activité 3

– Salut! Je m'appelle Luc. Moi, ce week-end, j'ai fait mon lit … et samedi matin, j'ai rangé ma chambre. Je déteste ranger!
– Salut! Je m'appelle Farida. Ce week-end, j'ai fait mon lit … et samedi … euh … samedi matin, je suis allée au supermarché et j'ai fait les courses.
– Salut! Je m'appelle Max. Moi, ce week-end, j'ai mis le couvert avant le dîner, et après j'ai fait la vaisselle.
– Salut! Je m'appelle Charlotte. J'aide ma mère à la maison. Par exemple, ce week-end, j'ai fait la cuisine … et dimanche matin, j'ai fait le ménage.
– Salut! Je m'appelle Kévin. Qu'est-ce que j'ai fait ce week-end? Eh bien, j'ai fait les courses … et … euh … j'ai rangé ma chambre.
– Salut! Je m'appelle Céline. Moi, ce week-end, j'ai fait la vaisselle deux fois! … et j'ai fait mon lit.

Feuille 57 Écoute En plus

Activity 1 provides listening practice on daily routine and the 12-hour clock and could be completed with pages 52–53 of the Students' Book. Activity 2 focuses on household chores in the present tense with expressions of frequency, and could be completed with pages 54–55. Activity 3 should be used with pages 56–57: it focuses on household chores in the perfect tense, including negative forms, together with other language, e.g. leisure activities.

AT 1.2/3 1 *Écoute. Dessine les aiguilles sur les horloges.*
Students listen to Thomas answering questions about his daily routine. They draw in the times on the clock faces to show when he does each activity.

Answers: 1 6.30; 2 6.40; 3 6.50; 4 7.00; 5 9.30

CD 3, track 28
Cassette 4, side 2
Feuille 57, activité 1

– Thomas, à quelle heure est-ce que tu te réveilles?
– Généralement, je me réveille à six heures et demie.
– Six heures et demie?
– Oui.
– Et ensuite?
– Je me lève et je me lave à sept heures moins vingt.
– Oui … Et après?
– Je m'habille dans ma chambre à sept heures moins dix … et … euh … je prends mon petit déjeuner …
– À quelle heure est-ce que tu prends ton petit déjeuner?
– À sept heures.
– OK! Et le soir, à quelle heure est-ce que tu te couches?
– Je me couche à neuf heures et demie le soir.
– Neuf heures et demie …
– Oui, pendant la semaine, je me couche toujours à neuf heures et demie.

AT 1.4 2 *Écoute et prends des notes.*
Students listen to the four teenagers being interviewed about what they do to help at home. They make notes in French in the grid provided.

Answers:

	tous les jours	de temps en temps	jamais
Karine	lit	cuisine	courses
Marc	courses	met le couvert	vaisselle
Isabelle	vaisselle	le ménage	range sa chambre
Antoine	lit	courses	cuisine

Tous les jours 4

CD 3, track 29 **Feuille 57, activité 2**
Cassette 4, side 2

– Qu'est-ce que tu fais pour aider à la maison, Karine?
– Je fais mon lit tous les jours … le matin … et … je fais la cuisine de temps en temps … parce que c'est amusant … mais je ne fais jamais les courses.
– Qu'est-ce que tu fais pour aider à la maison, Marc?
– Moi, je fais les courses tous les jours – j'achète du pain tous les matins à la boulangerie. Je ne fais jamais la vaisselle, par contre, je mets le couvert de temps en temps.
– Qu'est-ce que tu fais pour aider à la maison, Isabelle?
– Je fais le ménage de temps en temps – le samedi matin, par exemple – mais je ne range jamais ma chambre parce que je déteste ça. Je fais la vaisselle tous les jours après le dîner.
– Qu'est-ce que tu fais pour aider à la maison, Antoine?
– Je ne fais jamais la cuisine parce que je suis trop nul! Par contre, je fais les courses de temps en temps – je vais au supermarché avec mon père. Et je fais mon lit tous les matins, avant le petit déjeuner.

AT 1.4/5

3 *Écoute et réponds aux questions.*
Students listen to the conversation about what Charlie has and hasn't done today. They answer questions in French.

Answers: 1 Non, parce qu'il lit un magazine intéressant. 2 Il a retrouvé des copains et ils sont allés en ville. 3 Non (parce qu'il n'a pas d'argent). 4 Non, parce qu'il a fait ses devoirs. 5 Il a fait un sandwich.

CD 3, track 30 **Feuille 57, activité 3**
Cassette 4, side 2

– Tu n'as pas fait la vaisselle, Charlie?
– Euh, non, je n'ai pas fait la vaisselle. Je lis ce magazine. C'est très intéressant.
– Mais tu n'as pas fait le ménage non plus?
– Euh non, je n'ai pas fait le ménage. Cet après-midi, j'ai retrouvé des copains. Nous sommes allés en ville.
– Et en ville, tu as fait les courses?
– Euh non, je n'ai pas fait les courses. Je n'avais pas d'argent.
– Tu as rangé ta chambre ce matin, au moins?
– Ah non, ce matin, j'ai fait mes devoirs. Je n'ai pas rangé ma chambre, non.
– Oh là là!
– Mais j'ai fait la cuisine.
– Tu as fait la cuisine! C'est bien. J'ai faim. Qu'est-ce qu'il y a pour le dîner?
– Un sandwich.
– Un sandwich … c'est tout?
– Euh, oui. Voilà … Tu aimes les sandwichs?
– Grrrrr!

Feuille 58 Parle Encore

This information-gap speaking activity could be used with pages 56–57 of the Students' Book. It gives students practice in describing household chores, using the perfect tense. Revise the days of the week in advance, if necessary.

AT 2.3/4

1 *Lis le planning. Réponds aux questions de ton/ta partenaire.*
2 *Pose des questions à ton/ta partenaire et complète le planning.*
Students take turns to ask and answer questions about what the four characters have done on each day of the week to help at home. They fill in the gaps in their own rota using the information provided by their partner. Encourage students to sit back-to-back if you think they might be tempted to look at each other's rota.

Feuille 59 Parle En plus

This copymaster should be used with pages 56–57 of the Students' Book. Activities 1a and 1b practise the vocabulary for household chores with the perfect tense, including negatives; activity 2 practises the language of the whole unit.

AT 2.3/4

1a *Qu'est-ce que ton/ta partenaire a fait le week-end dernier? Pose des questions et écris ✔ ou ✘.*
1b *Réponds aux questions de ton/ta partenaire.*
Students use the symbols as cues for asking each other what jobs they did to help at home at the weekend. They should give personal answers, using full sentences, not just yes/no answers.

AT 2.4/5

2 *Tu es journaliste pour une émission de radio. Interviewe un(e) camarade de classe. Enregistre l'interview. Ensuite, changez de rôle.*
This activity provides an opportunity to practise the language of the whole unit. Students interview each other on a variety of topics, including sports, musical instruments, daily routine and household chores. Encourage them to add in as much detail as possible, e.g. reasons, explanations, opinions, time expressions, etc. If necessary, have a brainstorming session beforehand.

Feuille 60 Lis et écris Encore 1

This copymaster can be used with pages 50–51 of the Students' Book. It is a game designed to encourage accuracy in writing. At the same time, it keeps the whole class involved and provides a motivating reason to write and to read. Here, it practises and contrasts *jouer à/jouer de/faire de* + sport/musical instrument, but it could be adapted to suit any context where grammatical accuracy is required.

4 Tous les jours

AT 3.2
AT 4.2
Students play in teams of four or five. Each team writes three sentences, following the criteria given on the copymaster, i.e. each sentence must be about a person playing (or not playing) a sport or a musical instrument, include two time expressions, and have correct grammar and spelling. Team members choose one person to do the writing, although everyone in the team should be involved in suggesting phrases, spellings, etc.

The team members then imagine they have 50 euros to bet on their sentences. They choose the sentence that they think is most likely to be correct in terms of spelling and grammar. If they feel very confident about it, they bet a lot of money; if they are less confident, they bet only a little. One team member is then nominated to call out the bets: as well as being recorded on the copymaster, all bets must be announced to the teacher, which provides an opportunity to revise numbers.

Once all the bets are in, each team chooses a member to write their sentence on the board or OHP. Allow the "scribe" to copy from the sheet, then give the copymaster back to the team for 30 seconds so that they can check that the scribe has reproduced the sentence correctly and can make any necessary adjustments.

The other teams read the sentence looking for mistakes and appraise it according to agreed criteria: the criteria can be adjusted to suit the ability level of the class. This provides a motivating reason to read and keeps the whole class involved. Bets are won and lost as described on the copymaster.

When one sentence from each team has been appraised, move on to round two, in which the whole process is repeated for each team's second sentence; then move on to round three for the third sentence. If time is short, however, you need only play one round or two.

Feuille 61 Lis et écris Encore 2

This copymaster practises daily routine and can be used with pages 52–53 of the Students' Book.

AT 3.2
1a *Écris les lettres. Trouve le message de Charlie.*
Students fill in the missing letters to complete the sentences about daily routine. They then rearrange the letters in the order indicated to find out what Charlie's secret message is. This activity provides reading practice and at the same time encourages students to focus on accurate spelling.

Answers: 1 m; 2 e; 3 c; 4 o; 5 c; 6 h; 7 e; 8 j; 9 e; 10 u; Charlie's message is: je me couche

AT 3.2
1b *Traduis les phrases 1–10 en anglais sur une feuille.*
To check comprehension, students translate the sentences from activity **1a** into English.

Answers: 1 I wake up at 7.20. 2 Max gets up at 8.05. 3 When do you go to bed? 4 My father is brushing his teeth. 5 I get dressed in my bedroom. 6 Where do you get dressed? 7 She gets washed in the bathroom. 8 I never get washed. 9 We have breakfast. 10 Are you getting ready for school?

AT 4.3/4
2 *Regarde les symboles. Écris un article sur le samedi de Clément.*
Students write a brief description of Clément's Saturday morning routine, using the information provided in the pictures. If appropriate, ask them to include some names of rooms.

Possible answer: Le samedi, Clément se réveille à dix heures. Il se lève à dix heures vingt. Il se lave à dix heures vingt-cinq (dans la salle de bains) et il s'habille à dix heures et demie (dans sa chambre). À onze heures moins le quart, il prend le petit déjeuner (dans la salle à manger) et à onze heures, il se brosse les dents.

AT 4.3/4
3 *Décris ton samedi.*
Students write a similar description of their own Saturday morning routine.

Feuille 62 Lis et écris En plus 1

This copymaster focuses on the vocabulary for household chores with the perfect tense, including negatives, and could be used with pages 56–57 of the Students' Book.

AT 3.2/3
1a *Trouve une illustration pour chaque question.*
Students match the questions to the illustrations.

Answers: 1 a; 2 d; 3 c; 4 e; 5 b; 6 f

AT 4.2/3
1b *Regarde les cercles. Réponds aux questions.*
The tick or cross beside each illustration indicates whether students should give a positive or negative answer to each question. In preparation for the written work, students could first do this activity orally in pairs.

Answers: 1 Non, je n'ai pas fait mon lit. 2 Oui, j'ai fait les courses. 3 Non, je n'ai pas rangé ma chambre. 4 Non, je n'ai pas fait le ménage. 5 Oui, j'ai fait la vaisselle. 6 Oui, j'ai mis le couvert dans la salle à manger.

AT 3.3/4
2 *Lis les textes, puis complète les phrases.*
Students fill in the gaps in the sentences, referring to the four texts for the information required. If appropriate, ask some comprehension questions beforehand, e.g. *Martin a fait la cuisine? Qui a rangé sa chambre?*

Answers: a Martin et Nathalie; b Martin et Karima; c Martin et Nathalie; d fait les courses; e ont fait le ménage; f ont mis le couvert

Follow-up activity: You could exploit the texts further by asking questions relating to more specific detail, e.g. *Quand est-ce que Martin a préparé le petit déjeuner? Karima a fait les courses où/avec qui? Karima a fait la vaisselle quand? Nathalie a fait le ménage où? Nathalie a fait la cuisine: qu'est-ce qu'elle a préparé?*

Tous les jours

Feuille 63 Lis et écris En plus 2

This copymaster provides practice of household chores in the present tense, together with daily routine, and could be used with pages 54–55 of the Students' Book.

AT 3.5
AT 4.2

1 *Lis la lettre de Marie en entier.*
2 *Écris les bons mots dans les trous.*
Students read through Marie's letter in full, then fill in the gaps, choosing from the panel of words provided.

Answers: fait; mais; lève; fais; courses; déteste; met; range

AT 4.4

3 *Réponds aux questions.*
Students answer questions in French on Marie's letter.

Answers: 1 Parce que la mère est malade et le père travaille à Paris. 2 Elle fait son lit, elle prépare le petit déjeuner et elle fait la vaisselle. 3 Elle prend des tartines et du café. 4 Thibault fait les courses. 5 Non, il déteste faire la cuisine. 6 Il met le couvert et il fait la vaisselle.

AT 4.4

4 *Écris six questions sur la lettre de Marie. Échange avec un(e) partenaire.*
Students write six questions about Marie's letter for a partner to answer.

Feuille 64 Grammaire 1

This copymaster focuses on the first, second and third person singular and plural forms of reflexive verbs. It could be used either with the *Zoom grammaire* on page 53 of the Students' Book or with *Super-challenge!* on page 60.

1 *Complète les phrases.*
Students fill in the gaps with the correct parts of the verbs, using the Flashback panel to help them.

Answers: 1 me réveille; 2 te lèves; 3 se brossent; 4 m'habille; 5 se prépare; 6 se réveillent

2 *Trouve une phrase de l'exercice 1 (1–6) pour chaque illustration.*
To check their comprehension of the sentences in activity 1, students match each one with an illustration.

Answers: a 6; b 1; c 5; d 2; e 4; f 3

3 *Invente une ou deux phrases pour ces illustrations.*
Students make up sentences using reflexive verbs to describe the pictures.

Possible answers: Je me réveille/Il se réveille/Je me lève/Il se lève à huit heures et quart. 2 Je me brosse les dents/Elle se brosse les dents.

Feuille 65 Grammaire 2

This copymaster focuses on negative and positive statements in the perfect tense and could be used with the *Zoom grammaire* panel on page 57 of the Students' Book.

1 *Suis les lignes. Fais des phrases sur une feuille.*
Students follow the tangled lines to find out whether they need to give a positive or negative answer. This activity could be done orally or in writing.

Answers: 1 Non, il n'a pas fait la vaisselle. 2 Non, je n'ai pas fait mon lit. 3 Oui, ils ont fait le ménage. 4 Non, je n'ai pas mis le couvert. 5 Non, ils n'ont pas fait les courses. 6 Oui, elles ont fait le ménage. 7 Non, elle n'a pas rangé sa chambre. 8 Non, je n'ai pas visité Paris.

2 *Décris ce que tu as fait hier et ce que tu n'as pas fait.*
Working in pairs, students take turns to make up sentences based on the picture cues, saying what they did and didn't do to help at home yesterday.

Answers: Partenaire A: J'ai fait mon lit, j'ai rangé ma chambre, je n'ai pas fait les courses, je n'ai pas fait la cuisine, je n'ai pas mis le couvert. Partenaire B: J'ai fait les courses, j'ai fait la cuisine, je n'ai pas mis le couvert, je n'ai pas fait la vaisselle, je n'ai pas fait le ménage.

3 *Pierre et Paul sont paresseux. Décris ce qu'ils ont fait ce week-end (choisis deux activités) et ce qu'ils n'ont pas fait (les autres activités).*
Students use the text prompts to make additional statements about household chores in the perfect tense (some positive, but mainly negative), using the third person plural.

Feuille 66 Guide pratique 1

This copymaster accompanies the *Guide pratique* on page 53 of the Students' Book. It provides further guidance on adding more detail and interest to written work.

AT 3.3
AT 4.3/4

1a *Imagine la réponse d'Amina au prof. Utilise toutes les briques et fais des phrases.*
Students follow the advice given to write a paragraph of text about Amina's Saturday routine, based on the phrases provided in the bricks.

Possible answer: Normalement, je me lève à 10 heures et je m'habille dans ma chambre. Ensuite, je prends le petit déjeuner dans la salle à manger. De temps en temps, je regarde la télé. L'après-midi, je joue au foot avec mon frère parce que j'aime ça.

1b *Trouve d'autres détails (unité 4) et réponds pour toi.*
Students describe their own weekend routine, looking back at the Students' Book to remind themselves of other details and language that they could incorporate.

147

4 Tous les jours

2 *Réponds aux questions.*
Students answer each question in as much detail as possible, following the guidance given. This activity revises language from previous units: clothes (Unit 1), health and fitness (Unit 2), plans for next weekend (Unit 3).

Feuille 67 Guide pratique 2

This copymaster explains and practises the steps involved in adapting a model text to talk about oneself. It accompanies the *Guide pratique* section on page 57 of the Students' Book.

1 *Pour chaque description: (1) Lis le texte. (2) Souligne les mots à changer. (3) Recopie la description avec tes détails personnels.*
There are three texts here to be adapted. In each case, students read through the text, underlining the parts that refer specifically to the writer. They then write out the framework, substituting their own details for the underlined words and phrases.
The example shows how this works. Go through it with students, making sure they understand what they are supposed to do, before they start working on their own adaptation of the texts.

Feuille 68 Ça se dit comme ça!

This copymaster focuses on silent endings and should be used with page 60 of the Students' Book.

1a *Avec un(e) partenaire, prononcez les phrases suivantes.*
Working with a partner, students read aloud the sentences, focusing on correct pronunciation.

1b *Écoute et vérifie.*
Students listen to the recording to check their pronunciation.

CD 3, track 31
Cassette 4, side 2
Feuille 68, activité 1b

1 – Elle se couche à dix heures, mais ils se couchent à minuit.
2 – On s'amuse, mais ils ne s'amusent pas.
3 – Je joue au foot et mes parents jouent au tennis.

2a *Écoute bien. La prononciation des verbes soulignés dans chaque phrase est la même ou différente?*
Students listen to the recording while following the text on the copymaster. For each sentence, they indicate whether the two underlined verbs are pronounced differently or the same.

Answers: 1 same; 2 same; 3 different; 4 same; 5 different; 6 same; 7 same; 8 different

CD 3, track 32
Cassette 4, side 2
Feuille 68, activité 2a

1 – Pierre joue avec moi, mais ses copains ne jouent pas.
2 – Je joue au foot quand tu joues au golf.
3 – Je joue du piano et vous jouez de la guitare.
4 – Tu fais du judo, mais Marc fait du karaté.
5 – On aime faire de la voile et vous aimez faire du surf.
6 – Je regarde la télé tous les jours, mais mes parents regardent la télé le week-end seulement.
7 – Il se réveille à sept heures. À quelle heure est-ce que tu te réveilles?
8 – Vous vous brossez les dents, mais il ne se brosse pas les dents.

2b *Barrez pour compléter la règle.*
Students cross out the incorrect words to complete the pronunciation rules relating to present tense verbs.

Answers: the *-ent* at the end of verbs with *ils* or *elles* is usually silent; the *-s* at the end of verbs with *tu* is usually silent; the *-ez* at the end of verbs with *vous* is not usually silent

2c *Lis les phrases de l'activité 2a à haute voix. Attention à la prononciation!*
Students read aloud the sentences from activity **2a**, focusing on correct pronunciation.

3 *Invente cinq phrases similaires et échange avec un(e) partenaire qui les lit.*
Students make up five sentences similar to those in activity **2a**, in which the verb endings are spelt differently but sometimes sound the same. They exchange their sentences with a partner, who reads them aloud focusing on correct pronunciation.

Encore Workbook

Page 34 (4.1)

Use with pages 50–51 of the Students' Book.

AT 3.1 **1** *Trouve huit sports.*
Students separate out the words in the string of letters to find eight sports.

Answers: le hockey, le football, le tennis, la natation, la voile, la pêche, l'équitation, le ping-pong

AT 4.2 **2** *Écris des bulles pour les musiciens avec les éléments des colonnes 1 à 5.*
Students write a speech bubble for each musician. All the words are provided in the panel at the bottom of the page: students build their sentences by combining phrases from each of the five columns, making sure they choose the correct instrument and expression of frequency.

Answers: a Je joue du piano une fois par semaine. b Je joue de la guitare deux fois par jour. c Je joue du violon trois fois par semaine. d Je joue de la batterie deux fois par semaine. e Je joue du clavier une fois par jour. f Je joue de la flûte quatre fois par semaine.

Page 35 (4.2)

Use with pages 52–53 of the Students' Book.

AT 3.2 1 *Coche la bonne phrase.*
This activity checks comprehension of some of the reflexive verbs used to describe daily routine. Students tick the sentence that goes with each picture.

Answers: 1 b; 2 b; 3 b; 4 a

AT 4.2 2 *Écris une phrase pour chaque image.*
Students fill in the crossword grid. They could refer to activity **1a** for spellings if necessary.

Answers:

		j	e	m	e	l	è	v	e											
j	e	m	e	l	a	v	e													
						j														
e	m	e	b	r	o	s	s	e	l	e	s	d	e	n	t	s				
						u														
j	e	p	r	e	n	d	s	l	e	p	e	t	i	t	d	é	j	e	u	n	e	r
j	e	m	e	r	é	v	e	i	l	l	e									
				j	e	m	'	h	a	b	i	l	l	e						

AT 4.2/3 3 *Et toi? Qu'est-ce que tu fais le matin? Écris quatre phrases à la page 43.*
Students write about their own daily routine. More able students should be encouraged to add details of time and place, e.g. *Je me réveille à sept heures dix. Je m'habille dans ma chambre*, etc.

Page 36 (4.3)

Use with pages 54–55 of the Students' Book.

AT 3.2 1 *Lis les phrases et écris le bon nom sous chaque dessin.*
Students match the phrases to the illustrations of household chores.

Answers: a Christophe; b Isabelle; c Alexandre; d Jonathan; e Claire; f Marine; g David

AT 4.2/3 2 *Remets les mots dans l'ordre et fais des phrases.*
Students rearrange the jumbled words in the correct order to make sentences.

Answers: a Je mets le couvert. b Tu fais les courses? c Elle fait son lit le matin. d Je range ma chambre tous les jours.

Page 37 (4.4)

Use with pages 56–57 of the Students' Book.

AT 3.2/3 1 *Lis les textes et complète la grille.*
This activity provides practice of the first person singular of perfect tense verbs, including negatives. Students read the speech bubbles and tick or cross the grid to show what each person did/didn't do last weekend to help at home.

Answers: Martin: he set the table, didn't wash the dishes, didn't do the shopping; Estelle: she made her bed, washed the dishes, didn't tidy her room, didn't do the cooking; Baptiste: he didn't do the cooking, didn't make his bed, didn't tidy his room, didn't set the table

AT 4.3/4 2 *Et toi? Qu'est-ce que tu as fait le week-end dernier? Qu'est-ce que tu n'as pas fait? Écris six phrases à la page 43.*
Students write positive and negative statements to describe what they did and didn't do to help at home last weekend.

Page 38 Grammaire

Use with pages 52–53 of the Students' Book.

1 *Coche les phrases avec un verbe pronominal.*
Students tick the sentences that contain a reflexive verb.

Answers: sentences a, c and e contain reflexive verbs

2 *Complète.*
Students fill in the missing reflexive pronouns and subject pronouns.

Answers: a me; b te; c se; d se; e je; f tu

3a *Colorie les bonnes flèches.*
Students start at the word *je* and work their way around the maze, gathering words to make a sentence and colouring in the arrows to show their route. There is only one correct route.

Answer: Je me lève à sept heures et je m'habille.

3b *Écris la phrase.*
Students write the sentence from activity **3a**.

Page 39 Méli-mélo

This page pulls together and mixes much of the language and grammar of the whole unit. It should therefore be used towards the end of the unit, either with or after pages 56–57.

AT 3.3 / AT 4.3 1a *Recopie chaque phrase sous le bon dessin.*
Students copy the correct caption beneath each picture.

Answers: 1 Claire se lève à sept heures trente. 2 Je joue de la batterie tous les jours. 3 Tu n'as pas fait la vaisselle? 4 Max joue au ping-pong au club des jeunes. 5 Je ne me brosse pas les dents le matin. 6 Samedi, j'ai rangé ma chambre.

4 Tous les jours

1b *À la page 43, traduis les phrases a–f en anglais.*
Students translate into English the sentences from **1a**.

Answers: a I play the drums every day. b Max is playing table tennis at the youth club. c Claire gets up at half past seven. d I don't brush my teeth in the morning. e On Saturday I tidied my bedroom. f Haven't you washed the dishes?

[AT 4.3] **2** *Écris des phrases.*
Students write a sentence to describe each picture.

Answers: a Je joue de la guitare. b Je joue au football/Je fais du football. c Je m'habille.

Page 40 Challenge!

Use with page 60 of the Students' Book.

[AT 3.3/4] **1** *Lis le journal. Qui l'a écrit: un garçon ou un fantôme?*
Students read the text and decide whether it has been written from the point of view of the ghost or the boy.

Answer: the ghost

2 *Souligne les verbes au présent et entoure les verbes au passé composé.*
Students underline all the present tense verbs in the text and circle all the perfect tense verbs.

Answers: (present tense verbs are underlined; perfect tense verbs are in bold): Je me réveille … et je me lève … Toute la famille est au lit. J'aime le noir … Je vais dans la salle de bains, mais je ne me lave pas et je ne m'habille pas. Je vais dans la cuisine. Papa **n'a pas fait** la vaisselle … Maman **n'a pas fait** les courses – le frigo est presque vide. Je joue au football … Je joue au golf … Hier, **j'ai joué** avec un œuf … Je vais dans le salon. On aime beaucoup la musique: il y a un piano, … Hier, **j'ai joué** du violon. Ce soir, je joue du piano … Tout d'un coup, la porte s'ouvre. J'avance … C'est Julien. **Il m'a vu**! … ce n'est pas bien …

3 *Réponds en anglais à la page 43.*
Students answer comprehension questions about the story in English.

Answers: a He gets up. b The father hasn't done it. c Because the mother hasn't been shopping. d He plays football with it. e He plays golf with it. f Yesterday. g The bathroom, the kitchen and the living room. h Piano, violin, guitar and drums.

En plus Workbook

Page 34 (4.1)

Use with pages 50–51 of the Students' Book.

[AT 4.3] **1a** *Écris des bulles, comme dans l'exemple.*
Students write a speech bubble for each musician, responding to the pictures and symbols provided.

Answers: a Je joue du piano une heure par semaine. b Je joue de la guitare deux heures par jour. c Je joue du violon trois heures par semaine. d Je joue de la batterie deux heures par semaine. e Je joue du clavier une heure par jour. f Je joue de la flûte quatre heures par semaine.

[AT 3.3] **1b** *Lis les phrases. Relis les messages de l'activité 1a et devine l'instrument!*
Students look back at what they wrote in activity **1a** to work out which instrument is being referred to in each sentence.

Answers: a drums; b piano; c guitar; d flute

[AT 4.4/5] **2** *Imagine: ces détails sont vrais pour toi. Regarde les symboles et écris le plus possible de détails à la page 43.*
Using the model text and the symbols as prompts, students write about their imaginary leisure activities.

Page 35 (4.2)

Use with pages 52–53 of the Students' Book.

[AT 4.2] **1** *Écris la bonne phrase de la boîte dans chaque bulle.*
This activity checks comprehension of some of the reflexive verbs used to describe daily routine. Students copy the appropriate sentence into each speech bubble.

Answers: a Je m'habille. b Je me réveille. c Je me brosse les dents. d Je prends le petit déjeuner. e Je me lave.

[AT 3.4] **2** *Lis l'article et coche: vrai, faux ou on ne sait pas.*
Students read the article about the daily routine of a swimming champion and tick the columns to show their comprehension.

Answers: a vrai; b faux; c on ne sait pas; d faux; e faux/on ne sait pas; f faux

[AT 4.3/4] **3** *Et toi? Qu'est-ce que tu fais le matin? Écris un paragraphe à la page 43.*
Students write about their own morning routine. Encourage them to add details of time and place, as in the article in activity **2**, e.g. *Je me réveille à sept heures dix. Je m'habille dans ma chambre*, etc.

Tous les jours 4

Page 36 (4.3)
Use with pages 54–55 of the Students' Book.

AT 4.2/3

1 *Remets les mots dans l'ordre et fais des phrases.*
Students rearrange the jumbled words in the correct order to make sentences. Point out that, in answers b–e, the time expressions could begin the sentences instead of being placed at the end.

Answers: a Je mets le couvert. b Marc fait son lit le matin. c Elle fait la cuisine de temps en temps. d On fait la vaisselle le soir. e Nous faisons les courses tous les jours.

AT 4.3

2 *Écris une phrase sous chaque dessin.*
Students write a caption for each picture.

Answers: a À deux heures, il fait son lit. b À deux heures et demie, il fait le ménage. c À trois heures moins dix, il fait les courses. d À trois heures dix, il fait la cuisine. e À trois heures et demie, il met le couvert.

Page 37 (4.4)
Use with pages 56–57 of the Students' Book.

AT 3.3

1 *Lis les textes et coche la grille. Qui est Élodie: numéro 1, 2, 3 ou 4?*
This activity provides practice of household chores and perfect tense verbs, including negatives, in the form of a puzzle. Using the information provided, students work out which of the four characters is Élodie.

Answers: numéro 2

AT 4.4

2 *Et toi? Qu'est-ce que tu as fait le week-end dernier? Qu'est-ce que tu n'as pas fait? Écris un paragraphe à la page 43.*
Students write a paragraph about what they did and didn't do last weekend to help at home.

Page 38 Grammaire
This page could be used with pages 52–53 of the Students' Book. Alternatively, you might prefer to use it with the *Super-challenge!* page (page 60 of the Students' Book) because it includes the *nous*, *vous* and *ils/elles* forms of reflexive verbs, which are not formally dealt with until the *Zoom grammaire* panel on that page.

1a *Colorie les bonnes flèches.*
Students start at the word *je* and work their way around the maze, gathering words to make a sentence and colouring in the arrows to show their route. There is only one correct route.

Answer: Je me lève à sept heures et je m'habille.

1b *Écris la phrase.*
Students write the sentence from activity **1a**.

2a *Complète avec le bon verbe.*
Students fill in the correct forms of the reflexive verbs.

Answers: a me réveille; b te lèves; c se lave; d se brosse; e me repose; f vous préparez; g s'habillent; h nous entraînons

2b *Traduis les phrases a–h en anglais à la page 43.*
Students translate into English the sentences from activity **2a**.

Answers: a I wake up at six o'clock. b When do you get up? c He gets washed in the bathroom. d Marie is brushing her teeth. e I'm resting for five minutes. f Are you getting ready for the match? g The children are getting dressed in the bedroom. h We are training for the tennis match.

3 *Traduis ces phrases en français.*
Students translate the English sentences into French.

Answers: a Je me lève à sept heures. b Marc s'habille dans la salle de bains. c Nous nous lavons et nous nous brossons les dents. d Tu te réveilles/Vous vous réveillez à huit heures. e Je me repose dans ma chambre. f Ils/Elles s'entraînent pour le match?

Page 39 Méli-mélo
This page pulls together and mixes much of the language and grammar of the whole unit. It should therefore be used towards the end of the unit, either with or after pages 56–57.

AT 3.3

1 *Coche la bonne légende.*
Students tick the correct choice of caption for the picture.

Answer: c

AT 3.4

2 *Lis les bulles et réponds aux questions en anglais.*
Students answer comprehension questions in English on the two texts about last weekend's activities.

Answers: a She cleaned up/did the housework in the living room and went shopping. b She washed the dishes. c She met her friends and they played table tennis at the youth club. d She listened to music. e He made his bed, tidied his room and watched television. f He set the table and washed the dishes. g He played cards and Scrabble® with his brother.

Page 40 Super-challenge!
Use with page 60 of the Students' Book.

AT 3.5

1 *Lis le journal. Qui l'a écrit: un garçon ou un fantôme?*
Students read the text and decide whether it has been written from the point of view of the ghost or the boy.

Answer: the ghost

2a *Trouve trois expressions qui parlent du futur.*
Students search the text for three examples of *aller* + infinitive.

Answers: see **2b**

4 Tous les jours

2b *Souligne les verbes au présent et entoure les verbes au passé composé.*
Students underline all the present tense verbs in the text and circle all the perfect tense verbs.

Answers: (present tense verbs are underlined, perfect tense verbs are in bold, *aller* + infinitive is shown in italic):
Je me réveille … et je me lève … Toute la famille est au lit. J'aime le noir … Je vais dans la salle de bains, mais je ne me lave pas et je ne m'habille pas. *Qu'est-ce que je vais faire?* Ah, j'ai une idée – *je vais aller dans la cuisine.*
Dans la cuisine, je vois que Papa **n'a pas fait** la vaisselle … Et Maman **n'a pas fait** les courses … le frigo est presque vide. Je joue au football … Je m'amuse. Je joue au golf … Hier, **j'ai joué** avec un œuf …
À minuit et demi, je vais dans le salon. *Je vais jouer de la musique*: il y a un piano, … Hier, **j'ai joué** du violon. Pff, **je n'ai pas bien joué**. Ce soir, *je vais jouer du piano* … Je commence …
Tout d'un coup, la porte s'ouvre. Qui est là? J'avance … C'est Julien. **Il m'a vu**! … ce n'est pas bien …

3 *Réponds aux questions à la page 43.*
Students answer questions in French about the story.

Answers: a Il se lève à minuit dix. b Parce que toute la famille est au lit. c Parce que Maman n'a pas fait les courses aujourd'hui. d Un melon et une orange. e Il joue au football avec le melon et il joue au golf avec l'orange. f Hier. g Il joue du piano. h Parce que le fantôme joue du piano/fait du bruit. i Non, parce que Julien a vu le fantôme.

Révisions Unités 3–4

This revision spread provides consolidation and further practice of language from Units 3–4. You can take students through the activities as a whole class, or they can work independently or in pairs. The activities should help students prepare for the assessment for Units 3–4.

Resources

Students' Book, pages 63–64
CD 2, tracks 21–23
Cassette 2, side 2

AT 3.3 **1a** *Trouve la bonne réponse pour chaque message.*
Students match the invitations to the replies.

Answers: 1 b; 2 c; 3 d; 4 a

AT 4.3/4 **1b** *Écris un message comme Jasmine, Manon, Antoine ou Mustafa.*
Students write an invitation similar to those in activity **1a**.

AT 4.3/4 **1c** *Échange ton message avec un(e) partenaire. Écris une réponse.*
Students exchange their invitation with a partner and write a reply to their partner's invitation.

AT 1.3/4 **2a** *Écoute. Pour chaque conversation, note: quel film? heure? on se retrouve où?*
Students listen to the invitations/arrangements and note down the key details of each.

Answers: 1 film romantique, 7 h 30, chez moi; 2 film policier, 7 h 25, au cinéma; 3 film d'horreur, 19 h 40, au café; 4 film de science-fiction, 7 h 15, au cinéma

CD 2, track 21 — page 63, activité 2a
Cassette 2, side 2

1 – Tu veux aller au cinéma ce soir?
  – Oui, c'est quel film?
  – C'est un film romantique.
  – Ça commence à quelle heure?
  – À sept heures trente.
  – Et on se retrouve où?
  – Chez moi?
  – D'accord.
2 – Salut! Dis … Tu aimes les films policiers?
  – Les films policiers? Oui, j'adore ça!
  – Alors, on va au cinéma ce soir?
  – D'accord. Le film commence à quelle heure?
  – À sept heures vingt-cinq.
  – On se retrouve au cinéma?
  – Bonne idée. À ce soir!
3 – Tu veux venir au cinéma ce soir?
  – C'est quel film?
  – C'est un film d'horreur.
  – Super! J'aime bien les films d'horreur. Le film commence à quelle heure?
  – À dix-neuf heures quarante.
  – Et on se retrouve où?
  – On se retrouve au café?
  – Bonne idée! On se retrouve au café à dix-neuf heures.
  – D'accord. À plus tard!
4 – Il y a un bon film de science-fiction au cinéma ce soir.
  – J'aime bien les films de science-fiction. On y va?
  – Oui, d'accord, le film commence à sept heures et quart.
  – Sept heures et quart? D'accord.
  – On se retrouve où?
  – On se retrouve chez moi?
  – Euh non! On se retrouve au cinéma! C'est plus pratique!
  – D'accord.

AT 2.4 **2b** *Invente des conversations.*
Students follow the model dialogue to make up their own conversations.

AT 1.3 **3a** *Écoute et lis. Numérote les questions dans l'ordre où tu les entends.*
AT 3.3 Students listen to the interview with Esmée while focusing on the list of questions. They number the questions in the order in which they occur.

Answers: 1 c; 2 i; 3 a; 4 h; 5 d; 6 b; 7 g; 8 f; 9 e

CD 2, track 22 — page 64, activité 3
Cassette 2, side 2

1 – Bonjour, Esmée. On va un peu parler du week-end.
  – Oui, d'accord.
  – À quelle heure est-ce que tu te réveilles le week-end?
  – Ça dépend, mais normalement je me réveille à huit heures et demie et je prends le petit déjeuner avec ma famille vers neuf heures.
2 – Et tu te couches à quelle heure?
  – À onze heures, onze heures et demie, ça dépend.
3 – Et qu'est-ce que tu fais pour aider à la maison?
  – Je fais mon lit tous les jours et, le week-end, je range ma chambre. J'aime aussi faire la cuisine!
4 – Tu fais du sport le week-end?
  – Oui, bien sûr! Je suis très sportive. Je fais du judo deux fois par semaine, le samedi matin et le lundi soir, et je joue au tennis tous les jours.
5 – Tu joues d'un instrument de musique?
  – Ah non, je ne joue pas d'instrument. Je suis nulle en musique.
6 – Tu regardes souvent la télé?
  – Bof! Pendant la semaine, non, mais le week-end, je regarde beaucoup la télé!
7 – Tu aimes les émissions pour la jeunesse?
  – Oui, j'adore ça parce que c'est drôle.
8 – Tu aimes aller au cinéma?
  – Oui, je vais au cinéma tous les week-ends.
9 – Qu'est-ce que tu aimes voir au cinéma?
  – J'adore tous les films, surtout les films d'aventure et d'horreur.

Révisions Unités 3–4

AT 4.2 **3b** *Réécris les questions dans le bon ordre.*
Students write out the questions from activity **3a** in the correct order.

AT 1.4 **3c** *Réécoute et note les réponses d'Esmée.*
Students listen again to the recording from activity **1a** and note down Esmée's answers to the questions.

Answers: 1 à 8 h 30 (normalement); 2 à 11 h 00 ou à 11 h 30; 3 je fais mon lit (tous les jours), je range ma chambre (le week-end), j'aime faire la cuisine; 4 je fais du judo et je joue au tennis; 5 non; 6 pendant la semaine – non, le week-end – beaucoup; 7 oui (c'est drôle); 8 oui (tous les week-ends); 9 surtout les films d'aventure et d'horreur

AT 2.3/4 **3d** *Écris/Enregistre le week-end d'Esmée.*
AT 4.3/4 Students use their answers from activity **3c** to write or record a longer description of Esmée's weekend, using the third person singular. A wide variety of outcomes are possible; encourage able students to incorporate as much detail as they can. The activity could be done in pairs, if appropriate, instead of individually.

AT 1.4 **4a** *Écoute et complète l'emploi du temps d'Hugo.*
Students listen to Hugo describing his routine and complete the timetable to show what he does at certain times. Because of the monologue format, students may find this activity rather challenging and may need to listen to the recording several times in order to complete their answers.
The recording is set within the context of an English teenager who is working at a ski resort in France. If you think students might be motivated by the idea of working in France, discuss it with them: you can earn money while improving your French and seeing something of another country/travelling, and you can often combine the work with something that you enjoy doing (skiing, in Hugo's case).

Answers: 06 h 30: me réveille, me lève, me lave, m'habille; 07 h 30: mets le couvert, prépare le petit déjeuner; 09 h 00: fais la vaisselle; 09 h 30: fais les lits; 10 h 00: range le chalet; 10 h 30: fais les courses; 11 h 30: fais du ski; 18 h 00: travaille dans le chalet, prépare le dîner; 20 h 00: mange (avec les clients); 21 h 00: vais au café/au cinéma avec mes amis; 23 h 00: me couche

---

CD 2, track 23   **page 64, activité 4a**
Cassette 2, side 2

Bonjour! Je m'appelle Hugo et j'ai dix-neuf ans. Je suis anglais, mais je travaille en France. Maintenant, je parle très bien français! Je travaille pour une compagnie de ski et je m'occupe d'un chalet. C'est génial!
Normalement, je me réveille à six heures et demie, je me lève, je me lave et je m'habille. À sept heures et demie, je mets le couvert et je prépare le petit déjeuner dans le chalet. C'est pour dix personnes! À neuf heures, je fais la vaisselle et à neuf heures et demie, je fais les lits. Après ça, à dix heures, je range le chalet, et à dix heures et demie, je fais les courses. C'est intéressant d'aller dans un supermarché en France!
Puis, à onze heures et demie, je fais du ski. Super! Génial! J'adore ça! Je fais du ski tous les jours!
À dix-huit heures, je travaille encore dans le chalet où je prépare le dîner. À vingt heures, je mange avec les clients. C'est sympa.
À vingt et une heures, je vais au café ou au cinéma avec mes amis. J'adore les films français! À vingt-trois heures, je me couche! C'est fatigant, mon travail, mais c'est génial.

AT 2.4 **4b** *A pose les questions (trois minimum). B répond pour Hugo.*
In pairs, students take turns to play the roles of Hugo and an interviewer. They ask and answer questions about Hugo's routine, using their notes from activity **4a**.

AT 4.4/5 **4c** *Qu'est-ce qu'Hugo a fait au travail hier? Écris six activités.*
Students write a report using the third person singular of the perfect tense, describing what Hugo did at work yesterday. Encourage able students to invent as much detail as possible.

Contrôle Unités 3–4

For general comments on assessment, see page 22 of the Introduction.

Resources
Copymasters 111–118
CD 3, tracks 49–55
Cassette 2, side 2

AT 1.2/3

Feuille 111   Écoute Encore

1 *Écoute. Relie les émissions et les heures. Attention: les émissions ne sont pas en ordre.*
Students listen to the short conversations about TV programmes and times. They match the clock faces to the pictures to show what time each programme begins.

Answers: 1 f; 2 b; 3 e; 4 a; 5 d; 6 c

Mark scheme: 1 mark for each = 5 marks

Assessment criteria: Students who achieve 5 marks show evidence of performance at AT 1.3; those who achieve 3–4 marks show evidence of performance at AT 1.2.

CD 3, track 49   Feuille 111, activité 1
Cassette 2, side 2

– Le documentaire sur les extra-terrestres, c'est à quelle heure?
– Le documentaire? C'est à 22 heures.

– Le film, c'est à quelle heure ce soir?
– Le film? Le film policier? C'est à vingt heures trente.

– J'adore les émissions sportives. Il y a une émission sportive aujourd'hui?
– Oui, il y a une émission sportive à dix-huit heures vingt.
– Dix-huit heures vingt … OK!

– Je veux regarder la météo.
– La météo, c'est à quelle heure?
– C'est à vingt et une heures.

– Tu veux regarder les infos?
– C'est à quelle heure, les infos?
– À dix-neuf heures vingt-cinq … dans cinq minutes!

– Ah, il y a un bon dessin animé sur France 3.
– C'est quand?
– C'est à dix-sept heures.
– Cool!

AT 1.3

2 *Écoute l'interview. Réponds aux questions en anglais.*
Students listen to the telephone conversation in which two young people are making arrangements to go out. They answer questions in English.

Answers: 1 to the cinema; 2 Wednesday; 3 has to do his homework; 4 Saturday; 5 to the swimming pool; 6 yes; 7 11 o'clock; 8 at the park

Mark scheme: 1 mark for each correct answer = 8 marks

Assessment criteria: Students who achieve 6 marks or more show evidence of performance at AT 1.3.

CD 3, track 50   Feuille 111, activité 2
Cassette 2, side 2

– Allô.
– Salut, Paul, c'est Élise. Tu veux aller au cinéma mercredi?
– Ah non, mercredi je ne peux pas. Je dois faire mes devoirs.
– Oh …
– Tu veux sortir samedi?
– Samedi … euh …
– Tu veux aller à la piscine?
– Oui, j'adore la natation. On se retrouve à quelle heure?
– À onze heures?
– Et on se retrouve où?
– On se retrouve au parc?
– OK, samedi au parc à onze heures. À samedi!

AT 1.3

3 *Écoute. Coche les activités du mari idéal pour Isabelle.*
Students listen to Isabelle describing what her ideal husband would do to help around the house. They tick the activities that she mentions.

Answers: 1, 2, 6, 4, 5, 7

Mark scheme: 1 mark for each correct answer = 6 marks

Assessment criteria: See activity **4** below.

CD 3, track 51   Feuille 111, activité 3
Cassette 2, side 2

– Pour vous, Isabelle, le mari idéal fait quoi?
– Alors, pour moi, le mari idéal se lève tôt. Il prépare le petit déjeuner. Après, il fait le ménage. Il fait la cuisine à midi. Il fait aussi la vaisselle! Et puis, il fait les courses parce que moi, je déteste ça.

AT 1.3

4 *Écoute. Coche les activités de la femme idéale pour Marc.*
Students listen to Marc describing the household chores that his ideal wife would do. They tick the activities that he mentions.

Answers: 1, 2, 3, 6, 7, 8

Mark scheme: 1 mark for each correct answer = 6 marks

Assessment criteria: Assess activities 3 and 4 together. Students who achieve 9 marks or more for the two activities show evidence of performance at AT 1.3.

Contrôle Unités 3–4

CD 3, track 52
Cassette 2, side 2
Feuille 111, activité 4

– Pour vous, Marc, la femme idéale fait quoi?
– Alors, pour moi, la femme idéale se lève tôt. Elle prépare le petit déjeuner. Après elle fait le lit et elle fait le ménage. Elle fait aussi les courses. Et le soir, elle se repose avec moi, devant la télé.

Feuille 112   Écoute En plus

AT 1.3 1 *Écoute les trois jeunes. Ils parlent de leur émission préférée le lundi. Prends des notes.*
Students listen to three people giving details of their favourite TV programmes. For each one, they note down the type of programme, an opinion, and the time the programme begins.

Answers: 1 dessin animé, super, 9 h 05; 2 jeu, intéressant, 12 h 15; 3 émission sportive, génial, 20 h 35

Mark scheme: 1 mark for each correct answer = 9 marks

Assessment criteria: Students who score 7 or more marks show evidence of performance at AT 1.3.

CD 3, track 53
Cassette 2, side 2
Feuille 112, activité 1

1 – Quelle est ton émission préférée aujourd'hui?
– C'est lundi et mon émission préférée s'appelle *Jeanne et Serge*. C'est un dessin animé. J'adore les dessins animés parce que c'est super.
– C'est à quelle heure?
– À neuf heures cinq.

2 – Et toi, quelle est ton émission préférée aujourd'hui?
– *Le juste prix.*
– C'est quelle sorte d'émission?
– C'est un jeu. Les jeux, c'est intéressant.
– C'est à quelle heure?
– À midi et quart.

3 – Tu as une émission préférée le lundi?
– Oui, j'aime bien *Tout le sport*. J'adore les émissions sportives – c'est génial.
– C'est à quelle heure?
– Ce soir à vingt heures trente-cinq.

AT 1.3/4 2 *Écoute l'interview. Remplis la grille.*
Students listen to the interview with Nathalie. They note down details of the sports and musical instruments she plays, when she does them, and her opinion of each activity.

Answers: tennis: pas beaucoup/de temps en temps (par exemple, le week-end dernier), aime bien/génial; trompette: cours le mercredi, doit jouer tous les jours à la maison, n'aime pas/difficile/elle est nulle

Mark scheme: 1 mark for each correct answer = 6 marks

Assessment criteria: Students who achieve 5–6 marks show evidence of performance at AT 1.4; those who achieve 3–4 marks show evidence of performance at AT 1.3.

CD 3, track 54
Cassette 2, side 2
Feuille 112, activité 2

– Tu fais du sport, Nathalie?
– Oui, je joue au tennis.
– Tu joues quand?
– Euh … je ne joue pas beaucoup, je joue de temps en temps avec ma copine. On a joué ce week-end, mais j'ai perdu.
– Tu aimes jouer au tennis?
– Oui, j'aime bien. C'est génial!
– Et tu as d'autres passe-temps?
– Euh … je joue de la trompette.
– De la trompette!
– Oui, j'ai un cours le mercredi et en plus je dois jouer tous les jours à la maison.
– Alors, tu aimes bien ça?
– Ah non, je n'aime pas vraiment parce que c'est difficile et je suis nulle.

AT 1.4/5 3 *Écoute. Vrai ou faux?*
Students listen to Lucie and Yann talking about household chores. They tick or cross the statements to show whether they are true or false.

Answers: 1 vrai; 2 faux; 3 vrai; 4 faux; 5 faux; 6 faux; 7 vrai; 8 vrai; 9 faux; 10 vrai

Mark scheme: 1 mark per correct response = 10 marks

Assessment criteria: Students who achieve 9–10 marks are beginning to show evidence of performance at AT 1.5; students who achieve 5–8 marks show evidence of performance at AT 1.4.

CD 3, track 55
Cassette 2, side 2
Feuille 112, activité 3

– Salut! Je m'appelle Lucie. Normalement, j'aide ma mère à la maison le soir ou le week-end. Ce matin, par exemple, j'ai fait mon lit – comme tous les matins – et … après, j'ai fait les courses en ville. Avec ma mère, on est allées au supermarché. En plus, le mercredi après-midi, je fais les courses pour ma grand-mère parce qu'elle ne peut pas sortir. De temps en temps, je fais le ménage, mais je ne fais jamais la vaisselle parce que je déteste ça. C'est nul!

– Salut! Je m'appelle Yann. À la maison, c'est ma mère qui fait le ménage en général et mon père fait la cuisine. Mais hier, comme mon père n'était pas là, j'ai fait la cuisine. J'ai fait une omelette au fromage … et après le repas, j'ai fait la vaisselle. Je fais mon lit tous les matins et j'aime bien ranger ma chambre parce que j'aime bien que chaque chose soit à sa place.

Feuille 113   Parle Encore

AT 2.2/3

1 *Regarde le planning. Choisis un personnage. Ton/Ta partenaire devine qui tu es. Ensuite, changez de rôle.*
Students choose a role from the grid and tell their partner what they do to help around the house. The partner consults the grid to find out who they are. They continue until each partner has named all the activities shown.

Mark scheme: 1 mark for each activity (apart from the example) = 7 marks

Assessment criteria: Students who achieve 5 or more marks show evidence of performance at AT 2.3; students who achieve 3–4 marks show evidence of performance at AT 2.2.

AT 2.3

2 *Complète les heures pour toi. Pose des questions à ton/ta partenaire et note ses réponses.*
Students draw in the clock hands to show the times at which they themselves do each of these activities. Working with a partner, they then take turns to ask and answer questions on their daily routine, following the model question provided. They draw in their partner's times on the second column of clock faces.

Mark scheme: half a mark for each question correctly asked; half a mark for each correct response = 6 marks

Assessment criteria: Students who are score 4 or more marks show evidence of performance at AT 2.3.

AT 2.4

3a *Téléphone à ton/ta partenaire. Suis les instructions.*
3b *Ton/Ta partenaire t'invite au cinéma. Accepte son invitation et réponds à ses questions/suggestions.*
Students perform a role-play in which they make arrangements to go to the cinema, responding to the bulleted list of instructions provided.

Mark scheme: 2 marks for each bullet point (1 mark for communicating the information, 1 mark for accuracy of language and pronunciation) = 12 marks

Assessment criteria: Students who achieve 8 or more marks show evidence of performance at AT 2.4.

Feuille 114   Parle En plus

Students work in pairs for these activities. Give the top half of the sheet to one student and the bottom half to their partner.

AT 2.3

1a *Invite ton/ta partenaire.*
1b *Réponds aux questions de ton/ta partenaire.*
Students take turns to invite each other to do an activity. Visual cues are given for the questions, and there are two responses for students to choose between. Note that marks are awarded for the questions only.

Mark scheme: 2 marks for each question correctly asked (1 mark for content, 1 mark for accuracy of language) = 8 marks

Assessment criteria: Students who achieve 6 or more marks show evidence of performance at AT 2.3.

AT 2.3/4

2a *Pose des questions à ton/ta partenaire et note les réponses.*
2b *Réponds aux questions de ton/ta partenaire.*
The question forms are provided for this interview on favourite television programmes, so marks are awarded for the answers only.

Mark scheme: 1 mark for each answer = 5 marks

Assessment criteria: Students who achieve 4 or 5 marks show evidence of performance at AT 2.4; students who achieve 2 or 3 marks show evidence of performance at AT 2.3.

AT 2.4/5

3a *Qu'est-ce que tu as fait le week-end dernier? Explique à ton/ta partenaire.*
3b *Écoute ton/ta partenaire. Prends des notes.*
Students take turns to tell each other what they did last weekend to help around the house, responding to the visuals provided. Their partner notes down what they say.

Mark scheme: 2 marks for each activity (1 mark for the idea successfully conveyed, 1 mark for accuracy of language) = 12 marks

Assessment criteria: Students who achieve 10 or more marks and who are able to use the perfect tense correctly are beginning to show evidence of performance at AT 2.5; students who achieve 5–9 marks show evidence of performance at AT 2.4.

Feuille 115   Lis Encore

AT 3.2

1 *Relie.*
Students match the visuals to the statements about activities.

Answers: 1 b; 2 d; 3 c; 4 f; 5 e; 6 a

Mark scheme: 1 mark for each correct answer = 6 marks

Assessment criteria: Students who achieve 4 marks or more show evidence of performance at AT 3.2.

AT 3.3

2 *Choisis et entoure les bons mots.*
Students read the e-mail and circle the correct choices of words/phrases.

Answers: hier, au cinéma, nul, nous sommes allés, les émission sportives, veux, on se retrouve, du skate, je dois

Mark scheme: 1 mark per correct choice = 9 marks

Assessment criteria: Students who achieve 7 marks or more show evidence of performance at AT 3.3.

AT 3.4/5

3 *Lis la brochure et la bulle. Trouve et <u>souligne</u> cinq erreurs dans la bulle.*
Students read the holiday camp brochure, comparing it with the speech bubble about Marion's stay at the camp. They underline the five errors in the speech bubble.

Answers: Marion est allée dans un camp de vacances. Elle a fait son lit et <u>elle a rangé sa chambre tous les jours</u>. Elle a joué <u>au tennis</u> et elle a nagé à la piscine.

Contrôle Unités 3–4

Malheureusement, <u>il n'était pas possible de faire de la voile</u>. Le soir, <u>elle a fait la cuisine</u> et elle a fait la vaisselle. Ensuite, elle a joué <u>du violon</u>.

Mark scheme: 2 marks per error identified = 10 marks

Assessment criteria: Students who achieve 9 or 10 marks are beginning to show evidence of performance at AT 3.5; students who achieve 4–8 marks show evidence of performance at AT 3.4.

Feuille 116   Lis En plus

AT 3.4/5

1 *Qu'est-ce que Grégoire mentionne dans sa lettre?*
Students read Grégoire's letter about his weekend. They tick the pictures to show the activities he mentions.

Answers: 1, 2, 4, 5, 7

Mark scheme: 1 mark for each correct answer = 5 marks

Assessment criteria: See activity **3** below.

AT 3.4/5

2 *Complète.*
Students complete the sentences in French to give information about Grégoire's weekend activities.

Answers: 1 les émissions sportives/*Sport Dimanche*; 2 dimanche/le week-end; 3 le piano; 4 faire du skate; 5 fait le ménage

Mark scheme: 2 marks for each correct answer = 10 marks

Assessment criteria: See activity **3** below.

AT 3.4/5

3 *Souligne la bonne réponse.*
Students underline the correct words/phrases in each sentence.

Answers: 1 prendre son petit déjeuner au lit; 2 l'après-midi; 3 génial; 4 Dracula; 5 a fait ses devoirs

Mark scheme: 2 marks for each correct response = 10 marks

Assessment criteria: Assess activities 1–3 together. Students who achieve 20 marks or more are beginning to show evidence of performance at AT 3.5; students who achieve 14–19 marks show evidence of performance at AT 3.4.

Feuille 117   Écris Encore

AT 4.2

1 *Complète la phrase avec cinq activités. (Invente si tu veux!)*
Students complete the sentence, giving details of five more activities.

Mark scheme: 2 marks for each activity (1 mark only if grammar or spelling is incorrect) = 10 marks

Assessment criteria: Students who achieve 7 marks or more show evidence of performance at AT 4.2.

AT 4.3

2 *Adapte le message de Yann pour inviter ton/ta partenaire à une boum. Change les détails soulignés.*
Students adapt the message, changing the underlined phrases to write an invitation to a party.

Mark scheme: 1 mark for "une boum", 2 marks each for the time and the meeting place = 5 marks

Assessment criteria: Students who achieve 4 or 5 marks show evidence of performance at AT 4.3.

AT 4.3/4

3 *Qu'est-ce que tu as fait hier? Complète les bulles.*
In response to the visuals, students write five sentences in the perfect tense to say what household chores they have done.

Answers: 1 Moi, j'ai fait la cuisine. 2 Moi, j'ai fait mon lit. 3 Moi, j'ai fait la vaisselle. 4 Moi, j'ai mis le couvert. 5 Moi, j'ai fait les courses.

Mark scheme: 2 marks for each speech bubble (1 mark for the correct vocabulary, e.g. *la cuisine, la vaisselle*, etc., 1 mark for accurate grammar and spelling) = 10 marks

Assessment criteria: Students who achieve 7 marks or more show evidence of performance at AT 4.4; those who achieve 4–6 marks show evidence of performance at AT 4.3.

Feuille 118   Écris En plus

AT 4.3

1 *Complète les phrases.*
Students fill in the blanks in the sentences about daily routine.

Answers: a Je me réveille à sept heures. b Je me lève à sept heures dix. c Je me lave dans la salle de bains à sept heures et quart. d Je prends le petit déjeuner à sept heures et demie. e À huit heures moins cinq, je me brosse les dents.

Mark scheme: 2 marks for each picture = 10 marks

Assessment criteria: Students who achieve 7 marks or more show evidence of performance at AT 4.3.

AT 4.4

2 *Réponds aux questions.*
Students answer questions on sport, musical instruments, household chores and preferred types of film.

Mark scheme: 1 mark for each answer + 1 mark overall for general accuracy = 5 marks

Assessment criteria: Students who achieve 4 or 5 marks show evidence of performance at AT 4.4.

AT 4.4/5

3 *Regarde les illustrations et raconte tes activités du week-end dernier sur une feuille (minimum cinq choses). Écris 100 mots environ. Donne tes opinions et utilise les connecteurs: et, mais, parce que, par contre, aussi.*
Students describe a past weekend, using the visuals as prompts. Draw their attention to specific instructions given in the rubric (they are asked to mention at least five activities, write approximately 100 words, express opinions and use connectives) and point out that they will lose out on marks if they do not follow the instructions.

Mark scheme: 1 mark for each activity to a maximum of 5 marks, 2 marks for opinions, 3 marks for correct use of three connectives = 10 marks

Assessment criteria: Students who demonstrate ability to express themselves in the perfect tense and who achieve at least 8 marks are beginning to show evidence of performance at AT 4.5; students who achieve 4–7 marks show evidence of performance at AT 4.4.

Unit 5 Overview grid

National Curriculum

Pages/Contexts/ Cultural focus	Objectives	Grammar	Skills and Pronunciation	Key language	Framework	PoS	AT level
66–67 **5.1 À l'étranger** Countries and capital cities French-speaking countries	Name countries and capital cities; say which countries you are going to or have been to; say which countries you'd like to go to; use the correct preposition	*aller à* + *ville* *aller en/au/aux* + *pays*		*Je suis allé(e)/Je ne suis jamais allé(e)/Je vais/J'aimerais aller …* *à l'étranger* *à* + *ville, en/au/aux* + *pays* Names of countries and towns		1a, 1b, 1c, 2b, 2c, 2d, 2f, 3c, 3e, 4a, 4c, 4d, 5a, 5c, 5d, 5e, 5f, 5g, 5i	1.3, 2.1–3, 3.1–3, 4.1–4
68–69 **5.2 À pied ou en voiture** Transport	Name means of transport you use/don't use to go to places; say what you think of different means of transport; use the correct preposition	*à/en* + transport		*J'aime bien/Je n'aime pas prendre/Je prends/Je ne prends jamais …* *le bus, le train, l'Eurostar, le tramway, le métro, le car, le taxi, le vélo, le bateau, l'avion, la moto, la voiture, la mobylette* *parce que c'est très/trop/assez/un peu … pratique/cher/rapide/long/ confortable/dangereux* *Je vais (au collège)/Je ne vais pas … … à pied/vélo/moto/mobylette … en voiture/taxi/bus/car/métro/train,* etc.	8S5, 8L6 – R	1b, 1c, 2a, 2c, 2d, 2f, 2g, 2i, 3a, 3b, 3c, 3e, 4a, 4d, 5a, 5c, 5d, 5e, 5f, 5i	1.2–3, 2.1–4, 3.1, 3.3, 4.1–4
70–71 **5.3 Vacances de rêve!** Past holidays	Say where you went on holiday; say when you left; say how long you stayed and how you travelled; use the perfect tense with *être*	The perfect tense with *être*		*Tu es allé(e) où?* *Je suis allé(e) en/au/aux/à …* *Tu es parti(e) quand?* *Je suis parti(e) le* + date. *Tu es resté(e) combien de temps?* *Je suis resté(e) une semaine/un mois.* *Tu as voyagé comment? J'ai pris (l'avion).*	8W4, 8W5, 8S1, 8S7 – R	1b, 1c, 2a, 2c, 2d, 2f, 2i, 3a, 3c, 3e, 4a, 4d, 5a, 5d, 5e, 5f, 5i	1.3–4, 2.3–4, 3.1–3, 4.1–5
72–73 **5.4 C'était vraiment sympa!** Descriptions and opinions of past holidays	Ask what someone did during the holidays; describe a holiday in more detail; ask and say how it was and whether you liked it; read aloud, using sound-spelling links; understand comments about own work		Writing a detailed description	*Qu'est-ce que tu as fait pendant les vacances?* *D'abord … Après …* *J'ai fait/vu/joué/visité/mangé/bu …* *On est allé(e)s (à la plage), on a fait des excursions, on a visité (la région), on a fait du sport.* *C'était comment? C'était (vraiment) sympa/super/génial/moche/nul.* *J'ai (bien) aimé. J'ai adoré. Je n'ai pas aimé. J'ai détesté.*	8W3, 8S2, 8S4, 8S6, 8T5, 8L4 – R	1a, 1c, 2a, 2b, 2c, 2d, 2f, 2h, 2i, 2j, 3a, 3c, 3e, 4a, 4d, 5a, 5b, 5c, 5d, 5e, 5f, 5i	1.4, 2.3–5, 3.2, 3.4, 4.3–5
74–75 **5.5 La belle équipe, épisode 5** Soap story	Develop listening and reading skills via a soap story; understand some simple colloquialisms				8C5 – R	1a, 1c, 2a, 2b, 2g, 2h, 3b, 3c, 3e, 4a, 4d, 5a, 5d, 5e, 5g, 5i	1.4–5, 2.4, 3.4–5
76 **Super-challenge!** A visit to Burkina Faso	Use plural forms of the perfect tense; learn some expressions in the imperfect tense	Plural forms of the perfect tense				1a, 1b, 1c, 2a, 2b, 2c, 2h, 2i, 3c, 3e, 4a, 4c, 4d, 5d, 5e, 5i	1.4–5, 3.4–5, 4.4–5

ÉQUIPE NOUVELLE 2 UNIT 5 MEDIUM TERM PLAN

About this unit: In this unit students work in the context of travel and holidays. They learn about different means of transport and learn to ask about, describe and understand descriptions of journeys and holidays (both in France and in other countries). Whilst working in these contexts, students further develop their understanding and use of the *passé composé*, especially with the use of *être* as an auxiliary verb. The unit also provides opportunities for students to formulate a wider range of questions, build more complex sentences, read and write extended accounts in the past and research aspects of French-speaking countries and culture.

Framework objectives (reinforce)	Teaching and learning	Week-by-week overview (assuming 6 weeks' work or 10–12.5 hours)
8W3: words about progress	Use *c'était* + adjective to comment on quality of work and progress.	**Week 1** Introduction to unit objectives. Name countries and capital cities. Say which countries you are going to, have been to and would like to go to, using the prepositions *à/en/au/aux* correctly. Find out about French-speaking countries.
8W4: word endings	Make feminine and plural agreements in the perfect tense.	
8W5: verb tenses	Perfect tense of verbs using *être*.	
8S1: word, phrase and clause sequencing	Word order using verbs in the perfect tense.	**Week 2** Name means of transport. Say what transport you use/don't use to go to places, using the prepositions *à/en* correctly. Say what you think of different means of transport.
8S2: connectives in extended sentences	Use connectives to write a detailed description about a trip in the past.	
8S4: question types	Ask questions in different tenses.	**Week 3** Say where you went on holiday. Say when you left, how long you stayed and how you travelled. Use the perfect tense with *être*.
8S5: negative forms and words	Transport you don't use.	
8S6: substituting and adding	Write a detailed description.	**Week 4** Ask what someone did during the holidays. Describe a holiday in more detail. Ask and say how it was, using the imperfect tense, and whether you liked it. Read aloud, using sound–spelling links.
8S7: present, past and future	Use the perfect tense with auxiliaries *avoir* and *être*, and use set phrases in the imperfect tense, e.g. *C'était comment?, C'était* + adjective.	
8T5: writing continuous text	Write a detailed description.	**Week 5** Develop listening and reading skills via a soap episode.
8L4: extending sentences	Describe a holiday in more detail.	
8L6: expression in speech	Express opinions using qualifiers and intensifiers.	**Week 6** *Super-challenge!* for more able students. Recycle language of the unit via *Encore, En plus* and *Point lecture* pages. Students check progress via the *Podium* self-assessment checklist in the Students' Book and on Feuille 70.
8C5: colloquialisms	Understand some simple colloquialisms in the context of a soap episode, e.g. *à la limite, ciao, ça va hein, les mecs*.	
	Teaching and learning (additional)	
	à + ville, en/au/aux + pays. Countries. Means of transport. *à/en* + transport. Revision of places in town.	

5 Voyages et vacances

Unit objectives
Contexts: travel and holidays
Grammar: the perfect tense with *avoir* and *être*; prepositions *à/en/au/aux*
Language learning: detailed descriptions
Pronunciation: reading aloud (revision of sound–spelling links); *-ille*, *-eil*, *-agne* sounds
Cultural focus: French-speaking countries; travelling in France

Assessment opportunities
Reading: Students' Book, page 69, activity 4a; (and **writing**) Students' Book, page 72, activity 2a
Writing: Students' Book, page 73, *Challenge!* activity A or C

This opening page sets the context for Unit 5 and formally establishes the notion of *la Francophonie*. Students may remember some French-speaking countries from Part 1 of the course: see *Équipe nouvelle 1* Unit 6, in particular the *Point culture* panel on page 89 together with the corresponding section in the Teacher's Book.
This opening page also provides an opportunity to revise names of countries, genders of countries and use of the prepositions *en/au* before countries. If appropriate, students could investigate some rules for working out the genders: for example, they might deduce that countries ending in *-ie* are usually feminine (e.g. *l'Algérie, la Tunisie, la Nouvelle-Calédonie, l'Italie, l'Australie, la Russie*) as are small islands (e.g. *la Guadeloupe, la Martinique, la Réunion*).

AT 3.3 **1a** *Lis le quiz et réponds aux questions.*
Students could work with a partner on this activity. They complete the quiz on French-speaking countries, using various strategies (cognates, context, predicting, etc.) to work out any unknown language. For example, in question 6, they know that *pied* means "foot", so they should be able to deduce that *à pied* means "on foot/walking"; they might be able to connect this with *le train onze*, which is so called because the double figure one in eleven looks like two legs.
Remind students briefly about the prepositions that are used before names of countries (*en/au/aux*). There will be more on this on the following spread.

Answers: 1 c; 2 a, b; 3 c; 4 c; 5 c; 6 c

AT 1.2 **1b** *Écoute et vérifie.*
Students listen to the recording to check their answers to the quiz.

CD 2, track 24 **page 65, activité 1b**
Cassette 3, side 1

1 – Quel pays francophone n'est pas sur les photos?
 a le Maroc   b le Québec   c la Belgique
 d la Suisse   e le Congo   f la France
 – C'est la Belgique.
2 – Quelles sont les deux îles des Antilles françaises?
 a la Martinique   b la Guadeloupe   c la Corse
 – C'est la Martinique et la Guadeloupe!
3 – Dans quel pays africain on ne parle pas français?
 a au Sénégal   b au Cameroun   c au Nigeria
 – Au Nigeria.
4 – Dans quel pays "bonjour" veut quelquefois dire "au revoir"?
 – a en France   b aux Antilles   c au Québec
 – C'est au Québec!
5 – Au Sénégal, un chéri-coco, c'est:
 a une boisson   b un poisson   c un fiancé
 – C'est un fiancé.
6 – Au Niger, si on prend "le train onze" …
 a on va en train   b on va en taxi   c on va à pied
 – On va à pied.

AT 2.2 **2** *De mémoire, nomme: a) les cinq pays sur les photos; b) trois îles françaises; c) trois pays africains francophones.*
Students close their books and try to complete this activity from memory.

Answers: a le Maroc, le Québec, la Suisse, le Congo, la France; b la Martinique, la Guadeloupe, la Corse; c le Maroc, le Congo, le Sénégal, le Cameroun, le Niger

5 Voyages et vacances

AT 4.2 **3** *Remue-méninges. À deux, faites une liste de pays francophones.*

Students work with a partner to list all the French-speaking countries they know. This could either be done from existing knowledge within a time limit, or you could ask them to research French-speaking countries using the Internet (see www.francophonie.org/membres/etats or www.diplomatie.gouv.fr/francophonie/oif/pays-fr.html). The winning pair is the one with the longest list.

Answers: the main French-speaking countries are: en Europe: la France, la Belgique, la Suisse, le Luxembourg, Monaco, la Corse (point out that Corsica is a region of France); au Canada: le Québec, le Nouveau-Brunswick; en Amérique: Saint-Pierre-et-Miquelon, la Guadeloupe, la Martinique, Sainte-Lucie, la Dominique, l'Haïti, la Guyane française; en Afrique: l'Algérie, le Maroc, la Tunisie, le Sénégal, le Niger, le Mali, le Burkina Faso, le Togo, les Comores, Mayotte, les Seychelles, la Maurice, la Mauritanie, la Réunion, Madagascar, la Côte d'Ivoire, le Cameroun, le Congo, la République démocratique du Congo; en Asie: le Laos, le Cambodge, le Viêt-nam; dans les îles du Pacifique: la Nouvelle-Calédonie, la Polynésie française, Vanuatu, Wallis-et-Futuna

Voyages et vacances 5

Planning Page

5.1 À l'étranger
pages 66–67

Objectives
- Name countries and capital cities
- Say which countries you are going to or have been to
- Say which countries you'd like to go to
- Use the correct preposition

Resources
Students' Book, pages 66–67
CD 2, track 25
Cassette 3, side 1
Encore/En plus Workbooks, page 44
OHTs 20A, 20B, 20C and 21
Copymaster 77

Key language
Je suis allé(e)/Je ne suis jamais allé(e)/Je vais/J'aimerais aller …
à l'étranger, à + ville, en/au/aux + pays
Names of countries and towns

Programme of Study reference
1a, 1b, 1c, 2b, 2c, 2d, 2f, 3c, 3e, 4a, 4c, 4d, 5a, 5c, 5d, 5e, 5f, 5g, 5i

Starters
- *À vos marques*, page 66.
- Use **OHTs 20A** and **20B** to introduce the concept of European and French-speaking countries. First, display **OHT 20A** and ask students to name the countries (in English, if they can't name them in French). Check their answers by adding on overlay **20B**. Complete the overlay by adding the article in front of each country (*le/l'/la/les*).
- To introduce the capital cities, display **OHTs 20A** and **20B** and ask students to name the capital of each country. Copy and cut up **OHT 20C** and place the capital cities next to the appropriate country for students to check their answers.
- Speed dual: two students stand up. You say either *au* or *à la* and students must say the name of a country that matches the preposition. The winner is the one who answers first; the other student sits down and is replaced by someone else.

ICT suggestions
- Students do a quick survey in the class to find out which countries everyone has visited. They then present the results on a bar chart or using PowerPoint®.
- In groups of two or three, students research photos and some simple information about a French-speaking country of their choice (see www.francophonie.org/membres/etats or www.diplomatie.gouv.fr/francophonie/oif/pays-fr.html). They prepare a PowerPoint® presentation.

Creative activities
- In groups, students design a board game based on *Jeu de l'Oie* (similar to Snakes and Ladders) to revise the language of the unit: *Je suis allé(e)/Je ne suis jamais allé(e)/Je vais/J'aimerais aller à + ville, en/au/aux + pays*. First, they design a board with 22 squares: the first square says *Départ*, the last square says *Arrivée*, 10 squares contain the names of countries, the remaining 10 contain the names of capital cities. Students then play the game with a die, e.g. if they land on *le Maroc*, they have to say an appropriate sentence: *Je suis allé(e)/Je ne suis jamais allé(e)/Je vais/J'aimerais aller au Maroc*. The winner is the first one to reach *Arrivée*, having made correct sentences each time he/she landed on a square.
- In pairs, students invent a rap or a rhyming chant, e.g.
A: *Je suis allé(e) en Tunisie.*
B: *Je suis allé(e) en Italie.*
A: *Je ne suis pas allé(e) au Portugal.*
B: *Je ne suis pas allé(e) au pays de Galles …* etc.

Plenaries
- *Challenge!* page 67.
- You think of a French-speaking country, say how many letters in its name and students guess the country.
- Play a game using **OHTs 20A**, **20B** and **20C**: copy the names of the countries and cities on to an acetate and cut them all up; place the map of Europe on the OHP. Divide the class into two teams, each sending two students to the OHP. Members of the first team instruct their two students on where to put the names of the countries and the capital cities. They try to place all the names correctly on the map. Time them. Can the other team improve on their time?
- Recap on the use of *en/au/aux* + country, together with questions about which countries people have visited, by playing the game *Le tour de Padipado*. Students ask you questions to find out which countries this mysterious person Padipado has been to (answer: countries that have neither "i" nor "o" in their name: *pas d'"i", pas d'"o"*). For example:
Student A: *Est-ce que Padipado est allé en France?*
Teacher: *Oui, il est allé en France.*
Student B: *Est-ce que Padipado est allé au Maroc?*
Teacher: *Non, il n'est pas allé au Maroc …* etc.

Homework suggestions
- Students research and write a few lines about their favourite international stars: where they were born, where they live, where they've travelled. For example: *Pierce Brosnan est né en Irlande. Il habite aux États-Unis. Il est allé* + various countries.
- Students create an odd-one-out game using names of countries. For example: *le Portugal, le Danemark, la Grèce, le Canada* (the odd-one-out is *la Grèce* because it is the only feminine country).

5 Voyages et vacances

5.1 À l'étranger
pages 66–67

À vos marques

AT 3.1 **a** *Relie les capitales aux pays en 30 secondes.*
Students have 30 seconds to match the capital cities to the countries.

Answers: Copenhague: le Danemark; Bruxelles: la Belgique; Lisbonne: le Portugal; Amsterdam: les Pays-Bas; Berlin: l'Allemagne; Oslo: la Norvège; Berne: la Suisse; Athènes: la Grèce

AT 2.1/2 **b** *Vérifie avec la classe.*
Students feed back their answers to the class. Before doing this, remind them of *en/au/aux* + countries by referring them to the *Zoom grammaire* panel on page 67.

Follow-up activity: If you have time, ask students, in pairs, to come up with a different list of cities and countries in French. Suggest that they use a dictionary to look up any names they don't know. Pairs then swap their lists. This will be useful for activity **1d** below.

AT 1.3 / AT 3.3 **1a** *Écoute et lis le dialogue à droite.*
Students listen to the recording while following the text in the Students' Book. The four teenagers are discussing countries they've visited and where they are going or would like to go.

CD 2, track 25   page 66, activité 1a
Cassette 3, side 1

– Ah là là! J'aimerais bien aller en Martinique!
– Moi aussi!
– Tu es déjà allée dans quels pays, Juliette?
– Je suis allée aux États-Unis et au Canada, avec mon père … et je vais à Londres en octobre! Et toi, tu es allé où?
– Moi, je suis allé en Espagne et au Maroc, avec mes parents. J'aimerais bien aller à New York. Et toi Matthieu, tu es allé à l'étranger?
– Oui, je suis allé en Italie. À Noël, je vais à Vienne, en Autriche, avec ma mère!
– Super! J'aimerais bien voyager! Je ne suis jamais allée à l'étranger.
– Alors, il faut absolument gagner le concours de théâtre pour aller aux Antilles!!!

AT 3.2 **1b** *Trouve …*
Students search the text for the French equivalents of the English phrases.

Answers: a je suis allé(e); b je vais; c j'aimerais (bien) aller

AT 2.3 **1c** *À quatre, jouez la scène avec l'intonation!*
Students act out the conversation in groups of four, paying attention to correct intonation. Suggest that they at first repeat only the "melody" of the conversation, i.e. instead of worrying about the actual words, they imitate the sounds and intonation, using "lalalalala". Once they have done this, they can then move on to include the words.

AT 2.3 **1d** *À quatre, adaptez la conversation. Changez les pays et les villes soulignés. Attention aux prépositions!*
Working in groups of four again, students adapt the conversation, replacing the underlined words with other towns and countries from *À vos marques*. Point out that they will need to choose countries of the same gender as those used in the existing conversation, so that the prepositions *en/au/aux* remain the same.
Alternatively, if you wish to extend this activity beyond the towns and countries listed in *À vos marques*, students could use their own choice of destinations and alter the prepositions accordingly.

Follow-up activities:
▶ Use **OHT 21** for further front-of class exploitation of the conversation by blanking out words (e.g. prepositions, names of towns, countries, etc.).
▶ Photocopy **OHT 21** on to acetate and cut up each sentence for students to reorder.

AT 3.3 / AT 4.2 **2** *Recopie et complète la lettre de Matthieu, à droite, avec les mots.*
Students copy out and complete Matthieu's letter to his mother following his friends' visit, using the correct verb forms and prepositions. This activity requires students to think about past participle agreement, appropriateness of tense and prepositions. You may wish to complete the *Zoom grammaire* section (see below) before beginning this activity.

Answers: 1 aux; 2 n'est jamais allée; 3 est allé; 4 aimerait bien aller; 5 est allée; 6 au; 7 va; 8 à

Zoom grammaire

This grammar section focuses on how to say "to" + a town or country.

1 Students list the countries from *À vos marques* according to whether they are masculine, feminine or plural.

Answers: masculin: le Danemark, le Portugal; féminin: l'Allemagne, la Belgique, la Grèce, la Norvège, la Suisse; pluriel: les Pays-Bas

2 Students then match the prepositions *en/au/aux* to the correct category.

Answers: en + pays féminin; au + pays masculin; aux + pays pluriel

3 Using their answers to the grammar activities **1** and **2** above, students now look back to the conversation between the four teenagers in activity **1a** and work out the genders of the countries mentioned. Point out that *à la Martinique* and *à la Guadeloupe* are also possible (in addition to *en Martinique/Guadeloupe* used in the conversation), because they are small islands.

Answers: féminin: Martinique, Espagne, Italie, Autriche; masculin: Canada, Maroc; pluriel: États-Unis, Antilles

4 Students write sentences saying they would like to go to each of the countries listed in *À vos marques*.

Answers: J'aimerais aller … en Allemagne, au Danemark, en Belgique, en Grèce, au Portugal, en Norvège, aux Pays-Bas, en Suisse.

Refer students to the grammar sections on pages 135–136 of the Students' Book for further information on these points.

Point culture

This section provides information in French about French-speaking countries. Students summarize the information in English and compare with a partner.

Answer: There are about 170 million French-speaking people in the world, compared with 460 million English speakers. There are more than 51 French-speaking countries and 10 French-speaking territories (shown on the map).

The term *Francophonie* was coined in 1880 by French geographer Onésime Reclus to describe the linguistic and cultural community that France was building with its colonies. It extended to other French-speaking countries that were not colonies, e.g. Belgium, etc.
The origins of the presence of the French language in the world are various:
▶ the French administrative zones overseas (DOM-TOM), the legacy of former colonies of France in parts of the world such as the Caribbean, Canada, South America and the South Pacific;
▶ countries that were either former colonies of France and Belgium or were at one point or other touched by French culture.
These countries use French as their mother tongue and official language or co-official language, their language of administration, and have chosen French as their international language. Some countries (e.g. Vietnam) use the French language for diplomatic purposes, as a language of international exchange and cultural expression.

C77 Further practice of the language of this spread is provided on Feuille 77 *Lis et écris Encore 1*.

W44 Page 44 of the *Encore* and *En plus* Workbooks provides additional reading and writing practice on French-speaking countries and *en/au/aux*.

Challenge!

AT 2.2 **A** *Écris le nom de six pays où tu aimerais aller. Ton/Ta partenaire devine.*
AT 4.1/2 Students list six countries that they would like to visit, and their partner tries to guess them using the model question provided: *Tu aimerais aller en/au/aux …?*

AT 4.3 **B** *Réponds aux questions.*
Students answer the questions, giving information (real or imaginary) about any countries they have visited, whether they are going abroad soon, and which countries they would like to visit.

AT 4.4 **C** *Écris un texte sur le(s) pays où tu aimerais aller et dis pourquoi. Utilise toutes les Expressions-clés!*
Students write about the countries they would like to visit, giving reasons. If necessary, brainstorm some possible reasons beforehand, e.g. weather, food.

5 Voyages et vacances

Planning Page

5.2 À pied ou en voiture — pages 68–69

Objectives

- Name means of transport
- Say what transport you use/don't use to go to places (8S5 – R)
- Say what you think of different means of transport (8L6 – R)
- Use the correct preposition

Resources

Students' Book, pages 68–69
CD 2, tracks 26–28; CD 3, track 33
Cassette 3, side 1; cassette 4, side 2
Encore/En plus Workbooks, page 45
OHT 22
Flashcards 142–155
Copymasters 71, 73, 78 and 81

Key language

J'aime bien/Je n'aime pas prendre/Je prends/Je ne prends jamais …
le bus, le train, l'Eurostar, le tramway, le métro, le car, le taxi, le vélo, le bateau, l'avion, la moto, la voiture, la mobylette
parce que c'est très/trop/assez/un peu …
pratique/cher/pas cher/rapide/long/confortable/dangereux
Je vais (au collège)/Je ne vais pas …
… à pied/vélo/moto/mobylette
… en voiture/taxi/bus/car/métro/train, etc.

Programme of Study reference

1b, 1c, 2a, 2c, 2d, 2f, 2g, 2i, 3a, 3b, 3c, 3e, 4a, 4d, 5a, 5c, 5d, 5e, 5f, 5i

Starters

- *À vos marques*, page 68.
- Copymaster 71 *À vos marques*, activity 1.
- Play a speed game using **Flashcards 142–155**. Show a card; students in small groups race to each say a different sentence containing the word represented by the card. The class check that all the sentences are correct, and one point is awarded per correct sentence. Increase the challenge by timing each group.
- Using **Flashcards 142–155** again, distribute the 14 cards to 14 students and ask them to arrange themselves alphabetically in the shortest possible time, e.g. *avion*, *bateau*, *bus*, *car*, etc. (This can be done with fewer students sticking the flashcards on the board with putty adhesive.)
- Divide the class into two groups: *Les Contents* (always happy) and *Les Grincheux* (always grumpy). Show **Flashcards 142–155**. A student from each group must make a comment about the means of transport featured using the *Expressions-clés*: a positive comment if he/she is one of the *Contents*, a negative comment if he/she is a *Grincheux*.

ICT suggestions

- Using desktop publishing, students create lists of their top 10 means of transport according to different criteria: *c'est cher, pas cher, rapide, long, pratique, confortable*. They could add their own categories, e.g. *c'est écologique*.
- Working in groups, students do some research on the Internet into Jules Verne's *Le Tour du monde en quatre-vingts jours* (*Around the World in Eighty Days*). They produce a poster or PowerPoint® presentation showing the countries visited by Phileas Fogg and the means of transport used.

Creative activities

- In groups, students prepare a leaflet explaining about local transport for potential visitors to their area, incorporating texts, pictures, interviews, etc.
- In groups, students present their ideal "Around the World" trip, explaining which countries they would go to and the means of transport they would use. The class then select their favourite trip.

Plenaries

- *Challenge!* page 69.
- In pairs, students write a list of as many transport-related words as they can. They compare their list with that of another pair and categorize the words on each other's list according to whether they are *verbes, noms, adjectifs*, etc.
- Recap on the prepositions *à* and *en* by asking students to draw mind maps about their different uses, e.g. *à* + time/place/etc., *en* + country/transport/language, etc.
- Use **OHT 22** to play a stepping stone game: students race to go from one side of the road to the other, making sentences as they go along using the elements given on the OHT. This could be followed up by highlighting certain words that students must use to make their way across the road. Extend the activity by adding the verbs *aimer*, *ne pas aimer* and *prendre* alongside *aller* in the top row and by adding the construction *pour aller* between the modes of transport and the prepositions.

Homework suggestions

- Students prepare a word snake or wordsearch using the transport vocabulary, for their partner to solve during the next lesson.
- Give students the text of the rap from *Zoom grammaire*. They learn it and perform it in groups in class. Alternatively, they use the rap as a model to create their own version.
- Students write a text explaining in detail how they would go from their front door to Paris, e.g. *Je vais à la gare en taxi*, etc.
- Students write a paragraph describing their journey to school, giving their opinion. They then write the same paragraph as if they are Léo, the boy in the wheelchair, imagining his opinion.

Voyages et vacances

5.2 À pied ou en voiture — pages 68–69

À vos marques

AT 2.1
AT 4.1 *Regarde les Mots-clés pendant 20 secondes. Ferme le livre. Tu t'en rappelles combien?*
Students play a memory game: they study the transport vocabulary and pictures for 20 seconds then close their books and see how many they can remember. This could be done orally in pairs, with students testing each other, or it could be done individually as a written exercise.

AT 4.2 **1a** *Choisis tes cinq moyens de transport préférés.*
Students note down their five favourite means of transport: *J'aime bien prendre …*

AT 2.2/3 **1b** *Devine les transports préférés de ton/ta partenaire en premier!*
Working in pairs, students take turns to try to guess their partner's favourite means of transport, following the model question and answer provided. The use of negatives to express how they don't like to travel (*je n'aime pas prendre …*) reinforces **8S5**.

AT 1.2 **2a** *Sondage: "Comment est-ce que tu vas au collège?" Écoute et note les moyens de transport mentionnés.*
Students listen and note down how each person travels to school. Before playing the recording, ask students to predict the means of transport that are likely to be mentioned.

Answers: 1 à pied; 2 en voiture; 3 en bus; 4 à mobylette; 5 en car; 6 à vélo; 7 en bateau

AT 1.2 **2b** *Réécoute. Quel mot tu entends devant les noms de transport?*
Students listen again to the recording and note down the preposition that precedes each means of transport. You may want to look at the *Zoom grammaire* at this stage (see below) as it focuses on this language point.

Answers: see **2a**

🎧 CD 2, track 26 — page 68, activité 2
Cassette 3, side 1

– Comment est-ce que tu vas au collège?
– Je vais au collège à pied.

– Comment est-ce que tu vas au collège?
– En voiture, avec ma mère.

– Comment est-ce que tu vas au collège?
– Je vais au collège en bus.

– Et toi?
– Moi, je vais au collège à mobylette.

– Et toi, comment est-ce que tu vas au collège?
– Moi? Je vais au collège en car.

– Toi aussi?
– Non, moi, je vais au collège à vélo.

– Comment est-ce que tu vas au collège?
– Ah! Moi, je vais au collège … en bateau!
– En bateau?
– Oui, j'habite sur une île!
– Hum … je vois!

AT 2.2
AT 4.2-4 **2c** *Fais le sondage en classe et écris les résultats.*
Students conduct a survey to find out how everyone in the class travels to school. The results could be presented either as a written report or in the form of a graph/bar chart.

Zoom grammaire

This grammar section focuses on the use of *à* and *en* with means of transport.

1 Students listen to the recorded rap and note each means of transport together with its accompanying preposition. They attempt to come up with a rule to indicate when to use *à* and when to use *en*.

Answers: see underlining in transcript below; *en* is used with means of transport that you sit in; *à* is used (a) with means of transport that you sit on (b) for going on foot/walking

🎧 CD 2, track 27 — page 69, Zoom grammaire, activité 1;
Cassette 3, side 1 — page 69, activité 3

<u>À vélo</u> et <u>à pied</u>,
c'est bon pour la santé.
<u>En métro</u> et <u>en tramway</u>
c'est pratique et pas cher.
<u>À mobylette</u>, <u>à moto</u>,
c'est un peu dangereux.
<u>En voiture</u> et <u>en taxi</u>
c'est rapide, mais c'est cher!
<u>En bus</u> ou bien <u>en car</u>
ce n'est pas confortable!
<u>En bateau</u> et <u>en train</u>,
c'est vraiment bien!
<u>En avion</u>, <u>en Eurostar</u>
c'est cher, mais c'est super!

2 Students play Word Tennis using the means of transport and prepositions, following the example given in the Students' Book.

Refer students to the grammar section on page 136 of the Students' Book for further information on this point.

5 Voyages et vacances

C81 Feuille 81 *Grammaire 1* could be used here. It practises *à/en* + means of transport, together with *à/en/au/aux* + countries/towns from the previous spread.

AT 1.3 **3** *Écoute encore le rap dans Zoom grammaire. Recopie et coche les mots que tu entends. Traduis en anglais.*
Students listen again to the rap from *Zoom grammaire*. This time, they listen for the adjectives used to describe the transport. They then translate the adjectives into English.

Answers: (all these adjectives feature in the recording: see transcript above): *pratique*: practical; *cher*: expensive; *pas cher*: cheap/not expensive; *dangereux*: dangerous; *rapide*: fast; *confortable*: comfortable

AT 3.3 **4a** *Lis et complète la lettre de Léo à droite avec les mots de l'activité 3.*
Students complete Léo's letter using the adjectives from activity **3**. The use of qualifiers and intensifiers in the letter (*très, un peu, trop, assez*) reinforces **8L6**.

Answers: see underlining in transcript below (but note that *confortable* and *pratique* are interchangeable here – discuss alternatives with the class, if appropriate)

AT 1.3 **4b** *Écoute Léo et vérifie.*
Students listen to the recording to check their answers to activity **4a**.

🎧 **CD 2, track 28**　　　　　　　　　　**page 69, activité 4b**
Cassette 3, side 1

Je vais au collège en voiture avec ma mère. Quand je vais en ville, je ne prends jamais le bus: ce n'est <u>pas cher</u>, mais pour moi, ce n'est pas très <u>pratique</u>. Je ne prends pas le métro parce que c'est un peu <u>dangereux</u> quand on est en fauteuil roulant.
Pour voyager, j'aime bien prendre l'avion, c'est <u>rapide</u>, mais c'est trop <u>cher</u>. Alors, je prends le train, c'est assez <u>confortable</u>.

AT 3.1 **4c** *Traduis en anglais les mots surlignés.*
Students translate into English the highlighted words from Léo's letter.

Answers: très: very; *un peu*: rather, a little, a bit; *trop*: too; *assez*: quite, rather

AT 2.3/4 **5** *Qu'est-ce que tu penses des transports? Discute avec ton/ta partenaire.*
In pairs, students discuss their own opinions of the different means of transport. This provides further opportunities for reinforcement of Framework objectives **8S5** and **8L6**.

C73 Feuille 73 *Écoute Encore* provides additional listening and speaking practice of means of transport, including opinions, and could be used at this point.

C78 Feuille 78 *Lis et écris Encore 2* could also be used here. It practises means of transport with places in town and other destinations.

W45 Further reading and writing practice of transport is provided on page 45 of the *Encore* and *En plus* Workbooks.

Challenge!

AT 4.2/3 **A** *Invente une phrase pour chaque moyen de transport (Mots-clés).*
Students write a sentence about each means of transport featured in the *Mots-clés*.

AT 4.3 **B** *Écris des phrases comme dans l'activité A et ajoute une opinion.*
Students write a sentence about each means of transport featured in the *Mots-clés* (as in activity **A**), but here they go on to express their opinion of each.

AT 4.4 **C** *Écris un texte comme celui de Léo pour: une dame de 80 ans (en ville); une femme d'affaires (au bureau); un étudiant (à l'université).*
Using Léo's text as a model, students write about different means of transport from the perspectives of three different people.

Planning Page

5.3 Vacances de rêve! pages 70–71

Objectives
- Say where you went on holiday
- Say when you left
- Say how long you stayed and how you travelled
- Use the perfect tense with *être* (**8W4, 8W5, 8S1, 8S7 – R**)

Resources
Students' Book, pages 70–71
CD 2, tracks 29–30
Cassette 3, side 1
Encore/En plus Workbooks, pages 46 and 48
OHTs 4, 23A, 23B and 23C
Copymasters 71, 72, 75, 79 and 82

Key language
Tu es allé(e) où?
Je suis allé(e) en/au/aux/à …
Tu es parti(e) quand?
Je suis parti(e) le + date.
Tu es resté(e) combien de temps?
Je suis resté(e) une semaine/un mois.
Tu as voyagé comment?
J'ai pris (l'avion).

Programme of Study reference
1b, 1c, 2a, 2c, 2d, 2f, 2i, 3a, 3c, 3e, 4a, 4d, 5a, 5d, 5e, 5f, 5i

Starters
- *À vos marques*, page 70.
- Copymaster 71 *À vos marques*, activity 2.
- In small groups, students perform (as a rap or using mimes) the song "Aventure à Tahiti!" from the *Zoom grammaire* section.
- Use the grid given in the answers to activity **1b** (see page 170 of this book) to play a game of Three-in-a-Row (copy the grid on to acetate so that you can play the game as a whole class on the OHP). The aim is make correct sentences using the coordinates of the grid, e.g. *Fatia est allée à l'Alpe d'Huez, Jérémy est parti le 1er juillet*, etc.
- Play a "No Hesitation" game. Using the *Expressions-clés*, students describe a journey (imaginary or real). To score a point for their team, they must speak without any hesitation.

ICT suggestions
- Using desktop publishing, word processing and clip art, students create a "travel alphabet" based on the *Expressions-clés*, e.g. *A = Annie est allée en Allemagne. Elle est partie en avril. Elle est restée un an. Elle a voyagé en avion*. Divide the class into groups and give each group a certain number of letters to work on (not all letters will be possible).

Creative activities
- Using **OHTs 23A, 23B** and **23C**, ask students in pairs to come up with their own scenario, e.g. *Pierre est allé à la tour Eiffel pour voir Hélène. Hélène n'est pas venue. Il est monté seul. Hélène est arrivée très en retard. Elle est restée en bas*, etc. Pairs then present their stories to the class.

Plenaries
- *Challenge!* page 71.
- Copymaster 72 *Challenge!* activity 1.
- Make photocopies of **OHT 4** and distribute to students, one copy per pair. Ask each pair to write a speech bubble for each character using a verb in the perfect tense. They present their bubbles to the class. Suggest that they make them as wacky as possible!

Homework suggestions
- Students imagine and write the diary of a French boy or girl who has come on holiday to London. How did they travel, what did they do, where did they go? Start: *Je suis allé(e) en vacances à …*
- Students write a short dialogue between two famous explorers (see Creative activities on page 172), using the language learned so far in the unit. They can then act out their script with a partner in the next lesson.

5 Voyages et vacances

5.3 Vacances de rêve! pages 70–71

À vos marques

AT 3.1
AT 4.1
Complète les suites logiques.
This starter activity revises months and dates. Students work out the sequences and fill in the missing words.

Answers: a le 21 décembre (start of each season/every third month); b mai, septembre (every second month); c janvier, juillet, mars, novembre (alphabetical order)

Presentation

You may want to complete the activities in the *Zoom grammaire* section (see notes below) at an early stage during work on this spread.
OHTs 23A, **23B** and **23C** could be used to present and practise the perfect tense verbs of movement, requiring the use of *être* + past participle and agreement of the past participle with feminine and plural subjects. Suggestions for use:

- Cut out the shape of a boy and the shape of a girl to move around on the OHP. The text of the speech bubbles (**OHT 23C**) can be used as an overlay to check answers or, if you copy it on to acetate and cut it up, it will allow further practice.
- First, display only **OHT 23A**. Using the girl and boy shapes, act as a narrator, suggesting verbs of movement first in the present tense by showing the actions (*il/elle monte*, etc.), then in the perfect tense (e.g. *il/elle est monté(e)*, etc.). Invite students to come out and move the cut-outs on the OHP according to what you are describing.
- Place **OHT 23B** over **23A** and ask students what they think each person is saying. Then remove **23B** and add **23C** over **23A**, revealing one bubble at a time and asking students to "animate" the cut-out shapes of the boy and girl according to what they read in the bubbles.
- Display all three OHTs together and ask students to read the bubbles and make the appropriate agreement for each past participle according to whether a male or female character is doing the action.

AT 3.2 **1a** *Relie les réponses aux questions dans les Expressions-clés.*
Students match the questions to the answers in the *Expressions-clés* panel.

Answers: 1 b; 2 c; 3 d; 4 a

AT 1.3/4 **1b** *Écoute et note les réponses des trois personnes.*
Students listen to the three conversations and note down each person's answers to the questions from the *Expressions-clés*. The second and third conversations are less controlled. Ask students to note down any extra information they hear, e.g. Fatia went skiing, Jérémy's father goes sailing, Céline says she flew from Paris to Mumbai then took the train, which was cheap, practical but uncomfortable.

Answers:

	Où?	Départ?	Durée?	Transport?
a Fatia	Alpe d'Huez	20 décembre	1 semaine	car
b Jérémy	Guadeloupe	1 juillet	2 mois	avion, bateau
c Céline	Inde	2 août	1 mois	avion, train

CD 2, track 29 page 70, activité 1b
Cassette 3, side 1

a – Salut Fatia! Ça va?
  – Oui, super!
  – Tu es allée où en vacances?
  – Je suis allée à l'Alpe d'Huez, faire du ski.
  – Ouah! Tu es partie quand?
  – Je suis partie le 20 décembre.
  – Et tu es restée combien de temps?
  – Je suis restée une semaine.
  – Tu as voyagé comment?
  – J'ai pris le car.
  – Oh là là, j'aimerais bien faire du ski …

b – Tiens, Jérémy! Ça va? Tu es allé en vacances?
  – Oui oui!
  – Ah bon! Et tu es allé où en vacances?
  – Je suis allé en Guadeloupe.
  – Oh! Super! Et tu es parti quand?
  – Je suis parti le 1er juillet.
  – Et tu es resté combien de temps?
  – Je suis resté deux mois.
  – Deux mois? Ouah! Tu as voyagé comment?
  – J'ai pris l'avion et après, le bateau.
  – Super! Quelle chance tu as!
  – Oui, c'est vrai. Mon père fait de la voile, alors …

c – Ah! Céline, bonjour!
  – Bonjour!
  – Alors, tu es allée en vacances cet été?
  – Oui!
  – Tu es allée où?
  – Je suis allée en Inde!
  – Ouah!!! En Inde, mais c'est génial! Tu es partie quand?
  – Je suis partie le … euh … le 2 août.
  – Ah, et tu es restée combien de temps là-bas, en Inde?
  – Je suis restée un mois, jusqu'au 2 septembre.
  – Super! Tu as voyagé comment?
  – Eh bien, j'ai pris l'avion à Paris pour aller à Mumbai et là, j'ai pris le train. J'ai pris beaucoup de trains! Et le train en Inde, ce n'est pas cher, c'est pratique, mais ce n'est pas toujours très confortable!
  – Quelle aventure! Moi, j'aimerais tellement aller en Inde ou en Chine, enfin faire un long voyage comme ça …

AT 2.3/4 **1c** *À deux, faites les interviews de Fatia, Jérémy et Céline. Adaptez les Expressions-clés.*
Using their answers from activity **1b** together with the *Expressions-clés*, students work in pairs to interview each other, taking turns to play the roles of Fatia, Jérémy, Céline and the interviewer.

AT 2.3/4 **2** *Invente une destination de rêve. Ton/Ta partenaire t'interviewe.*
Students imagine they have just returned from a dream holiday. Their partner interviews them, using the questions from the *Expressions-clés*.

Zoom grammaire

This grammar section focuses on verbs that use the auxiliary verb *être* in the perfect tense. It reinforces **8W4** (word endings), **8W5** (verb tenses), **8S1** (word order using verbs in the perfect tense) and **8S7** (present, past and future).

1 Students search page 70 for verbs that use *être* instead of *avoir* in the perfect tense.

Answers: partir, rester

2 Students pick out the 10 verbs from the list that use *être* instead of *avoir*.

Answers: aller, arriver, descendre, entrer, monter, partir, rester, sortir, tomber, venir

3a Students are asked to consider ways of remembering which verbs need *être* instead of *avoir* in the perfect tense. They listen to the song "Aventure à Tahiti!" and draw arrows to represent the different types of movement.
You could suggest some well-known mnemonics, e.g. Mr Van Der Tramps (or Mrs Van Der Tramp), which includes the verbs *naître*, *mourir*, *rentrer* and *retourner* in addition to the verbs used here. You could also ask students to come up with their own mnemonics for this, either using the first letters of verbs (as in Mr Van Der Tramps) or making up sentences to tell a story, using the verbs themselves (following the Tahiti song model).

CD 2, track 30   page 71, Zoom grammaire, activité 3
Cassette 3, side 1

Aventure à Tahiti!
Je suis parti(e) de Paris
Je suis arrivé(e) à Tahiti
Je suis entré(e), je suis sorti(e)
je suis allé(e), je suis venu(e)
je suis monté(e), je suis descendu(e)
Je suis tombé(e), aïe, aïe, aïe!
Je suis resté(e) deux jours au lit
Et je suis rentré(e) à Paris.

3b Students listen again to the song, join in, and try to learn the words.

Refer students to the grammar section on page 142 of the Students' Book for further information on the perfect tense.

C82 Feuille 82 *Grammaire 2* could be used at this point. It provides additional grammar practice of verbs that take *être* in the perfect tense.

W48 Further grammar practice of the perfect tense is provided on page 48 of the *Encore* and *En plus* Workbooks.

C75 Feuille 75 *Parle Encore* could also be used here. It provides speaking practice on means of transport and the perfect tense of *aller*, including negatives, together with *au/à l'/à la* plus places in town.

C79 Feuille 79 *Lis et écris En plus 1* is a puzzle practising the perfect tense together with means of transport and countries, and could also be used at this point.

W46 Further reading and writing practice of the perfect tense in the context of past holidays is provided on page 46 of the *Encore* and *En plus* Workbooks.

Challenge!

AT 3.3 **AT 4.2** **A** *Recopie et complète la bulle.*
Students copy out and complete Charlie's speech bubble about a recent holiday. This activity focuses on agreement of the past participle.

Answers: Je suis <u>allé</u> en vacances à la montagne avec Noémie. Je suis <u>parti</u> le 2 février. Le premier jour, Noémie est <u>montée</u> et elle est <u>descendue</u> sur les pistes, super! Moi, je suis <u>monté</u>, mais je suis <u>tombé</u>! Aïe aïe aïe! Je suis <u>resté</u> à l'hôpital six jours. Je suis <u>rentré</u> à la maison en ambulance! Noémie est <u>restée</u> à la montagne … Grrr!

AT 4.3/4 **B** *Choisis des vacances p. 70 (A, B ou C). Invente les détails et réponds aux questions des Expressions-clés.*
Students choose one of the holidays described by Fatia, Jérémy and Céline in activity **1b**. They answer the questions from the *Expressions-clés*, imagining that they have just returned from that holiday.

AT 4.4/5 **C** *Invente une destination de rêve, comme dans l'activité 2. Raconte.*
Students imagine they have just returned from a dream holiday: this could be the same holiday as in activity **2**. They write a description of the holiday, incorporating as much detail as possible.

5 Voyages et vacances

Planning Page

5.4 C'était vraiment sympa!
pages 72–73

Objectives
- Ask what someone did during the holidays (**8S4 – R**)
- Describe a holiday in more detail (**8S2, 8S6, 8T5, 8L4 – R**)
- Ask and say how it was and whether you liked it
- Read aloud, using sound–spelling links
- Understand comments about own work (**8W3 – R**)

Resources
Students' Book, pages 72–73
CD 2, track 31; CD 3, tracks 34–37
Cassette 3, side 1; cassette 4, side 2
Encore/En plus Workbooks, pages 47 and 49
OHTs 24 and 25
Flashcards 61–78, 98–106 and 142–155
Copymasters 72, 74, 76, 80, 83, 84 and 85

Key language
Qu'est-ce que tu as fait pendant les vacances?
D'abord … Après …
j'ai fait/vu/joué/visité/mangé/bu …
on est allé(e)s (à la plage), on a fait des excursions, on a visité (la région), on a fait du sport
C'était comment?
C'était (vraiment) sympa/super/génial/moche/nul.
J'ai (bien) aimé. J'ai adoré. Je n'ai pas aimé. J'ai détesté.

Programme of Study reference
1a, 1c, 2a, 2b, 2c, 2d, 2f, 2h, 2i, 2j, 3a, 3c, 3e, 4a, 4d, 5a, 5b, 5c, 5d, 5e, 5f, 5i

Starters
- *À vos marques*, page 72.
- In pairs, students come up with as many holiday activities as they can think of in a limited time (e.g. two minutes). Recap with the whole class. For example: *aller à la plage, faire du sport, visiter un musée*, etc.
- Using **Flashcards 61–78** (types of leisure activities), **98–106** (places to stay) and **142–155** (transport), make three piles. Student A picks a card from each pile. Others must ask questions to find out how A travelled, what he/she did and where he/she stayed. Student A can answer only yes or no.
- Divide the class into two groups: *Les Contents* (always happy) and *Les Grincheux* (always grumpy). Students from each group must answer the six questions from *Expressions-clés*, either very positively if they are one of the *Contents*, or very negatively, if they are a *Grincheux*.

ICT suggestions
- In groups, students use word processing, desktop publishing, clip art, Internet research, etc. to produce a poster display or a PowerPoint® presentation about a holiday: either a "dream holiday" or a "holiday from hell". Encourage them to give as many details as possible.

Creative activities
- Working in groups, students research the travels of famous explorers and present the information either visually (via a poster or PowerPoint® presentation) or orally (via a mock interview, mini-play, etc.), reusing as much known language as possible (description, where they went, how, when, what they did, their opinions, etc.). Explorers might include Marco Polo, Hernando Cortés, Christophe Colomb, Vasco de Gama, Jacques Cartier, James Cook, Robert E. Peary, David Livingstone, Roald Amundsen.

Plenaries
- *Challenge!* page 73.
- Copymaster 72 *Challenge!* activity 2.
- Give a verb in the infinitive and ask students to write the past participle on mini-whiteboards. To make this more challenging, use a timer. Ask students to predict how many verbs they will be able to do in one minute. Check. Repeat the activity for another minute and see if students can improve their score.
- Repeat the previous activity but this time give the past participle and ask students to write the infinitive. You could perhaps extend more able students by including some unfamiliar verbs (*voyagé, vu, admiré, découvert*, etc.).
- Students recap on how best to understand comments made on their work (see notes on reinforcement of **8W3** on page 174), focusing on how to go about improving areas identified as needing improvement.

Homework suggestions
- Students write a short text using the notes they made after working on **OHT 25** (see page 174).
- Students exchange their texts and write some feedback on each other's work in preparation for the next session (using words such as *très bien, excellent, bonne utilisation du passé, bon effort, en progrès*, etc.).
- Students write a paragraph in the past tense, on any subject, using three verbs with *avoir* as their auxiliary and three verbs with *être* as their auxiliary.
- Students create a mind map of key language and language-learning points from the unit.

Voyages et vacances 5

5.4 C'était vraiment sympa!

pages 72–73

À vos marques

AT 3.2 *En deux minutes, trouve dans les textes: a) deux pays et trois villes; b) quatre moyens de transport; c) quatre activités que tu aimes faire; d) quatre activités que tu n'aimes pas.*

Students have two minutes to find various details in the three texts about past holidays.

Answers: a les États-Unis, l'Espagne, New York, Miami, Dieppe; b l'avion, la voiture, le car, le vélo; c/d any of the following activities: visiter des musées/châteaux, aller à la plage, faire des excursions dans la région, faire de l'équitation, faire du kayak, sortir avec des copains, faire du vélo, jouer au foot, aller au centre commercial, aller au cinéma, regarder la télé, jouer sur une console

AT 1.4 **1** *Écoute les interviews et note les questions (voir Expressions-clés). Traduis "C'était comment?" en anglais.*

Students listen to the interviews with Emmanuelle, Élodie and Corentin about their recent holidays. They note the questions asked: all the questions are listed in *Expressions-clés*. This focus on question types in the perfect and the imperfect tense reinforces Framework objective **8S4**.

Answers: see questions in transcript below; C'était comment? = What was it like?

CD 2, track 31 page 72, activité 1
Cassette 3, side 1

- Emmanuelle, tu es allée où en vacances?
- Pendant les vacances, je suis allée aux États-Unis avec mes parents.
- Tu es partie quand?
- On est partis le 3 août.
- Tu es restée combien de temps?
- On est restés deux semaines.
- Tu as voyagé comment?
- On a pris l'avion pour New York.
- Qu'est-ce que tu as fait pendant les vacances?
- D'abord, on est restés quatre jours à New York. On a visité beaucoup de musées.
- C'était comment, New York?
- Moi, je n'ai pas aimé. C'était vraiment moche! Après, on est allés à Miami en avion. Là, on est restés une semaine. On a visité la région en voiture et on est allés à la plage.
- C'était comment?
- J'ai beaucoup aimé Miami, c'était vraiment génial.

- Élodie, tu es allée où en vacances?
- Cet été, je suis allée dans un camp de vacances en Espagne.
- Tu es partie quand?
- Je suis partie le 2 juillet.
- Tu es restée combien de temps?
- Je suis restée deux semaines.
- Tu as voyagé comment?
- J'ai pris le car.
- Qu'est-ce que tu as fait pendant les vacances?
- La première semaine, on a fait des excursions dans la région et on a visité des châteaux et des musées.
- C'était comment?
- Ça, j'ai adoré, c'était super! La deuxième semaine, on est restés dans le camp et on a fait du sport. D'abord, on a fait de l'équitation, c'était sympa, mais après, on a fait du kayak, et ça, j'ai détesté!

- Corentin, tu es allé où en vacances?
- Moi, je ne suis pas parti, je suis resté à la maison.
- Qu'est-ce que tu as fait pendant les vacances?
- D'abord, je suis sorti avec mes copains: on a fait du vélo et on a joué au foot au parc. C'était sympa. On est aussi allés au centre commercial, mais c'était nul parce que moi, je déteste les magasins! On est allés au cinéma. Le soir, j'ai regardé la télé ou joué sur ma console avec mon frère. Voilà!
- C'était comment?
- Ce n'était pas super. Moi, j'aimerais vraiment partir parce que je ne suis jamais allé à l'étranger.

AT 3.4
AT 4.3 **2a** *Lis les textes. Réponds aux questions pour chaque personne.*

Students answer the questions from *Expressions-clés* on behalf of Emmanuelle, Élodie and Corentin, referring back to the three texts for the information. When they have completed this activity, they should have three interviews similar to the ones on the recording. They will use these texts in activity **2b**.

Answers: see questions and answers in transcript above

C85 Feuille 85 *Ça se dit comme ça!* could be used before the next activity. It provides guidance on reading aloud, focusing in particular on liaisons and intonation.

AT 2.3/4 **2b** *Lis le texte à haute voix.*

Students read aloud their texts from activity **2a**. Take this opportunity to revise the work on sound–spelling links done in *Équipe nouvelle 1*, e.g. vowel sounds *u/ou*, *eau*, *ai*, etc.; nasal sounds *en/an*, *ain*, *ion*, etc.; accents è, é; liaisons with *-s*, *-t*, *-n*, etc.

AT 2.4/5 **2c** *A choisit un rôle. B pose les questions 1–6 (Expressions-clés). A répond de mémoire (1 point par bonne réponse). Changez de rôle.*

In pairs, students take turns to ask each other the questions from the *Expressions-clés*. The person answering the questions takes on the role of Emmanuelle, Élodie or Corentin, and must try to answer from memory.

Follow-up activities:
▶ Use **OHT 24** for extra practice. Blank out various elements you want students to practise, e.g. all auxiliaries, all past participles, actual details about the holiday, etc. You could do this gradually, as a challenge.

5 Voyages et vacances

- Ask students to assess how many missing elements they feel comfortable with. If, for example, they decide they can fill in all the auxiliary verbs, blank them all out. Award a certain number of points, depending on how many auxiliaries students are able to fill in correctly.
- If students then decide they can also recall all the past participles, blank these out too, giving points for correct recall.
- Continue in the same way until there is practically nothing left of the text and students can recall most of it from memory.

AT 4.3 3 *À trois. A: Réponds à la question 1 dans les Expressions-clés sur une feuille, puis plie et passe la feuille à B. B: Réponds à la question 2 sur la feuille pliée, puis plie encore et passe à C, etc. À la fin, dépliez et lisez.*
This is based on the game of Consequences (called *Cadavres exquis* in French) and is played in the same way. Organize groups of three students. Each student has a sheet of paper and starts by answering the first question (*Tu es allé(e) où?*), then folds the paper and passes it to the next student who answers the second question. They continue until all six questions have been answered. Each student then reads out the whole sequence on the sheet they end up with.
One of the aims here is to encourage students to produce more detailed descriptions, which is the focus of the *Guide pratique* panel. The activity also reinforces **8S4** through its focus on different question types in the perfect tense.

Guide pratique
This section gives step-by-step guidance on how to produce more detailed descriptions. It reinforces Framework objectives **8S2** (connectives in extended sentences), **8S6** (substituting and adding), **8T5** (writing continuous text) and **8L4** (extending sentences).

1 In pairs, students invent a holiday, following the model provided and taking turns to add extra details.

Follow-up activities:
- Students write up their imaginary holiday. To reinforce Framework objective **8W3**, provide written feedback in French on their work. Discuss the feedback with the class the following week, discussing what sort of language they can expect to see on their written work. Identify typical words for positive feedback (e.g. *C'était très bien, excellent, bonne utilisation du passé*), encouraging words (e.g. *bon effort, en progrès*) and words that point out areas for improvement (e.g. *améliorer*).

OHT 25 could also be used here for extra practice:
- Play a memory game: using a sticky note, hide one square and ask students to identify what it was and say the relevant sentence.
- Photocopy the OHT and cut out the squares. Narrate a story based on the pictures. Students come to the OHP and either place the frames in the correct order or point at the frames as you mention them.)

- Photocopy the OHT and cut out the squares. Place the frames in a different order on the OHP; students look at them for one minute. Then switch off the OHP and ask students to recall in which order events took place.
- Divide students into two teams and play a game of Noughts and Crosses. One student from team A asks the relevant question about a frame (e.g. *Tu es allé(e) où? Tu es parti(e) quand?*) and a student from team B must provide the correct answer in order to secure that frame.
- At the end of the session with this OHT, ask students to note down something about each of the nine frames. They will use these notes to write a text (see Homework suggestions on page 172).

C83 Feuilles 83 and 84 *Guide pratique 1* and *2* could both be used at this point. *Guide pratique 1* focuses on using
C84 connectives to make written work more fluent and interesting, while *Guide pratique 2* provides further guidance on writing a more detailed description.

C74 Feuille 74 *Écoute En plus*, Feuille 76 *Parle En plus* and Feuille 80 *Lis et écris En plus 2* could also be used here.
C76 They all provide additional practice of the language of
C80 this spread.

W47 Further reading and writing practice in this context is provided on page 47 of the *Encore* and *En plus* Workbooks

W49 Page 49 of the *Encore* and *En plus* Workbooks draws together and practises much of the language of the whole unit and could be used either with or after this spread.

Challenge!

AT 4.3/4 **A** *Écris une description des vacances d'Emmanuelle, Élodie ou Corentin. Utilise "il" ou "elle".*
Students refer back to the texts on page 72 to help them write a description of Emmanuelle's, Élodie's or Corentin's holiday, using the third person singular.

AT 2.4/5 **B** *Jeu du "Ni oui ni non". A pose des questions: B ne doit pas dire "oui" ou "non"!*
Students play a question-and-answer game in which they take turns to ask and answer questions about a past holiday. The person answering the questions is not allowed to say *oui* or *non*, so in order to win the game students have to give complete sentences in the perfect tense. To extend the activity beyond the topic of holidays, encourage students to reuse questions from previous units/contexts.

AT 4.4/5 **C** *Imagine: un(e) touriste français(e) est venu(e) en vacances dans ta ville. Écris sa lettre. Donne le plus de détails possible!*
Students imagine they are a French tourist who has just been on holiday in your home area. They write a letter from the tourist, describing the holiday in detail.

Voyages et vacances **5**

5.5 La belle équipe, épisode 5

pages 74–75

Objectives
▶ Develop listening and reading skills via a soap story based on the language of the unit
▶ Understand some simple colloquialisms (**8C5 – R**)

Resources
Students' Book, pages 74–75
CD 2, track 32
Cassette 3, side 1

Programme of Study reference
1a, 1c, 2a, 2b, 2g, 2h, 2i, 3b, 3c, 3e, 4a, 4d, 5a, 5d, 5e, 5g, 5i

For general information on introducing and exploiting the soap story, refer to page 19 of the Introduction.

Following Arnaud's disastrous performance in rehearsals at the end of the previous episode, the story continues here with Natacha, Juliette and Matthieu discussing how to deal with the problem of Arnaud's dreadful singing. They agree that although Arnaud can't sing, he does have rhythm so could probably cope with a rap. Luckily, Matthieu is a rap expert, so Juliette suggests doing the final rehearsals at Matthieu's house so that he can help. After a minor accident on his moped, Arnaud arrives at the next rehearsal and immediately becomes angry and indignant to find that Matthieu ("Mr Know-it-all", according to Arnaud) is going to help with the rap. The two boys begin to lose their temper with each other but Juliette manages to calm the situation down.

On the day of the audition, Juliette and Matthieu travel to the theatre together by taxi. Arnaud happens to spot Juliette helping Matthieu out of the taxi (Matthieu is still quite weak after his operation), and he wonders whether something is going on between them.

The episode ends with the announcement that the Pieds-Nus have won the competition and the trip to the West Indies! This is wonderful news for Natacha, Juliette and Arnaud ... but a shame for poor Matthieu who will not be going with them.

AT 1.4/5
AT 3.4/5

1 *Écoute et regarde les photos!*
Students listen to the recording and follow the photos in the Students' Book.

CD 2, track 32 page 74, La belle équipe, épisode 5
Cassette 3, side 1

1 Une semaine plus tard ...
– Alors, Arnaud est allé à toutes les répétitions? C'était comment?
– C'était affreux!!! Il est nul!
– Il ne chante pas bien, mais il a du rythme! À la limite, il peut faire un rap.
– Super idée! Tu es génial en rap, toi! On fait les dernières répétitions ici et tu donnes tes idées! D'accord?
– Moi, je veux bien ... si Arnaud est d'accord.
2 – Arnaud? Tu es où? Tu es en retard!
– Je suis à la pharmacie! J'ai eu un accident de mobylette quand je suis rentré du collège.
– Oh non! C'était grave?
– Non, mais j'ai mal au bras.
– Ah, rien de grave? Alors, viens vite chez Matthieu! On t'attend. Prends le bus! Ciao!
3 Plus tard ...
– Arnaud, Matthieu va t'aider à faire un rap.
– Ah, je vois! Monsieur "Je-sais-tout-faire" va m'aider! Quel honneur! Oh, merci, merci, votre Grandeur!
– Oh, ça va, hein! Si tu n'es pas content ...
– Grrrrrrrrr! Les mecs, arrêtez!
4 Le jour de l'audition ...
– Tu vas au théâtre? Super! Tu vas en voiture avec ton père?
– Non, il est parti en ville. Je prends un taxi. C'est cher, mais c'est moins fatigant que le bus. Viens avec moi!
– Euh ... D'accord! Je préfère le taxi à la mobylette d'Arnaud ... c'est moins dangereux!
5 – Juliette et Matthieu??? Mais, qu'est-ce qui se passe?
6 Après les auditions ...
– Quel talent vous avez tous! La décision finale est difficile. Les gagnants du premier prix sont ... Les Pieds-Nus!!! Félicitations aux nouvelles stars! Juliette, Natacha et Arnaud!!!
7 – Oui, bravo! Et bravo, Arnaud. Bien joué! À toi, le voyage aux Antilles ... avec Natacha et Juliette ...
À suivre ...

---

2 *Écoute et lis. Trouve ...*
Students listen again while reading the text. They search the text for the French equivalents of the English colloquial expressions. This reinforces **8C5**.

Answers: at a push: *à la limite*; bye!: *ciao!* (the French use the Italian word for "bye!"); that's enough!: *ça va, hein!*; guys!: *les mecs!* (point out that this is used to refer to males only)

3 *Remets les phrases de ce résumé dans l'ordre.*
Students arrange sentences a–h into the correct order to give a summary of the text.

Answers: e, c, d, a, h, f, g, b

AT 2.4 **4** *À cinq, jouez l'épisode!*
Students act out the episode in groups.

5 Voyages et vacances

Super-challenge! page 76

This extension page is intended to stretch more able students who are confident with the core language of the unit. It combines language from the unit with unfamiliar language and develops grammar points introduced in the main body of the unit. It can be used flexibly either as part of a teacher-led lesson or as alternative independent class and homework material.

Objectives
▶ Use the plural forms of the perfect tense
▶ Learn some expressions in the imperfect tense

Resources
Students' Book, page 76
CD 2, track 33
Cassette 3, side 1
Encore/En plus Workbooks, page 50

Programme of Study reference
1a, 1b, 1c, 2a, 2b, 2c, 2h, 2i, 3c, 3e, 4a, 4c, 4d, 5d, 5e, 5i

AT 1.4/5
AT 3.4/5
1a *Lis et écoute le texte. Trouve deux pays, trois villes, quatre moyens de transport.*
Students listen to the recording while reading the text about a visit to Burkina Faso. They search the text for specific details.

Answers: deux pays: France, Burkina Faso; trois villes: Paris, Ouagadougou, Bobo-dioulasso; quatre moyens de transport: l'avion, le bus, le taxi, la mobylette

CD 2, track 33 — Cassette 3, side 1 — page 76, activité 1a

Nous sommes parties avec ma mère en juillet. Nous avons pris l'avion pour Ouagadougou, la capitale. Quand nous sommes descendues de l'avion, il faisait très très chaud! Nous avons pris un bus pour Bobo-dioulasso et là, un taxi pour le village de maman. C'était long! Nous sommes restées deux mois au village.
Quand nous sommes arrivées, notre grand-mère a fait un repas typique. Maman et Azéla ont aidé et moi, j'ai pris des photos! Tous les gens du village sont venus manger et faire la fête! C'était génial! Le soir, nous sommes allées dormir chez ma grand-mère. Les femmes et les filles sont restées en bas, les hommes et les garçons sont montés à l'étage. Nous avons fait des excursions dans la région. Ma préférée? Le lac de Tengrela avec les hippopotames! Nous sommes aussi sorties avec nos cousins à mobylette pour aller à Bobo-dioulasso. Là, nous sommes allés au restaurant et au cinéma. Un soir, il y avait une fête au village: on a chanté, dansé et joué du tambour! C'était génial!
Nous sommes rentrées à Paris avec de bons souvenirs du Burkina!

1b *Relis et trouve …*
Students search the text for the French translations of the English phrases.

Answers: a il faisait très très chaud; b c'était long; c c'était génial; d il y avait une fête

1c *Relis. Trouve les phrases qui répondent aux questions.*
Students find, in the text, the sentences that contain answers to the questions a–e.

Answers: a Nous sommes parties avec ma mère en juillet. b Nous avons pris l'avion pour Ouagadougou, la capitale. c Nous sommes restées deux mois au village. d Quand nous sommes arrivées, notre grand-mère a fait un repas typique. Maman et Azéla ont aidé et moi, j'ai pris des photos! e Nous avons fait des excursions dans la région. Ma préférée? Le lac de Tengrela avec les hippopotames! Nous sommes aussi sorties avec nos cousins à mobylette pour aller à Bobo-dioulasso.

AT 4.4/5
1d *Écris un résumé du texte à partir des questions de l'activité 1c.*
Students summarize the text in French, using the questions in activity **1c** as a framework.

Zoom grammaire
This grammar section focuses on the plural forms of verbs in the perfect tense.

1 Students search Amina's text for all the perfect tense verbs.

Answers: <u>verbs with auxiliary *être*</u>: Amina Kayendé et sa sœur Azéla sont nées, elles sont allées, nous sommes parties, nous sommes descendues, nous sommes restées, nous sommes arrivées, tous les gens du village sont venus, nous sommes allées, les femmes et les filles sont restées, les hommes et les garçons sont montés, nous sommes aussi sorties, nous sommes allés, nous sommes rentrées; <u>verbs with auxiliary *avoir*</u>: nous avons pris, maman et Azéla ont aidé, nous avons fait

2 Students consider what is different about the plural forms of the past participle.

Answers: They should notice that when the auxiliary verb is *être*, an "s" is added to the past participle when the people doing the action are male or a mixed group of both male and female, and that "es" is added when the people doing the action are all female.

3 Students consider what happens to the past participle when the subject is *nous*.

Answer: as in activity **2** above

4 Students fill in the gaps using the correct forms of *être* and past participle endings. Point out that various answers are possible for c, depending on whether *vous* refers to a single person (*Monsieur X, Madame X*) or to several people (either all male or all female, or a mixture of both).

Answers: a sommes allés; b sont allées; c êtes tombé(e)(s); sommes allés

Refer students to the grammar section on page 142 of the Students' Book for further information on the perfect tense.

W50 Page 50 of the *Encore* and *En plus* Workbooks could be used at this point.

Vocabulaire
page 77

This page provides a summary of the key language covered in this unit. It could be used as a handy reference for students as they work through the unit. Alternatively, students could use its clear French–English format with language organized thematically when learning vocabulary.

C69 Feuille 69 *Vocabulaire* also contains a summary of the key language of the unit and could be given to students at this point for revision purposes. See page 7 of the Introduction for ideas on how to use this copymaster.

W51 Page 51 of the *Encore* and *En plus* Workbooks also provides a summary of the key language of the unit.

Podium
page 78

The *Podium* page provides students with an end-of-unit checklist of learning objectives in French and English. At the foot of the page are activities at three levels of difficulty (bronze, silver and gold) to extend the work of the unit. Encourage students to select an activity at the most appropriate level.

C70 Feuille 70 *Podium* could also be used at this point. This worksheet contains activities to help students keep track of their progress. See page 7 of the Introduction for ideas on how to use it to help self- and peer-assessment.

W52 Page 52 of the *Encore* and *En plus* Workbooks also provides an end-of-unit checklist in French and English with activities to help students keep track of their progress.

Encore Unité 5
pages 104–105

Objectives

These reinforcement pages are intended for those students requiring further practice of core language from the unit. They can be used by students who finish other activities quickly or as alternative class and homework material.

Resources
Students' Book, pages 104–105
CD 2, track 34
Cassette 3, side 1

Programme of Study reference
1c, 2a, 2c, 2d, 2h, 2i, 3e, 4a, 4d, 5a, 5c, 5d, 5e, 5f, 5i

AT 1.3 **1a** *Écoute et relie.*
Students listen to the four interviews about holidays. They match each interview to the corresponding *fiche*.

Answers: 1 Valentine; 2 Alex; 3 Elsa; 4 Julien

AT 1.3
AT 4.1 **1b** *Réécoute. Recopie et complète les fiches.*
Students copy out the *fiches*, then listen again and fill in the missing details.

Answers:

	Alex	Valentine	Julien	Elsa
Où?	pays de Galles	États-Unis	Écosse	Londres
Départ?	le 8 août	le 15 août	le 3 juillet	le 21 juillet
Durée?	deux semaines	une semaine	un mois	un week-end
Transport?	bateau, train	avion	avion, train	car

CD 2, track 34 page 104, activité 1
Cassette 3, side 1

1 – Bonjour, tu es allée où en vacances?
 – Je suis allée aux Etats-Unis.
 – Tu es partie quand?
 – Euh … je suis partie le 15 août.
 – Et tu es restée combien de temps?
 – Je suis restée une semaine.
 – Tu as voyagé comment?
 – J'ai pris l'avion.
 – Super!
2 – Salut! Tu es allé où en vacances?
 – Je suis allé au pays de Galles.
 – Tu es parti quand?
 – Je suis parti le 8 août.
 – Tu es resté combien de temps?
 – Je suis resté deux semaines.
 – Tu as voyagé comment?
 – J'ai pris le bateau et le train.
 – Génial.
3 – Alors, tu es allée où en vacances?
 – Je suis allée à Londres.
 – Tu es partie quand?
 – Je suis partie le 21 juillet.
 – Tu es restée combien de temps?
 – Je suis restée un week-end.
 – Tu as voyagé comment?
 – J'ai pris le car.
 – Super!

5 Voyages et vacances

4 – Tu es allé où en vacances?
 – Je suis allé en Écosse.
 – Tu es parti quand?
 – Je suis parti le 3 juillet.
 – Tu es resté combien de temps?
 – Je suis resté un mois.
 – Tu as voyagé comment?
 – J'ai pris l'avion et le train.

AT 2.2/3 **1c** *Dis une phrase. Ton/Ta partenaire devine qui tu es.*
Referring to their answers for activity **1b**, students work in pairs, taking turns to make statements about one of the holidays, e.g. *Je suis parti le trois juillet*. The partner consults their completed *fiches* to find out which person is being referred to.
This can be extended to longer exchanges by using the answer grid from activity **1b** to play a game of Three-in-a-Row (copy the grid on to acetate so that you can play the game as a whole class on the OHP). The aim is to make correct sentences using the coordinates of the grid, e.g. *Alex est allé au pays de Galles*.

AT 4.2-4 **2** *Invente des vacances. Remplis une fiche et écris une carte postale.*
Students write out a *fiche* about their own (real or imaginary) holiday. They use this as a framework for writing a postcard describing the holiday.

AT 3.3 **3a** *Lis les quatre lettres. De qui sont les dessins?*
Students read four letters in which people describe recent holiday experiences. They decide which holiday is best represented by the assortment of photos and symbols.

Answer: letter 3

AT 2.3/4 **3b** *A choisit une personne. B pose les questions pour deviner qui.*
Students choose an identity from the four people who have written the letters in activity **3a**. Their partner asks a series of questions to find out their identity.

AT 4.4/5 **4** *Raconte des vacances (réponds aux questions 1–6). Lis ton texte à ton/ta partenaire. Il/Elle devine si c'est vrai ou faux.*
Students write a description of a past holiday, real or imaginary. They read out their text to a partner, who decides whether or not it is true.

En plus Unité 5 pages 116–117

Objectives
These extension pages are intended for more able students who are confident with the core language of the unit. They can be used by students who finish other activities quickly or as alternative class and homework material.

Resources
Students' Book, pages 116–117

Programme of Study reference
1c, 2c, 2d, 2e, 2h, 2i, 3b, 3c, 3e, 4a, 4d, 5a, 5d, 5e, 5g, 5i

AT 3.4/5 **1a** *Lis l'article et trouve …*
Students search the text for specific details.

Answers: a Claude, Françoise, Manon; b avril, mai; c Lyon, Paris; d la France, le Pakistan, l'Inde, la Chine, l'Australie, la Nouvelle-Zélande, les États-Unis, le Maroc, l'Espagne; e du hérisson, du singe, des coléoptères

1b *Ça se dit comment en français?*
Students search the text for the French translations of some English expressions.

Answers: a un voyage extraordinaire; b ils sont allés en Asie; c ils sont restés six ans; d ils ont campé dans des déserts et dans la jungle; e ils sont arrivés en Australie; f ils ont continué leur aventure

2 *Vrai ou faux? Corrige si c'est faux.*
Students answer true/false questions on the text. They correct the false statements.

Answers: a vrai; b faux – they got married while travelling; c faux – they had their baby in New Zealand/carried on travelling; d vrai; e vrai; f vrai

3 *Lis l'article et recopie les phrases dans l'ordre chronologique.*
Students copy out the statements in chronological order to produce a summary of the text.

Answer: c, e, d, a, f, b

AT 4.3 **4** *Imagine: tu es Claude ou Françoise. Un reporter fait une interview sur Internet. Réponds à ses questions.*
Students give written replies to the questions, imagining they are Claude or Françoise.

AT 2.4/5 **5** *A est Claude ou Françoise. B est reporter et prépare 10 questions. Imaginez l'interview.*
In pairs, students conduct an interview. One student plays the role of the interviewer and prepares 10 questions. Their partner answers as if they are Claude or Françoise. The six questions from activity **4** could form the basis of the interview, with students deciding on the additional four questions themselves.

Voyages et vacances **5**

Point lecture
pages 128–129

These pages are intended to encourage independent reading. Students should attempt them once they are confident with the core language of the unit. They can be used by students who finish other activities quickly or as alternative class and homework material.

Objectives
▶ Develop reading for information and pleasure via song lyrics (**8C4**) and a magazine article about holiday destinations

Resources
Students' Book, pages 128–129
CD 2, tracks 35–38; CD 3, tracks 35–37
Cassette 3, side 1; cassette 4, side 2
Copymaster 85

Programme of Study reference
1a, 1c, 2a, 2b, 2c, 2h, 2i, 3b, 3c, 3d, 3e, 4a, 4c, 4d, 5a, 5d, 5e, 5g, 5i

AT 1.3 / AT 3.3 **1a** *Écoute et lis le texte "La Ronde des pays". Numérote les dessins dans l'ordre.*
Students listen to the poem while following the words in the Students' Book (**8C4**). They list the illustrations in the order in which they are mentioned.

Answers: j, c, k, e, i, b, g, a, h, f, d

🎧 **CD 2, track 35** page 128, activité 1a
Cassette 3, side 1

La ronde des pays
Ta montre est faite en Suisse
Ta chemise est faite en Inde
Ta radio est faite en Chine
Et ta voiture au Japon
Ta pizza vient d'Italie
Ton couscous vient d'Algérie
Tes chiffres viennent d'Arabie
Et ton café du Brésil
Tu vas en vacances en Espagne
au Maroc ou aux États-Unis,
Alors, avec tout ça, impossible d'être raciste!

AT 4.1 **1b** *Fais la liste des pays mentionnés. Attention, masculin ou féminin? Vérifie dans un dictionnaire.*
Students list all the countries mentioned in the poem, together with their genders, using a dictionary to check where necessary.

Answers: la Suisse, l'Inde (f), la Chine, le Japon, l'Italie (f), l'Algérie (f), l'Arabie (f), le Brésil, l'Espagne (f), le Maroc, les États-Unis (m)

1c *Explique la dernière ligne du poème en anglais.*
Students explain the last line of the poem in English.

Answer: It is impossible to be racist when so much of what we have comes from other countries.

AT 1.4/5 **2a** *Écoute la chanson "Voyage aux Antilles". Mets les dessins dans l'ordre.*
Students listen to the song and list the drawings in the order they are mentioned (**8C4**). Point out that the French often use the phrase *quinze jours* (in the first verse) to mean a fortnight.

Answers: g, h, a, f, i, e, d, b, c

🎧 **CD 2, track 36** page 129, activité 2a
Cassette 3, side 1

Voyage aux Antilles
Refrain:
Je suis allée aux Antilles
Chapeau de paille et espadrilles.
Je suis allée aux Antilles
Couleur café, parfum vanille.

Je suis partie en juillet
J'ai acheté mon billet
Un billet aller-retour
Je suis restée quinze jours.
Refrain

J'ai pris l'avion à Marseille
Ciel tout gris, pas de soleil
Je suis arrivée aux Antilles
Là, toujours le soleil brille.
Refrain

Je suis montée en montagne
J'ai campé à la campagne
J'ai mangé du chou coco
J'ai dansé le calypso.
Refrain

AT 2.3 **2b** *A pose les questions des Expressions-clés, p. 70. B réponds avec les mots de la chanson.*
Students refer back to the questions listed in the *Expressions-clés* panel on page 70 of the Students' Book. They ask each other the questions, giving their answers in the words of the song.

Answers: Tu es allée où?: Je suis allée aux Antilles. Tu es partie quand?: Je suis partie en juillet. Tu es restée combien de temps?: Je suis restée quinze jours. Tu as voyagé comment?: J'ai voyagé en avion.

AT 3.4/5 **3** *Lis "Vacances en Europe". Choisis la bonne option.*
Students answer multiple-choice questions on an article about the preferred holiday destinations of Europeans.

Answers: 1 a; 2 b; 3 b; 4 b; 5 a; 6 b

5 Voyages et vacances

Ça se dit comme ça!

This section focuses on the pronunciation of *-ille*, *-eil(le)* and *-agne*.

1 Students listen to the recording and repeat the words.

CD 2, track 37 — page 129, Ça se dit comme ça! activité 1
Cassette 3, side 1

-ille … Antilles … espadrille … vanille … brille
-eil(le) … Marseille … soleil
-agne … montagne … campagne

2 Students read the three sentences aloud then listen to the recording to check their pronunciation.

CD 2, track 38 — page 129, Ça se dit comme ça! activité 2
Cassette 3, side 1

a – L'Espagne et l'Allemagne.
b – Camille, la fille de la famille, aime la vanille des Antilles.
c – Les abeilles sommeillent au soleil.

C85 Feuille 85 *Ça se dit comme ça!* could be used here, if not already used with page 72 of the Students' Book. It provides guidance on reading aloud, focusing in particular on liaisons and intonation.

Copymasters

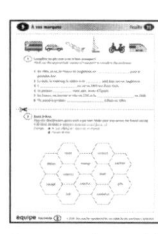

Feuille 71 À vos marques

There are two starter activities on this copymaster.
Activity 1 focuses on transport and could be completed with pages 68–69 of the Students' Book. Activity 2 practises the perfect tense with auxiliaries *avoir* and *être*, and could be used with pages 70–71.

1 *Complète les phrases avec le bon transport!*
Students fill in the correct words to complete the historical facts about transport. Students could work individually on this activity or brainstorm the answers in pairs or groups. Point out the use of the perfect tense and the past participle agreement in *né/nés* (sentences 2 and 3).

Answers: 1 Eurostar; 2 bus; 3 avion; 4 bateau; 5 mobylette; 6 taxi

2 *Jouez à deux.*
Students play a Blockbusters-style game with a partner. In order to "win" squares and make their way across the board, they must say sentences incorporating the past participles featured. They could either use counters or colour the squares to mark their route.

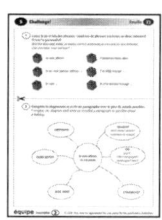

Feuille 72 Challenge!

There are two plenary activities on this copymaster.
Activity 1 practises the perfect tense with auxiliaries *avoir* and *être*, including negatives, together with *je vais* and *j'aimerais aller*. It could be used with pages 70–71 of the Students' Book. Activity 2 combines much of the language of Unit 5 and should be used towards the end of the unit, at any point after the *Guide pratique* on page 73.

1 *Lance le dé et fais des phrases. Combien de phrases correctes en deux minutes? Et ton/ta partenaire?*
This is a dice game played in pairs. Students take turns to roll the die; the number they throw represents one of the phrases shown on the copymaster. Students then have two minutes to say as many correct sentences as they can beginning with the phrase shown.

2 *Complète le diagramme et écris un paragraphe avec le plus de détails possible.*
Students complete the diagram using ideas from Unit 5 or from their previous learning. They use it as a framework for writing a detailed paragraph about a past holiday.

Feuille 73 Écoute Encore

This copymaster provides listening and speaking practice of means of transport, including opinions, and could be used with pages 68–69 of the Students' Book.

AT 1.3

1a *Écoute le sondage sur les transports. Entoure les lettres dans la grille.*
Students listen to a survey on means of transport. Each opinion expressed is represented by a letter in the grid on the copymaster: students circle one letter for each means of transport.

Answers: t, y, w, a, a, r, m

CD 3, track 33 — Feuille 73, activité 1a
Cassette 4, side 2

– Qu'est-ce que vous pensez des transports dans votre ville?
– Moi, je vais partout à pied! Au moins, ce n'est pas cher!

– Qu'est-ce que vous pensez des transports dans votre ville?
– Moi, je vais au travail à vélo, mais c'est très dangereux, à cause des voitures.

– Qu'est-ce que vous pensez des transports dans votre ville?
– Moi, j'aime bien prendre le bus … mais c'est long!

– Qu'est-ce que vous pensez des transports dans votre ville?
– J'aime bien prendre le métro parce que c'est rapide.

– Qu'est-ce que vous pensez des transports dans votre ville?
– Moi, je prends la voiture parce que … euh … c'est pratique.

– Qu'est-ce que vous pensez des transports dans votre ville?
– Moi, j'habite assez loin, en banlieue, alors je prends le train pour venir en ville. J'aime bien le train parce que c'est confortable.

– Qu'est-ce que vous pensez des transports dans votre ville?
– Moi, quand je vais en ville, je prends un taxi. C'est bien, mais c'est cher.

1b *Mets les lettres dans l'ordre et découvre le nom d'un moyen de transport écologique.*
Students rearrange the letters from activity **1a** to find the name of an ecologically friendly means of transport.

Answer: tramway

AT 1.3
AT 2.3
2 *À deux: A donne des opinions sur les transports pour former le nom d'un moyen de transport avec les lettres de la grille. B entoure les lettres sur sa grille et trouve le nom. Changez de rôle.*
In pairs, students make up their own puzzles for each other, similar to the one in activities **1a** and **1b**.

Feuille 74 Écoute En plus

This copymaster provides listening and speaking practice on detailed descriptions of past holidays and could be used with pages 72–73 of the Students' Book.

AT 1.4/5
1a *Écoute trois jeunes raconter leurs dernières vacances organisées par trois agences de voyage. Coche la grille.*
Students listen to three young people being interviewed about recent holidays. They tick the grid to indicate various aspects of each holiday, e.g. when they went, for how long, how they travelled, what they did.

Answers: Samuel: été, un mois +, avion, activités sportives, plage; Clara: hiver, 1–4 semaines, train, excursions culturelles et touristiques, activités sportives; Benoît: printemps/automne, moins d'une semaine, car, excursions culturelles et touristiques

CD 3, track 34
Cassette 4, side 2
Feuille 74

– Samuel, parle-nous de tes dernières vacances. Où es-tu allé?
– Pendant mes dernières vacances? Je suis allé dans le sud de la France.
– Avec qui?
– Avec un groupe de copains.
– Vous êtes partis quand?
– On est partis le 1er juillet.
– Et vous êtes restés combien de temps?
– On est restés un mois et demi.
– Comment avez-vous voyagé?
– On a pris l'avion. C'était cher, mais rapide et très pratique.
– Et qu'est-ce que vous avez fait?
– On est allés à la plage, bien sûr, et on a aussi fait beaucoup de sport: de la natation, de la voile et du jetski.
– C'était comment?
– Moi, j'ai adoré. C'était super!!
– Alors, tu recommandes les vacances "Mer et soleil"?
– Ah oui, c'était vraiment génial!

– Clara, parle-nous de tes dernières vacances. Où es-tu allée?
– Moi, je suis allée dans les Alpes, tout près de la frontière suisse, avec mes parents.
– Oui, c'était quand?
– On est partis le 19 décembre et on est restés une semaine.
– Comment avez-vous voyagé?
– On a pris le train. C'était pratique et rapide.
– Et qu'est-ce que vous avez fait?
– Eh bien, on a fait du ski, du ski et encore du ski!!! On a aussi fait deux excursions intéressantes, mais moi, j'ai surtout aimé le ski!
– Alors, tu recommandes les vacances "En piste"?
– Ah oui, tout à fait, c'était super bien.

– Benoît, parle-nous de tes dernières vacances.
– Oui, alors, moi, je suis allé à Paris avec un groupe de jeunes. Je suis parti le 15 mai et je suis resté cinq jours. J'ai pris le car. C'était bien parce que ce n'était pas cher, mais c'était un peu long. À Paris, on a visité beaucoup de choses très intéressantes: des monuments, des musées. On a aussi fait des excursions, comme au château de Versailles. On avait un guide, il était génial.
– Alors, tu recommandes les vacances "Arts et villes"?
– Ah oui, bien sûr!

1b *Quelles vacances aimes-tu? Coche la grille. Quelle agence de vacances voudrais-tu contacter?*
Students tick the grid to show the type of holiday they themselves would prefer and indicate which of the three travel agents they would contact.

AT 1.4
AT 4.2
2a *Réécoute Samuel et note les questions.*
Students listen again to the interview with Samuel and note down the questions.

Answers: see transcript above

5 Voyages et vacances

AT 2.3-5

2b *Pose les questions de l'activité 2a à ton/ta partenaire. Il/Elle imagine les vacances qu'il/elle a choisies en 1b. Ensuite, changez de rôle.*
Using the questions they noted down in activity **2a**, students work in pairs to interview each other about the ideal holiday they chose in activity **1b**. The level achieved will depend on the quality of students' answers: encourage them to respond in as much detail as possible.

Feuille 75 Parle Encore

This copymaster could be used with pages 70–71 of the Students' Book. It practises means of transport and the perfect tense of *aller*, including negatives, but uses *au/à l'/à la* plus places in town instead of countries/holiday destinations.

The activities are based on the game of Battleships and follow the same principles.

1 *Coche deux destinations et deux moyens de transport.*
Students choose two destinations and two means of transport and tick the grid accordingly.

AT 2.3

2 *Devine les deux destinations et les deux moyens de transport de B. Réponds aussi aux questions de B. Le premier à deviner gagne!*
Students try to guess their partner's destinations and how they travelled by asking and answering questions following the examples on the copymaster. The winner is the first person to guess both the transport and the destinations.

Feuille 76 Parle En plus

This copymaster provides speaking practice on describing a past holiday and should be used with pages 72–73 of the Students' Book.

AT 2.4/5

A interviewe B sur ses vacances. Ensuite, B interviewe A. Prépare tes réponses à l'avance. Note les réponses de ton/ta partenaire.
Students interview each other about a previous holiday (real or imaginary). They prepare their answers in advance, writing them in the spaces provided on the copymaster. When they interview their partner, they note down their partner's answers too.
Various ideas are scattered around the outside of the copymaster as prompts, but more able students may prefer to use their own details. The level achieved will depend on the quality of students' answers, so encourage them to respond in as much detail as possible.
As a follow-up activity, students could report back to the class on their partner's holiday, using *il/elle*.

Feuille 77 Lis et écris Encore 1

This copymaster practises names of countries and towns and could be used with pages 66–67 of the Students' Book.

AT 3.2

1 *Lis et complète les phrases avec les noms de pays.*
Students complete the sentences using the names of countries. All the names are provided as anagrams.

Answers: 1 France; 2 Maroc; 3 Belgique; 4 Sénégal; 5 Afrique du Sud; 6 Antilles; 7 Québec; 8 Tunisie; 9 États-Unis

AT 3.2
AT 4.2

2 *Complète les phrases pour toi avec des noms de villes et de pays. Choisis les bonnes prépositions.*
Students complete the sentences to provide information (real or imaginary) about where they have been, where they have never been, and where they would like to go. They need to make sure they have chosen the correct gender of country, etc. to follow each preposition.

Feuille 78 Lis et écris Encore 2

This copymaster practises means of transport with places in town and other destinations. It could be used with pages 68–69 of the Students' Book.

AT 3.2
AT 4.2

1 *Réponds comme dans l'exemple.*
Students complete the sentences with destinations and means of transport.

Answers: 2 Non, je vais à la plage à pied. 3 Il va à la poste en bus. 4 Non, on va au marché en voiture. 5 Nous allons en Angleterre en bateau. 6 Mais non! Vous allez à Paris en car! 7 Elles vont aux États-Unis en avion.

Feuille 79 Lis et écris En plus 1

This copymaster could be used with pages 70–71 of the Students' Book. It is a puzzle practising the perfect tense together with means of transport and countries

AT 3.2

1 *Qui est allé où et comment?*
Students work out who went where and how they travelled by reading the clues given in the style of a logic puzzle. Tell students to make sure they tick the grid as they go along when they find a piece of correct information, but also (and perhaps more importantly) to make a cross when they find information that is definitely false: for example, they know from clue number 4 that it is a girl who went to Spain, so they can cross out all three boys in the *Espagne* column.

Answers: Léa: Espagne, mobylette; Lucie: Irlande, avion; Agnès: Angleterre, bateau; Marc: Belgique, train; Luc: Allemagne, voiture; Pierre: Italie, car

Voyages et vacances 5

AT 4.2/3

2 *Regarde la grille et fais des phrases. Compare tes résultats avec un(e) partenaire.*
Students write sentences stating where each person went and how they travelled. They compare their own sentences with those of a partner.

Answers: Léa est allée en Espagne à mobylette. Lucie est allée en Irlande en avion. Agnès est allée en Angleterre en bateau. Marc est allé en Belgique en train. Luc est allé en Allemagne en voiture. Pierre est allé en Italie en car.

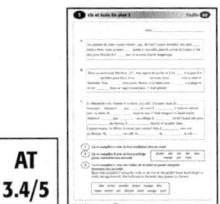

Feuille 80 Lis et écris En plus 2

This copymaster practises the perfect tense with both *avoir* and *être*; it could be used with pages 72–73 of the Students' Book.

AT 3.4/5

1 *Lis et complète A avec le bon auxiliaire: être ou avoir.*
Students read text A and fill in the gaps using the correct form of the auxiliaries *être* or *avoir*.

Answers: ont, est, est, a

AT 3.4/5

2 *Lis et complète B avec le bon participe passé. Attention aux accords!*
Students read text B and fill in the gaps, choosing from the past participles supplied in the box. They need to decide themselves what endings, if any, to add to the past participles.

Answers: pris, allé, acheté, allé, allé, resté, allés, mangé

AT 3.4/5

3 *Lis et complète C avec les verbes de la boîte au passé composé. Attention aux accords!*
Students read and complete text C using the verbs supplied in the box. The verbs are listed in the order in which they appear in the text. Students need to put the infinitives into the correct form of the perfect tense, taking care with agreement of past participles where necessary.

Answers: sont allés, sont arrivés, a pris, est rentré, ont voyagé, est allé, est resté, est rentré, a vu, a discuté, ont bu, ont mangé, sont sortis

Feuille 81 Grammaire 1

This copymaster practises *à/en/au/aux* + names of countries/towns together with *à/en* + means of transport. It should be used once these two grammar points have been taught, after the *Zoom grammaire* on page 69 of the Students' Book.

1 *Tire des traits pour faire des phrases correctes (au moins 15). Écris-les sur une feuille.*
Students draw lines joining items in the three columns, trying to make as many correct sentences as they can. They need to make sure that their choice of preposition in column 2 matches the destination, means of transport or other element in the third column.

2 *Lis le récit des vacances de Sophie et complète avec à/au/aux ou en.*
Students complete Sophie's account of her holiday using the correct prepositions.

Answers: en, à, en, en, à, en, en, à, à, en, à, au, en, en, à, au, à, en, en, au, au, à, à

Feuille 82 Grammaire 2

This copymaster focuses on agreement of the past participle in verbs that need *être* in the perfect tense. It could be used with the *Zoom grammaire* section on page 71 of the Students' Book.

1 *Complète les phrases avec les verbes au passé composé.*
Students complete the sentences using the correct perfect tense forms of the infinitives. Remind them to be careful with the agreement of the past participles.

Answers: 1 sont partis; 2 sont montés; 3 est descendue; 4 est tombée; 5 sont arrivés; 6 sont allés; 7 est entré; 8 est sorti; 9 est rentrée; 10 est resté

Feuille 83 Guide pratique 1

This copymaster accompanies the *Guide pratique* on 73 of the Students' Book. It focuses on using connectives to make written work more fluent and interesting.

1 *Entoure le bon connecteur.*
Students choose the correct connective for each sentence.

Answers: 1 parce que; 2 et; 3 mais; 4 parce que; 5 quand; 6 et; 7 quand; 8 mais; 9 d'abord, après

2 *Transforme les phrases en une. Utilise un connecteur.*
Students rewrite each pair of sentences, using a connective to make a single sentence.

Answers: 1 Je suis allée à Paris, mais je n'ai pas visité Disneyland./Quand je suis allée à Paris, je n'ai pas visité Disneyland. 2 J'ai fait de l'équitation et (j'ai fait) de la natation./D'abord, j'ai fait de l'équitation, après j'ai fait de la natation. 3 J'ai déjà voyagé en train, mais je n'ai jamais voyagé en avion. 4 Je suis allé en vacances en train parce que c'était rapide et pas cher. 5 J'ai bien aimé mes vacances au ski parce que je suis allée faire du ski avec mon père.

Feuille 84 Guide pratique 2

This copymaster provides guidance on writing a detailed description and should be used with the *Guide pratique* section on page 73 of the Students' Book.

AT 3.4

1 *Lis la description et complète le schéma.*
Students read the description of the Christmas holidays and fill in the mind map.

5 Voyages et vacances

AT 4.4/5

2 *Réponds à la question pour toi (tu peux inventer!). Utilise le schéma pour t'aider.*
Students now produce a detailed description (real or imaginary) of what they themselves did during the Christmas holidays, using the mind map to help them.

Feuille 85 Ça se dit comme ça!

This copymaster provides guidance on reading aloud, focusing in particular on liaisons and intonation. It could be used before students attempt activity 2b on page 72 of the Students' Book, or with the *Ça se dit comme ça!* section on page 129 (*Point lecture*). Remind students of the work they have already done on liaisons (on Feuille 51 and, prior to that, in *Équipe nouvelle 1* Unit 6) and intonation (in *Équipe nouvelle 2* Unit 2).

1a *Lis le texte A tout haut. Attention aux liaisons!*
Following the guidance in the Flashback panel, students read aloud text A, focusing in particular on the liaisons.

1b *Écoute et répète.*
Students listen to the recording to check their pronunciation. Liaisons are indicated by underlining in the transcript below.

CD 3, track 35   Feuille 85, activité 1b
Cassette 4, side 2

A – L'année dernière, je suis_allée en vacances en Guadeloupe avec mes parents. La Guadeloupe, c'est_une île des_Antilles. Je suis partie le deux_août. Je suis restée deux semaines. Nous_avons pris l'avion à Paris. Huit_heures après, nous sommes_arrivés à Pointe-à-Pitre. C'était long, mais l'avion était confortable. On_a loué une voiture et on_est_allés à Sainte-Anne en voiture.

2a *Écoute et lis le texte B.*
Students read text B while listening to the recording. Point out that they should listen carefully to the intonation.

CD 3, track 36   Feuille 85, activité 2a
Cassette 4, side 2

B – Pourquoi Sainte-Anne? Parce que Sainte-Anne, c'est le paradis, bien sûr! C'est la plus jolie plage de l'île. Ici, il y a tout: du sable blanc, de l'eau claire, des poissons multicolores, des palmiers et des petits restaurants sur la plage. C'est génial!

2b *Lis le texte B tout haut. Attention à l'intonation.*
Students read text B aloud, focusing in particular on correct intonation.

3 *Lis le texte C tout haut, puis écoute et répète.*
Students read aloud text C, focusing on intonation and liaisons, then listen to the recording to check.

CD 3, track 37   Feuille 85, activité 3
Cassette 4, side 2

C – Je suis_allée à la plage matin et soir. Là, je me suis fait deux_amies, deux filles de Sainte-Anne. On_a fait des excursions en bateau. On_a même vu des dauphins! Qu'est-ce qu'on_a mangé en Guadeloupe? Des spécialités des_Antilles, du poisson, des_ananas et beaucoup d'autres choses. Tout_était bon! C'était vraiment de super vacances!

4 *Dis ces phrases très très vite!*
Students practise saying the two tongue-twisters as fast as they can.

Encore Workbook

Page 44 (5.1)

Use with pages 66–67 of the Students' Book.

AT 3.1
AT 4.1

1 *C'est quel pays?*
Students solve the anagrams to find the names of French-speaking countries.

Answers: a la France; b la Belgique; c la Suisse; d le Québec; e les Antilles; f le Maroc; g le Sénégal; h le Niger; i le Cameroun; j le Congo

AT 4.2 **2** *Écris une phrase pour chaque pays à la page 53.*
Students write a sentence for each of the 10 countries, using *Je vais* + the correct preposition *en*, *au* or *aux*.

Answers: a Je vais en France. b Je vais en Belgique. c Je vais en Suisse. d Je vais au Québec. e Je vais aux Antilles. f Je vais au Maroc. g Je vais au Sénégal. h Je vais au Niger. i Je vais au Cameroun. j Je vais au Congo.

Page 45 (5.2)

Use with pages 68–69 of the Students' Book.

AT 3.1 **1** *Trouve les dix moyens de transport dans la grille.*
Students find 10 means of transport in the wordsearch grid.

Answers:

```
J L A V O I T U R E E
L E M É T R O V A I S
E B N L A V I O N F R
L A M O B Y L E T T E
E T A L L E T R A I N
B E L E T R A M W A Y
U A N C C E E N A É R
S U O A G L I S S E U
L ' E U R O S T A R R !
```

AT 4.1   **2** *Avec les autres lettres, découvre le message secret!*
Students copy out the unused letters from the grid to spell out a mystery message.

Answer: Je vais en France en aéroglisseur!

AT 4.2   **3** *Et toi? Réponds aux questions.*
Students write their own answers to the questions about how they travel to various places.

Page 46 (5.3)

Use with pages 70–71 of the Students' Book.

AT 3.2   **1** *Relie.*
Students match the sentence halves to produce four sentences in the perfect tense.

Answers: 1 b; 2 c; 3 d; 4 a

AT 3.2   **2** *Lis les bulles et relie aux bons dessins.*
Students match each holiday description to the correct set of symbols.

Answers: 1 b; 2 a

AT 4.3   **3** *Écris dans les bulles.*
Students write a speech bubble to describe each person's holiday, using the symbols as prompts and adapting the sentences from activities **1** and **2**.

Answers: Je suis allée à Londres. Je suis partie le six juin. Je suis restée deux semaines/quinze jours. J'ai pris l'Eurostar. Je suis allé en Angleterre. Je suis parti le premier juillet. Je suis resté une semaine. J'ai pris le car.

Page 47 (5.4)

Use with pages 72–73 of the Students' Book.

AT 3.3   **1** *Laure et Luc sont allés en Angleterre. Lis les lettres.*
Students read the two letters about holidays in London.

AT 3.3   **2a** *C'est qui, Luc ou Laure?*
Referring to the two letters in activity **1**, students decide whose holiday is depicted in each illustration.

Answers: a Luc; b Luc; c Laure; d Laure; e Luc; f Laure

AT 4.2   **2b** *Écris la bonne phrase pour chaque dessin (a–f).*
Students write a caption for each of the six illustrations, taking care with agreement of the past participles. They can refer back to the two letters in activity **1** for help in writing the sentences.

Answers: a J'ai pris le bateau. b J'ai fait du vélo. c Je suis allée au théâtre/voir une comédie musicale. d J'ai visité des musées. e Je suis resté à la maison. f J'ai joué au golf.

AT 4.4/5   **3** *Invente un séjour dans une famille en France. C'était super ou nul? Écris une lettre à la page 53.*
Students imagine they have just returned from a stay with a French family. They write a letter about it, using the two letters provided in activity **1** as models.

Page 48 Grammaire

Use with pages 70–71 of the Students' Book.

1 *Écris l'équivalent anglais de ces verbes.*
Students translate the infinitives into English.

Answers: a to go; b to arrive; c to return/come back; d to go up; e to leave; f to stay

2 *Complète avec "je suis" ou "j'ai".*
Students complete each sentence using either *je suis* or *j'ai*.

Answers: a je suis; b j'ai; c je suis; d j'ai; e je suis; f je suis

3 *Écris la bonne forme du participe passé.*
Students fill in the gaps using the correct past participles, taking care with agreement where necessary.

Answers: a parti; b resté; c rentré; d monté; e allé; f partie; g restée; h rentrée; i montée; j allée

Page 49 Méli-mélo

This page pulls together and mixes much of the language and grammar of the whole unit. It should be used towards the end of the unit, either with or after pages 72–73.

1 *Barre le mauvais participe passé.*
Students cross out the incorrect form of the past participle in each sentence.

Answers: the correct forms are: a allé; b arrivée; c venu; d rentrées; e parties; f allées; g montée; h tombés

2 *Prends un élément de chaque colonne en lançant le dé. Tu peux faire une phrase? Si oui, écris-la à la page 53. (Attention à la préposition!)*
This is a dice game. The first number thrown indicates a phrase in the first column; the second number thrown indicates a phrase in the second column. If the two phrases match up, the student writes down the sentence. Point out that the preposition at the end of the first phrase must "agree" with the word that follows it.

Answers: the following combinations of numbers are possible: 1 + 4 or 6; 2 + 5; 3 + 3; 4 + 4; 5 + 1 or 2; 6 + 1 or 2

3 *Écris dix phrases correctes à la page 53.*
Students write 10 grammatically correct sentences, choosing different combinations of words and phrases from the four columns. They need to make sure that the past participles (column 2) agree with the subjects/verbs (column 1), and that the destinations and means of transport (column 4) agree with the prepositions (column 3).

Page 50 Challenge!

Use with page 76 of the Students' Book.

AT 3.4   **1** *Lis le texte. Numérote les dessins dans l'ordre.*
Students read the story about an unusual journey home. They number the pictures in the order in which they are mentioned in the text.

Answers: left to right: 2, 4, 3, 1

5 Voyages et vacances

2 *Relis le texte et souligne: a) en noir des verbes au passé composé avec "être"; b) en rouge des verbes au passé composé avec "avoir"; c) en bleu l'équivalent français de* it (she/he) was.
Students search the text for perfect tense verbs with *avoir* and *être* and for examples of the imperfect form *était*.

Answers: <u>perfect tense with *être*</u>: Pierre est rentré, sa voiture est tombée en panne, il est sorti de la voiture, il est arrivé, il est entré, Pierre est allé au garage, il est reparti, il est arrivé à la maison, il est retourné au village, il est allé chez le voisin, elle est morte, il est allé dans les ruines; <u>perfect tense with *avoir*</u>: il a marché, il a parlé, il a bu un café, il a mangé des gâteaux, elle a beaucoup parlé, le garagiste a réparé sa voiture, il n'a pas trouvé sa clé, le voisin a dit, il a trouvé sa clé; <u>imperfect tense</u>: il était tard, elle était très sympa, c'était intéressant, sa clé était chez la vieille dame, c'était la maison de Mademoiselle Bertin, c'était impossible

AT 4.4 **3** *Imagine que tu es Pierre. Raconte ton histoire. Écris les dix premières phrases à la page 53.*
Students write out the first 10 sentences of the story from the point of view of Pierre. They will need to change the third person forms (*il a/est …*) into the first person singular, and there is one possessive adjective that will need to change from *sa* to *ma*.

Answers: Hier soir, <u>je suis</u> rentré de voyage. Il était tard. <u>Ma</u> voiture est tombée en panne … oh non, pas de téléphone portable! <u>Je suis</u> sorti de la voiture. <u>J'ai</u> marché. <u>Je suis</u> arrivé devant une maison, à l'entrée d'un village. <u>J'ai</u> parlé à une vieille dame. Elle était très sympa: <u>je suis</u> entré, <u>j'ai</u> bu un café et <u>j'ai</u> mangé des gâteaux avec elle. Elle a beaucoup parlé. C'était intéressant.

En plus Workbook

Page 44 (5.1)

Use with pages 66–67 of the Students' Book.

AT 3.1
AT 4.1 **1** *C'est quel pays? Note la lettre et complète avec "le", "la", "l'" ou "les".*
Students complete the key to the map, labelling the countries with their correct identification letters from the map. They then fill in the missing articles *le, la, l'* or *les*.

Answers: 1 e: les Antilles; 2 l: l'Australie; 3 b: la Belgique; 4 i: le Cameroun; 5 j: le Congo; 6 n: les États-Unis; 7 a: la France; 8 k: l'Inde; 9 f: le Maroc; 10 h: le Niger; 11 d: le Québec; 12 m: la Russie; 13 g: le Sénégal; 14 c: la Suisse

AT 4.2 **2** *Écris une phrase pour chaque pays à la page 53.*
Students write a sentence for each of the 14 countries, using *Je vais* + the correct preposition *en, au* or *aux*.

Answers: 1 Je vais aux Antilles. 2 Je vais en Australie. 3 Je vais en Belgique. 4 Je vais au Cameroun. 5 Je vais au Congo. 6 Je vais aux États-Unis. 7 Je vais en France. 8 Je vais en Inde. 9 Je vais au Maroc. 10 Je vais au Niger. 11 Je vais au Québec. 12 Je vais en Russie. 13 Je vais au Sénégal. 14 Je vais en Suisse.

AT 4.2 **3** *Quels pays ne sont pas francophones? Écris à la page 53.*
Students complete the sentence, giving the names of the countries from the map that are not French-speaking.

Answers: On ne parle pas français aux États-Unis, en Australie, en Inde ou en Russie.

AT 4.3 **4** *Tu aimerais aller dans quel(s) pays (parmi les 14)? Écris à la page 53.*
Students write sentences stating which countries out of the 14 on the map they would like to visit.

Page 45 (5.2)

Use with pages 68–69 of the Students' Book.

AT 3.1 **1a** *Trouve les dix moyens de transport dans la grille.*
Students find 10 means of transport in the wordsearch grid.

Answers:

```
J L A V O I T U R E E
  L E M É T R O V A I S
E B N L A V I O N F R
L A M O B Y L E T T E
E T A L L E T R A I N
B E L E T R A M W A Y
U A N C C E E N A É R
S O A G L I S S E E U
  L' E U R O S T A R R !
```

AT 4.1 **1b** *Avec les autres lettres, découvre le message secret!*
Students copy out the unused letters from the grid to spell out a mystery message.

Answer: Je vais en France en aéroglisseur!

AT 4.2 **2** *Et toi? Réponds aux questions.*
Students write their own answers to the questions about how they travel to various places.

Page 46 (5.3)

Use with pages 70–71 of the Students' Book.

AT 3.2
AT 4.1 **1a** *Complète les bulles avec les bons verbes au passé composé.*
Students fill in the gaps in the holiday descriptions using the perfect tense verbs from the box. They need to make sure they select the correct masculine and feminine forms of the past participles.

Answers: a Je <u>suis allé</u> en Allemagne. Je <u>suis parti</u> le vingt et un juin. Je <u>suis resté</u> quatre jours. J'<u>ai pris</u> le train. b Je <u>suis allée</u> en Italie. Je <u>suis partie</u> le onze août. Je <u>suis restée</u> un week-end. J'<u>ai pris</u> l'avion.

AT 3.2 **1b** *Lis les bulles et relie aux bons dessins.*
Students match each holiday description from activity **1a** to the correct set of symbols.

Answers: a Sonia; b Paul

186

| AT 4.3 | **2** *Écris une bulle pour chaque personne. Attention aux accords!*
Students write a speech bubble to describe each person's holiday, using the symbols as prompts and adapting the texts from activity **1**.

Answers: 1 Je suis allée à Londres. Je suis partie le six juin. Je suis restée deux semaines/quinze jours. J'ai pris l'Eurostar.
Je suis allé en Angleterre. Je suis parti le premier juillet. Je suis resté une semaine. J'ai pris le car.

| AT 4.3-5 | **3** *Invente un voyage! Écris une description à la page 53.*
Students write a description of a past journey (real or imaginary). Encourage them to expand their descriptions beyond those featured in activities **1** and **2**: they could include opinions and reasons, e.g. *J'ai pris l'avion parce que c'est rapide.*

Page 47 (5.4)

Use with pages 72–73 of the Students' Book.

| AT 3.3 | AT 4.2 | **1** *Laure et Luc sont allés en Angleterre. Lis les lettres et complète avec la bonne forme des verbes au passé composé.*
Students read the two letters about visits to London, filling in the gaps with the correct perfect tense verbs. Here, students need to decide whether to use *avoir* or *être* as the auxiliary verb, then add the correct form of the past participle, with agreement if necessary.

Answers: <u>Laure</u>: je suis allée, je suis partie, je suis restée, j'ai pris, j'ai visité, je suis allée, j'ai joué, tu as fait; <u>Luc</u>: je suis allé, je suis parti, j'ai pris, je suis resté, je n'ai pas visité, j'ai fait du vélo, je suis resté, j'ai regardé

| AT 3.3 | **2a** *C'est qui, Luc ou Laure?*
Referring to the two letters in activity **1**, students decide whose holiday is depicted in each illustration.

Answers: a Luc; b Luc; c Laure; d Laure; e Luc; f Laure

| AT 4.2 | **2b** *Écris la bonne phrase pour chaque dessin (a–f).*
Students write a caption for each of the six illustrations, taking care with agreement of the past participles. They can refer back to the two letters in activity **1** for help in writing the sentences.

Answers: 1 J'ai pris le bateau. 2 J'ai fait du vélo. 3 Je suis allée au théâtre/voir une comédie musicale. 4 J'ai visité des musées. 5 Je suis resté à la maison. 6 J'ai joué au golf.

| AT 4.4/5 | **3** *Imagine un séjour dans une famille en France. C'était super ou nul? Écris une lettre à la page 53.*
Students imagine they have just returned from a stay with a French family. They write a letter about it, using the two letters provided in activity **1** as models.

Page 48 Grammaire

Use with pages 70–71 of the Students' Book.

1 *Entoure les verbes qui se conjuguent avec "être" au passé composé.*
Students circle the verbs that take *être* in the perfect tense.

Answers: rentrer, aller, monter, rester, arriver, partir, sortir

2 *Complète avec "je suis" ou "j'ai".*
Students complete each sentence using either *je suis* or *j'ai*.

Answers: a je suis; b j'ai; c j'ai; d je suis; e je suis; f j'ai; g je suis; h j'ai; i je suis; j j'ai; k je suis; l je suis

3 *Relie les moitiés de phrases.*
Students match the sentence halves, taking care that each past participle agrees with the subject of its sentence.

Answers: 1 c; 2 b; 3 d; 4 a

4 *Complète les phrases avec la bonne forme du verbe "aller" au passé composé.*
Students complete each sentence using the correct perfect tense form of *aller*.

Answers: a je suis allée; b elles sont allées; c je suis allé; d ils sont allés

Page 49 Méli-mélo

This page pulls together and mixes much of the language and grammar of the whole unit. It should be used towards the end of the unit, either with or after pages 72–73.

1 *Écris le participe passé correct.*
Students complete the sentences with the correct past participles, making sure that they add the correct agreement where necessary.

Answers: a allé(e); b arrivé(e); c venu; d rentré(e)s; e parti(e)s; f allées; g montée; h tombés

2 *Prends un élément de chaque colonne en lançant le dé. Tu peux faire une phrase? Si oui, écris-la à la page 53 et gagne un point. (Attention à l'accord du participe passé et à la préposition!)*
This is a dice game. The first number thrown indicates a phrase in column 1, the second number a past participle in column 2, the third number a preposition in column 3, and the fourth number a destination or means of transport in column 4. If the four items match up to make a grammatically correct sentence, the student writes it down.

Answers: there are many possible combinations of numbers

3 *Traduis en français à la page 53.*
Students translate the sentences into French.

Answers: a Je suis allé(e) à Paris en avion. b Mes parents sont arrivés en Belgique. c Ma sœur et moi sommes resté(e)s à Paris un week-end. d Ma correspondante française Lucie est venue à Londres en Eurostar. e Matthieu n'est pas allé à l'hôpital à pied. f Lucas et Sophie sont déjà allés aux États-Unis en bateau?

5 Voyages et vacances

Page 50 Super-challenge!
Use with page 76 of the Students' Book.

AT 3.5 1 *Lis le texte. Numérote les dessins dans l'ordre.*
Students read the story about an unusual journey home. They number the pictures in the order in which they are mentioned in the text.

Answers: left to right: 2, 4, 3, 1

AT 3.5 2 *Réponds aux questions en français à la page 53.*
Students answer questions in French on the text.

AT 4.3 *Answers:* a Il est sorti de la voiture et il a marché vers un village. Il est arrivé devant une maison et il a frappé à la porte. b Il n'était pas chargé. c Il est entré, il a bu un café, il a mangé du gâteau au chocolat et il a parlé avec elle. d Il a oublié sa clé chez la vieille dame/Sa clé était chez la vieille dame. e Elle est morte en 1950/C'est un fantôme et sa maison est en ruines. f Il y avait sa clé et un gâteau au chocolat.

AT 4.4 3 *Imagine, c'est ton histoire. Adapte et raconte! Écris sur une feuille.*
Students rewrite the story in the first person singular from the point of view of Pierre. They will need to change the third person forms (*il a/est ...*) into the first person singular, and the possessive adjectives from *son/sa* to *mon/ma*.

Unit 6 Overview grid

Pages/Contexts/ Cultural focus	Objectives	Grammar	Skills and Pronunciation	Key language	Framework	PoS	AT level
80–81 **6.1 Qu'est-ce qu'il y a ici?** Places in town Dieppe	Revise talking about what's available in town; understand a publicity brochure; improve your dictionary skills		Dictionary skills	un château, un hôpital, un marché, un musée, un office de tourisme, un supermarché, un zoo une banque, une boulangerie, une église, une mairie, une pharmacie, une plage, une poste Est-ce qu'il y a … près d'ici? Oui, il y a … Non, il n'y a pas de/d' … C'est loin? Non/Oui, c'est à deux cents mètres/kilomètres. C'est près du/de l'/de la/des …	8W7, 8T1, 8T3, 8T4 – R	1a, 1c, 2a, 2b, 2c, 2d, 2f, 2g, 2h, 2i, 3b, 3c, 3d, 3e, 4a, 4c, 4d, 5a, 5d, 5e, 5f, 5g, 5i	1.2–3, 2.3, 3.1–4, 4.2–4
82–83 **6.2 C'est où, la plage?** Directions	Ask for and give directions; understand directions	Imperative (revision)		C'est où, (le port)? Tourne(z) à gauche/droite. Prends/Prenez la première/deuxième/troisième rue à gauche/droite. Va/Allez tout droit. Aux feux/Au carrefour, tourne(z) à gauche/droite. C'est près/C'est en face/C'est à côté du/de l'/de la/des …		1a, 1b, 1c, 2a, 2b, 2c, 2d, 2e, 2f, 2h, 3a, 3b, 3c, 3e, 4a, 5a, 5d, 5e, 5f, 5i	1.3, 2.2–4, 3.1–3, 4.2–4
84–85 **6.3 Visite à Paris** Paris	Say what you are going to see and do during a visit to Paris; understand some information on the main tourist attractions in Paris; pronounce the r sound		The French r sound	le Centre Pompidou, le musée du Louvre, la cité des Sciences et de l'Industrie, la tour Eiffel, la cathédrale de Notre-Dame, la basilique du Sacré-Cœur, la place du Tertre, Montmartre, l'Arc de Triomphe, l'arche de la Défense, les bateaux-mouches	8W5, 8W8, 8S7, 8S8, 8L3, 8C1–R	1a, 1c, 2a, 2b, 2f, 2h, 2i, 3a, 3b, 3c, 3e, 4a, 4c, 4d, 5a, 5d, 5e, 5f, 5g, 5i	1.4, 2.2–3, 3.1, 3.3, 4.3–5
86–87 **6.4 C'était vraiment super!** A visit to France Souvenirs	Write about a visit to France; say how it was; say what souvenirs and presents you bought; improve your written work	c'est/c'était + adjective	Improving writing skills	Pour mon père/ma mère, j'ai acheté … Pour ton père/ta mère, tu as acheté … Pour son père/sa mère, il/elle a acheté … un crayon, un foulard, un porte-clés, un poster, un tee-shirt, une cravate, une poupée, une tasse, du parfum, des bonbons, des cartes postales	8T5, 8T6, 8T7 – R	1a, 1b, 1c, 2a, 2b, 2c, 2f, 2h, 2i, 2j, 3a, 3b, 3c, 3d, 3e, 4a, 4d, 5a, 5c, 5d, 5e, 5f, 5i	1.1, 1.4, 2.3, 3.1, 3.3, 4.1, 4.3–6
88–89 **6.5 La belle équipe, épisode 6** Soap story	Develop listening and reading skills via a soap story based on the language of the unit					1a, 1c, 2a, 2b, 2g, 2h, 2i, 3b, 3c, 3e, 4a, 4d, 5a, 5d, 5e, 5g, 5i	1.5, 2.4, 3.5
90 **Super-challenge!** An exchange visit to Strasbourg	Use a variety of tenses together within the same piece of work; improve dictionary use		Dictionary skills			1c, 2f, 2g, 2h, 2i, 2j, 3b, 3c, 3d, 3e, 4c, 4d, 5c, 5d, 5e, 5f, 5g, 5i	3.5–6, 4.5–6

National Curriculum

ÉQUIPE NOUVELLE 2 UNIT 6 MEDIUM TERM PLAN

About this unit: In this unit students work in the context of places in town and the main tourist attractions of Paris. They learn some new vocabulary for places in town as well as revising words they already know; they also learn how to understand and give directions, which revises the imperative. Progress continues to be made on different tenses: the unit practises the perfect tense, the imperfect (*c'était* + adjective), the future (*aller* + infinitive) and the present tense, and also provides opportunities for students to use a variety of tenses together within the same piece of work. There is a strong focus on dictionary skills, and students receive step-by-step guidance on how to improve their written work, including checking for errors. Pronunciation skills are further developed through work on the French *r* sound.

Framework objectives (reinforce)	Teaching and learning	Week-by-week overview (assuming 6 weeks' work or 10–12.5 hours)
8W5: verb tenses	Comparison of past, present and future tenses.	**Week 1** Introduction to unit objectives. Revise talking about what's available in town. Understand a publicity brochure. Improve dictionary skills.
8W7: dictionary detail	Look in detail at how certain words from the Dieppe text are recorded in a dictionary, e.g. use of abbreviations and examples.	
8W8: non-literal meanings	Compare the different meanings of *à* and *de* in the context of a letter about a weekend in Paris (*Je vais passer le week-end à Paris. Le train part de Dieppe à 8 h 38 et arrive à Paris à 11 h 40*). Compare also *on arrive à Paris* and *on arrive de Paris*.	**Week 2** Ask for directions. Understand and give directions. Revise the imperative.
8S7: present, past and future	Comparison of past, present and future tenses.	
8S8: using high-frequency words and punctuation clues	Prepositions change meaning: *il arrive à Paris, il arrive de Paris*.	**Week 3** Say what you are going to see and do during a visit to Paris. Understand some information on the main tourist attractions in Paris. Pronounce the *r* sound.
8T1: meanings in context	In text on Dieppe, look at words and phrases that have different meanings in different contexts, e.g. *chouette, boîte, pêche*.	
8T3: language and text types	Understand a publicity brochure.	**Week 4** Write about a visit to France, and say how it was using *c'était* + adjective. Say what souvenirs and presents you bought. Improve your written work.
8T4: dictionary use	Improve your dictionary skills.	
8T5: writing continuous text	Plan a description about a visit to France.	**Week 5** Develop listening and reading skills via a soap episode.
8T6: text as model and source	Students use a description of a visit to France as a model to write their own description.	
8T7: checking inflections and word order	Techniques for checking written work for errors.	**Week 6** *Super-challenge!* for more able students. Recycle language of the unit via *Encore*, *En plus* and *Point lecture* pages. Students check progress via the *Podium* self-assessment checklist in the Students' Book and on Feuille 87. Use the *Révisions* and *Contrôles* sections for formal assessment of student progress.
8L3: relaying gist and detail	Understand information about the main tourist attractions in Paris.	
8C1: historical facts	Information about the main tourist attractions in Paris.	
	Teaching and learning (additional)	
	Revise places in town. Directions. Buying souvenirs/presents.	

6 Une visite en France

Unit objectives
Contexts: town; directions; trip to France
Grammar: imperatives; *c'était* + adjective
Language learning: understanding a text; improving your dictionary skills; improving your writing
Pronunciation: the sound *r*
Cultural focus: Paris

Assessment opportunities
Listening: Students' Book, page 82, activity 1a; Students' Book, page 118, *En plus*, activity 2
Speaking: Students' Book, page 106, *Encore*, activity 3; Students' Book, page 118, *En plus*, activity 3

AT 3.3 **1** *Relie les textes et les images.*
Students match the postcard texts to the corresponding photos.

Answers: 1 b; 2 a; 3 d; 4 c

AT 3.2 **2a** *Trouve …*
Students search the postcard texts for the French translations of the English time expressions. Emphasize the importance of time phrases, because they determine the tense to be used – this links directly with the following activity.

Answers: a tous les jours; b aujourd'hui; c hier; d demain

AT 3.2 **2b** *Recopie les verbes dans la bonne colonne.*
Students identify all the present, past and future tense verbs in the postcard texts. This activity revises all the tenses that students have learned so far: the present tense, perfect tense, and the future tense formed with *aller* + infinitive. It also includes one phrase in the imperfect tense (*c'était*), which can be included in the *passé* column without further explanation.

Answers: présent: j'adore les animaux sauvages, la neige est fantastique, l'hôtel est à côté de l'hôpital, ça va, je m'amuse, il fait super beau, je fais de la natation, notre hôtel est bien situé, j'adore la capitale de la France, mon hôtel a une vue superbe, on est en face du métro; passé: j'ai vu des éléphants, j'ai fait du ski, je suis beaucoup tombé, j'ai visité le château, c'était intéressant; futur: je vais visiter le musée du Louvre

AT 3.2 **3a** *Relie le français et l'anglais.*
Students match the French to the English prepositions. Encourage them to find the phrases in the postcards to see how *de* changes in different situations. This leads directly on to the following revision activity.

Answers: 1 b; 2 a; 3 c

Follow-up activity:
OHT 26 could be cut up and the pictures used to practise the position phrases *à côté de*, *près de* and *en face de*. For example, begin with the pictures of the beach and park, and move them around to make a variety of sentences, e.g. *la plage est en face du parc, le parc est en face de la plage*. Stress the changes each time and see if students can identify the rule.

AT 4.2 **3b** *Recopie correctement.*
Students join the prepositional phrases and the nouns (places in town), to practise *de + le/la/l'/les*. Draw their attention to the *Rappel* panel, which focuses on this grammar point.

Answers: a en face de la piscine; b près du parc; c en face de l'hôpital; d à côté de l'église

6 Une visite en France

Planning Page

6.1 Qu'est-ce qu'il y a ici?

pages 80–81

Objectives

▶ Revise talking about what's available in town
▶ Understand a publicity brochure (**8T3 – R**)
▶ Improve your dictionary skills (**8W7, 8T1, 8T4 – R**)

Resources

Students' Book, pages 80–81
CD 2, tracks 39–41
Cassette 3, side 2
Encore/En plus Workbooks, page 54
OHT 26
Copymasters 88, 89 and 100

Key language

un château, un hôpital, un marché, un musée, un office de tourisme, un supermarché, un zoo
une banque, une boulangerie, une église, une mairie, une pharmacie, une plage, une poste
Est-ce qu'il y a … près d'ici?
Oui, il y a …
Non, il n'y a pas de/d' …
C'est loin?
Non/Oui, c'est à deux cents mètres/kilomètres.
C'est près du/de l'/de la/des …

Programme of Study reference

1a, 1c, 2a, 2b, 2c, 2d, 2f, 2g, 2h, 2i, 3b, 3c, 3d, 3e, 4a, 4c, 4d, 5a, 5d, 5e, 5f, 5g, 5i

Starters

▶ *À vos marques*, page 80.
▶ Copymaster 88 *À vos marques*, activity 1.
▶ When students are familiar with the places in town, use **OHT 26** for a variety of revision games, e.g. allow students 30 seconds to look at the OHT, then turn off the OHP and cover up some places with sticky notes. Turn the OHP back on again for students to guess which ones are missing. This is a good opportunity to practise the phrase *il n'y a pas de …*
▶ Display **OHT 26** again (or write the words for places in town on the board without their genders) and ask students to organize the places into two columns according to gender.

ICT suggestions

▶ Students design a poster or a PowerPoint® presentation saying what there is and what there isn't in their nearest town, using *il y a/il n'y a pas de …*
▶ Students could visit the Dieppe tourist office website (www.dieppetourisme.com) for further information about Dieppe.

Creative activities

▶ Students make up a rap to aid learning of the places in town, focusing particularly on gender.
▶ Students work in pairs or small groups to write a short tourist brochure for their nearest town, using ICT if possible.

Plenaries

▶ *Challenge!* page 81.
▶ Copymaster 89 *Challenge!* activity 1.
▶ Discuss how short sentences can be improved by the use of simple connectives, e.g. *Dans ma ville, il y a une piscine. Il n'y a pas de centre sportif. – Dans ma ville, il y a une piscine, mais il n'y a pas de centre sportif.*
▶ Play a memory game in small groups to see who can remember the most places in town, e.g.
A: *Dans ma ville, il y a une piscine.*
B: *Dans ma ville, il y a une piscine et une poste.*
C: *Dans ma ville, il y a une piscine, une poste et …*

Homework suggestions

▶ Students learn the spelling and gender of places in town. It might be worth brainstorming with the class to remind them of effective ways of learning vocabulary.
▶ Students prepare a tourist brochure for their own town.
▶ *Encore/En plus* Workbooks, page 54.

Une visite en France **6**

6.1 Qu'est-ce qu'il y a ici?

pages 80–81

À vos marques

AT 3.1 **a** *Relie les symboles aux Mots-clés. Qu'est-ce qu'il n'y a pas?*
Students match the words listed in the *Mots-clés* to the symbols representing places around town. They indicate which words are not featured among the symbols.
This activity provides an opportunity to revise places around town from *Équipe nouvelle 1* (pages 62 and 91 of the Students' Book) as well as introducing some new vocabulary.

Answers: a une banque; b une pharmacie; c une boulangerie; d une poste; e une mairie; f un hôpital; g un supermarché; h un marché; i un zoo; j un château (there are no symbols for *un musée, un office de tourisme, une église* and *une plage*)

AT 1.2 **b** *Écoute et vérifie.*
Students listen to the recording to check their answers.

CD 2, track 39 — page 80, À vos marques
Cassette 3, side 2

– Voici le plan de ma ville idéale.
  Voici la banque, c'est a …
  … et en face, il y a la pharmacie, b.
  À gauche, nous avons la boulangerie, c …
  … et à droite, il y a la poste, d.
  Voici la mairie, e …
  … et à côté de la mairie, il y a l'hôpital, f.
  À droite, il y a le supermarché, g …
  … et à gauche, il y a le marché, h.
  Voici le zoo, i …
  et puis, près du zoo, il y a un monument historique, le château, j. Bienvenue à Bonneville!
– Il n'y a pas d'église, de plage, de musée ou d'office de tourisme?
– Ah, non! J'ai oublié! Ah, zut!!!

Follow-up activities:
▶ Students could work in pairs to list as many places around town as they can remember (including those already learned in *Équipe nouvelle 1*), and to organize them into lists of masculine and feminine nouns.
▶ **OHT 26** could also be used at this point to revise the places in town. Use sticky notes to cover up certain places on the OHT, so that students have an opportunity to practise *il y a un/une* and *il n'y a pas de …*
▶ Project **OHT 26** onto a whiteboard and ask students to identify the genders of the places, circling the pictures in different colours according to whether they are masculine or feminine.
▶ Using **OHT 26** again with a blank overlay, add some distances in metres for each place on the OHT to practise the phrases (especially the pronunciation of *loin* and *mètres*) needed for activity **3**:
A: *Le musée, c'est loin?*
B: *Non, c'est à deux cents mètres.*

AT 1.3
AT 3.3 **1a** *Lis et écoute. Note cinq endroits en ville.*
Students listen to the conversation and follow the text in the Students' Book. They note down the five places around town that are mentioned.

Answers: la plage, un supermarché, l'office de tourisme, la pharmacie, le cinéma

CD 2, track 40 — page 80, activité 1a
Cassette 3, side 2

– Salut, Natacha!
– Salut! Je vous présente Mélanie. Elle vient de Suisse, mais elle est chez mon voisin pendant deux semaines.
– Bonjour, Mélanie. Tu aimes Dieppe?
– Oui, beaucoup. J'adore la plage! Mais je dois faire du shopping. Est-ce qu'il y a un bon supermarché près d'ici?
– Oui, il y a un supermarché à 200 mètres, à côté de l'office de tourisme.
– Et la pharmacie, c'est loin?
– Tu connais le cinéma? Il y a une pharmacie en face du cinéma.
– Merci. Bon, j'y vais … À bientôt!

AT 3.2 **1b** *Trouve …*
Students search the text for the French translations of the English phrases.

Answers: a Est-ce qu'il y a un bon supermarché près d'ici?; b à 200 mètres; c à côté de l'office de tourisme; d c'est loin?; e en face du cinéma

AT 1.3 **2a** *Écoute les cinq conversations et note la destination.*
Students listen to the five conversations and note down where each person is going.

Answers: see **2b** below

AT 1.3 **2b** *Réécoute. Note les distances. Quel est l'endroit le plus proche?*
Students listen again, this time noting down the distances. Make sure students keep a record of their answers: they will use the information gathered in this and the previous activity in order to carry out the role-plays in activity **3**.

Answers: 1 le musée: à 200 mètres; 2 la poste: à 50 mètres; 3 la plage: à deux kilomètres; 4 l'hôpital: à cinq kilomètres; 5 l'office de tourisme: à 100 mètres; the nearest place is *la poste*

6 Une visite en France

CD 2, track 41
Cassette 3, side 2
page 80, activité 2

1 – Pardon, monsieur. Est-ce que le musée est près d'ici?
  – Le musée? Oui, le musée est à 200 mètres à gauche.
  – Merci, monsieur.
2 – Excusez-moi, madame, la poste, c'est loin?
  – Non, la poste, c'est tout près, à 50 mètres à droite.
  – Merci, madame.
3 – Bonjour, monsieur. Où est la plage, s'il vous plaît?
  – La plage? C'est assez loin, c'est à deux kilomètres d'ici.
  – Il y a un bus qui va à la plage?
  – Oui … voilà … il arrive.
4 – Bonjour, madame. Où est l'hôpital, s'il vous plaît?
  – L'hôpital.
  – Oui, je dois aller à l'hôpital!
  – Mmm, l'hôpital, c'est loin …
  – C'est loin?
  – Oui, l'hôpital est à cinq kilomètres.
  – Cinq kilomètres! Aïe! Je prends un taxi …
5 – Excusez-moi, madame.
  – Oui, je peux vous aider?
  – Je voudrais aller à l'office de tourisme. C'est près d'ici?
  – Oui, l'office de tourisme est dans la mairie, rue du Port, à 100 mètres d'ici.

AT 2.3 3 *A choisit trois symboles et trois distances en secret. B pose les questions des Expressions-clés pour deviner les symboles. Vous avez 60 secondes.*
Working in pairs, students take turns to play a guessing game, asking and answering the questions from the *Expressions-clés*. Student A chooses a place in town and a distance, referring back to their answers from activities **2a** and **2b**; student B tries to work out what they have chosen, following the model provided; then the roles are reversed.

AT 3.4 4 *Lis les informations touristiques. Qu'est-ce qu'il y a à Dieppe? Fais une liste.*
Students read the Dieppe publicity brochure and list the attractions mentioned. More able students could go on to identify places that Dieppe doesn't have (according to the brochure), e.g. *il n'y a pas de patinoire*. These activities based on the publicity brochure reinforce Framework objective 8T3.

Answers: un château-musée, un centre culturel, une vidéothèque, une bibliothèque, un théâtre, une salle de danse, un cinéma, la Cité de la mer (un musée des techniques de pêche), un monument historique (les Tourelles), le port, la plage, une piscine chauffée, un mini-golf, des courts de tennis, une aire de jeux, des églises, une vieille ville, un marché, des cafés, des restaurants, des magasins, un casino, des salles de jeux, un parc, un centre sportif, des boîtes

Guide pratique

This section focuses on improving dictionary skills and reinforces Framework objectives **8W7**, **8T1** and **8T4**. It looks at words that have different meanings in different contexts.

1 Students are asked how they can tell what part of speech a word is, when they look it up in a dictionary or glossary.

Answers: Students should be aware of abbreviations such as n, adj, adv, v, etc., which are used to indicate parts of speech.

2 Students look up each word in a dictionary or glossary and note down its different meanings. They then choose the most appropriate meaning of each word for use in the Dieppe brochure. Students should recognize some of the words from earlier in the course.
Answers may vary here depending on the dictionaries used for this activity.

Answers: (most appropriate meanings for use in the Dieppe brochure are indicated in bold): a <u>pêche</u>: *nf* peach, **fishing**, fishery, fishing ground, *adj* peach-coloured; b <u>aire</u>: *nf* **area/ground**, floor, eyrie; c <u>boîte</u>: *nf* box, can/tin, **nightclub**; d <u>chouette</u>: *nf* owl, *adj* **great, fantastic**; e <u>front</u>: *nm* forehead, front/façade (of building), impudence, **seafront**, weather front, front (political movement); f <u>jeux</u>: *mpl* games/sports, **amusements, gambling**, card games

C100 Feuille 100 *Guide pratique 1* provides further activities to practise dictionary skills and could be used at this point.

W54 Page 54 of the *Encore* and *En plus* Workbooks provides further practice on places in town and could also be used here.

Challenge!

AT 4.2/3 **A** *Qu'est-ce qu'il y a dans une ville près de chez toi?*
Students list the attractions that are available in their own area. This might be a good opportunity to remind students of how to form noun plurals in French: most of the words in the *Mots-clés* (on Students' Book page 80) are straightforward and add an *-s* in the plural; the exceptions are *châteaux* and *hôpitaux*.

AT 2.3 **B** *Fais dix phrases, vraies ou fausses, sur ta ville. Ton/Ta partenaire trouve les erreurs!*
AT 4.3/4 Students make 10 statements, some of them correct and some incorrect, about what is and isn't available in their own area. Their partner must identify what is true and what is false. This could be done orally or in writing.

AT 4.4 **C** *Prépare un dépliant touristique pour une ville près de chez toi.*
Students create a tourist brochure for their own area, using ICT if appropriate. Encourage them to focus on using a wide variety of language, e.g. adjectives, connectives and linking phrases (*en face de la piscine, il y a …*).

Planning Page

6.2 C'est où, la plage?
pages 82–83

Objectives
▶ Ask for directions
▶ Understand and give directions

Resources
Students' Book, pages 82–83
CD 2, tracks 42–43; CD 3, track 38
Cassette 3, side 2; cassette 4, side 2
Encore/En plus Workbooks, page 55
OHTs 27A, 27B, 27C and 28
Copymasters 90, 92, 94, 96 and 98

Key language
C'est où, (le port)?
Tourne(z) à gauche/droite.
Prends/Prenez la première/deuxième/troisième rue à gauche/droite.
Va/Allez tout droit.
Aux feux/Au carrefour, tourne(z) à gauche/droite.
C'est près du/de l'/de la/des …
C'est en face du/de l'/de la/des …
C'est à côté du/de l'/de la/des …

Programme of Study reference
1a, 1b, 1c, 2a, 2b, 2c, 2d, 2e, 2f, 2h, 3a, 3b, 3c, 3e, 4a, 5a, 5d, 5e, 5f, 5i

Starters
▶ *À vos marques*, page 82.
▶ Hide an object in the class after sending a student out. The others have to give directions in French in order to lead the student to the hidden object.
▶ Play *Jacques a dit* (Simon says) with the class. Agree on directions first, e.g. *Allez tout droit* – both arms together pointing forwards; *prenez la deuxième rue à gauche* – left arm out with two fingers pointing).

ICT suggestions
▶ Students could create a text with gaps (as in *Challenge!* activity **A**) for other students to complete. If the texts are saved, they will be a useful departmental resource for other groups.
▶ Students use ICT (e.g. clip art, drawing programs, scanned images) to create their treasure island maps: see Creative activities below.

Creative activities
▶ Students prepare and perform short sketches (including bringing in a key prop), as in the cartoons in the *Zoom grammaire* section (Students' Book page 83). Other students watch the performances and note the destination and directions.
▶ Students design their own treasure island map, modelled on page 55 of the *Encore/En plus* Workbooks, with directions leading to the buried treasure. They exchange their map with a partner, who tries to work out where the treasure is hidden.

Plenaries
▶ *Challenge!* page 83.
▶ Hold a class discussion on the imperative, focusing on the need for different forms of the imperative in different contexts. Students could discuss in pairs first, before discussing the issue as a whole class.
▶ Draw some symbols of places in the town (next to and opposite each other) on the board for students to make up sentences, e.g. *La piscine est en face du port.*

Homework suggestions
▶ Students write directions to places within the school, e.g. how to get from the French classroom to the hall. You may need to provide them with a few additional phrases, depending on the layout of your school, e.g. *Montez/Descendez l'escalier, traversez la cour.*
▶ In class, students work in pairs to write a conversation asking for and receiving directions; they learn it for homework. The conversations could then be performed in the following lesson. Encourage more able students to use a greater variety of language, e.g. *aux feux, au carrefour*.
▶ *Encore/En plus* Workbooks, page 55.

6 Une visite en France

6.2 C'est où, la plage?
pages 82–83

À vos marques

AT 3.1
a *Regarde et mémorise le plan de Dieppe pendant deux minutes.*
Students study the street plan and the key for a couple of minutes, attempting to memorize the location of the places. This starter aims to familiarize students with the map, which will be crucial for the direction-giving activities that follow on this spread.

AT 2.2/3
b *B couvre la légende. A pose cinq questions et B indique les destinations sur le plan.*
Working in pairs, one student questions the other on the location of each place, e.g. *C'est où, la piscine?* Without looking at the key, the partner tries to point out where each place is, e.g. *Voilà. La piscine, c'est le numéro quatre.* They score a point for each place correctly identified.

AT 2.2/3
c *Changez de rôles.*
Students swap roles.

Presentation

▶ Use **OHT 27A** to present and practise the direction phrases. It is worth focusing on the first seven symbols first, before progressing to the other position phrases.

▶ The overlays **27B** and **27C** focus on the different imperative forms (*tu*, *vous*): it is important to introduce these separately so that students are not confused. With less able students, perhaps focus on one form of the imperative only for speaking activities: the *vous* form is the most useful as students are more likely to ask for or give directions to someone they don't know well.

▶ **OHT 28** is also available for use during work on this spread to further practise asking for and giving directions. Model short conversations with the class and allow students to practise in pairs.

▶ Using **OHT 28** again, give directions to a place on the map and ask students to identify the destination. If students find it difficult to keep track of the route on the map, project the OHT onto a whiteboard or use a blank OHT as an overlay, so that you or a student can trace the route as directions are given. Students could then do this activity in pairs.

AT 1.3
1a *Quatre personnes sont à Dieppe et regardent le plan. Écoute. Qui va à l'office de tourisme? Qui va au centre culturel? Au mini-golf? À l'église St Rémy?*
Students listen to the four people describing their routes. They follow each route on the map to find out where each person is going. Remind students to start from *Vous êtes ici* each time. This could be a paired listening activity, with students tracing each route with a finger on the map.

Answers: 1 l'église St Rémy; 2 l'office de tourisme; 3 le mini-golf; 4 le centre culturel

CD 2, track 42
Cassette 3, side 2
page 82, activité 1a

1 – Bon, voilà le plan … Vous êtes ici … Alors, je vais tout droit et je prends la troisième rue à droite. Oui, la troisième rue à droite. Puis, c'est tout près, à gauche. Bon, on y va.

2 – Tiens, voilà un plan de Dieppe! Alors, je vais tout droit et je prends la troisième rue à droite. Oui, la troisième rue à droite. Puis je vais tout droit … et c'est la cinquième rue à droite. C'est tout près, à gauche, devant le port.

3 – Oh là là, je suis perdue … Ah, voilà un plan! Alors … je vais tout droit, tout droit, tout droit, jusqu'à la plage. Je tourne à droite et continue tout droit. C'est à côté de la piscine, à droite.

4 – Je vais regarder le plan, je crois. Bon, je prends la deuxième rue à droite. Puis je vais tout droit, passe l'aire de jeux et c'est à droite, à côté du cinéma.

AT 2.2/3
1b *Travaille avec un(e) partenaire. A pose une question sans regarder le plan. B donne les explications et A les note, puis regarde le plan pour vérifier.*
Working in pairs, students take turns to ask for and give directions to places on the Dieppe map. Partner A asks questions without looking at the map; partner B refers to the map in order to give the directions, while A notes down what B says; the two then check A's notes against the map. The roles are then reversed.
Students could use *tu* forms only or the dialogues could be extended to include *vous* forms, polite greetings, etc., e.g. *Excusez-moi, monsieur. C'est où, le port, s'il vous plaît?* Encourage more able students to provide as much detail as possible in their directions.

AT 1.3
AT 3.3
2a *Écoute et lis. Mélanie veut aller où?*
Students listen to and read the conversation, in which Mélanie is being given directions. They note down her destination.

Answer: le château-musée

CD 2, track 43
Cassette 3, side 2
page 83, activité 2a

– Excusez-moi, monsieur. C'est où, le château-musée, s'il vous plaît?
– Le château-musée? C'est assez loin. Prenez la deuxième rue à gauche, puis la première rue à droite. Allez tout droit pendant deux cents mètres. Au carrefour, tournez à droite. Puis, aux feux, tournez à gauche. Allez tout droit et le château-musée est à gauche à côté du café et en face de la pharmacie. D'accord?
– Euh, ben … merci, monsieur.
– Au revoir.
– Oh là là! C'est compliqué à Dieppe. Je crois que je vais acheter un plan.

Follow-up activity: Students could act out the conversation in pairs, focusing on pronunciation and intonation.

AT 3.3 **2b** *Dessine le chemin pour Mélanie.*
Referring back to the text of **2a**, students draw a sketch of Mélanie's route. If appropriate, they could work on this in pairs and then compare their sketch with that of another pair. Refer students to the *Expressions-clés* or to the glossary for the meanings of the new words (*carrefour, feux*).

AT 2.3/4 **2c** *Adapte la conversation.*
AT 4.3/4 Working individually, students adapt the conversation from **2a**. Encourage them to make their conversation as long as possible and to give detailed directions. Students then work with a partner to read out their conversation: the author should play the role of the person giving the directions, because he/she will be more familiar with this section, having written it.

Follow-up activity: The conversations from activity **2c** could be used to give the class additional listening practice. Pairs could read out the texts while the class listen and either draw a sketch map of the route or note the destination.

Zoom grammaire

This grammar section revises the imperative, which was taught in Unit 2 in the context of health and fitness.

1 Students consider the uses of the imperative, referring back to Unit 2 (page 25) to check their answer.

Answer: students should be aware that the imperative is used to give instructions and advice

2 Students list the imperatives according to whether they are the *tu* or the *vous* form.

Answers: tu: tourne, va, prends; vous: tournez, allez, prenez

3 Students complete the speech bubbles using the correct imperative forms.

Answers: conversation 1: va, tourne, prends; conversation 2: prenez, tournez, allez

Refer students to the grammar section on page 143 of the Students' Book for further information on the imperative.

C98 Feuille 98 *Grammaire 1* provides further practice of the imperative and could be used together with the *Zoom grammaire* section.

C90 Activity 1 on Feuille 90 *Écoute Encore* provides additional listening practice on directions and could also be used at this point.

C92 Further speaking practice on directions is provided on Feuille 92 *Parle Encore*.

C94 Feuilles 94 *Lis et écris Encore 1* and 96 *Lis et écris En plus 1*
C96 provide reading and writing practice on directions and could be used towards the end of this spread.

W55 Page 55 of the *Encore* and *En plus* Workbooks also provides additional reading and writing practice on directions.

Challenge!

AT 3.2 **A** *Recopie et complète les explications.*
AT 4.2 Students copy out and complete the directions.

Answers: Sortez de l'office de tourisme. Tournez <u>à</u> gauche et <u>prenez</u> la deuxième <u>rue</u> à droite. <u>Allez</u> tout droit. L'église St Jacques <u>est</u> près du cinéma.

AT 3.3 **B** *Commence au point "Vous êtes ici" sur le plan de Dieppe, choisis une destination en secret et écris des explications.*
AT 4.3/4 *Échange-les avec ton/ta partenaire. Il/Elle peut deviner la destination?*
Referring back to the Dieppe street map, students choose a destination and write directions to it, starting from *Vous êtes ici*. They exchange their directions with a partner, who follows the route and works out the destination.

AT 4.4 **C** *Écris à ton correspondant/ta correspondante comment aller de chez toi au collège. Quels mots tu changes si tu écris à un adulte?*
Students write a letter to a penfriend giving directions from their home to school. They then show how they would adapt the letter if they were writing a formal letter to an adult instead of to a friend.

6 Une visite en France

Planning Page

6.3 Visite à Paris
pages 84–85

Objectives
- Say what you are going to see and do during a visit to Paris (8W5, 8W8, 8S7, 8S8 – R)
- Understand some information on the main tourist attractions in Paris (8L3, 8C1 – R)
- Pronounce the *r* sound

Resources
Students' Book, pages 84–85
CD 2, tracks 44–46; CD 3, tracks 39 and 42
Cassette 3, side 2; cassette 4, side 2
Encore/En plus Workbooks, page 56
OHT 29
Copymasters 88, 90 and 102

Key language
le Centre Pompidou
le musée du Louvre
la cité des Sciences et de l'Industrie
la tour Eiffel
la cathédrale de Notre-Dame
la basilique du Sacré-Cœur
la place du Tertre, Montmartre
l'Arc de Triomphe
l'arche de la Défense
les bateaux-mouches

Programme of Study reference
1a, 1c, 2a, 2b, 2f, 2h, 2i, 3a, 3b, 3c, 3e, 4a, 4c, 4d, 5a, 5d, 5e, 5f, 5g, 5i

Starters
- *À vos marques*, page 84.
- Copymaster 88 *À vos marques*, activities 2a and 2b.
- As a quick warm-up activity, call out the sights listed in the *Mots-clés* section (on Students' Book page 84) and ask students to point to the relevant pictures as you say them. Students could work in pairs to see who can be the quickest to point to the correct picture.
- Use **OHT 29** to match the pictures and words of the main tourist attractions in Paris. Perhaps do this as a timed challenge: which student can place the labels next to the pictures in the shortest time?

ICT suggestions
- Students prepare a poster for one or more of the Paris sights from the spread, searching the Internet for pictures and adding their own labels and opinions, e.g. *C'est super!* More able students could search for additional facts about Paris (as in the *Point culture* section) and incorporate these into a classroom display.
- Students could find the opening times of another Paris sight (see the Eiffel Tower times in activity **3**) and prepare their own true/false statements to test a partner. The Paris tourist office website (www.parisinfo.com) gives information on/links to all the attractions mentioned on this spread.

Creative activities
- Students design a poster to advertise one or more of the Paris tourist attractions: see ICT suggestions above.
- Students work together in pairs or small groups to prepare a short radio advert encouraging tourists to visit Paris.

Plenaries
- *Challenge!* page 85.
- Describe some of the famous places in Paris for students to identify (see transcript for activity **1a**), e.g. *C'est un musée moderne – le Centre Pompidou*. More able students may like to describe one of the places for the rest of the class to guess.
- After activity **2b**, students could evaluate the written work of their peers, focusing on criteria previously agreed: content, range of language, accuracy, presentation, etc.

Homework suggestions
- Students learn the main Paris sights, focusing particularly on good pronunciation of the *r* sound.
- Activity **2b** is ideally suited as a homework activity. Students should be encouraged to draft and redraft their work and to focus on agreed criteria (see plenary suggestion above).
- *Encore/En plus* Workbooks, page 56.

Une visite en France 6

6.3 Visite à Paris
pages 84–85

À vos marques

AT 3.1 *Tu reconnais les photos de Paris? Relie les photos et les Mots-clés.*

The cultural information about Paris given on this spread provides an opportunity to reinforce Framework objective **8C1**.

In this starter activity, students match the photos of Paris attractions to the *Mots-clés*. Brainstorm what they know about each place, then students could research additional information for homework. If you have access to *France Live**, see pages 48–49.

(*France Live is published by Oxford University Press. See the latest Oxford University Press Modern Languages catalogue for details.)

Answers: a le Centre Pompidou; b l'arche de la Défense; c la cathédrale de Notre-Dame; d la tour Eiffel; e l'Arc de Triomphe; f la place du Tertre, Montmartre; g le musée du Louvre; h la cité des Sciences et de l'Industrie; i les bateaux-mouches; j la basilique du Sacré-Cœur

AT 1.4 **1a** *Écoute. C'est quelle photo?*

This activity provides an opportunity to reinforce Framework objective **8L3** (relaying gist and detail). Students listen to the tour guide talking about the Paris tourist attractions and indicate the photo that represents each one. You could pause the recording after each item so that students can check their answers; at the same time, you could provide some simple information about each place. Focus strongly on pronunciation, particularly of the places that students will already know in English, e.g. the Eiffel Tower, Notre-Dame.

Answers: 1 d; 2 e; 3 b; 4 j; 5 f; 6 h; 7 a; 8 g; 9 c; 10 i

CD 2, track 44 — page 84, activité 1a
Cassette 3, side 2

1 – Bienvenue à bord du bus touristique … Amusez-vous bien! Regardez à gauche. Vous voyez le monument le plus célèbre de Paris. C'est une tour de 320 mètres, avec un restaurant panoramique! C'est la tour Eiffel.
2 – Maintenant, regardez à droite. Au bout des Champs-Élysées, vous voyez un monument historique! Une arche construite pour fêter les victoires de Napoléon. C'est l'Arc de Triomphe.
3 – Maintenant, nous sommes à l'ouest de Paris, dans un quartier moderne avec beaucoup de bureaux et de magasins. Regardez cette grande arche! C'est l'arche de la Défense.
4 – Nous sommes maintenant à Montmartre. En face de vous, il y a une église blanche où il y a des messes tous les jours. C'est la basilique du Sacré-Cœur.
5 – Nous sommes toujours à Montmartre. Cette place est idéale pour se relaxer: il y a des cafés et des restaurants bien sûr, mais il y a aussi beaucoup d'artistes qui travaillent. C'est amusant! C'est la place du Tertre.
6 – Bienvenue dans le quartier où la technologie est super et où il y a un grand cinéma dans la Géode. C'est la cité des Sciences et de l'Industrie.
7 – Regardez ce bâtiment moderne, avec beaucoup de couleurs! Si vous aimez l'art moderne, ce centre est idéal pour vous! C'est le Centre Pompidou.
8 – Vous aimez les musées? Ce bâtiment contient beaucoup de peintures célèbres, comme la Joconde, "The Mona Lisa". C'est le musée du Louvre.
9 – Vous avez vu le film avec Quasimodo, le bossu qui habite dans cette grande église dans le centre de Paris, près de la Seine? Eh bien, l'église, la voilà, c'est la cathédrale Notre-Dame.
10 – Vous aimez l'eau? Vous voulez faire un tour sur la Seine? C'est fantastique, regardez! Ce sont les bateaux-mouches.

Follow-up activities:

▶ To focus on the detail of the tour guide commentary, write on the board or OHP some key phrases relating to each extract, e.g. *Vous aimez l'eau?*, *C'est une tour de 320 mètres*, etc. and ask students to guess which tourist attraction each phrase refers to. Play the recording again so that students can check their answers and hear the phrases in the correct context.
▶ **OHT 29** can be used to provide further practice of the sights of Paris. The pictures can be cut up and used for matching games with the words, for a Bingo game, for memory games (good preparation for activity **1b**), etc.
▶ Using the cut-up pictures from **OHT 29** again, place one of the pictures on the OHP, making sure it is out of focus, and ask students to identify it, e.g. *C'est la tour Eiffel? Non, c'est la place du Tertre à Montmartre.*

AT 2.2/3 **1b** *Jeu de mémoire. Qu'est-ce que tu vas visiter à Paris?*
Students play a memory game in pairs to practise *Je vais visiter …* with the Paris tourist attractions. As the main focus here is pronunciation, it might be appropriate to complete the *Ça se dit comme ça!* panel (see page 200) beforehand. This activity might be suitable for peer-assessment: students could assess different aspects of each other's performance, e.g. pronunciation, memory. The use of *aller* + infinitive here and in activities **2a** and **2b**, together with the future tense and past tense activities in *Challenge!* **A**, **B** and **C**, reinforces Framework objectives **8W5** and **8S7**.

Point culture

This section provides some facts about the population of Paris and the number of visitors to the city. Students are asked to recall what else they have learned about Paris and its famous monuments.

AT 1.4 **2a** *Natacha parle avec Mélanie. Écoute et mets les lettres des images à droite dans le bon ordre.*
Students listen to Mélanie's plans for her visit to Paris and note down the pictures in the order in which they are mentioned.

Answers: b, a, f, d, c, e, g, h

6 Une visite en France

CD 2, track 45
Cassette 3, side 2
page 85, activité 2a

– Salut, Mélanie! Qu'est-ce que tu vas faire ce week-end?
– Ce week-end, j'ai de la chance. Je vais visiter Paris!
– Super! Tu vas prendre le train?
– Oui, le train de Dieppe part à 8 h 38 et arrive à Paris à 11 h 40.
– Tu vas aller à l'hôtel?
– Non, je vais aller chez mon cousin.
– C'est pratique. Et qu'est-ce que tu vas faire à Paris?
– Beaucoup de choses! Je vais visiter le Centre Pompidou parce que j'adore l'art moderne.
– L'art moderne? Ah non, moi, je déteste ça!
– Je vais aussi visiter le musée du Louvre et la cathédrale de Notre-Dame.
– Bonne idée! Mais tu dois absolument faire un tour en bateau aussi.
– Oui, je vais prendre un bateau-mouche le samedi soir, je crois, pour voir Paris de nuit!
– Tu vas monter en haut de la tour Eiffel?
– Oui, mais je vais prendre l'escalier. C'est bon pour la forme.
– Tu vas manger au restaurant au sommet de la tour Eiffel?
– Non! C'est trop cher!
– Et dimanche, qu'est-ce que tu vas faire?
– Je vais aller à la messe au Sacré-Cœur et je vais acheter des souvenirs à Montmartre – des cartes postales, des posters …
– Les artistes font des caricatures amusantes sur la place du Tertre. Tu vas y aller?
– Oui, bien sûr! Et puis c'est tout, je crois, parce que je dois rentrer dimanche soir.
– Ben, bon week-end!
– Merci. À bientôt!

AT 4.3/4 **2b** *Continue la lettre de Mélanie.*
Students are given the opening lines of a letter from Mélanie to her mother, describing what she plans to do during her visit to Paris. They complete the letter, using the information from activity **2a**. Some will find this a very challenging writing task, so it could be done in pairs or small groups with students drafting and redrafting their work at the computer.

The letter in this activity provides an opportunity to reinforce Framework objectives **8W8** (non-literal meanings) and **8S8** (high-frequency words and punctuation clues). Look at the beginning of the letter and ask students to give the different meanings of *à* and the meaning of *de* in this context. Ask them to consider the phrases *on arrive à Paris* and *on arrive de Paris* and then to explain how high-frequency words can change the meaning of a sentence.

AT 3.3 **3** *Mélanie a surfé sur Internet (www.tour-eiffel.fr). Lis les phrases. Vrai (V) ou faux (F)?*
Students read the statements about opening times at the Eiffel Tower and compare them with the details obtained from the Internet. They indicate whether each statement is true or false.

Answers: a vrai; b faux; c vrai; d faux

Follow-up activity: Students could use the Internet to research another Paris attraction and could prepare questions or true/false statements to test a partner. The Paris tourist office website (www.parisinfo.com) gives information on/links to all the attractions mentioned on this spread.

Ça se dit comme ça!

This section focuses on pronunciation of the French *r* sound.

1a Students listen to the recorded details of Paris tourist attractions while following the text in the Students' Book. Each letter *r* is highlighted in the text, apart from one (in the verb *visiter*): students are asked to consider why this one is not highlighted.

Answer: It is not highlighted because it is not pronounced – students should be aware that the infinitive ending *-er* has the same sound as *é* or *ez*.

CD 2, track 46
Cassette 3, side 2
page 85, Ça se dit comme ça! activité 1

Bienvenue à Paris! C'est une ville romantique, historique, célèbre!
On doit absolument visiter la tour Eiffel, Notre-Dame, le Sacré-Cœur, Montmartre, l'Arc de Triomphe, le musée du Louvre, le Centre Pompidou.

1b Students listen again and read the text aloud. This activity could be used for peer-assessment. There are 13 examples of the *r* sound in the text: students award each other a point for each one pronounced well.

C102 Feuille 102 *Ça se dit comme ça!* provides further practice of the French *r* sound.

C90 Activity 2a on Feuille 90 *Écoute Encore* provides additional listening practice based on Paris tourist attractions and could be used at this point.

W56 Page 56 of the *Encore* and *En plus* Workbooks provides further reading practice on Paris tourist attractions and could also be used here.

Une visite en France

Challenge!

AT 4.3/4

A *Tu vas à Paris. Qu'est-ce que tu vas faire? Écris six phrases.*
Students write six sentences stating what they are going to do during an imaginary visit to Paris.

AT 4.4/5

B *Tu vas passer un week-end à Paris. Qu'est-ce que tu vas faire? Si possible, donne des raisons.*
Students write a longer text outlining their plans for an imaginary visit to Paris, giving reasons for their choice of activities.

AT 4.4/5

C *Qu'est-ce que Mélanie a fait à Paris? Décris sa visite.*
Students write a description of Mélanie's visit to Paris, using the third person singular of the perfect tense.

6 Une visite en France

Planning Page

6.4 C'était vraiment super!

pages 86–87

Objectives

- Write about a visit to France (**8T5, 8T6 – R**)
- Say how it was
- Say what souvenirs/presents you bought
- Improve your written work (**8T7 – R**)

Resources

Students' Book, pages 86–87
CD 2, tracks 47–48; CD 3, tracks 40–41
Cassette 3, side 2; cassette 4, side 2
Encore/En plus Workbooks, pages 57, 58 and 59
OHTs 29, 30 and 31
Copymasters 89, 90, 91, 93, 95, 97, 99 and 101

Key language

Pour mon père/ma mère, j'ai acheté …
Pour ton père/ta mère, tu as acheté …
Pour son père/sa mère, il/elle a acheté …
un crayon, un foulard, un porte-clés, un poster, un tee-shirt
une cravate, une poupée, une tasse
du parfum
des bonbons, des cartes postales

Programme of Study reference

1a, 1b, 1c, 2a, 2b, 2c, 2f, 2h, 2i, 2j, 3a, 3b, 3c, 3d, 3e, 4a, 4d, 5a, 5c, 5d, 5e, 5f, 5i

Starters

- *À vos marques*, page 86.
- Reuse **OHT 29** to practise the phrase *Le week-end dernier, j'ai visité …* in preparation for describing activities in the past tense on this spread. As a tourist attraction is mentioned, remove the picture, so that all the key language is revised. If appropriate, the phrase *je suis allé(e) à …* could be practised, too, and opinions could be added, e.g. *C'était super!*
- Use **OHT 31** to play a variety of games to practise the souvenir vocabulary, e.g. cover the OHT with a piece of paper with a small hole cut out. Students try to guess the souvenir item that is partly showing – the odder the angle the better, perhaps even placing **OHT 31** upside down!

ICT suggestions

- Students draft and redraft their writing work for the *Guide pratique* section and *Challenge!* activities on this spread.
- Students word-process a dossier of language learned, using colour to highlight the differences in gender: *un/une/des, mon/ma/mes*, etc.
- Using an appropriate ICT package, students prepare the mind map for the writing activity suggested in the *Guide pratique* (see Students' Book page 87).
- Students prepare a PowerPoint® presentation to describe a past holiday (see activity **6**).

Creative activities

- Students design a postcard from a holiday. The picture on the front could be drawn by students or clip art/magazine pictures/holiday brochures/old postcards could be used. Students write the text of the postcard on a separate piece of paper (postcard-style). The pictures and texts can then be used for a display, perhaps with a reading quiz based on the postcards, or as a matching activity where groups of students read the postcard texts and match them to the appropriate pictures.
- Students record an interview with a partner about a recent holiday (real or imaginary). If necessary, brainstorm possible questions with the students first, e.g. *Où es-tu allé(e)? Tu as acheté des souvenirs?* This is a useful activity to recycle language from Unit 5. The recorded interviews can be used as additional listening practice for the rest of the class.

Plenaries

- *Challenge!* page 87.
- Copymaster 89 *Challenge!* activity 2.
- Play the game *Qu'est-ce qui manque?* using the cut-up souvenir pictures on **OHT 31**. Display the souvenirs and ask students to study them carefully. Then switch off the OHP and remove an item. Switch the OHP back on and ask students to identify which item has gone. Encourage them to respond using full sentences, e.g. *J'ai acheté le tee-shirt!*
- Write a word on the board, e.g. *Paris*. Ask a student to come to the board and add an extra word (or words) to make a phrase, e.g. *À Paris*. Another student then comes to the board to lengthen the phrase further, e.g. *À Paris, le week-end dernier, …* and so on. Encourage students to use connectives, adjectives and opinions. A follow-up activity might be to write a single word on the board and to give students one minute to see who can come up with the longest sentence containing the word.

Homework suggestions

- Students learn the souvenir vocabulary (meaning, pronunciation, gender and spelling). Encourage them to try out different ways of learning the vocabulary (e.g. making a Pairs game, typing up the words on the computer, teaching someone else, making up a rap) and discuss the effectiveness of the different methods in a following lesson.
- Following classwork (see suggestion below after activity **1c**), make a photocopy of **OHT 30** and ask students to annotate it with a key, e.g. underline in green all past tense expressions, circle all adjectives, highlight all time phrases/connectives.
- *Encore/En plus* Workbooks, page 57.

6.4 C'était vraiment super!

pages 86–87

À vos marques

AT 4.1 *Fais une liste d'adjectifs en deux minutes! Compare avec ton/ta partenaire. Qui a la liste la plus longue?*
This activity aims to refresh students' memories of opinions in preparation for work on this spread. Students have two minutes to note down as many adjectives/opinions as they can, e.g. *intéressant, ennuyeux*, etc. The activity follows the "Think – Pair – Share" model: each student works individually at first, then pairs up with another student to compare and share answers. Each pair could then join with another pair to share even more answers. By the end of the activity, each student should have a long list of opinion words.

AT 3.3 **1a** *Trouve la bonne photo pour chaque jour.*
Students read Mélanie's holiday diary and match each day to a photo.

Answers: photo a: samedi; photo b: vendredi; photo c: mercredi; photo d: jeudi

AT 3.1 **1b** *Lis le texte et note tous les adjectifs. Compare avec ta liste d'À vos marques.*
Students list all the adjectives used by Mélanie in her holiday diary. They compare these with their own list in the *À vos marques* activity.

Answers: mal, froid, marrant, intéressant, délicieux, cher, fantastique, historique, génial

AT 2.3 **1c** *A pose des questions. B répond de mémoire!*
In pairs, students take turns to ask each other questions about Mélanie's activities. The person answering the questions must try to do so from memory, with the Students' Book closed.
Although the model question and answer in the Students' Book uses the third person singular, less able students could ask questions using *tu* and give their answers using the *je* form, enabling them to lift the language straight from Mélanie's text. Instead of doing the activity from memory, they could be allowed to refer to Mélanie's text.

Follow-up activities:
Use **OHT 30** (an enlarged version of Mélanie's diary from Students' Book page 86) to focus on use of language. The following suggestions may be helpful:
▶ Project the OHT onto a whiteboard or use a blank overlay to underline key language, focusing on one aspect at a time, e.g. adjectives, past tense expressions, time phrases, connectives, opinions, places in the town.
▶ When students are familiar with the text, use small pieces of paper or blobs of putty adhesive to cover up parts of the diary. Students try to read the text aloud.
▶ Turn off the OHP and ask students simple questions, e.g. *Elle est allée en ville quel jour?* Turn the OHP back on for students to check their answers.

AT 4.3-5 **2** *Imagine les trois derniers jours de Mélanie à Dieppe. Continue son journal.*
Before students begin this activity, brainstorm some useful phrases in the perfect tense. You could use a "Think – Pair – Share" approach, similar to that described in the *À vos marques* activity. A list of phrases could be left on display, on the board or OHP, for students to refer to if necessary. Students imagine what Mélanie did during her final three days in Paris. They continue her diary, using the perfect tense. Encourage students to look back at the previous spread if they need some ideas.
Students may find it helpful to work on the *Zoom grammaire* section (see below) before doing this activity.

Zoom grammaire

This section focuses on expressing opinions using *c'est* and *c'était* followed by an adjective.

1 Students read the two speech bubbles and work out the difference between *c'est* and *c'était*.

Answer: C'est refers to the present tense; *c'était* refers to what something was like in the past.

2 Students copy out the sentences, filling in the gaps with *c'est* or *c'était*.

Answers: a c'était; b c'est; c c'est; d c'était; e c'était; f c'était

Refer students to the grammar section on page 143 of the Students' Book for further information on *c'était* + adjective.

C99 Feuille 99 *Grammaire 2* could be used at this point. It focuses on the perfect tense and the use of *c'était* to express opinions in the past tense.

W58 Further practice of these grammar points is provided on page 58 of the *Encore* and *En plus* Workbooks

AT 1.1 / AT 3.1 **3** *Relie les Expressions-clés et les images. Puis écoute et vérifie.*
Students match the souvenir items listed in the *Expressions-clés* to their corresponding pictures. They then listen to the recording to check their answers.

Answers: see transcript below

CD 2, track 47
Cassette 3, side 2
page 87, activité 3

a – un tee-shirt
b – des cartes postales
c – un poster
d – un foulard
e – du parfum
f – des bonbons
g – une poupée
h – une tasse
i – une cravate
j – un crayon
k – un porte-clés

6 Une visite en France

Follow-up activities: Use **OHT 31** to practise the vocabulary for souvenir items: see Starter and Plenary suggestions on the Planning Page. See also page 17 of the Introduction for further ideas on how to present and practise new language using OHTs or flashcards.

AT 1.4 **4** *Écoute. Quels souvenirs est-ce que Mélanie a acheté et pour qui?*
Students listen to Mélanie talking about the souvenirs she has bought. They note down what she has bought and for whom. Note that Mélanie does not actually say what she has bought for Natacha, so students have to work it out by a process of elimination: it is the only item in the picture that has not yet been mentioned.

Answers: mère: parfum, tasse; père: cravate (moderne), porte-clés; grand-mère: foulard (en soie); copine/Nadia: poupée; "pour moi": tee-shirt, poster, cartes postales, crayon; Natacha: bonbons

CD 2, track 48   page 87, activité 4
Cassette 3, side 2

– Salut, Natacha!
– Salut! Tu pars ce soir?
– Oui, c'est ça.
– Tu as acheté des souvenirs?
– Oui, bien sûr! J'ai acheté beaucoup de souvenirs et de cadeaux! Pour ma mère, j'ai acheté du parfum et une tasse.
– Et pour ton père?
– Je lui ai acheté une cravate moderne et un porte-clés!
– Et quoi d'autre?
– Pour ma grand-mère, j'ai acheté un foulard en soie. C'était cher!
– Mais c'est une bonne idée!
– Et pour ma copine, Nadia, j'ai acheté une poupée. Elle a une belle collection de poupées.
– Et pour toi?
– Pour moi? À Paris, j'ai acheté un tee-shirt, un poster, des cartes postales, un crayon … et quelque chose pour toi.
– Pour moi?
– Oui, voilà.
– C'est gentil, Mélanie. Merci beaucoup!

AT 2.3 **5** *Imagine. Tu rentres de vacances en France. Qu'est-ce que tu as acheté?*
Students imagine they have just returned from a trip to France and have brought back souvenirs for friends and family. They tell their partner what they have bought and for whom.

AT 4.4/5 **6** *Écris une lettre à ton correspondant français/ta correspondante française pour décrire tes dernières vacances. Voir Guide pratique.*
Students imagine they are writing a letter to a French penfriend about a recent holiday (real or imaginary). Refer them to the step-by-step advice given in *Guide pratique*. This activity, together with the *Guide pratique* panel, reinforces Framework objectives **8T5**, **8T6** and **8T7**.

Guide pratique

This section gives guidance on how students can improve their written work. Encourage them to follow this systematic advice when they do any piece of writing, drafting and redrafting their work (on computer, if possible).

C101 Feuille 101 *Guide pratique 2* provides further activities to give students practice in drafting and redrafting their written work.

C90 Activity 2b on Feuille 90 *Écoute Encore* provides additional listening practice on the vocabulary for souvenirs and could be used at this point.

C91 Feuille 91 *Écoute En plus* could also be used here. It provides extended listening practice on describing a past holiday and future holiday plans.

C93 Feuille 93 *Parle En plus* provides speaking practice on a wide variety of topics drawn from the whole of *Équipe nouvelle 2*. It could be used at this point or later in the unit.

C95 Extra reading and writing practice on describing a past holiday is provided on Feuille 95 *Lis et écris Encore 2* and
C97 Feuille 97 *Lis et écris En plus 2*.

W57 Page 57 of the *Encore* and *En plus* Workbooks provides additional reading and writing practice in this context.

W59 Page 59 of the *Encore* and *En plus* Workbooks draws together much of the language of the whole unit. It could be used at any point from now on.

Challenge!

AT 4.3 **A** *Relis les textes de la page 86. Maintenant, à toi! Tu es en vacances à Dieppe. Écris une carte postale.*
Students look back at Mélanie's diary on page 86 and use one of the short texts as a model to help them write a postcard about a visit to Dieppe. Refer them to the Dieppe brochure on page 81 for additional ideas.

AT 4.4/5 **B** *Décris les vacances de Mélanie.*
Students write a longer perfect tense description of Mélanie's holiday, using the third person singular.

AT 4.5/6 **C** *Regarde l'affiche à droite. Écris un texte de 100 mots environ.*
Students imagine they are taking part in a competition to win a holiday. This activity provides an opportunity for students to write using a variety of tenses: the perfect tense, the imperfect tense (*c'était* + adjective), the future using *aller* + infinitive, and the present tense (*J'adore ça parce que …*).

6.5 La belle équipe, épisode 6

pages 88–89

Objectives

▶ Develop listening and reading skills via a soap story based on the language of the unit

Resources

Students' Book, pages 88–89
CD 2, track 49
Cassette 3, side 2

Programme of Study reference

1a, 1c, 2a, 2b, 2g, 2h, 2i, 3b, 3c, 3e, 4a, 4d, 5a, 5d, 5e, 5g, 5i

For general information on introducing and exploiting the soap story, refer to page 19 of the Introduction.

This episode begins where the previous episode ended: the judges have just announced that the Pieds-Nus are the winners of the competition. Natacha and Juliette are jubilant, while Matthieu tries to put on a brave face by congratulating them on their success; but meanwhile Arnaud seems to have something on his mind. He explains to the judges that it is Matthieu who deserves the trip to the West Indies, because he composed the rap and is the real singer with the group. After a discussion, the judges decide that all four friends should go to the West Indies! The two boys now seem to have put all their differences behind them and are the best of friends again … and Matthieu, hoping to eliminate Arnaud as a rival for Juliette's affections, secretly tells Arnaud that his considerate gesture seems to have made a very good impression on Natacha! The four of them decide to go out to a pancake restaurant to celebrate. But who will Juliette choose … Arnaud or Matthieu?

AT 1.5
AT 3.5
1 *Écoute et lis. Choisis le bon titre pour l'épisode.*
Students listen to the recording and follow the text in the Students' Book. They choose an appropriate title for the episode from the three that are given.

Answer: b

CD 2, track 49 — page 88, La belle équipe, épisode 6
Cassette 3, side 2

1 – Ouah! Les nouvelles stars, c'est nous!
  – Génial, non! Quand je pense qu'on part aux Antilles!!! Arnaud … tu vas où?
  – Je dois parler aux juges.
2 – Félicitations, Arnaud! Ton rap était genial!
  – Merci, madame, mais il y a un problème. Ce n'est pas mon rap. Le vrai chanteur des Pieds-Nus, c'est mon copain Matthieu, là-bas.
  – Je ne comprends pas.
  – Il était très malade après la première audition, alors j'ai fait son rap. C'est Matthieu qui doit partir aux Antilles, pas moi.
3 – Félicitations! Et bon voyage aux Antilles! Achetez-moi un souvenir, hein? Un tee-shirt, un poster, une carte postale!
  – Matthieu …
  – On est vraiment désolées pour toi.
4 – … Pas Arnaud … Matthieu … première audition … très malade … un rap génial … que faire?
5 – Nous avons bien considéré la proposition d'Arnaud …
  – Quoi? Qu'est-ce qui se passe?
  – … et nous avons une solution. Le premier prix va aux Pieds-Nus, y compris Matthieu. Un groupe de quatre, c'est idéal pour la tournée aux Antilles.
6 – On part tous les quatre, avec Matthieu, mais c'est le top!!!!
  – Arnaud! Tu es génial!
  – Mais, non, c'est normal! Matthieu, c'est mon meilleur pote!
7 – Merci, Arnaud. C'est super sympa de ta part. Et tu as vraiment impressionné Natacha!
  – Ah bon? Tu crois?
  – Ah oui oui oui! Elle t'adore, c'est clair!
8 – On va fêter ça? Je vous invite à la crêperie!
  – Bonne idée! La crêperie près de la bibliothèque, au coin de la rue Lafayette, est super sympa.
  – Bon, on y va! Tu n'es pas trop fatigué, Matthieu?
  – Non, j'ai plein d'énergie maintenant, avec toi … merci, Juliette.

Fin

2 *Trouve …*
Students search the text for the French translations of the English expressions.

Answers: a tu vas où?; b il faut m'acheter un souvenir, hein?; c je ne comprends pas; d y compris; e c'est mon meilleur pote; f j'ai plein d'énergie maintenant

3 *Qui …?*
Students answer questions on the text.

Answers: a Arnaud; b Matthieu; c les Pieds-Nus (Matthieu, Arnaud, Natacha, Juliette); d Natacha; e Matthieu

AT 2.4 **4** *À cinq, jouez l'épisode.*
Students act out the episode in groups.

Super-challenge!

page 90

This extension page is intended to stretch more able students who are confident with the core language of the unit. It combines language from the unit with unfamiliar language and develops grammar points introduced in the main body of the unit. It can be used flexibly either as part of a teacher-led lesson or as alternative independent class and homework material.

6 Une visite en France

Objectives
- Use a variety of tenses together within the same piece of work
- Improve dictionary use

Resources
Students' Book, page 90
Encore/En plus Workbooks, page 60

Programme of Study reference
1c, 2f, 2g, 2h, 2i, 2j, 3b, 3c, 3d, 3e, 4c, 4d, 5c, 5d, 5e, 5f, 5g, 5i

AT 3.5/6

1 *Lis le rapport de Danny. Trouve un titre pour chaque paragraphe.*
Students read Danny's report and select an appropriate title for each paragraph. The text and activities on this page practise familiar language within the new context of an exchange visit to Strasbourg.

Answers: paragraphe 1: c Pierre et sa famille; paragraphe 2: f le voyage; paragraphe 3: a les repas; paragraphe 4: e les activités; paragraphe 5: d conclusion; paragraphe 6: b le futur

2 *Fais une liste de phrases au présent, au passé et au futur. Compare avec un(e) partenaire.*
Students search the text for verbs in the past tense, the present and the future. They compare their list with that of a partner.

Answers: passé composé: j'ai fait un échange, j'ai passé deux semaines chez eux, je suis parti, j'ai pris le train, j'ai fait bon voyage, j'ai lu, j'ai écouté mon baladeur, j'ai bien aimé les repas, j'ai fait du shopping, j'ai acheté des souvenirs, j'ai choisi des chocolats, j'ai aussi acheté un tee-shirt, je me suis bien entendu avec mon correspondant, j'ai beaucoup parlé français; imparfait: la famille était vraiment sympa, c'était fatigant, c'était la tarte aux pommes, l'échange était super, c'était génial; présent: il a quinze ans, il aime le vélo …, il habite avec ses parents, les repas sont longs en France, c'est une ville super dynamique, … sa grand-mère qui habite sur la côte; futur: je vais faire un échange, ça va être amusant, nous allons visiter Madrid, nous allons passer une semaine chez sa grand-mère

AT 4.5/6

3a *Prépare un rapport comme celui de Danny. Note des expressions utiles.*
Students plan out a report like Danny's. Point out that they can "lift" useful phrases from Danny's text, adapting where necessary. Encourage them to follow the guidance given in the *Guide pratique* panel on page 87.

AT 4.5/6

3b *Invente un rapport: "Mon échange à Paris".*
Students now expand their ideas from activity **3a** to write a report about an imaginary exchange visit to Paris.

Guide pratique
This section focuses on making effective use of a dictionary to cope with unfamiliar language in a French text. It advises students to look up just one word of an unknown phrase instead of trying to find every single word in a dictionary.

W60 Page 60 of the *Encore* and *En plus* Workbooks could be used at this point.

Vocabulaire *page 91*

This page provides a summary of the key language covered in this unit. It could be used as a handy reference for students as they work through the unit. Alternatively, students could use its clear French–English format with language organized thematically when learning vocabulary.

C86 Feuille 86 *Vocabulaire* also contains a summary of the key language of the unit and could be given to students at this point for revision purposes. See page 7 of the Introduction for ideas on how to use this copymaster.

W61 Page 61 of the *Encore* and *En plus* Workbooks also provides a summary of the key language of the unit.

Podium *page 92*

The *Podium* page provides students with an end-of-unit checklist of learning objectives in French and English. At the foot of the page are activities at three levels of difficulty (bronze, silver and gold) to extend the work of the unit. Encourage students to select an activity at the most appropriate level.

C87 Feuille 87 *Podium* could also be used at this point. This worksheet contains activities to help students keep track of their progress. See page 7 of the Introduction for ideas on how to use it to help self- and peer-assessment.

W62 Page 62 of the *Encore* and *En plus* Workbooks also provides an end-of-unit checklist in French and English with activities to help students keep track of their progress.

Encore Unité 6 *pages 106–107*

Objectives
These reinforcement pages are intended for those students requiring further practice of core language from the unit. They can be used by students who finish other activities quickly or as alternative class and homework material.

Une visite en France 6

Resources
Students' Book, pages 106–107
CD 2, track 50
Cassette 3, side 2

Programme of Study reference
1a, 1b, 1c, 2b, 2c, 2d, 2e, 2f, 2h, 3e, 4a, 4c, 5a, 5d, 5e, 5f, 5g, 5i

AT 3.2 **1** *Lis les phrases. Recopie et complète le plan.*
Students copy out the diagram of the street plan. They read sentences a–g describing the location of various places and mark the places on to the plan.

Answers:

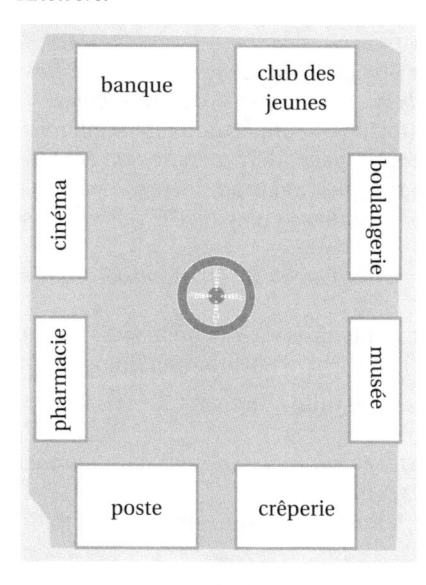

```
    banque          club des
                    jeunes

cinéma                      boulangerie

pharmacie                   musée

    poste           crêperie
```

AT 3.3 **2a** *Lis et complète la conversation avec les mots de la boîte.*
Students read and complete the conversation with words from the box. This activity could be done in pairs, with students reading the text aloud as they work out the correct words to fill the gaps.

Answers: see underlining in transcript below

AT 1.3 **2b** *Écoute et vérifie.*
Students listen to the recording to check their answers.

CD 2, track 50 page 106, activité 2b
Cassette 3, side 2

– Excusez-moi. Où <u>est</u> la poste, s'il vous plaît?
– La poste? <u>Allez</u> tout droit et aux <u>feux</u> tournez à gauche. Puis, <u>prenez</u> la première <u>rue</u> à droite et la poste est à <u>côté</u> du parc.
– C'est <u>loin</u>?
– Non, c'est à cinq cents <u>mètres</u>.
– <u>Merci</u> et au revoir.

AT 2.3 **2c** *Jouez la conversation avec un(e) partenaire. Attention à la prononciation!*
Students act out the conversation with a partner, focusing on pronunciation and intonation.

AT 2.3 **3** *Invente des conversations avec un(e) partenaire (voir les images).*
In pairs, students make up their own conversations, following the model provided and using the panel of *Destinations/Explications* as prompts. The model conversation uses the *tu* form of the imperative, whereas activity **2** above used the *vous* form: you may need to remind students of the difference between *prends* and *prenez*.
Less able students could omit the last line of the conversation, which provides an opportunity to give a more open-ended response using the future tense. Encourage students to use their imagination to come up with a reason for going to each of the places.

AT 3.3 **4** *Tu reconnais les monuments à Paris? Qu'est-ce que c'est (a–h)?*
Although this is a reading activity, it also revises what students have learned about Paris tourist attractions. Students study the descriptions and photos of locations in Paris and try to remember the name of each. If they find this difficult, you could replay the recording for activity **1a** on Students' Book page 84: this will provide them with all the information they need to complete the activity.

Answers: a la tour Eiffel; b la cathédrale de Notre-Dame; c le musée du Louvre; d la Défense; e l'Arc de Triomphe; f la basilique du Sacré-Cœur; g le Centre Pompidou; h la cité des Sciences et de l'Industrie

AT 4.2 **5a** *Recopie et complète avec la bonne forme du verbe "aller".*
This activity revises the future tense using *aller* plus infinitive. Students copy and complete the sentences using the correct form of *aller*.

Answers: a vais; b vas; c va; d allons; e allez; f vont

AT 4.3/4 **5b** *Qu'est-ce que tu vas faire pendant les prochaines vacances? Écris cinq phrases minimum.*
Students write at least five sentences saying what they are going to do during the next holidays. They should be able to cope with this more open-ended activity because it is very similar to *Challenge!* activity **A** on page 85 of the Students' Book.

En plus Unité 6 pages 118–119

Objectives
These extension pages are intended for more able students who are confident with the core language of the unit. They can be used by students who finish other activities quickly or as alternative class and homework material.

6 Une visite en France

Resources
Students' Book, pages 118–119
CD 2, track 51
Cassette 3, side 2

Programme of Study reference
1c, 2a, 2c, 2d, 2e, 2f, 2h, 2i, 3e, 4a, 4d, 5a, 5c, 5d, 5e, 5f, 5i

AT 4.3/4

1 *Décris la place de la Fontaine. Utilise "en face de", "près de" et "à côté de".*
Students study the plan of the town square and write as many sentences as they can to describe the location of the buildings. You could hold a competition to see who can make up the most sentences within a set time.

AT 1.4

2 *Écoute les cinq conversations et dessine le chemin. Puis, compare avec un(e) partenaire.*
Students listen to five conversations in which people are given directions. They sketch out the route for each one, then compare with a partner.

Answers: 1 second street on the right, straight ahead at traffic lights, turn left, beach is in front of you; 2 straight ahead, then straight ahead again at the crossroads, post office is on the left opposite the museum; 3 first street on the left, then second street on the right, church is on the left beside the supermarket; 4 turn left, then turn right at the traffic lights, then take the second street on the left, tourist information centre is in the castle; 5 first street on the left, hospital is on the right opposite the park

---

CD 2, track 51
Cassette 3, side 2
page 118, activité 2

1 – C'est où, la plage, s'il vous plaît?
– La plage? Prenez la deuxième rue à droite.
– La deuxième rue à droite … oui …
– Aux feux, allez tout droit.
– Oui, aux feux, tout droit.
– Puis, tournez à gauche et la plage est en face de vous.

2 – Excusez-moi, madame. C'est où, la poste, s'il vous plaît?
– Allez tout droit. Au carrefour, continuez tout droit.
– Tout droit … au carrefour, tout droit … oui …
– Et la poste est à gauche en face du musée.
– À gauche en face du musée. Merci, madame.

3 – Pardon, monsieur. Où est l'église Saint-Jean?
– L'église Saint-Jean? C'est tout près. Prenez la première rue à gauche et la deuxième rue à droite.
– La première rue à gauche et la deuxième rue à droite?
– Oui, c'est ça. L'église est à gauche à côté du supermarché.
– À gauche à côté du supermarché. Merci, monsieur.

4 – Excusez-moi, madame. C'est où, l'office de tourisme?
– L'office de tourisme? Tournez à gauche. Puis, aux feux, à droite. Après ça, c'est la deuxième rue à gauche.
– Merci. C'est loin?
– Bof … à cinq cents mètres environ. L'office de tourisme est dans le château.
– Merci et au revoir.

5 – Aïe! C'est où, l'hôpital?
– Hmm … l'hôpital …
– Aïe! Oui, l'hôpital, s'il vous plaît. Aïe!
– L'hôpital … Ah oui, il y a un hôpital dans la rue des Vignes.
– Oui? Aïe! C'est loin?
– Non, c'est assez près.
– Aïe! C'est par où? … Aïe! … s'il vous plaît.
– Prenez la première rue à gauche.
– Aïe!
– L'hôpital est à cinquante mètres à droite en face du parc. Ça va?
– Non, ça ne va pas. Je dois aller à l'hôpital. Au revoir.

AT 2.5/6

3 *Imagine que tu es en vacances à Paris et que tu rencontres ton prof de français devant la tour Eiffel. A est le prof qui pose beaucoup de questions et B répond.*
This activity provides an opportunity for students to use a variety of tenses. In pairs, they prepare and act out a role-play based on the question prompts provided. Make sure that everyone has a turn at playing the role of the student.

AT 3.5/6

4a *Lis les trois textes. Quel texte est au passé? Au présent? Au futur?*
Students look at the three texts (a postcard, an e-mail and a letter) and decide which tense is used for each.

Answer: a présent; b futur; c passé

4b *Relis les textes et trouve (a) les mots qui indiquent le temps et (b) les connecteurs.*
Students search the texts for time expressions and connectives.

Answers: <u>time expressions</u>: tous les jours, aujourd'hui, demain soir, d'abord, ensuite, après ça, pendant les vacances; <u>connectives</u>: parce que, et, comme, pour (+ infinitive), si (s'il fait beau), où, mais

AT 3.5/6

4c *Réponds aux questions.*
Students answer questions in French on the three texts. Draw their attention to the tense of the questions because this may help them to locate the correct answers. For example, the first question mentions *monuments historiques*, but all three texts refer to historic buildings so where should students look for the answer? If they notice that the question is in the past tense, they will realize that text b cannot contain the answer because this text is all written in the future tense; so the answer must be in text c (written in the past tense) or text a (although Marilyne writes in the present tense, she implies that she has been visiting historic buildings every day).

Answers: a Marilyne, Susie; b à Montmartre, près du Sacré-Cœur; c Marc; d non (la capitale de la France, c'est Paris); e Susie, parce qu'elle a nagé tous les jours en Bretagne et elle a fait de longues promenades et de l'escalade à Chamonix; f accept any reasonable answer

AT 4.5/6 **4d** *Et toi? Complète ces phrases. Donne un maximum de détails!*
Students expand each phrase to give details about holidays using the past tense, the present tense and the future. Encourage them to use the three texts (postcard, e-mail and letter) as models, and to use time phrases and connectives to make their writing more detailed and interesting.

Follow-up activity: More able students could research an area of France, imagining they have just been holiday on there, and write a reply to letter b.

Point lecture   pages 130–131

These pages are intended to encourage independent reading. Students should attempt them once they are confident with the core language of the unit. They can be used by students who finish other activities quickly or as alternative class and homework material.

Objectives
▶ Develop reading for information and pleasure

Resources
Students' Book, pages 130–131

Programme of Study reference
1c, 2h, 2i, 3e, 4a, 4c, 4d, 5c, 5d, 5e, 5g, 5i

AT 3.4 **1a** *Lis les informations. Vrai ou faux?*
Students read the statements about the Orsay Museum and compare with the information given in the leaflet. They indicate whether the statements are true or false.

Answers: a faux (c'est un musée d'art); b faux (le musée est ouvert jusqu'à 21 h 15 le jeudi); c vrai; d faux (7 euros c'est plein tarif, l'entrée est gratuite pour les enfants); e faux (l'entrée est gratuite le premier dimanche du mois); f vrai

AT 4.2 **1b** *Corrige les phrases fausses.*
Students correct the false statements from **1a**.

Answers: see **1a** above

AT 3.3 **1c** *Qui …*
Students answer questions on the opinions expressed in the speech bubbles.

Answers: a Laure; b Jérôme; c Aline; d Laure

AT 4.3/4 **1d** *Tu voudrais visiter le musée d'Orsay? Pourquoi?*
Students write a few sentences to explain why they would or wouldn't like to visit the Orsay Museum.

AT 3.5 **2a** *Lis les textes. Où sont-ils allés en France?*
Students read the descriptions of holidays in different regions of France. They match each description to a location on the map.

Answers: 1 Julien; 2 Camille; 3 Sarah; 4 Marion; 5 Paul; 6 Julie; 7 Benoît

AT 4.3-5 **2b** *Qui a passé les vacances les plus intéressantes, à ton avis? Pourquoi?*
Referring again to the holiday descriptions in **2a**, students explain who they think had the most interesting holiday, and why.

Follow-up activity: Students could research another holiday destination, either in France or in a different French-speaking region of the world, and write a short text describing an imaginary holiday there.

Copymasters

Feuille 88 À vos marques

There are two starter activities on this copymaster.
Activity 1 focuses on places in town and could be completed with pages 80–81 of the Students' Book. Activities 2a and 2b practise talking about Paris tourist attractions and could be used with pages 84–85.

1 *Relie.*
Students match the places in town to the list of activities. This activity also revises vocabulary from other contexts, e.g. food, leisure activities. As a follow-up, students could make up similar sentences about other places in town.

Answers: 1 d; 2 h; 3 j; 4 i; 5 a; 6 b; 7 c; 8 g; 9 f; 10 e

2a *A pose les questions pour samedi et B répond. Puis, B pose les questions pour dimanche et A répond.*
Working in pairs, students take turns to ask and answer questions about what they have done during an imaginary visit to Paris, using the illustrated diary pages as prompts.

2b *Jouez la conversation de mémoire devant la classe.*
Students attempt to perform their conversation from activity **2a** in front of the class, from memory.

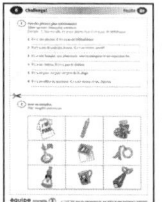

Feuille 89 Challenge!

There are two plenary activities on this copymaster.
Activity 1 focuses on places in town and could be used towards the end of pages 80–81 of the Students' Book. Activity 2 could be used with pages 86–87: it practises the vocabulary for souvenirs.

6 Une visite en France

1 *Fais des phrases plus intéressantes.*
Students attempt to improve the sentences by using connectives, opinions, etc. to make them longer and more interesting. Refer them back to the *Guide pratique* section on connectives on page 37 of the Students' Book. Students could work in pairs on this and you could hold a competition, with the class voting for the most interesting phrases.

Possible answers: 2 Dans ma ville, il n'y a pas de club des jeunes, mais il y a un centre sportif – c'est super! 3 Dans ma ville, il y a beaucoup de magasins: par exemple, il y a une banque, une pharmacie et une boulangerie (j'adore les croissants!), et il y a aussi un grand supermarché – c'est pratique. 4 À …, il y a un grand cinéma (j'adore les films!); par contre, il n'y a pas de théâtre. 5 À …, il y a un joli parc près de la plage. 6 Près de l'office de tourisme, il y a un musée très intéressant et un vieux château.

2 *Joue au morpion.*
Students play Noughts and Crosses to practise the vocabulary for souvenirs. This provides an opportunity to focus on the gender of the new vocabulary: in order to "win" one of the squares, students have to give the French word, including the gender. More able students could be encouraged to form sentences, e.g. *Pour mon père, j'ai acheté une cravate. C'est génial! Pour sa mère, il/elle a acheté …*

Feuille 90 Écoute Encore

This copymaster provides three listening activities for use at different points in Unit 6.
Activity 1 practises directions and could be used with pages 82–83 of the Students' Book. Activity 2a focuses on Paris tourist attractions and could be used with pages 84–85. Activity 2b practises the vocabulary for souvenirs and could be used with pages 86–87.

AT 1.3 **1** *Écoute les six conversations et identifie les destinations sur le plan.*
Students listen to six conversations in which people are being given directions. They follow the routes and mark the location of each place on the street map.

Answers: a église; b centre sportif; c parc; d château; e boulangerie; f pharmacie

CD 3, track 38 — Feuille 90, activité 1
Cassette 4, side 2

1 – Excusez-moi, madame. Où est le parc, s'il vous plaît?
  – Le parc? Prenez la deuxième rue à gauche et le parc est à gauche.
  – La deuxième rue à gauche et …
  – Oui, et le parc est à gauche.
  – Merci, madame. Au revoir.

2 – Excusez-moi, monsieur. Est-ce qu'il y a une boulangerie près d'ici, s'il vous plaît?
  – Une boulangerie? Aux feux, prenez la première rue à droite et la boulangerie est à gauche.
  – Aux feux, la première rue à droite et …
  – … et la boulangerie est à gauche.
  – Merci, monsieur. Au revoir.

3 – Pardon, madame. Où est le centre sportif, s'il vous plaît?
  – Continuez tout droit et prenez la troisième rue à droite. Le centre sportif est dans cette rue à gauche.
  – Merci, madame.
  – Je vous en prie.

4 – Excusez-moi, monsieur. Où est l'église, s'il vous plaît?
  – L'église? Hmm … Ah oui, continuez tout droit et prenez la deuxième rue à gauche.
  – La deuxième rue à gauche?
  – Oui, c'est ça, et l'église est à droite.
  – Merci, monsieur. Au revoir.

5 – Pardon, monsieur. Est-ce qu'il y a une pharmacie près d'ici?
  – Une pharmacie? Oui, c'est tout près. Tournez à droite et la pharmacie est en face de la boulangerie.
  – La première rue à droite, en face de la boulangerie …
  – Oui, c'est ça!

6 – Excusez-moi, madame. Où est le château, s'il vous plaît?
  – Le château? C'est facile! Continuez tout droit, tout droit, tout droit, et vous voyez le château en face de vous.
  – Merci, madame. Au revoir.

AT 1.4 **2a** *Qu'est-ce que Sandrine va faire à Paris. Écoute et coche les activités.*
Students listen and tick the pictures to show what Sandrine plans to do in Paris.

Answers: the following pictures should be ticked: Eiffel Tower, Sacré-Cœur, restaurant symbol, boat on Seine, market

CD 3, track 39 — Feuille 90, activité 2a
Cassette 4, side 2

– Tu vas à Paris le week-end prochain, Sandrine?
– Oui, j'y vais avec mes parents et mon frère.
– Et qu'est-ce que tu vas faire à Paris?
– Je vais visiter les monuments historiques, bien sûr! La tour Eiffel, Sacré-Cœur …
– Tu vas regarder les artistes qui travaillent à Montmartre près du Sacré-Cœur?
– Oui, ça va être intéressant! Et le samedi soir, on va manger au restaurant et on va faire une promenade en bateau-mouche sur la Seine.
– Génial!
– Je vais aussi visiter le marché pour acheter un souvenir pour toi.
– Merci! Tu es gentille, Sandrine!

Une visite en France 6

AT 1.4 **2b** *Sandrine fait une liste de souvenirs. Qu'est-ce qu'elle a acheté à Paris? Pour qui?*
Students listen to Sandrine talking about the souvenirs she has brought back from Paris. They note down the items and who they are intended for.

Answers: mère: port-clés; père: (grande) tasse; frère: tee-shirt; copine: (grand) poster de la tour Eiffel; Sandrine: 10 cartes postales

CD 3, track 40 **Feuille 90, activité 2b**
Cassette 4, side 2

Mon week-end à Paris est fini, mais j'ai acheté des souvenirs super! Pour ma mère, j'ai acheté un porte-clés … et pour mon père, j'ai acheté une grande tasse … J'adore ce tee-shirt – c'est pour mon frère … Et pour ma copine, j'ai acheté un grand poster de la tour Eiffel. Génial! Et les cartes postales … j'ai acheté dix cartes postales … les cartes postales sont pour moi! Un bon souvenir de mon week-end à Paris!

Feuille 91 Écoute En plus

This copymaster provides listening practice on describing a past holiday and future holiday plans. It could be used with pages 86–87 of the Students' Book.

AT 3.2 **1a** *Avant d'écouter, relie et fais neuf questions comme dans l'exemple.*
Students match the beginnings and the endings of the sentences to make nine questions.

Answers: 1 c; 2 b; 3 g; 4 e; 5 i; 6 h; 7 a; 8 f; 9 d

AT 1.2 **1b** *Écoute et vérifie.*
Students listen to the recording to check their answers.

CD 3, track 41 **Feuille 91**
Cassette 4, side 2

– Salut, Marie! Tu es allée où en vacances? En Angleterre?
– Non, je suis restée en France, mais je suis allée voir ma tante et mon oncle qui habitent à Blois.
– Tu as voyagé comment?
– J'ai pris le train de Paris à Blois. C'est direct et très rapide.
– Tu es restée combien de temps?
– Deux semaines.
– C'était comment?
– C'était génial parce que ma tante et mon oncle sont vraiment sympa et j'ai fait plein de choses.
– Qu'est-ce qu'il y a à Blois? C'est une ville intéressante?
– Oui, il y a un beau château, de bons magasins et un musée. On peut faire beaucoup de sport aussi!
– Et qu'est-ce que tu as fait?
– J'ai visité le château, bien sûr! C'était très beau et le guide était intéressant. J'ai fait du vélo presque tous les jours sur les bords de la Loire, j'ai mangé au restaurant avec ma tante et mon oncle et j'ai aussi fait les magasins.

– Le château est loin du centre-ville?
– Mais non! Le château est bien situé au centre-ville, près des magasins.
– Tu as acheté des souvenirs?
– Oui, j'ai acheté des cartes postales, un livre sur le château et un tee-shirt avec un motif moderne.
– Super! Et qu'est-ce que tu vas faire pendant les prochaines vacances?
– Pendant les prochaines vacances? Je vais aller voir des amis à Rome. Ça va être super!

AT 1.5 **2** *Réécoute. Entoure la bonne réponse à chaque question.*
Students listen again and answer multiple-choice questions about Marie's holiday.

Answers: 1 b; 2 b; 3 a, b, f; 4 a, d, e, h; 5 c

AT 1.5 **3** *Écoute encore une fois et complète les phrases.*
Students listen a third time and note down the information needed to complete the sentences.

Possible answers: 1 en France; 2 génial; 3 le château; 4 des cartes postales, un livre sur le château et un tee-shirt avec un motif moderne; 5 elle va voir des amis

Feuille 92 Parle Encore

This copymaster provides speaking practice on directions and could be used with pages 82–83 of the Students' Book.

AT 2.3 **1a** *C'est où? Pose des questions à ton/ta partenaire. Écris l'endroit sur le plan.*
1b *Réponds aux questions de ton/ta partenaire.*
This is an information-gap activity. Students take turns to ask and answer questions to complete their maps. They use the directions given by their partner in order to locate and fill in the missing places.

Feuille 93 Parle En plus

This copymaster should be used towards the end of Unit 6, either on or after pages 86–87.

AT 2.4-6
Partenaire A: Tu es journaliste et tu travailles pour l'émission de radio "Petits Potins". Interviewe un(e) camarade de classe. Enregistre l'interview. Ensuite, changez de rôle.
Partenaire B: Réponds aux questions de ton/ta partenaire. Donne le plus possible de détails pour l'interview! Ensuite, changez de rôle.

This interview provides extended speaking practice on a wide variety of topics drawn from the whole of *Équipe nouvelle 2*. Encourage students by telling them that they have made considerable progress towards GCSE if they are able to answer these questions in any detail. Less able students might prefer to select 15 questions to ask and answer instead of tackling the whole lot.
To provide a model for students, you could arrange to carry out this interview with a Foreign Language Assistant (if your school has one) or with a suitable Sixth Form

6 Une visite en France

student or French-speaking member of staff. Perhaps your volunteer interviewee could be videoed giving detailed answers to the questions (based on the language of *Équipe nouvelle 2*) and this would provide additional listening practice for students as well as a helpful model for students' own interviews.

Feuille 94 Lis et écris Encore 1

This copymaster provides reading and writing practice on directions and could be used with pages 82–83 of the Students' Book.

AT 3.3

1 *Suis les instructions et note les lettres. C'est où?*

Students follow the directions on the plan and note down the letters of the destinations.

Answers: 1 plage; 2 parc; 3 poste

AT 3.1

2a *Gare, c'est quel symbole?*

Students choose the symbol that represents a railway station.

Answer: b

AT 4.3

2b *Où est la gare? Écris les instructions comme dans l'activité 1. Compare avec un(e) partenaire.*

Students write a series of directions, similar to those in activity **1**, that will spell out the word *gare* on the street plan.

Answers: Va/Allez tout droit (G). Prends/Prenez la quatrième rue à droite (A). Aux feux, tourne/tournez à droite (R). Va/Allez tout droit et prends/prenez la troisième rue à droite.

Feuille 95 Lis et écris Encore 2

This copymaster provides reading and writing practice on a visit to Paris. It could be used with pages 86–87 of the Students' Book.

AT 3.3

1 *Lis la carte postale. Relie les symboles.*

Students read a postcard about a visit to Paris. They link up the symbols to show the opinions expressed about the different activities and the times at which two of the activities are to take place.

Answers: 1 c; 2 a; 3 e; 4 b; 5 d

AT 4.3

2 *Décris ton week-end à Paris. N'oublie pas de donner tes opinions!*

Students fill in the holiday diary, in response to the picture prompts, to describe an imaginary weekend in Paris. Some phrases are provided in the perfect tense, for support. Encourage students to include time expressions in their sentences, as in the example, together with opinions.

Feuille 96 Lis et écris En plus 1

This copymaster could be used with pages 82–83 of the Students' Book. It provides reading and writing practice on directions.

AT 3.3

1 *Lis les instructions. Dessine l'itinéraire sur le plan.*

Students read the directions for a guided tour of Dieppe. They draw the route on the plan.

Answers:

AT 4.4

2 *Regarde le plan. Retrouve de mémoire les instructions de la visite guidée. Écris-les sur une feuille.*

Without looking at the *Visite guidée* text, students now attempt to rewrite the directions following the route they have just drawn on the plan. They then compare their version with the *Visite guidée* text.

AT 4.4

3 *Écris un autre itinéraire pour une visite de Dieppe ou une visite de ta ville sur une feuille.*

Students write their own guided tour, either for Dieppe or for their own town.

Feuille 97 Lis et écris En plus 2

This copymaster could be used with pages 86–87 of the Students' Book. It provides reading and writing practice on describing past holidays.

AT 3.5/6

1a *Lis l'e-mail.*

Students read the e-mail about a holiday in Corsica.

1b *Trouve le français.*

Students search the e-mail for the French translations of the English expressions.

Answers: 1 en vacances en Corse; 2 mes amis me manquent beaucoup; 3 je suis (presque) championne de planche à voile; 4 il faisait trop chaud; 5 on est allés au cinéma ensemble; 6 tôt demain matin

1c *Relis l'e-mail d'Aurélie et prends des notes en anglais sur les trois thèmes.*
Students make notes in English on different aspects of Aurélie's holiday.

Answers: the hotel: there's a computer in the hotel so she can send e-mails to her friends, the hotel is modern, is situated beside the beach and is 500 metres from the shops; windsurfing: she's been going to the beach every morning to do a windsurfing course, she found it very difficult at first but now (after two weeks of hard work) she's quite good at it and has built up muscles in her arms and legs; other activities: tennis with father, shopping with mother, played in hotel swimming pool with her brothers, walking in the mountains – very tiring because too hot, has been to the cinema four times with a boy she's met at the hotel, has bought souvenirs for all her friends

AT 4.5/6

2 *Imagine que tu es en vacances. Utilise les images et écris un e-mail à un(e) ami(e) sur une feuille.*
Using the pictures as prompts, students write an e-mail to a friend describing a holiday in Paris.

Feuille 98 Grammaire 1

This copymaster focuses on the imperative and should be used with the *Zoom grammaire* section on page 83 of the Students' Book.

1 *Complète les bulles.*
Students fill in the gaps in the speech bubbles with the correct imperative forms (*tu* or *vous* forms).

Answers: 1 va/continue, tourne, prends; 2 prenez, allez/continuez, tournez, prenez; 3 prenez, tournez, tournez, allez/continuez; 4 va/continue, tourne, prends

2 *Fais un dessin, comme dans l'activité 1, et écris la conversation.*
Students sketch a situation similar to the pictures in activity **1** and write out a conversation to practise asking for and giving directions.

Feuille 99 Grammaire 2

This copymaster focuses on when to use *c'était* and when to use the perfect tense. It could be used with the *Zoom grammaire* section on page 86 of the Students' Book.

1 *Complète comme dans l'exemple.*
Students complete the sentences, deciding when to use *c'était* and when to use the perfect tense.

Answers: 1 Pendant mes vacances à Paris, j'<u>ai fait</u> une promenade en bateau sur la Seine. C'<u>était</u> super bien! 2 Je <u>suis allé(e)</u> au cinéma voir le film de James Bond. C'<u>était</u> nul! 3 J'<u>ai fini</u> mes devoirs de français. C'<u>était</u> très difficile! 4 La musique à la boum, c'<u>était</u> nul! C'est Léon qui <u>a choisi</u> du disco! 5 Pour Noël, mon petit frère <u>a mis</u> ses vêtements préférés. C'<u>était</u> horrible! 6 J'<u>ai fait</u> les courses. C'<u>était</u> amusant!

Feuille 100 Guide pratique 1

This copymaster focuses on dictionary skills and could be used with the *Guide pratique* section on page 81 of the Students' Book. It points out that words often have more than one meaning and that, when using a dictionary, it is important to select the correct translation for the context.

1 *Trouve le bon sens du mot pour chaque phrase.*
Students read the sentences, each of which features a different meaning of the word *pièce*. Referring to the Flashback panel, they choose the correct meaning of *pièce* in each sentence.

Answers: a coin; b room; c play; d document, paper; e rooms

2 *Cherche ces mots dans le dictionnaire. Donne deux traductions possibles pour chaque mot.*
Students look up the words in a dictionary and note down two possible translations for each. Answers will vary depending on the dictionaries used and the choices made by students.

Possible answers: a *un terrain*: piece of land, soil, ground, (football) pitch/field, (golf) course, (camp) site, terrain; b *une chambre*: bedroom, room, chamber, house (of Commons/Representatives, etc.); c *la cuisine*: kitchen, cooking/cookery, wheeling and dealing/scheming; d *un séjour*: living room, stay/sojourn; e *un bureau*: office/study, desk, committee; f *l'argent*: money, silver

3 *Traduis en anglais.*
Students translate the French sentences into English, focusing on choosing the most appropriate meanings of some of the words from activity **2**.

Answers: a I love French cooking. b My brother is in the kitchen. c The dictionary is on my desk. d My mother is working in her office/study. e The living room is large and modern. f They stayed/had a stay in Provence.

Feuille 101 Guide pratique 2

This copymaster provides guidance on drafting and redrafting written work and should be used with the *Guide pratique* section on page 87 of the Students' Book.

1a *Lis et identifie les textes: 1 premier effort, 2 deuxième effort, 3 propre.*
Students study the three texts and decide which is the first draft, which is the second and which the third.

Answers: A 3; B 1; C 2

1b *À ton avis, c'est une lettre …?*
Students decide who the letter is intended for.

Answer: c

6 Une visite en France

2a *Lis le poster, puis imagine un week-end à Paris et prends des notes (premier effort).*
In response to the poster, students make notes in preparation for writing a description of an imaginary stay in Paris.

2b *Maintenant, écris une lettre à l'Office de Tourisme pour décrire ton séjour à Paris.*
Following the advice given in the Flashback panel, students prepare a second then a third draft of a letter to the Paris tourist information centre, based on their notes/first draft from activity **2a**.

Feuille 102 Ça se dit comme ça!

The activities on this copymaster practise the French *r* sound and should be used with the *Ça se dit comme ça!* section on page 85 of the Students' Book.

1 *Écoute. C'est un jeune anglais (A) ou un jeune français (F) qui parle?*
Students focus on the pronunciation of the different speakers and work out who is French and who is English. This activity is intended to be light-hearted, while helping students to distinguish between French and English sounds.

Answers: 1 F; 2 A; 3 A; 4 F; 5 A; 6 A; 7 F; 8 F; 9 F; 10 A

CD 3, track 42   **Feuille 102, activité 1**
Cassette 4, side 2

1 – J'adore Paris!
2 – Le premier jour, j'ai visité la tour Eiffel et la cathédrale Notre-Dame.
3 – La basilique du Sacré-Cœur était super belle.
4 – J'ai trouvé la place du Tertre à Montmartre vraiment intéressante.
5 – Le Centre Pompidou est trop moderne pour moi!
6 – Il y a une pyramide en verre devant le musée du Louvre.
7 – L'Arc de Triomphe est un monument historique important.
8 – Comme souvenir pour ma mère, j'ai trouvé un poster de Paris la nuit.
9 – J'ai acheté quatre porte-clés et treize cartes postales.
10 – Pour mon frère, j'ai acheté des crayons de couleur et une cravate verte.

2a *Dis les phrases à haute voix.*
Students practise saying the 10 sentences aloud.

2b *A dit les phrases 1–10 et B donne les points pour chaque phrase. Ensuite, changez de rôle. Qui gagne?*
In pairs, students award each other points on their pronunciation of the 10 sentences.

Encore Workbook

Page 54 (6.1)
Use with pages 80–81 of the Students' Book.

AT 3.1 **1** *Trouve huit endroits dans la ville.*
Students find the names for eight places in town in the string of letters.

Answers: un château, un hôpital, un marché, un musée, une banque, une boulangerie, une église, une mairie

AT 3.3 **2** *Remets les conversations dans le bon ordre.*
Students use the sentences supplied to complete the conversations about the location of places in town.

Answers:
1 – Pardon, monsieur. Est-ce que l'office de tourisme est près d'ici?
 – L'office de tourisme? Oui, l'office de tourisme est à 200 mètres à gauche.
 – À 200 mètres … Merci, monsieur.
2 – Excusez-moi, madame. Le marché, c'est loin?
 – Non, le marché, c'est tout près, à 50 mètres à droite.
 – À 50 mètres. Merci, madame.
3 – Bonjour, monsieur. Où est l'hôpital, s'il vous plaît?
 – L'hôpital? C'est assez loin, c'est à deux kilomètres d'ici.
 – Oh là là! Deux kilomètres, c'est loin!

AT 2.2 **3** *Lis les conversations à haute voix avec un(e) partenaire.*
Working in pairs, students read the conversations aloud.

Page 55 (6.2)
Use with pages 82–83 of the Students' Book.

AT 3.2/3 **1a** *Lis les instructions (A–D) et relie aux symboles.*
Students read the instructions given on the map of treasure island. They match each instruction to a symbol.

Answers: 1 D; 2 B; 3 A; 4 C

1b *Trouve le trésor! C'est quel numéro?*
Students follow the directions to work out where the treasure is hidden.

Answer: le trésor = numéro 9

AT 4.3 **2** *À toi de cacher le trésor dans l'île (aux numéros 1–15)! Écris des instructions pour ton/ta partenaire à la page 63.*
Students imagine they have hidden the treasure somewhere else on the map. They write directions to the treasure, for their partner to follow.

Page 56 (6.3)
Use with pages 84–85 of the Students' Book.

AT 3.4 **1** *Barre les mots qui ne vont pas.*
Students read the guided tour of Paris, crossing out the incorrect words.

Answers: Regardez à gauche. Vous voyez <u>le monument</u> le plus célèbre de Paris. C'est une tour de 320 mètres, avec un restaurant panoramique! C'est <u>la tour</u> Eiffel. Maintenant, regardez <u>à droite</u>. Au bout des Champs-Élysées, vous voyez un monument historique! Une arche construite pour fêter les victoires de Napoléon. C'est <u>l'Arc de Triomphe</u>.

Maintenant, <u>nous</u> sommes à l'ouest de Paris, dans un quartier moderne avec beaucoup de bureaux et de magasins. Regardez cette <u>grande</u> arche! C'est l'arche de la Défense.

Nous sommes maintenant à Montmartre. En face de vous, il y a <u>une église</u> blanche où il y a des messes tous les jours. <u>C'est</u> la basilique du Sacré-Cœur.

Nous sommes toujours à Montmartre. Cette <u>place</u> est idéale pour se relaxer: il y a des cafés et des restaurants, bien sûr, mais il y a aussi beaucoup <u>d'artistes</u> qui travaillent. C'est amusant! C'est la place du Tertre.

Bienvenue dans le quartier où la technologie est super et où il y a un grand <u>cinéma</u> dans la Géode. C'est la cité des <u>Sciences</u> et de l'Industrie.

Page 57 (6.4)

Use with pages 86–87 of the Students' Book.

AT 3.3 **1** *Voici les trois derniers jours de Mélanie à Dieppe. Complète son journal.*

Students read about the last three days of Mélanie's stay in Dieppe. They fill in the gaps in her diary using the opinions and perfect tense verbs supplied.

Answers: **dimanche**: (a) <u>J'ai fait</u> une promenade en mer avec Natacha et Matthieu. <u>C'était super</u>! Le soir, (b) <u>je suis allée</u> au cinéma avec Natacha et Matthieu. C'était un film avec Schwarzenegger. <u>C'était nul</u>!
lundi: Ce matin, (c) <u>je suis allée</u> à la piscine avec Natacha. <u>C'était super</u>! L'eau était chaude! Après, (d) <u>j'ai mangé</u> une pizza au Quick avec Natacha et ses copains, Matthieu, Arnaud et Juliette. <u>C'était sympa</u>.
mardi: Ce matin, (e) <u>je suis allée</u> au musée avec Natacha. <u>C'était intéressant</u>! Après, (f) <u>j'ai regardé</u> un match de foot avec Matthieu. Ah Matthieu!!!! <u>C'était super</u>!

AT 4.3/4 **2** *Invente les deux premiers jours de Mélanie à Dieppe. Écris son journal à la page 63. Adapte les modèles.*

Students imagine what Mélanie might have done during her first two days in Dieppe. They write two additional diary entries, adapting the texts from activity **1**.

Page 58 Grammaire

Use with pages 86–87 of the Students' Book.

1 *Écris les phrases au passé, comme dans l'exemple.*

Students rewrite the sentences in the past tense using the perfect tense and the imperfect, as in the example.

Answers: a J'ai joué au foot avec mes copains. C'était cool! b J'ai mangé une pizza au restaurant. C'était délicieux! c J'ai fait du shopping aux Halles. C'était sympa! d Je suis allé(e) au Centre Pompidou. C'était super! e J'ai vu la Joconde au musée du Louvre. C'était nul! f Je suis monté(e) en haut de la tour Eiffel. C'était genial!

Page 59 Méli-mélo

This page pulls together and mixes much of the language and grammar of the whole unit. It should be used towards the end of the unit, either with or after pages 86–87.

1a *Coche la bonne légende.*
Students choose a caption to best represent each picture.

Answers: a Je prends une photo de la tour Eiffel. b J'ai pris beaucoup de photos. c J'ai acheté des souvenirs et des cadeaux pour ma famille.

1b *Traduis les légendes en anglais.*
Students translate the captions from **1a** into English.

Answers: a I'm taking a photo of the Eiffel Tower. b I took lots of photos. c I bought souvenirs and presents for my family.

2 *Arrange les mots pour écrire des phrases.*
Students rearrange the words in the correct order to build sentences.

Answers: a Ce week-end, nous sommes allés à Boulogne. b Samedi, nous avons visité la ville. c Aujourd'hui, je vais à la plage avec mon frère. d Demain, je vais acheter des cartes postales et beaucoup de souvenirs.

Page 60 Challenge!

Use with page 90 of the Students' Book.

AT 3.4/5 **1** *Lis les opinions. Ils parlent …?*
Students read the three texts in which young people express opinions about holidays. They indicate whether the people are talking about past holidays, future holidays or the type of holiday they prefer.

Answers: all three young people mention past holidays, future holidays and their preferred type of holiday

2 *Vrai ou faux?*
Referring back to the three young people's texts, students decide whether each statement is true or false.

Answers: a vrai; b vrai; c vrai; d faux; e vrai; f faux; g faux; h vrai; i faux

3 *Choisis un compagnon/une compagne de vacances. Écris à la page 63.*
Students choose the person they would most like to go on holiday with. They explain why in English.

6 Une visite en France

En plus Workbook

Page 54 (6.1)
Use with pages 80–81 of the Students' Book.

AT 4.1 1 *Complète la grille.*
Using the symbols as prompts, students fill in the grid with the names of places in town. This type of activity encourages students to focus on accurate spellings: they need to spell the words correctly in order to fit them in the correct places in the grid.

Answers:

								p	
								o	
					m			s	
	m	m	é		a			t	
b	o	u	l	a	n	g	e	r	i	e
a		s	i		l	c		
n		é	r		i	h		
q		e	i		s	é		
u			e		e			
e								

AT 3.3 2a *Lis les conversations et regarde le plan. Les instructions sont bonnes?*
Students read the conversations about the location of places in town. Referring to the street map, they decide whether the information given in the conversations is correct.

Answers: a faux: le musée est à 200 mètres à droite, à côté du château; b faux: la poste est à 50 mètres à droite, en face de l'église

AT 2.3 2b *Invente des conversations similaires. Joue avec un(e) partenaire ou écris à la page 63.*
AT 4.3 Students write out similar conversations and perform them with a partner.

Page 55 (6.2)
Use with pages 82–83 of the Students' Book.

AT 3.2/3 1a *Lis les instructions (A–F) et relie aux symboles.*
Students read the instructions given on the map of treasure island. They match each instruction to a symbol.

Answers: 1 D; 2 E; 3 A; 4 F; 5 B; 6 C

1b *Trouve le trésor! C'est quel numéro?*
Students follow the directions to work out where the treasure is hidden.

Answer: le trésor = numéro 9

AT 4.3/4 2 *À toi de cacher le trésor dans l'île (aux numéros 1–15)! Écris des instructions pour ton/ta partenaire à la page 63.*
Students imagine they have hidden the treasure somewhere else on the map. They write directions to the treasure, for their partner to follow.

AT 4.3/4 3 *Invente une "île au trésor". Écris des instructions pour ton/ta partenaire.*
Students design their own treasure island with its own hidden treasure. They write directions for a partner to follow.

Page 56 (6.3)
Use with pages 84–85 of the Students' Book.

AT 3.4 1 *Complète le commentaire avec les mots de la boîte.*
Students use the words provided to fill in the gaps and complete the guided tour of Paris.

Answers: see above at *Encore* Workbook page 56

Page 57 (6.4)
Use with pages 86–87 of the Students' Book.

AT 3.3 1 *Voici les trois derniers jours de Mélanie à Dieppe. Complète son journal au passé composé. Ajoute les opinions!*
AT 4.2
Students read about the last three days of Mélanie's stay in Dieppe. They fill in the gaps in her diary using the correct opinions and perfect tense verbs. The infinitives are supplied but students have to form the perfect tense themselves.

Answers: **dimanche**: Le matin, (a) j'ai fait une promenade en mer avec Natacha et Matthieu. C'était super! Le soir, (b) je suis allée au cinéma avec Natacha et Matthieu. C'était un film avec Schwarzenegger. C'était nul!
lundi: Ce matin, (c) j'ai nagé à la piscine avec Natacha. C'était super! L'eau était chaude! Après, (d) j'ai mangé une pizza au Quick avec Natacha et ses copains, Matthieu, Arnaud et Juliette. (e) Je suis restée parler avec Matthieu pendant une heure. C'était intéressant.
mardi: Ce matin, (f) j'ai visité le musée avec Natacha. C'était nul! L'après-midi, (g) j'ai regardé un match de foot avec Matthieu. C'était sympa! Le soir, (h) je suis rentrée très tard à la maison. Ah Matthieu!!!! C'était super!

AT 4.4 2 *Invente les deux premiers jours de Mélanie à Dieppe. Écris son journal à la page 63. Adapte les modèles.*
Students imagine what Mélanie might have done during her first two days in Dieppe. They write two additional diary entries, adapting the texts from activity **1**.

AT 4.4/5 3 *Imagine que tu es allé(e) passer une journée à Dieppe. C'était comment? Raconte à la page 63.*
Students describe an imaginary day trip to Dieppe.

Page 58 Grammaire
Use with pages 86–87 of the Students' Book.

1 *Écris les phrases au passé, comme dans l'exemple.*
Students rewrite the sentences using the perfect tense and the imperfect, as in the example.

Answers: a J'ai joué au foot avec mes copains. C'était cool! b J'ai mangé une pizza au restaurant. C'était délicieux! c J'ai fait du shopping aux Halles. C'était sympa! d Je suis allé(e) au Centre Pompidou. C'était super! e J'ai vu la Joconde au musée du Louvre. C'était nul! f Je suis monté(e) en haut de la tour Eiffel. C'était genial!

2 *Réponds aux questions et ajoute une opinion.*
Students answer the questions and express an opinion about each.

Page 59 Méli-mélo

This page pulls together and mixes much of the language and grammar of the whole unit. It should be used towards the end of the unit, either with or after pages 86–87.

1a *Coche la bonne légende.*
Students choose a caption to best represent each picture.

Answers: a J'ai pris beaucoup de photos. b J'ai acheté des souvenirs et des cadeaux pour ma famille. c L'office de tourisme est en face de la pharmacie, à côté de l'église.

1b *Traduis les légendes en anglais.*
Students translate the captions from **1a** into English.

Answers: a I took lots of photos. b I bought souvenirs and presents for my family. c The tourist information centre is opposite the chemist, next to the church.

2 *Arrange les mots pour écrire des phrases.*
Students rearrange the words in the correct order to build sentences.

Answers: a Aujourd'hui, je vais à la plage avec mon frère. b Demain, je vais acheter de jolis souvenirs et des cartes postales. c Max est parti en vacances chez son oncle et sa tante. d Anne a acheté une petite poupée et un grand poster.

Page 60 Super-challenge!

Use with page 90 of the Students' Book.

AT 3.5

1 *Lis les phrases. Qui …?*
Students read the three texts in which young people express opinions about holidays. They decide which person is being referred to in each phrase.

Answers: a Jérôme; b Siheme; c Pauline

2 *Prends des notes en anglais. (Pour t'aider, souligne tous les verbes au passé et encercle tous les verbes au futur.)*
Students make notes in English about the three texts, focusing on past holidays, future holiday plans and preferred types of holiday.

Answers: <u>Siheme</u>: Last year she went camping to Le Lavandou in the south of France with her family; this year they're going to stay at home; she prefers holidays at the seaside. <u>Jérôme</u>: In February he went to the countryside with his father; in August he's going to stay with his aunt in Paris; he prefers active holidays, likes enjoying himself, doing sport, making friends. <u>Pauline</u>: During the summer she went to England; next year she's going to Rome with her school; she prefers going to see interesting things on holiday and taking lots of photos.

AT 4.5/6

3 *Donne ton opinion des vacances pour l'article à la page 63.*
Students write their own text about past holidays, future holiday plans and preferred types of holiday.

Révisions Unités 5–6

This revision spread provides consolidation and further practice of language from Units 5–6. You can take students through the activities as a whole class, or they can work independently or in pairs. The activities should help students prepare for the assessment for Units 5–6.

Resources
Students' Book, pages 93–95
CD 2, tracks 52–54
Cassette 3, side 2

AT 1.3 **1a** *Écoute et regarde le plan. C'est quelle destination?*
Students listen to the recording and follow the four sets of directions on the street plan to find out where each person is going.

Answers: 1 le parc; 2 le cinéma; 3 l'église; 4 la pharmacie

CD 2, track 52 — page 93, activité 1a
Cassette 3, side 2

1 – Vous allez tout droit et vous prenez la deuxième rue à gauche. C'est à droite.
2 – Continuez tout droit. Aux feux, tournez à droite et puis prenez la première rue à gauche. C'est à droite en face de la piscine.
3 – Prends la troisième rue à gauche et, au carrefour, tourne à droite. C'est à gauche.
4 – Prenez la deuxième rue à droite et allez tout droit. Aux feux, tournez à gauche et continuez tout droit. C'est à cent mètres des feux, à droite.

AT 2.2/3 **1b** *A donne les explications et B devine la destination.*
Referring back to the street plan, students take turns to give directions for their partner to follow.

AT 4.2/3 **1c** *Ils vont où? Écris les explications.*
Students read the six sentences and first work out where each person wants to go. Then, referring to the street plan, they write directions to the places.

Answers: The destinations are: 1 le cinéma; 2 la pharmacie; 3 la piscine; 4 la boulangerie; 5 le parc; 6 l'office de tourisme. Accept any appropriate directions that lead to the correct destinations.

AT 1.4/5 **2a** *Lis les notes et écoute l'interview de Nicole. Corrige les quatre erreurs.*
Students listen to an interview with a young tour guide. They compare what she says on the recording with the notes in the Students' Book, and correct the four mistakes.

Answers: est allée aux États-Unis et <u>en Australie</u> (*not* en Chine); est restée <u>un an</u> aux États-Unis (*not* 15 ans); préfère <u>l'avion</u> (*not* le bateau); sa ville préférée est <u>Paris</u> (*not* Madrid)

AT 1.4/5 **2b** *Réécoute. Recopie et complète le texte avec les mots dans la boîte.*
AT 3.3 Students listen again to the interview with Nicole. They copy and complete a summary of what she says, using the words supplied.

Answers: allée, restée, an, deux, super, le bateau, transport, rapide, Paris, ville, acheté, poupée

CD 2, track 53 — page 93, activité 2
Cassette 3, side 2

– Vous aimez voyager?
– Oui, j'adore ça! Maintenant je suis guide de vacances. C'est idéal pour moi!
– Ah oui! Comme guide, vous êtes allée où?
– Je suis allée aux États-Unis et en Australie.
– Vous êtes restée combien de temps aux États-Unis et en Australie?
– Je suis restée un an aux États-Unis et deux ans en Australie.
– C'était comment?
– C'était super!
– Vous avez voyagé comment?
– J'ai pris l'avion, bien sûr!
– C'est quoi votre moyen de transport préféré?
– J'aime bien le bateau, mais je crois que je préfère l'avion! C'est plus rapide.
– C'est New York, aux États-Unis, votre ville préférée?
– Non. Moi, j'adore Paris! Je suis allée à Paris avec mon copain. C'est une ville très romantique! J'adore tous les monuments … Notre-Dame, la tour Eiffel, le Centre Pompidou …
– Oui, oui, oui. Et quel est votre souvenir préféré?
– Ah, c'est facile. J'ai acheté une poupée espagnole à Madrid il y a dix ans. Elle est très jolie!

AT 3.4 **3a** *Voici le journal de Claire Tondini. Recopie et complète.*
AT 4.3 Students read Claire's account of her holiday in a horse-drawn caravan in the south of France. They copy it out, adding in the correct past participles.

Answers: partie, allée, restée, allée, restée, rentrée

AT 1.4 **3b** *Écoute. Recopie la grille et complète pour la famille Tondini.*
Students listen to the Tondini family discussing the souvenirs they have bought. They note down what they have bought and for whom.

Answers: Claire: bonbons pour prof de français; Martial: cravate pour papa; M. Tondini: parfum pour sa mère (pour la grand-mère de Claire/Martial); Mme Tondini: un tee-shirt (très chic/moderne) pour elle-même

Révisions Unités 5–6

CD 2, track 54
Cassette 3, side 2
page 94, activité 3b

– Qu'est-ce que tu as acheté comme souvenir, Claire?
– J'ai acheté des bonbons pour mon professeur de français.
– Pour ton prof de français? C'est bizarre!
– Et toi, Martial, qu'est-ce que tu as acheté?
– J'ai acheté une cravate pour papa.
– Ah, c'est gentil, Martial. Merci beaucoup!
– Et, papa, qu'est-ce que tu as acheté comme souvenir?
– Moi, j'ai acheté du parfum.
– Super! C'est pour maman?
– Ah non, c'est pour ma mère, ta grand-mère. Je suis désolé, ma chérie.
– Ça ne fait rien parce que, moi, j'ai acheté un souvenir génial.
– Qu'est-ce que tu as acheté?
– Un tee-shirt très chic, très moderne.
– Et c'est pour qui, maman?
– C'est pour moi!

AT 2.4/5
3c *Imagine! Tu as passé des vacances en roulotte dans ta région. Écris une carte postale ou enregistre un message pour un copain/une copine. (Tu peux adapter le texte de Claire!)*
AT 4.4/5
Students imagine they have been travelling around their own region in a horse-drawn carriage. They write or record a description of their travels, using Claire's text as a model.

AT 4.4
4 *Regarde le puzzle, suis les lignes et écris des phrases intéressantes. Compare avec un(e) partenaire.*
Students follow the tangled lines and build sentences using the words and symbols given. They could work in pairs on this, if appropriate. Point out that there are several possibilities for each sentence, e.g. *Sophie va/aime/préfère/voudrait aller/est allée au collège à vélo.* Brainstorm the different possibilities beforehand and encourage students to use a variety of tenses and opinions in order to make their sentences as interesting as possible.

When students have completed their sentences, they compare with a partner. They could then work together to correct and improve each other's work. Partners could award each other points for the most interesting sentences, and students could then select a few sentences to share with the class, either on the board or on OHT.

AT 3.4/5
5a *Relie les questions aux réponses.*
Students match the questions 1–7 with Théo's answers a–g.

Answers: 1 d; 2 f; 3 e; 4 c; 5 g; 6 b; 7 a

AT 3.4/5
5b *Choisis six images qui illustrent les vacances de Théo.*
Students select six pictures to represent Théo's holiday.

Answers: a, c, f, g, i, l

AT 2.4/5
5c *Interviewe ton/ta partenaire à propos de ses vacances (vraies ou imaginaires). Attention: Les phrases en bleu sont les réponses de base. Donne plus de détails et fais des phrases plus intéressantes.*
In pairs, students interview each other about a past holiday (real or imaginary). To ensure that this activity is accessible to students of all abilities, some phrases are highlighted in blue in Théo's answers: students can use these as a starting point. However, do encourage more able students to respond in as much detail as possible.

Contrôle Unités 5–6

For general comments on assessment, see page 22 of the Introduction.

Resources

Copymasters 119–126
CD 3, tracks 56–60
Cassette 3, side 2

Feuille 119   Écoute Encore

AT 1.2 **1** *Écoute et relie les destinations aux instructions.*
Students listen to the directions to places around town. They match the direction symbols to the destinations.

Answers: 1 c; 2 a; 3 e; 4 f; 5 d; 6 b

Mark scheme: 1 mark for each = 5 marks

Assessment criteria: Students who achieve 4 or 5 marks show evidence of performance at AT 1.2.

CD 3, track 56   Feuille 119, activité 1
Cassette 3, side 2

1 – C'est où, la plage, s'il vous plaît?
  – La plage? Allez tout droit.
  – Merci, monsieur.
2 – C'est où, le château, s'il vous plaît, madame?
  – Le château? Prenez la première rue à gauche.
  – Merci, madame. Au revoir.
3 – Excusez-moi, monsieur. C'est où, le centre sportif?
  – Prenez la deuxième rue à droite.
  – Merci beaucoup.
4 – C'est où, l'église Saint-Denis, s'il vous plaît?
  – L'église? Ah, oui. Prenez la première rue à gauche et puis tournez à droite. L'église est dans cette rue.
  – Merci, madame. Au revoir.
5 – Pardon, madame. C'est où, le port?
  – Le port? C'est simple! Tournez à droite.
  – La première rue à droite?
  – Oui, c'est ça.
6 – C'est où, le musée, s'il vous plaît, monsieur?
  – Le musée?
  – Oui, le musée.
  – Hmmm … Ah oui, le musée. Prenez la deuxième rue à gauche.
  – Merci, monsieur.

AT 1.3 **2** *Écoute et relie.*
Students listen to the conversations about how people travel to various places. For each conversation, they indicate the destination and the means of transport.

Answers: 1 d, i; 2 f, l; 3 c, h; 4 a, g; 5 e, j; 6 b, k

Mark scheme: 1 mark for each destination, 1 mark for each means of transport = 10 marks

Assessment criteria: Students who achieve 8 marks or more show evidence of performance at AT 1.3.

CD 3, track 57   Feuille 119, activité 2
Cassette 3, side 2

1 – Comment est-ce que tu vas au collège, Daniel?
  – Quand je vais au collège, je vais en bus. C'est pratique.
2 – Quand tu vas à la piscine, tu prends le bus, Marie?
  – Non, quand je vais à la piscine, je vais à pied parce que la piscine est tout près de chez moi.
3 – Comment est-ce que tu vas au club des jeunes?
  – Au club des jeunes? Je vais à vélo.
4 – Tu vas au supermarché en bus?
  – Ah, non, je vais au supermarché en voiture. C'est plus pratique!
5 – Comment est-ce que tu vas à la plage?
  – Je vais à la plage à mobylette. J'adore ça!
6 – Comment est-ce que tu vas au centre-ville?
  – Au centre-ville? Je vais en métro parce que c'est rapide et pratique.

AT 1.4 **3** *On parle des voyages. Prends des notes sur une feuille: date de départ/transport.*
Students listen to the interviews about past holidays. They note down details of each person's departure date and how they travelled.

Answers: Lucie: le 25 juillet, bus; Yann: le 19 mai, voiture; Isabelle: le 2 avril, bateau; Marc: le 30 mars, avion; Stéphanie: le 16 août, train

Mark scheme: 1 mark for each date, 1 mark for each means of transport = 10 marks

Assessment criteria: Students who achieve 6 marks or more show evidence of performance at AT 1.4.

CD 3, track 58   Feuille 119, activité 3
Cassette 3, side 2

Exemple:
– Éric, tu es allé où pendant les grandes vacances?
– Je suis allé à Dieppe.
– Dieppe? Ah, bon. Tu es parti quand?
– Je suis parti le premier août, at puis on est restés deux semaines.
– Tu as voyagé comment?
– Je suis allé à Dieppe à vélo, avec deux copains. C'était super!
1 – Et toi, Lucie, tu es partie pendant les vacances?
  – Oui, je suis partie. Je suis allée à Paris.
  – J'adore Paris, moi. Tu es partie quand?
  – Euh, je suis partie le vingt-cinq juillet. Le vingt-cinq juillet, j'ai pris le bus. C'était long, le voyage en bus, mais Paris, c'était super!
2 – Yann, tu es allé en Espagne, n'est-ce pas?
  – Oui, c'est ça. Mon père est espagnol, alors …
  – Alors tu es parti en famille?
  – Oui, avec papa et mes deux sœurs … Six heures en voiture avec mes sœurs, oh là là!
  – Six heures en voiture, c'est pas marrant! Et vous êtes partis quand?
  – On est partis le dix-neuf mai.
  – Le dix-neuf mai.

Contrôle Unités 5–6

3 – Bonjour, Isabelle.
– Bonjour, madame. Ça va?
– Oui, ça va bien merci. Tu as passé de bonnes vacances? Tu es partie quand?
– Oui, pas mal. Je suis allée voir ma correspondante en Angleterre. Elle est super sympa! Je suis partie le deux avril … oui, le deux avril, et j'ai apporté un œuf en chocolat comme cadeau …
– Et tu as voyagé comment, Isabelle? Tu as pris le bateau ou le train?
– J'ai pris le bateau. La mer était assez calme, alors ça allait.
4 – Marc, tu es parti pendant les vacances de Pâques?
– Oui, je suis allé aux Antilles, pour voir mes grands-parents. J'adore ça!
– Tu es resté longtemps?
– Oui, nous sommes restés deux semaines, maman et moi. Nous sommes partis … le 30 mars, et nous sommes rentrés hier!
– Et le voyage, c'était comment?
– Oh, pas mal. On a vu de bons films dans l'avion.
5 – Tu es allée où pendant les vacances, Stéphanie?
– Je suis allée à Nice, pour passer une semaine chez ma tante.
– Et c'était quand, ça? Tu … tu es partie quand?
– Euh … je suis partie … je suis partie le seize août, je crois. Oui, voilà mon billet de train – le seize août.
– Alors, tu as pris le train.
– Oui, c'est ça.

AT 1.5 **2** *Écoute les quatre conversations et complète la grille.* Students listen to four interviews about past holidays. They fill in the grid in French, noting down details of destination, means of transport, dates, location of hotel, activities, and souvenirs bought.

Answers: items shown in brackets below are provided on the copymaster as examples:

	1	2	3	4
Où?	Dieppe	(Antilles)	Athènes/ Grèce	Pays-Bas
Transport?	train	avion	voiture	train
Dates?	(1–14 août)	15 juillet– 10 août	3–22 mai	5 septembre, est resté 2 semaines
Situation de l'hôtel?	(en face de la gare)	en face de la plage	au centre d'Athènes, près des magasins	en face d'une piscine chauffée
Activités?	plage tous les jours	voile tous les jours	monuments historiques	vélo
Souvenirs?	tee-shirt	(foulard)	5 posters	porte-clés

Mark scheme: 1 mark for each correct answer = 20 marks

Assessment criteria: Students who achieve 15 marks or more show evidence of performance at AT 1.5.

AT 1.4/5

Feuille 120   Écoute En plus

1 *Écoute la conversation et choisis la bonne réponse.* Students listen to the interview with Théo about his holiday in Paris. They select the correct word or phrase to complete each sentence.

Answers: 1 Paris; 2 le 15 août; 3 une semaine; 4 train; 5 historiques; 6 cartes postales

Mark scheme: 1 mark for each correct item = 5 marks

Assessment criteria: Students who achieve 4 or 5 marks after only one listening show evidence of performance at AT 1.5; those who score 4 or 5 marks but who need to hear the recording more than once show evidence of performance at AT 1.4.

CD 3, track 59   Feuille 120, activité 1
Cassette 3, side 2

– Tu es allé où en vacances, Théo?
– Je suis resté en France. Je suis allé à Paris. C'était super!
– Tu es parti quand?
– Je suis parti le quinze août et je suis resté une semaine.
– Tu as voyagé comment?
– J'ai voyagé en train. J'aime ça!
– Qu'est-ce que tu as fait?
– J'ai visité tous les monuments historiques! C'était fatigant!
– Tu as acheté des souvenirs?
– Non, mais j'ai acheté beaucoup de cartes postales.

CD 3, track 60   Feuille 120, activité 2
Cassette 3, side 2

1 – Tu es allée où en vacances, Manon?
– Je suis allée à Dieppe.
– Tu as voyagé comment?
– J'ai pris le train. C'était pratique parce que l'hôtel était en face de la gare.
– Tu es partie quand?
– Je suis partie le premier août et je suis restée jusqu'au quatorze août.
– Tu es partie le premier août et tu es restée jusqu'au quatorze août?
– Oui.
– Et qu'est-ce que tu as fait à Dieppe?
– Je suis allée à la plage tous les jours. C'était super!
– Tu as acheté des souvenirs?
– Oui, j'ai acheté un tee-shirt.
2 – Tu es allé où en vacances, Marc?
– Je suis allé aux Antilles.
– Tu as voyagé comment?
– J'ai voyagé en avion. C'est loin!
– Tu es parti quand?
– Je suis parti le quinze juillet et je suis resté jusqu'au dix août.
– Tu es parti le quinze juillet et tu es resté jusqu'au dix août?

Contrôle Unités 5–6

- Oui, c'est ça.
- L'hôtel était bien situé?
- Oui, en face de la plage!
- Qu'est-ce que tu as fait aux Antilles?
- J'ai fait de la voile tous les jours. C'était super!
- Tu as acheté des souvenirs?
- Oui, j'ai acheté un foulard pour ma grand-mère.

3 – Tu es allée où en vacances, Charlotte?
- Je suis allée en Grèce, dans la capitale, Athènes.
- Tu as voyagé comment?
- J'ai voyagé en voiture. C'est loin et c'était fatigant!
- Tu es partie quand?
- Je suis partie le trois mai et je suis restée jusqu'au vingt-deux mai.
- Tu es partie le trois mai et tu es restée jusqu'au vingt-deux mai?
- Oui.
- L'hôtel était bien situé?
- Oui, au centre d'Athènes, près des magasins!
- Qu'est-ce que tu as fait en Grèce?
- J'ai visité des monuments historiques. C'était intéressant!
- Tu as acheté des souvenirs?
- Oui, j'ai acheté cinq posters.

4 – Tu es allé où en vacances, Paul?
- Je suis allé aux Pays-Bas.
- Tu as voyagé comment?
- J'ai voyagé en train, mais j'ai mis mon vélo dans le train.
- Tu es parti quand?
- Je suis parti le cinq septembre et je suis resté deux semaines.
- Tu es parti le cinq septembre et tu es resté deux semaines?
- Oui, c'est ça.
- L'hôtel était bien situé?
- Oui, l'hôtel était en face d'une piscine chauffée. Super!
- Qu'est-ce que tu as fait aux Pays-Bas?
- J'ai fait du vélo, bien sûr! C'était génial!
- Tu as acheté des souvenirs?
- Oui, j'ai acheté un porte-clés.

Feuille 121   Parle Encore

Students work in pairs for these activities. Give the top half of the sheet to one student and the bottom half to their partner.

AT 2.3 **1a** *Demande à ton/ta partenaire: Qu'est-ce qu'il y a à Chatville/Poissonville? Note la réponse.*
1b *Réponds à la question.*
Students take turns to ask and tell each other what buildings there are in Chatville or Poissonville, responding to the visual prompts provided.

Mark scheme: 1 mark for each correct place = 5 marks

Assessment criteria: Students who are able to name 4 or 5 places show evidence of performance at AT 2.3.

AT 2.3 **2** *Fais des conversations avec ton/ta partenaire pour compléter le plan.*
This is an information-gap activity. Students ask and answer questions in order to find out the location of buildings on their street plan.

Mark scheme: 2 marks for each question, 2 marks for each answer = 20 marks

Assessment criteria: Students who achieve 15 or more marks show evidence of performance at AT 2.3.

Feuille 122   Parle En plus

AT 2.3 **1** *A pose les questions et B répond. Ensuite, changez de rôle.*
Students take turns to ask and answer questions about how they travel to various places. Note that marks are awarded for the answers only.

Mark scheme: 1 mark for each answer = 5 marks

Assessment criteria: Students who achieve 4 or 5 marks show evidence of performance at AT 2.3.

AT 2.4/5 **2a** *Qu'est-ce que tu as fait pendant les vacances? Choisis cinq symboles. Explique à ton/ta partenaire.*
2b *Écoute et coche les activités de ton/ta partenaire.*
Students take turns to tell each other about an imaginary past holiday, based on five of the visuals provided.

Mark scheme: 2 marks for each activity mentioned (1 mark for content, 1 mark for accurate use of the perfect tense) = 10 marks

Assessment criteria: Students who achieve 8 or more marks are beginning to show signs of performance at AT 2.5; students who achieve 5–7 marks show evidence of performance at AT 2.4.

AT 2.5 **3a** *Pose les questions à ton/ta partenaire.*
3b *Réponds aux questions.*
Students interview each other about a past holiday, real or imaginary.

Mark scheme: 2 marks for each answer (1 mark for content, 1 mark for accuracy of language/grammar) = 10 marks

Assessment criteria: Students who achieve 8 or more marks are beginning to show evidence of performance at AT 2.5.

Feuille 123   Lis Encore

AT 3.2 **1** *Relie.*
Students match the pictures to their corresponding sentences about travel to various places.

Answers: 1 e; 2 c; 3 a; 4 d; 5 b

Mark scheme: 2 marks for each correct answer = 10 marks

Assessment criteria: Students who achieve 8 marks or more show evidence of performance at AT 3.2.

AT 3.3 **2** *Dessine un petit plan pour chaque instruction comme dans l'exemple.*
Students draw a simple plan to represent each set of directions to places in town.

Answers: a the beach: third street on the left; b the swimming pool: first street on the right; c the port: second street on the left then turn right

Mark scheme: 3 marks for each answer (1 mark for the destination, 2 marks for the directions) = 9 marks

Assessment criteria: Students who achieve 7 marks or more show evidence of performance at AT 3.3.

AT 3.4 **3** *Lis la carte postale. Choisis la bonne réponse.*
Students answer multiple-choice questions about a holiday in Dieppe.

Answers: 1 c; 2 b; 3 a

Mark scheme: 2 marks per correct answer = 6 marks

Assessment criteria: Students who achieve 6 marks show evidence of performance at AT 3.4.

Feuille 124   Lis En plus

AT 3.4 **1** *Lis et remets le dialogue dans un ordre logique. Commence par c.*
Students arrange the sentences in the correct order to create a dialogue about a past holiday.

Answers: c, b, a, f, i, l, d, k, e, h, j, g, m

Mark scheme: 1 mark for each = 12 marks

Assessment criteria: Students who achieve 9 marks or more show evidence of performance at AT 3.4.

AT 3.5 **2** *Lis la lettre de Julien à sa copine Sandra. Réponds aux questions sur une feuille.*
Students answer questions in French about Julien's holiday in Paris.

Answers: 1 car, métro, bateau, vélo (4 marks); 2 le 5 juillet, le 1 août (2 marks); 3 une semaine (1 mark); 4 la tour Eiffel (1 mark); 5 il l'adore (1 mark); 6 un tee-shirt cool, un poster marrant (2 marks); 7 any two of: il est allé dans un camp de vacances en Normandie/il a fait du sport/il a fait des excursions en vélo (2 marks)

Mark scheme: marks as shown above = 13 marks

Assessment criteria: Students who achieve 10 marks or more show evidence of performance at AT 3.5.

Feuille 125   Écris Encore

AT 4.2 **1** *Qu'est-ce qu'il y a à Dieppe? Continue la liste.*
Students use the visuals as prompts to continue the list of places to visit in Dieppe.

Answers: des cafés, une plage, un château, un marché

Mark scheme: 2 marks for each answer (2 marks if spelling and gender are correct, 1 mark if there are mistakes in spelling or gender) = 8 marks

Assessment criteria: Students who write three of the four places accurately with the correct gender show evidence of performance at AT 4.2.

AT 4.3 **2** *Choisis un souvenir pour chaque personne.*
Students complete the sentences, giving details of the imaginary souvenirs they have bought and for whom.

Mark scheme: 2 marks for each sentence (1 mark for the person, 1 mark for the souvenir item) = 8 marks

Assessment criteria: Students who achieve 6 marks or more show evidence of performance at AT 4.3.

AT 4.4 **3** *Invente un autre voyage pour cet explorateur. Réponds aux questions.*
Students invent a different journey for the explorer and answer questions about it.

Mark scheme: 2 marks for each answer (1 mark for content, 1 mark for accuracy of language), plus 1 bonus mark for general creativity/accuracy = 9 marks

Assessment criteria: Students who achieve 6 or more marks show evidence of performance at AT 4.4.

Feuille 126   Écris En plus

AT 4.4/5 **1** *Qu'est-ce que tu as fait pendant les vacances? Choisis cinq activités.*
Students write a paragraph about what they did during the holidays, based on five of the visuals provided.

Mark scheme: 3 marks for each activity (2 marks for accurate use of the perfect tense, 1 mark for content) = 15 marks

Assessment criteria: Students who achieve 11 marks or more are beginning to show evidence of performance at AT 4.5; those who achieve 6–10 marks show evidence of performance at AT 4.4.

AT 4.5 **2** *Écris sur une feuille une lettre à un ami français, Alexandre. Regarde les illustrations et raconte tes dernières vacances.*
Students write a letter about an imaginary holiday in Paris, responding to the visuals provided.

Mark scheme: 5 marks for content and 5 marks for accuracy of language = 10 marks

Assessment criteria: Students who achieve 7 marks or more show evidence of performance at AT 4.5.